# Believers Church Bible Commentary

Elmer A. Martens and Howard H. Charles, Editors

**Believers Church
Bible Commentary**

# Jeremiah

Elmer A. Martens

**HERALD PRESS**
Scottdale, Pennsylvania
Kitchener, Ontario
1986

Library of Congress Cataloging-in-Publication Data

Martens, E. A.
    Jeremiah.

    (Believers church Bible commentary)
    Bibliography: p.
    1. Bible.  O.T.  Jeremiah—Commentaries.  I. Title.
    II. Series.
    BS1525.3.M37    1986       224'.207       86-9958
    ISBN 0-8361-3405-2 (pbk.)

BELIEVERS CHURCH BIBLE COMMENTARY: JEREMIAH
Copyright © 1986 by Herald Press, Scottdale, Pa.  15683
    Published simultaneously in Canada by Herald Press.
    Kitchener, Ont.  N2G 4M5. All rights reserved.
Library of Congress Catalog Card Number: 86-9958
International Standard Book Number: 0-8361-3405-2
Printed in the United States of America

91  90  89  88  87  86  10  9  8  7  6  5  4  3  2  1

## To Lauren, Frances, Vernon, and Karen

our children in their early twenties, who represent the
cresting generation. Their quality of life may be
dependent on whether the present generation
responds to the urgent message of a Jeremiah. This
volume is dedicated to them with much love and
affection.

# Contents

*For a more comprehensive outline of Jeremiah, see pages 281-289.

# Series Foreword

The Believers Church Bible Commentary Series makes available a new tool for basic Bible study. It is published for all who seek to understand more fully the original message of Scripture and its meaning for today—Sunday school teachers, members of Bible study groups, students, pastors, or other seekers. The series is based on the conviction that God is still speaking to all who will hear him, and that the Holy Spirit makes the Word a living and authoritative guide for all who want to know and do God's will.

The desire to be of help to as wide a range of readers as possible has determined the approach of the writers. No printed biblical text has been provided in order that readers might continue to use the translation with which they are most familiar. The writers of the series have used the *Revised Standard Version*, the *New International Version*, and the *New American Standard Bible* on a comparative basis and indicate which of these texts they have followed most closely, as well as where they have made their own translations. The writers have not worked alone, but in consultation with select counselors, the series' editors, and with the Editorial Council.

To further encourage use of the series by a wide range of readers the focus has been centered on illumination of the text, providing historical and cultural background, sharing necessary theological, sociological, and ethical meanings and, in general, making "the rough places plain." Critical issues have not been avoided, but neither have they been moved into the foreground as a debate among scholars. The series will aid in the interpretive process, but not attempt to provide the final meaning as authority above Word and Spirit.

The term "believers church" has often been used in the history of the church. Since the sixteenth century it has frequently been applied to the Anabaptists and later the Mennonites, as well as to the Church of the Brethren and similar groups. As a descriptive term it now includes more than Mennonites and Brethren. It represents specific theological understandings such as believers baptism, commitment to the Rule of Christ in Matthew 18:15-18 as part of the meaning of church membership, belief in the power of love in all relationships, and a willingness to follow the way of the cross of Christ. The writers chosen for the series stand in this tradition.

Believers church people have always been known for their emphasis on obedience to the simple, literal meaning of Scripture. Because of this, they do not have a long history of deep historical-critical biblical scholarship. This series attempts to be faithful to the Scriptures while also taking archaeology and current biblical studies seriously. Doing this means that at many points the writers will not differ greatly from interpretations which can be found in many other good commentaries. But basic presuppositions about Christ, the church and its mission, God and history, human nature, the Christian life, and other doctrines do determine a writer's interpretation of Scripture. Thus this series, like all other commentaries, stands within a specific historical church tradition. A felt need for help on the part of many is, therefore, understandable and justification enough to attempt its production.

The Holy Spirit is not bound to any tradition. May this series be an instrument in breaking down walls between Christians in North America and around the world, bringing new joy in obedience through a fuller understanding of the Word.

*The Editorial Council*

# Author's Preface

This commentary is intended to "give the biblical text its voice" and to help this generation hear it.

The text of Jeremiah is not reprinted here. Yet that text is primary and the serious student will want to read it, not only initially but repeatedly. My comments do not begin to exhaust the riches of this marvelous book. Occasionally questions are introduced to invite the reader to make new discoveries from the text.

The comments on an individual text are not complete without a look at the larger biblical context. Also, since the Bible is there for the Christian to live out life before God, the comments are not complete without an indication of present-day relevance. At the end of each chapter (though sometimes within it) two sections incorporate these concerns: "The Text in Biblical Context" and "The Text in the Life of the Church."

The "Glossary Notes" at the end of the volume present additional material of interest to selected readers. These notes minimize repetition and serve as a brief overview of a topic. Sometimes they elaborate on technical vocabulary.

I am indebted to the late Professor William H. Brownlee, who as a mentor encouraged me in a doctoral thesis which involved Jeremiah, and also to the growing cadre of recent Jeremiah scholars on whose works I have drawn. I am grateful to the Seminary Board of Directors for the study leave at Tyndale House in Cambridge, England. I extend my appreciation to the Believers Church Bible Commentary Editorial Council for its support. Professor Allen Guenther, one of its members and my teaching colleague, deserves special mention; as a coeditor for this volume he provided invaluable assistance. Several readers—

Professor Robert Neff, Professor John Miller, LaVerna Pauls, Pushpan-
gadan Pappu, Genet Yacob—made helpful suggestions. I acknowledge
with gratitude the painstaking work of Ray Wiebe, my teaching assistant.

In particular, I record with deep appreciation the help of Phyllis, my
wife, whose expertise in word crafting was given with enthusiasm and is
evident on every page.

This commentary is offered as a contribution to the church, whose
spiritual head is Jesus Christ the Lord. To him belongs endless praise!

> *Elmer A. Martens*
> *Mennonite Brethren Biblical Seminary*
> *Fresno, California*
>
> *Easter, 1985*

# Jeremiah

# Becoming Acquainted

We read a book like Jeremiah for its message and insights. This book has a weighty message. It may shock us into reassessments and realignments; it will almost certainly change our values. The story in this book may strike us as dark and dismal. We shall hear about Israel's failures, her fascination with substitute deities, her disregard for just dealings. We will hear passionate appeals for change, admonitions, laments, exhortations, and threats.

We will also hear promises. The underlying message has two faces: God disciplines people and punishes them; yet there is also forgiveness—the promise of new covenant. The gospel in Jeremiah reads: "I have loved you with an everlasting love" (31:3).

The book holds up a mirror to any and every society. It moves on a broad platform of world events; it addresses the nations, who are held accountable before God, and threatens annihilation of peoples who persist in evil. This ancient book is strangely relevant to our generation— a relevance which accounts, no doubt, for the recent explosion of dissertations, books, and commentaries on Jeremiah.

Yet here and there we are whisked, suddenly and swiftly, to a closet where the prophet is alone with his God. We hear his most intimate conversations. We learn about the prophet's pain and grief, his struggle to comprehend God's message to a faithless people. Thus the book is a mirror, not only of the international scene, but of an individual's life with God.

The more we learn about the stressful times in which Jeremiah lived, about the passionate prophet himself, and about the arrangement of the book that bears his name, the more forceful the message becomes.

15

## Upheavals at the Turn of the Century

The book spans Judah's history from the middle of the seventh to the beginning of the sixth century, i.e., 640-580 B.C. Judah rises in one last burst of energy under King Josiah; then a period of uncertainty sets in, followed by further national vacillation, decay, and sudden catastrophe.

King Josiah is the prominent figure in the last half of the seventh century. A century earlier the mighty Assyrian army had terrorized the land and humiliated Israel, the northern state, by capturing in 722 her capital city, Samaria. Now, however, the Assyrian empire was in difficulty. Josiah of Jerusalem seized the moment of Assyria's weakness and enlarged Judah's territory. Economically, times were briefly prosperous. Religious reforms were inaugurated after the remarkable discovery of the law scroll in the temple. Josiah wanted to serve God and led his people away from their evil ways.

Then, tragedy. In the battle at Megiddo in 609, this good king was killed. Jehoiakim, one of the important successors, despised Josiah's efforts at restoring godly living, and the long slide to disaster began. In the middle of his reign the Babylonians defeated the Egyptians at Carchemish and advanced southward to Israel in 605. They overpowered Jerusalem during Jehoiachin's three-month rule (598-597) and set up a king of their own choice, Zedekiah. His eleven-year rule was marked by vacillation: he would listen to his pro-Egyptian advisers, but also occasionally consult Jeremiah—who, of all things, advised surrender to the Babylonians! When Zedekiah finally attempted to throw off his vassal condition, Babylonian armies, Jeremiah's "foe from the north," moved swiftly in revenge. The armies seized Jerusalem, looted the temple, burned the city, and marched its citizens away captive. The year was 587. [Babylon/Babylonians, p. 291.]

From a religious point of view, such a tragedy was the outcome of the spiritual deterioration that had set in after King Hezekiah's reform a century earlier. This good and devout king had been followed by his son Manasseh, Judah's most godless monarch. His long reign (687-642) left Judah in spiritual shambles. He reintroduced Baal worship. [Baal, p. 291.] He built altars to foreign gods, and to make emphatic his rejection of the Lord, he built these altars in the temple at Jerusalem. The temple courtyard also was dotted with altars to the starry host. He resorted to divination. As an ultimate abomination he sacrificed his own son. "He did much evil in the eyes of the Lord, provoking him to anger" (2 Kings 21:6). Granted, Josiah, Manasseh's grandson, set an opposite course for Judah. Josiah introduced reforms in accordance with the book of the law found in the temple (2 Kings 22—23). While the reforms were sincere, they seem not to have reached deeply into the fabric of society, and they were ultimately short-lived. Jehoiakim, who followed shortly after Josiah, was not God-fearing (Jer. 36). Thus the kings and people paved their own way to the disaster that came with the fall of Jerusalem in 587.

For Judah, the turn of the century was clearly a time of transition marked by storm and stress. Judah had five different kings in its last two decades, few of them God-fearing. The prophets presented a false message, the priests were corrupt, the scribes wrote with a "lying pen." Jeremiah as God's spokesperson tried in vain to bring a spiritually wayward people back to God. He failed; they did not respond. The social fabric of society crumbled until national existence ended, not to be continued until the second century (and then only briefly) under the Maccabees. Jeremiah, then, is the book that recounts the final moments of a nation's 250-year history. [Chronology, p. 293, Kings of Judah, p. 300.]

## Jeremiah, an Unusual Prophet

The book begins as the international balance of power was shifting from Assyria to Babylon. God called a youth, probably in his late teens, Jeremiah by name, son of Hilkiah the priest, to be his prophet (627 B.C.). The young man wished to be excused and pleaded inexperience. However, before long he was preaching with passion. You have forsaken God, he told his people. You have forsaken the fountain of living waters, and as a second evil you have hewed out cisterns that can hold no water (2:13). You are an adulterous people. He declared, "An enemy is coming." He preached at the temple gate (7:1-15), pressed God's message upon the elders in the valley of Topheth (19:1-13), and had his message read in the king's court, where it was irreverently dissected with a penknife and cast into the fire (36:1-26). He wore an ox yoke in the streets to publicize coming bondage to an enemy power (27:2-11).

Then, in the middle of the gloom and doom, he spoke about God's consolation and comfort. Another day was coming, he said, when the land would be restored to the people and the people to their God, when brides and grooms would be celebrating in the streets (31:7-14). He purchased a field, even though he was in prison and the Babylonian army was at that moment laying siege to the city (32:1-15).

God gave him a message not only for Judah and Israel but for surrounding nations: Egypt, Babylon, Edom, Moab (46—51). This unusual prophet was involved in the international political scene of his day for a longer time (four decades) and with greater intensity than any other Old Testament prophet.

Still, he was not a politician, but God's servant. His true antagonists were the false prophets, whom he opposed with the claim that it was he, not they, who stood in God's council and proclaimed God's true message. It is not out of idle repetition that in his book "thus says the Lord," or similar phrases, occur more than 150 times.

Some of the events of Jeremiah's life can be briefly sketched. The book contains a surprising amount of information about the prophet personally. Jeremiah was born in the decade of 650-640 B.C. His call from God to be a prophet came in 627, though some scholars have suggested (but not compellingly) that 627 was the date of Jeremiah's birth.

He was of a priestly family in Anathoth, some three miles north of Jerusalem. This priestly family could trace its roots to Eli, who ministered at Shiloh, once the central worship place for Israel. King Solomon had disenfranchised this Levitical priestly family because Abiathar had supported Solomon's rival to the throne (1 Kings, 1:19; 2:27). As a sign to Judah of the terrible times soon to come, Jeremiah was forbidden to marry (16:1).

The reform by King Josiah beginning in 622 must have been followed by Jeremiah with interest, though direct statements about it are difficult to isolate. Some of the oracles in the early part of the book belong to Josiah's reign. Jeremiah became quite vocal during the reign of King Jehoiakim (609-598). In the roll call of kings, Jehoiakim receives major attention (22:11-23). Jeremiah's temple sermon was preached during his reign (7:1-15; 26:1-24). After Nebuchadnezzar of Babylon attacked Jerusalem in 597 and carried off captives, Jeremiah engaged in correspondence with the exiles, cautioning them against false prophets but also urging them not to participate in revolt-like activities (chapter 29).

During Zedekiah's rule (597-587) Jeremiah repeatedly counseled the king to submit to the world power, Babylon (e.g., 27:12). King Zedekiah, while occasionally seeking out the prophet's advice, did not deter his gate guards and other officials from arresting Jeremiah and confining him (37:16; 38:6). Zedekiah replied helplessly, "The king can do nothing to oppose you" (38:10). When Jerusalem fell, Jeremiah was given a choice: he could go with the exiles to Babylon or stay in the land (40:4). He stayed, lived through the assassination of Gedaliah the governor, and then despite his counsel to the contrary, went with the group that sought refuge in Egypt. It was in Egypt that Jeremiah died.

Rarely has there been a man so singularly pitted against the whole world. The people of his home city plotted his assassination. The general populace opposed him, mocking him for his gloomy message on a sunny day. The Jerusalem crowd of religious folk who heard his temple-gate sermon were ready to lynch him (26:7-11). His peers, the prophets, spoke an opposite message announcing peace—for example, the prophet Hananiah declared in God's name that the Babylonian domination would be only temporary (28:1-4). Pashhur the priest jailed him (20:1-3). The kings were (understandably) ill-disposed toward this prophet who urged treason. They imprisoned him with the intent of killing him; and had it not been for the help of a friend, Jeremiah would have died in a muddy dungeon (38:11-13). As if all this were not enough, Jeremiah felt at times opposed by the very almighty God whose message he faithfully carried (20:7-9).

Jeremiah was unique among the prophets in that he disclosed more of his private emotional life than any of the others. He was personally devastated when his message over a 25-year span was rejected out of hand. He felt trapped. In his "confessions" he described his spiritual anguish, his tussle with God. Moreover, he agonized because all along he saw clearly the coming disaster and the awful destruction of his people.

> O that my head were a spring of water
> and my eyes a fountain of tears!
> I would weep day and night
> for the slain of my people. (9:1)

Jeremiah preached in three modes: (1) he preached with his life, for by God's command he remained unmarried (16:1); (2) he preached orally; and (3) he wrote a book by dictating to Baruch what he had preached (36:4). That record was burned, but was rewritten.

## A Difficult Book

The book of Jeremiah is not only the longest prophetic book in the Bible (1,364 verses) but the most difficult to sort out. An initial encounter leaves the reader bewildered for several reasons. There is a strangeness in reporting: sometimes the book is about Jeremiah, at other times Jeremiah is the speaker. The book is chronologically disarranged. The principle of organization is neither fully chronological nor topical: its organization continues to be a challenge to all, especially to scholars who keep proposing organizational schemes and theories on how the book came about.

Certain blocks of material are readily distinguished. Judged by content we can distinguish threats against Judah and Jerusalem (chapters 1—20), stories about Jeremiah which illustrate the evil society (21—29; 34—45), a book of hope statements (30—33), and oracles against the nations (46—51). Generally speaking, the poetry predominates in all but the story section. The first chapter, which tells the story of Jeremiah's call to be a prophet, has its counterpart, so to speak, in the last chapter (52), which summarizes the story of the fall of Jerusalem and the deportation of the exiles. [Formation of Book, p. 296.]

Scholars also debate about the original text of the book. The standard English Bibles follow a venerable Masoretic Hebrew text. The Greek Septuagint, however, is one eighth shorter and has a different arrangement of material; for example, the segment about the nations (chapters 46—51) is inserted after 25:13. Is it possible to determine which text was the original? The debate continues. This commentary is based on the standard Masoretic Hebrew text. [Septuagint, p. 308.]

Scholars debate other issues. What is the relationship between the poetic and prose sections of the book, and does the answer to this question help decide issues about authorship? An unusual number of text blocks appear in more than one place: what does this signify? [Doublets, p. 296.] Furthermore the genre, that is, the literary forms of writing, are much less stereotyped than in the material from earlier prophets such as Amos and Micah. Recently the accuracy of the historical details about the person Jeremiah has been challenged by a British scholar—a debate similar to that about the historical details of Jesus. The outcome of all these debates is important, but because the conclusions are often tentative, these issues are not discussed in this commentary, though the comments take account of and frequently rely on recent scholarly insights.

For all its difficulty, the book of Jeremiah has great charm and power. "No Old Testament prophet used a wider variety of literary forms or showed more artistic skill than Jeremiah" (LaSor: 418). The book touches issues of life and death. It depicts the love of God in the face of the sin of the people; it shows the sin of a people in the face of the love of their God. It is a book of exclamation marks. It is a revelation of God's unfolding plans and purposes. Like a Picasso painting, it yields its contents slowly—but with what force!

## A Disturbing but Exciting Message

The themes tumble over each other to overwhelm the reader. The message is one of both judgment and deliverance. It is God who brings both about, and the reasons and settings for these actions are detailed, both for Judah and for other nations. A strong theme is the emphasis on knowing and clinging to God. Another is the grid of covenant, including the jeweled passage about the new covenant. Stranger to Western ears, perhaps, is the great significance placed on land.

What then is the enduring message of the book? The following is an attempt to present a theological digest.

## Judgment/Deliverance

To talk about deliverance is inspirational, but it is necessary sometimes to talk of judgment. Judah's problem was sin here, sin there, sin everywhere. The people bowed down before Baal and not the Lord; leaders as well as people spoke falsely; the rich exploited or ignored the poor; violence was the hallmark of society; military alliances were forged with Egypt; rulers lavished money upon themselves, and prophets could not be trusted (23:13; 9:3-6; 5:27-28; 7:6; 23:11-12). In all of this God was taken for granted, or worse, was marginal in the people's thinking. For all this and more, Jeremiah pronounced judgment.

> Hear, O earth:
> I am bringing disaster on this people,
>   the fruit of their schemes,
> because they have not listened to my words
>   and have rejected my law. (6:19)

The judgment as an expression of God's wrath would come in the form of an attack by the "foe from the north." Fields would be devastated and women taken; the men, both young and old, would lie dead in the streets. "Death has come into this city." Not only armies but famines would sweep the land. The anguish would bring moans and groans and sometimes shrill, piercing cries. [Wrath, p. 313; Judgment, Oracle, p. 299.]

It was always made clear that God did not desire the disintegration of the people—"he does not willingly bring affliction" (Lam. 3:33). When the destruction came and the exile also, the message in the Book of Comfort became one of appeal and promise. It took this form: Return to me and I will return you to the land; I am with you to deliver you; I will give you a satisfying life in your homeland (31:7-14). Judgment for sin would not be the last word. [Deliverance Oracles, p. 295.]

There are other books in the Old Testament that talk about deliverance. Chief of these is Exodus, which records a large-scale rescue of a slave people. But Jeremiah announced that the coming deliverance from the exile would be so glorious that by comparison the rescue from Egypt would look pale (23:7-8). In the Psalms, deliverance for both the individual and the people is a recurring theme. Ezekiel, Jeremiah's contemporary, spoke to the refugees in exile about deliverance, with this difference: Ezekiel stressed that God would physically bring the people out of their exile, after which they would repent (20:39-44); Jeremiah urged repentance first, following which the people would be returned to their land (31:15-19). Jeremiah preached judgment because of sin, but beyond judgment, hope.

## On Knowing God

Knowing God is a prime value. Jeremiah chastised his audiences because they pursued everything but God. He confronted kings with the importance of knowing God, and defined such knowledge, not as some esoteric mystery, but as dealing in justice and compassion with those who were powerless (22:15-16). In a classic statement he instructed his listeners not to boast in riches, might, or wisdom, but in their knowledge of a God who delights in covenant love, righteousness, and justice (9:23-24).

God's delight in righteousness holds center stage in the book. Being himself righteous, he will not tolerate evil and corruption. If there is a strong stand against falsehood and deception, it is because God is a God of truth.

> O Lord, do not your eyes look for truth? (5:3a)
> But the Lord is the true God;
>    he is the living God, the eternal King. (10:10a)

If God is intolerant of inconstancy, it is because God is faithful, reliable. The topic of God's righteous conduct is firmly rooted also in the Pentateuch, where, as in Isaiah, the more usual term is "holy." Given a righteous God and a corrupt people, it is clear why there is in this book so much about God's anger and wrath. [Justice, p. 299; Wrath, p. 313.]

> When he is angry, the earth trembles;
>    the nations cannot endure his wrath. (10:10b)

On the other hand, while God's integrity commits him to punish evil, still it allows him freedom to relent when the human response changes (18:1-12). Indeed the book underlines God's sovereignty over Israel and over all nations.

In his treatment of the kindness of God, Jeremiah drew especially on Hosea, who lived a hundred years earlier (of Jer. 31:18; Hos. 10:10-11;

11:3). Hosea had not only asserted God's kindness as a proposition but had symbolized it in a marriage with Gomer (Hos. 1—3). Jeremiah placed the kindness of God as a central affirmation in worship:

> Give thanks to the Lord Almighty,
>   for the Lord is good;
>   his love endures forever. (33:11b)

It was surely one of the greatest of catastrophes to hear God declare, "I have withdrawn my blessing, my love and my pity from this people" (16:5).

Talk about knowing God is frequent in the Psalms. That experience with God is reflected in the thanksgiving and praise psalms, but the difficulties of that experience are registered in the lament psalms, which make up one third of the psalms. With these Jeremiah's "confessions" or laments have much in common (e.g. 15:15-21; 20:7-13).

But Jeremiah's God, though a God of the individual, is by no means a parochial or tribal God. He is the creator God for whom nothing is impossible (32:17). No other gods and no idol representatives can be tolerated (10:6-16). To know him is to know of one who has jurisdiction over nations large and small, all of whom are subject to his sovereign will. [Knowing God, p. 301.]

## On Covenant

Covenant is a third major theme in Jeremiah. The accusations against Israel were based on covenant thinking. Jeremiah not only itemized the demands of covenant which Israel had disregarded (7:5, 6, 9), but he pointed often to the objective of covenant, namely intimacy with God. In no other book does the covenant formula, "I will be your God and you shall be my people," occur more frequently (e.g. 11:4; 30:22). This pithy expression proclaims that God takes initiative. It declares that God, in offering himself, purposes to bond a people to himself. It suggests that the people of God are peculiar, set-apart people. Its overtones are those of intimacy, privilege, and accountability. It contains both promise and demand. Its trajectory may be followed to the redeemed people in heaven (Rev. 21:3). [Covenant and Covenant Formula, p. 294.]

Explicit references in Jeremiah to God's earlier covenants are not frequent, possibly because "covenant," like "temple," had become a false security for the people, or because covenant was one of those strong words that was used rarely and certainly not lightly. Jeremiah shattered any security based on covenant by declaring essentially that the covenant was broken and its curses would now go into effect (cf. 11:8, 10). That harsh news was followed eventually by the good news: "I will make a new covenant." Then everyone would know him, said God, and the covenant purpose would be secured: "I will be their God, and they will be my people" (31:31-34).

Jeremiah drew covenant material from another Old Testament book, Deuteronomy, which, some maintain, in its arrangement exhibits an ancient treaty form, a "covenant." Deuteronomy, like Jeremiah, contains constant exhortations to obedience; it stipulates the blessings for covenant keeping and the curses for covenant breaking. When Jeremiah therefore had the uncomfortable task of facing his audiences with the curses that follow covenant breaking, for these curses he was dependent on Deuteronomy. The vocabulary and language style of the two books are so similar that scholars have framed a variety of theories about the possible connections between the two. [Style, p. 309.]

## On Land

One of the curses incorporated in covenant involves losing possession of land. Indeed land is a fourth theme, along with judgment/deliverance, knowing God, and covenant. In an early sermon Jeremiah used the terms of land to tell the story of Israel's history (chapters 2—3). In the temple sermon Jeremiah urged compliance with God's ways because only then could the people dwell on the land (7:3, 7). Because God's people did not comply, they lost their God-given land to the Babylonians and they themselves were deported to another country. But the story does not end there. In response to God's command Jeremiah purchased a plot of ground and with this symbolic action announced that God would restore his people to their land. The headline of chapters 30—31 is:

> . . . I will bring my people Israel and Judah back from captivity and restore them to the land I gave their forefathers to possess, says the Lord. (30:3)

In so saying, Jeremiah had more in mind than a geographical relocation, for "land" had become a symbol for the good life, the life with God. Land was part of that triangle—God, people, and land—that spoke of completeness. Families would live well since each had an apportioned territory. Corporate worship before God would proceed as commanded, and security from God would be a reality. "Land" was shorthand for the abundant life (cf. Martens, 1981: 242ff.).

Israel's history, as told in Numbers, Deuteronomy, and Joshua, books which recount entry into the land, God's gift, is clearly the background for much of the discussion about land. However, neither Jeremiah nor Ezekiel (who rivals Jeremiah in concern for land), invoked the Abrahamic covenant, which, after all, had been already fulfilled. Instead both prophets drew on such motifs as God's compassion, his reputation, his initiative and presence, and especially his purpose and design to form a people. [*Restoration Formula, p. 307; Land, p. 303.*]

It is around God's design—a design which has to do with judgment/ deliverance, knowledge of God, covenant, and land—that one can cluster the theological message of Jeremiah (cf. Exod. 5:22—6:8 and Martens, *God's Design*). That design is governed by a divine obsession to form a people for God's own possession. The pathos involved in this shaping process is nowhere clearer than in Jeremiah.

## Jeremiah Within the Bible

The book of Jeremiah is a miniature of the entire Old Testament, for it depicts the alienation of people from God, God's unceasing attempts to bring them back to himself, God's judgment on the evil through exile, the delights of restoration, and his actions not only on behalf of the people of Israel but for the benefit of the world of nations.

This redemption story is of course continued in the New Testament. There too one reads of a judgment on sin—Christ's death. The redemption blessings include the formation of God's people, the church, which is to be an exhibit of the kingdom of God to the nations.

Jeremiah as a person prefigured Jesus. Like Jesus, Jeremiah came to his own people, and his own people did not receive him (John 1:11). Like Jesus, Jeremiah preached a message of repentance. Like Jesus, Jeremiah had a special concern for Jerusalem. Like Jesus, Jeremiah faced mounting hostility in the course of his ministry, the most severe of which came from religious leaders. Chapters 26—44 could be called "The Passion of Jeremiah." Like Jesus, Jeremiah suffered rejection; and though he was not crucified, one tradition (perhaps not reliable) holds that in Egypt he was placed in a hollow log and sawn asunder.

The importance of this book for the New Testament is suggested in that, according to one count, there are 40 quotations and allusions from Jeremiah in the New Testament. Most of these occur in Revelation. The most striking reference is in Hebrews 8 where one finds the New Testament's longest quotation from the Old Testament.

## The Present-day Relevance of Jeremiah

As the Word of God, Jeremiah is not to be studied for historical interests only, but also for its present relevance. Each section of this commentary concludes with some reflections, "The Text in the Life of the Church." That feature of the commentary can be introduced here by some summary comments.

In suggesting the relevance of this ancient book for another time— our time—we can easily err by too quickly equating the political state then with the nation in which we live in now. Such an equation is problematic because, for example, the leaders of our government do not have the same responsibilities as those who led God's people. Yet God's dealings with a people, at once a religious community and a political unit, provide a window for us. We can look out upon a scene and recognize how God addresses a society. We soon become aware that he is addressing us too.

### Assessment of Culture

Repeated readings and study of the book are likely to put the reader in a mood sometimes of detachment and at other times of involvement. Jeremiah stood detached in his function of assaying lifestyles. He was atuned to both God and society, but always to God first. For this reason he understood the self-deception that characterized the people. He pinpointed the faults of the leaders. He X-rayed the culture so that all could see the falsehoods, the insincerities, the adulteries, both physical and spiritual, the violence . . . all of which had become part of the social fabric and were regarded by the populace as normal.

He critiqued authorities such as kings. He exposed the pitfalls of a civil religion. He raises for us the issue of church and state. At a minimum, his message insists that if church and state are to be separate, religion and politics cannot be. Those who speak in God's name must call government and politics to accountability on the basis of God's priorities.

The detachment which produces this analysis of society can also bring about an involvement. Jeremiah moved into the crowds, challenged their falsely based security, their double-think, their manipulative ways, their god-substitutes. He became an activist confronting his peers, the prophets, calling rulers and nobles to account and preaching at the cost of his life. Thus he holds a mirror to God's people today, inviting them to stand back and see their society as God sees it, but also to plunge into it to work for repentance and change.

### Dealing with Imminent Destruction

A prophet "knows what time it is," said Abraham Heschel, a Jewish scholar. Jeremiah announced the time very clearly: doom time. The nuclear threat for the twentieth century is not unlike the Babylonian threat for Judah. Nuclear warheads threaten more massive destruction than does an army of foot soldiers, to be sure. And nuclear war would likely be global rather than limited to a nation or two, but the end results would be identical: devastation, destruction, death.

The word for our times is the word Jeremiah and Jesus spoke to their times: repentance. Jeremiah keyed on the word "turn," with its meaning of "return," "repent." 'Change your ways," Jeremiah cried in the temple courts. "Stop your oppressions, stop your violence, stop your stealing and double talk" (cf. 7:1-11). The urgent message for a modern fear-ridden society is not psychological survival skills nor even hope in negotiations between superpowers for nuclear freezes and disarmaments, but *"Repent!" [Repentance, p. 306.]*

Despite flashes of generosity in nations and individuals, modern civilizations are enormously self-seeking. Present-day society is characterized by moralities of convenience, lack of moral scruples, a professed interest in religion but a simultaneous disregard of God's claims. Treaty-breaking, violence, lack of integrity in government and individuals invokes the wrath of a holy God. Our incredible fascination with military buildup has led us to the brink of an insane and final catastrophe. It is, once more, doom time. Unless we change our ways, turn, and repent, judgment may well be inevitable.

## Personal and Corporate Courage

Timidity and accommodation to prevailing culture continue too easily as the stance of church and individual Christians. Jeremiah is a summons to courage. Untiringly, Jeremiah called the people to accountability before God; unflinchingly, he confronted those in power, and let the chips fall where they might. By his example he calls for courage to risk it with God—all the way. Such courage entails boldness to confront evils in a world where evil is normalized; to protest against preachers of an "easy grace" which promises endless benefits without responsibility; to present a God who demands righteous living and sends his wrath against all evil.

Jeremiah's courage is also needed to speak a word of hope when according to all appearances there is little reason for hope. More than a courageous imagination is needed to depict a time beyond disaster when life will be joy-filled: the message of hope must come from God based on his unceasing faithfulness and concern. Paul Tillich wrote about "courage to be," Jeremiah about "courage to serve . . . in hope."

*The Significance of the Church*

Those refrains throughout Jeremiah, "I will be your God and you shall be my people" are refrains the church must hear (1 Peter 2:10). God's work in the world is largely carried on through the agency of God's people.

For a day beset with individualism, at least in the Western world, Jeremiah calls for people to recognize their collective responsibility. For a time in which loyalty means little, Jeremiah focuses on integrity. For a day when bewildered people, even people of the church, begin to depend for solutions on governments and militarism, Jeremiah insists that the history of the world is written in the last analysis as the history of God's people.

We shall fail with this book if we are captured only by the boldness of a prophet dauntlessly confronting his world. We need to understand that the objective of his ministry, while it entailed exposing all idolatries, was also to "build and to plant." The building and planting referred to the people whom God was shaping.

And more. The vision must not be dimmed. God is sovereign and desires the salvation of all. In a high moment of the book there is pictured a marvelous turnabout by the peoples of the world:

> . . . to you the nations will come
> from the ends of the earth and say,
> "Our fathers possessed nothing but false gods . . .
> Therefore I will teach them. . . .
> Then they will know
> that my name is the Lord." (16:19-21)

In short, a study of the book will raise these questions: How do Christians relate to their culture and their governments? What is to be done for a civilization on the brink of global blow-up? Is the message of repentance to be preached to a secularized people? Has the church and/or the individual courage to represent God? Is there a message of hope? Can the church maintain a spiritual perspective on its mission? The book of Jeremiah raises these questions for our day because in it are answers to some of these questions for Jeremiah's day. More will be at stake in our study than merely tossing about questions and answers in an intellectual game of volleyball. At stake is gutsy grappling with a word from God, which Jeremiah described as a "fire" and a "hammer that breaks a rock in pieces" (23:29).

Part 1

# God's Personal Message to Jeremiah

# Jeremiah 1

The first chapter is an introduction to the prophet, but even more to his message. An opening dialogue between God and his young, reluctant prophet sets up Jeremiah as a sparring partner with God in a tension that escalates later in the book. In Part 3 (chapters 11—20) we will get a firsthand report on how Jeremiah fared and how the dialogue begun here continued.

The message the prophet brings to his people is that disaster will come in the form of an invasion from a northern enemy because God's people have forsaken God (1:16). Both parts—the announcement and the accusation—will become the subject of Part 2 (chapters 2—10).

Jeremiah 1:1-19

# Meet the Prophet-Priest from Anathoth

## PREVIEW

The book of Jeremiah reports God's word to a people. Yet more than any other prophetic book it also records how the prophet himself felt, how he responded and what happened to him. Beginning with chapter 2 we are on public stage. But in chapter 1 we listen to a conversation in the privacy of Jeremiah's home and garden. The editorial heading prepares us for Jeremiah's first-person report of his call from God to the ministry.

The chapter anticipates what lies ahead for Jeremiah, namely trouble, and also signals the message for the book, largely judgment. It is the prelude to the entire book.

## OUTLINE

An Editorial Heading, 1:1-3

Grasped for Ministry, 1:4-19
    1:4-10   God's Call to Jeremiah
    1:11-12  The Vision of the Almond Rod
    1:13-16  The Vision of the Boiling Pot
    1:17-19  God's Charge to Jeremiah

EXPLANATORY NOTES

## An Editorial Heading 1:1-3

The opening sentence of the book, like a modern book's title page or dust jacket, introduces both the book and the man. Information is supplied about Jeremiah's family, his residence, his time, and his words.

Jeremiah came from a priestly family and from a town to which Abiathar, one of two priests under David the king, had been exiled (1 Kings 2:26-27). Whether Jeremiah was of Abiathar's lineage is not known. The town Anathoth was three miles north of Jerusalem and so was within an hour's walk of the capital. However, Jerusalem was in Judah and Anathoth was located in Benjaminite territory, where today there is an Arab village called Anata.

Jeremiah lived during the final decades of the seventh century B.C. He was born, so it is believed, about 645. This means that in his time the eight-year-old Josiah ascended the throne of Jerusalem (640). It was in 627, Josiah's thirteenth year, that Jeremiah received his call from the Lord. Jeremiah must have known about the reforms of the king in 622—reforms which got under way when a book of the law was found as the temple was being repaired (2 Kings 21-22). These reforms were virtually undone during Jehoiakim's reign (609-598). [Chronology, p. 293.]

Jeremiah witnessed the decadence of the Southern Kingdom and also its collapse. He would have heard about the Babylonians taking the Assyrian capital city of Nineveh in 612 and the subsequent dismantling of this powerful Assyrian Empire. He was there when in their westward march they besieged Jerusalem (598). He was aware that the victors had placed Zedekiah, their choice, on the throne. In the *eleventh year of Zedekiah* he saw the Babylonians return to deal decisively with the vacillating and subversive king (587). He saw the city burn and the citizens taken away to Babylon. [Kings of Judah, p. 300.]

The book contains *the words of Jeremiah* spoken during this exceedingly troublesome time. But verse 2 immediately makes clear that these are more than the words or opinions of a man. *The word of the Lord came* (lit., "was," "happened") to the prophet. This book has a divine quality. Therefore study of this book is an important as well as a sobering task.

God's Word does not come in abstract form, but it comes into historical situations, in a certain time and place and to certain people. Strictly speaking, the heading introduces chapters 1—39, or even only chapters 1—20. The collection of Jeremianic material grew, but we don't know the stages. The present book, for example, also contains God's words to Jeremiah which came *after* King Zedekiah's exile to Babylon as well as Jeremiah's later messages given in Egypt (chapters 40—44). [*Formation of Book, p. 296.*]

## Grasped for Ministry 1:4-19

How does a person get to be God's messenger? Jeremiah tells how it came about in his life. There are three distinct parts to his call: a dialogue, a set of visions, and a charge. First, in the dialogue Jeremiah learns that God had singled him out prior to his birth. Second, two visions are reported: one of an almond tree, another of a tilting boiling pot. Third, the Lord commissions Jeremiah.

### 1:4-10 God's Call to Jeremiah

No circumstances are described. Only the event, the happening of God's word to Jeremiah, is offered as the setting for this call. The prophetic revelation formula, *The word of the Lord came to me,* occurs often in Jeremiah (e.g., 1:11; 2:1; 14:1; 18:1; 21:1; 27:1). These passages use the name Yahweh, which English versions usually render not as a name but as a title—LORD. The personal element is retained in the name Yahweh. [*Revelation Formulae, p. 307; Yahweh, p. 314.*]

Dialogue between God and the hitherto unknown Hebrew teenager begins with a sudden but strong statement in which Yahweh discloses his intentions for his new prophet. God declares, *"Before I formed you . . . I knew you."* In Hebrew "to know" means to experience another individual. For this reason the word "know" is appropriate even for marital intimacy: "And Adam knew Eve his wife, and she conceived and bore Cain . . ." (Gen. 4:1, KJV). The word "know" was sometimes used in political treaties, where it meant commitment. The verb "formed," used in the call, is familiar from the shaping of the first man (Gen. 2:7). As a noun, it is the word for "potter" (Jer. 18:2; cf. Isa. 44:2).

Jeremiah would have known of God's call to Moses or Isaiah. Even non-Israelites recorded similar call stories. In the Egyptian Pianchi stele, from the time about 150 years prior to Jeremiah, the god Amun says: "It was in the belly of your mother that I said concerning you that you were to be ruler of Egypt; it was as a seed and while you were in the egg that I knew you, that (I knew) you were to be lord."

To be a prophet meant to be counted with such persons as Moses, Samuel, and Isaiah. A good glimpse into the work of a prophet comes from Exodus 7:1, where Aaron is called to be a prophet for Moses: his

assignment is to speak in behalf of another. Jeremiah obviously under-
stands speaking to be part of a prophet's function, for he at once objects:
*I do not know how to speak* (v. 6). While prophets such as Samuel and
Elijah were called to speak to Israel, Jeremiah's commission is to involve
him with nations. So it later proved (25:15; 36:2; 46—51). *[Prophet, p.
306.]*

Is this call to prominence as God's spokesperson eagerly accepted?
Not at all. Jeremiah exclaims, "Oh no!" He calls attention to his age: he is
not a veteran but a *child*. The term is not unlike our word "youngster,"
which could refer to an infant as well as an inexperienced adult. Judging
by his life span, Jeremiah may have been in his late teens.

God answers the excuse: He will assume responsibility for the
message content and the itinerary. But the prohibition, *Do not be afraid
of them*, comes as a surprise. Jeremiah has pleaded his inadequacy but
has not mentioned fear. God is now speaking, not to the given reason,
but to the real reason for resisting the call. God's answer to the fear is the
promise of his presence: *I am with you and will rescue you* (1:8). The
promise for deliverance is a reminder of the Exodus, since the same language is used for that event (Exod. 3:8; 5:23; 6:6). The phrase, "I am
with you," occurs in interesting settings (e.g., Gen. 28:15, Judg. 6:12).
*[Divine Assistance Formula, p. 295.]* God's reply demolishes both the
given reason, inability, and the real reason, fear. The call is anchored in
who God is.

The call account continues with an installation service. Following a
symbolic act of touching the mouth (cf. Isa. 6:7), the Lord announces,
*Now, I have put my words in your mouth* (1:9; cf. Deut. 18:18).
Jeremiah's task is to be first destructive, then constructive. He is to be a
verbal wrecking ball that smashes into well-preserved but erroneous
traditions (e.g., Jer. 7). The combination *uproot and tear down, build
and plant* occurs often in the book (18:7-9; 24:6; 31:27; 42:10; 45:4f.).

### 1:11-12 The Vision of the Almond Rod

The dialogue between the Lord and Jeremiah continues but at
another time and in another setting, possibly in an orchard. God's question, *What do you see?* could suggest a real object (cf. Jer. 24:3; Amos
7:7; 8:1). Or it might be a mental picture as in a trance. Our word "vision" includes both possibilities: a real object or a mental image. The
question-answer exchange rivets attention on the object—here a flower-
ing almond branch. The Lord's comment, which turns on a wordplay, is
therefore more memorable. The almond tree, a "watching tree"
*(shaqed)*, evokes the word "watching" *(shoqed)*. Just as the almond

tree, the first to blossom in spring, watches over all else, so God will keep a good lookout over his word—the message that God has put in Jeremiah's mouth (v. 9). [*Word Play, p. 313.*]

## 1:13-16 The Vision of the Boiling Pot

The Lord questions Jeremiah again—perhaps, so one can conjecture, as the evening meal is in preparation. The boiling pot, tilted so that the boiling water spills in a southerly direction, is to signify the spillover of nations, some of whom will descend on Judah from the north. A vivid picture indeed!

Enemy nations invading Palestine came from either the north or the south, but hardly from the east where lay the Arabian Desert. The northern foe is not the Scythian people, as has been argued, but Babylon, which, though located in the east, would be attacking from the north. Babylon's siege of Jerusalem in 598 B.C. and her destruction of the temple in 587/6 were to leave a permanent mark. For now the foe is not identified.

The tilted, boiling pot, gives rise to a speech about Judah's evils. The foremost evil is forsaking the Lord, a complaint Jeremiah will make frequently (2:13, 17, 19; 5:7, 19; 16:11; 17:13). This departure from the Lord is the reason, really, for all other evils. The worship of other gods or idols was prohibited in the first two of the Ten Commandments (Exod. 20:3-4; Deut. 5:7-8). The vision of the boiling pot stresses the judgment-type message which Jeremiah will speak and explains why the nature of his work will be to dismantle, and why it will involve other nations. This vision, like the former one, deals with the *content* of Jeremiah's message.

## 1:17-19 God's Charge to Jeremiah

In a final speech the Lord calls Jeremiah to action. To "gird up loins," as in some versions, is battle-readiness language. The customary long-flowing garments need to be tied up. The earlier assignment is now repeated: speak (cf. v. 7). The target audience is specified: he is to address political leaders, kings, and princes (e.g., 22:11-30). He is also to confront the religious leadership (cf. 20:1-6; 23:9ff. and 28:15f.). Like Luther of the Reformation and like Conrad Grebel, the Anabaptist leader in sixteenth-century Switzerland, Jeremiah is to confront state and religious officialdom. If such an assignment makes Jeremiah apprehensive and fearful, he is warned, "Don't lose your nerve because of them, lest I shatter your nerve right before them" (Bright: 4).

Military language predominates. These leaders will oppose, even *fight,* yet Jeremiah will be made a *fortified city, an iron pillar.* If Jeremiah is pictured by some as a weeping prophet, and tender, it should not be forgotten that he was also to be a soldier, a man of steel. The outcome is established. Jeremiah will overcome.

## THE TEXT IN BIBLICAL CONTEXT

*God's Call.* Jeremiah's call is much like Moses' call (cf. Deut. 18:18; Exod. 3:12), and can be compared with other calls to leadership (Boadt: 11).

|                        | Exodus  | Isaiah   | Jeremiah | Ezekiel   |
|------------------------|---------|----------|----------|-----------|
| Divine Meeting         | 3:1-4a  | 6:1-2    | 1:4      | 1:1-28    |
| Word of Identification | 3:4b-9  | 6:3-4    | 1:5a     | 1:29—2:2  |
| Commission             | 3:10    | 6:7b-10  | 1:5b     | 2:3-5     |
| Objection              | 3:11    | 6:5,11a  | 1:6      | 2:6, 8    |
| Reassurance            | 3:12a   | 6:11b-13 | 1:7-8    | 2:7-8     |
| Sign                   | 3:12b   | 6:6-7a   | 1:9-10   | 2:8—3:11  |

One may distinguish two types of call: (1) those with visions such as God's call to Isaiah and Ezekiel, and (2) those without visions such as the calls to Moses and Jeremiah.

In the New Testament Paul's reference to his divine call into ministry (Gal. 1:15) draws on language from this chapter. Points of similarity are: pre-birth consecration, a speaking ministry, and a Gentile assignment. While these calls to ministry are of a private nature, the New Testament shows how the congregation can become involved in another's call to ministry (Acts 13:1-3).

## THE TEXT IN THE LIFE OF THE CHURCH

*Grasped!* Wilbur Smith, a twentieth-century preacher and lecturer, tells how he cared little for ministers or the ministry. "Then circumstances arose so that one morning when I was standing in my bedroom on the third floor of our home, the Lord suddenly hit me. I wasn't praying, I wasn't weeping for my sins; I was rather perplexed as to what I should do, and the Lord just suddenly said to me, 'You are to go into the Christian ministry.' I can't explain it; it was just overwhelming, and it was from the Lord."

The person who is called is grasped. The call to the ministry leaves no room for wiggle. As one minister said, "When I was converted, I discovered that I had no choice. I had been decided upon."

## *"Are You Joking, Jeremiah?"*

Norman Habel, an Old Testament scholar, has given a contemporary ring to Jeremiah's call (Habel: 14-16).

Some years ago,
When I was young,
In the middle of my teens,
Sporting jeans
Or lounging on the rooftops
Back in Israel,
My life began to drag. . . .

My name is Jeremiah,
Or Jerry, if you like. . . .
I had no number I could dial,
No football and
No groove,
Until a frightening message
Was delivered to my house
By my God,
Yes, by God,
My God called Yahweh,
Lord of Hosts!. . .

"Young man," He said,
"I've chosen you
For a difficult assignment
To be My new ambassador
At large
To the people of your land. . . .

But I said, "God,
there must be some mistake.
I can't do work like that.
After all,
I'm only in my teens
Sporting jeans
And lounging on the rooftops.
I've had no training
In diplomacy
Or politics,
In how to speak,
Or how to pray in public. : . .

Then God replied,
"Keep quiet, son,
Don't answer Me like that.
Don't say you're only in your teens,
For you will go
Wherever I decide,
And you will say
The words which I supply. . . ."

Part 2

# Sermons Warning of Disaster

# Jeremiah 2—10

Two "sermons"—to use a modern label—are key to this section. In the first sermon, Jeremiah's theme is that the people have turned away from God (2:1—3:5). The material which follows, mostly poetry, calls for a spiritual return and warns repeatedly of the approaching disaster from the "foe from the north." The poetry is vivid: barked commands of army captains already seem to ring in the air.

In the second sermon Judah is confronted with two evils: bad theology and corrupt practice (7:1-15). Warnings continue as with prophetic perception Jeremiah describes the disaster of an enemy siege as though it were already taking place (chapters 8—10). The "foe from the north" has arrived. Jeremiah is heartbroken.

A third "sermon," or sermon summary, on the theme "You did not listen" (11:1-17) is followed by a third warning, this time of exile. But that is already to put us on the threshold of another division of the book.

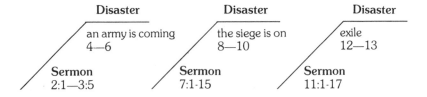

| Disaster | Disaster | Disaster |
|----------|----------|----------|
| an army is coming 4—6 | the siege is on 8—10 | exile 12—13 |
| Sermon 2:1—3:5 | Sermon 7:1-15 | Sermon 11:1-17 |

Jeremiah 2:1 – 3:5

# From Honeymoon to Divorce

## PREVIEW

From bride, to adulterous wife, to prostitute—the sequence is shocking. Jeremiah, now on public stage, begins his message abruptly. He describes the relationship between God and Israel with a marriage metaphor. Sadly, that once-beautiful relationship, is virtually in pieces. Following the attractive opening picture of deep attachment each partner had for the other, Jeremiah catapults his audience into an imaginary courtroom. Here the two partners hurl charges and counter charges in an emotionally packed encounter. Jeremiah pleads for a turnabout.

Most of the chapter turns on a court law case, technically called in Hebrew a *rib*. In the verb form that word occurs in *I bring charges* (v. 9 "contend," RSV). Four emotionally charged speeches given as court evidence follow the formal charge of Israel's unfaithfulness. The dialogue is laced with metaphors, with quotations by "innocent" Israel, and with the Lord's admonitions. A quick search for these features and a listing of them is an excellent way to discover the mood of the dialogue.

The topics raised in 2:1—3:5 will be treated in the book later; this chapter signals what is to come. Likely these words were spoken early in Jeremiah's career, probably before the reform under King Josiah in 621. Mention is made of Egypt and Assyria, but not of Babylon, already a noteworthy power by 620.

41

OUTLINE

An Early Portrait: The Lord and His Bride, 2:1-3

A Court Lawsuit: The Charge of Unfaithfulness, 2:4-13

The Court Evidence, 2:14—3:5
2:14-19    Israel Has Turned to Other Nations
2:20-28    Israel Has Turned to Baals
2:29-37    Israel Has Forgotten the Lord
3:1-5      Israel Presumes on the Lord

EXPLANATORY NOTES

**An Early Portrait: The Lord and His Bride  2:1-3**

Jeremiah's message about the early relationship between the Lord and Israel was not his own idea. The word of the Lord, almost like a tangible thing, carne to him as it had come before (1:4,11) and as it would many times more (7:1; 11:1; 14:1). The target audience was Jerusalem. The message was to deal with the apostasy or waywardness of God's people, a theme already sounded when Jeremiah was called (1:16). The short poem about marriage is in two parts. The first focuses on Israel (v. 2); the second on God (v. 3).

The Lord remembered to Israel's credit (lit., "I remember with regard to you") her keen devotion (ḥesed). Loyal love (ḥesed) often describes God's covenant love to people; less often it is used for the people's integrity in their covenant. The word, it has been claimed, suggests someone coming to help another who is in need. Israel's love for God in the wilderness following the memorable Exodus was like the love of a new bride. In the wilderness Israel did not (as she did later) follow after idols, except for the brief golden calf incident (Exod. 32; for a different view of the wilderness experience see Ezek. 20:10-17). Her devotion to the Lord was clear from her response to the covenant offer (Exod. 24:7).

God took pleasure in her since she belonged to him and to him only. Like the barley and wheat firstfruits, she was special to the Lord (cf. Num. 15:17-21; 18:12ff.; Lev. 23:9-21; Deut. 26:1ff.). God insured her safety. Evil would come on all who dared to molest her, such as the Amalekites and the Midianites (Exod. 17:8ff.; Num. 25:16ff.).

**A Court Lawsuit: The Charge of Unfaithfulness  2:4-13**

God asks the people some searching questions prior to filing a formal court charge. The target group has widened now beyond Jerusalem to *all you clans of the house of Israel.* "Israel" could mean those tribes to the north of Judah which had been captured by the Assyrians (722). Some had been removed to Assyrian-held territory. Others remained in the land under Assyrian rule there. Or "Israel" could mean the current political entity—strictly speaking, Judah. More likely Jeremiah has in view all those who are descendants of Jacob, the covenant people, whether they are in his home area of Judah or in northern Israel or in exile in Assyria.

In its full form the prophetic lawsuit *(rib)* includes a call to witnesses, a statement by the accuser or plaintiff, a recital of God's acts, a specific accusation or complaint, and a judicial sentence. Here the Lord, who is the prosecutor and later will appear also as judge, opens the case with a question. A general accusation calls attention to Israel's action, i.e., *they strayed so far from me,* and to their words, or better, their lack of words, for *they did not ask . . .* (v. 6).

Several accusations are then pinpointed: Israel has defiled the land; leaders have failed in their responsibility; and worst of all, Israel has exchanged God for other so-called gods. Most of these single accusations are summarized in *they have forsaken me* (v. 13). God files a lawsuit: *I bring charges against you* (v. 9). The atmosphere is intense because Israel's failure contrasts so sharply with God's faithfulness (v. 6). The accusations are grave—so grave that the heavens as witness shudder at the evidence (v. 12).

God the accuser at once disclaims that any guilt is attached to him. No, Israel has walked after worthless idols, emptiness, nothingness *(hebel)* (v. 5), the much-used term in Ecclesiastes meaning "vanity." The word *hebel* is also a wordplay on the god Baal. To go after worthless idols results in personal emptiness. One becomes like that which one pursues (Hos. 9:10).

The people are accused of failure to remember the Lord's actions in their behalf. To inquire, *Where is the Lord?* (v. 6) is not to ask for information but to seek orientation. Such orientation was to come from the priests, but they themselves have failed to say, *Where is the Lord?* (v. 8; cf. Isa. 63:11-14). Consequently the people have not been reminded of the Lord's (1) deliverance, or (2) guidance, or (3) gifts. God's accusation, *Israel defiled my land,* is even more grave in the light of such gracious activity. The land could be defiled with improper criminal procedures (Deut. 21:23), or through child sacrifice (Ps. 106:38), or by marriage irregularities (Deut. 24:1-4), or as here, through idolatry (Ezek. 36:18).

The accusation singles out four classes: priests, leaders, prophets, peoples (v. 8). Each of the first three is charged with failure in their chief assignment. The priests were to teach (Mal. 2:7), but they did not teach. The leaders (lit. "shepherds") were to safeguard commitments, but they broke the commitments (pesha'="cause a breach"). The prophets were to be spokespersons for the Lord, but they had become spokespersons instead for Baal. [Baal, p. 291.]

The people, it is charged, have bartered away their glory (a reference to the Lord God) and exchanged God for gods who are no gods. Such action is unnatural, for not even people of other religions, whether those in the west (Kittim originally referred to a place on Cyprus and by extension designated islands and coastlands) or those in the east (Kedar= Arabian tribes) would exchange their gods (v. 10f; cf. Isa. 8:19). The barter is worthless, without any advantage; it "does not profit" (v. 11, NASB), a frequent theme in the entire lawsuit (cf. vv. 5, 8, 13). Such apostasy is incredible, even preposterous. The heavens as witness have reason to be appalled (cf. Isa. 1:2; Mic. 6:1).

The lawsuit essentially charges that Israel has forsaken God, a term often found in Jeremiah (v. 13; 2:17, 19; 5:7, 19; 16:11; 17:13). Cisterns for holding water during the dry hot summer were dug into the porous limestone and lined with plaster. When the plaster cracked, the cisterns would leak. *Cisterns that cannot hold water* is a metaphor for the idolatry of Baalism (vv. 10-11) and perhaps also for reliance on Egypt and Assyria, nations to whom Israel went for help (2:18). The image of God as a fountain of living water is pervasive (Isa. 55:1; Ps. 36:9; John 4:10-14).

Despite the court language with its accusations and its severity, there is in Jeremiah's impassioned poetry a plaintive sound, a pleading note. God the accuser has no joy in prosecuting his covenant partner. He wishes to bring her to her senses, as the next stanza makes clear.

### The Court Evidence  2:14 — 3:5

Evidence for the lawsuit is in the form of disputations. The purpose of a disputation is to argue, to convict, but also to persuade. Here God dissuades Israel from her plan of seeking help from other nations.

The disputation speeches are marked by numerous quotations. Essentially God exposes their evil by playing back to them what they have said. These quotations from the people are everywhere imbedded in the Lord's speeches (vv. 20, 23, 25, 27, 31, 35, 3:4; cf. Mal. 1:2, 4, 6, 12; 2:17, etc.). An example:

*You say, "I am innocent. . . ."*
*But I will pass judgment on you (2:35).*

## 2:14-19 Israel Has Turned to Other Nations

The opening question is rhetorical and expects "No" for an answer. Israel was not originally a people in bondage, a born slave destined to be a slave. If Israel had once been free, why had she now become *plunder*, virtually in the grip of others?

Something must be seriously wrong, for her country has been devastated. The lion was the insignia or symbol for the Assyrians. It was the Assyrians, the longtime enemy from the east, that made Israel a wasteland. Memphis, a capital of the pyramid-building Pharaohs, is 14 miles from Cairo. Tahpanhes, where Jeremiah went later (43:9; 44:1), was a fortress city in the northeast delta of the Nile. Egypt, as represented by these two cities, *shaved* (lit., "grazed") *the crown of Israel's head*, either a reference to the way the Israelite kings had been exploited or to the choice lands in Israel from which Egypt had gained benefit. The cause of Israel's slavelike humiliation was her departure from the Lord, whose benefit of guidance (v. 17), as in 2:6, forms a backdrop for the implied accusation.

Ironically, despite being virtually controlled by these powers, Israel is headed toward Egypt to drink the waters (a metaphor for getting political or military help) of the Nile, Egypt's source of nourishment. On the other hand and in the opposite direction, Israel makes overtures to the Assyrians to drink the waters of the Euphrates. The image of drinking water at these foreign sources compares with the earlier charge that Israel had forsaken the fountain of living water, the Lord God (2:13).

The consequences of such reliance on Egypt and Assyria are given in verse 19 (cf. Isa. 30:1-5). Israel's attempts at such alliances will be shown by experience to be negative and evil. Again, as earlier, God draws up a ledger to show the people that to forsake the Lord is evil and bitter and also unprofitable to themselves (cf. vv. 5, 8). The ease with which Israel goes after other nations demonstrates that she lacks the proper awe for the Lord (cf. Deut. 32:17), whose title significantly is *Lord Almighty. [Lord of Hosts, p. 304.]* The title, synonymous with power and rulership, renders their reach for political alliances even more ironic.

## 2:20-28 Israel Has Turned to Baals

This disputation speech begins, not with a question, but with an accusation, *Long ago you broke off your yoke.* "You" is grammatically possible and from the context is to be preferred (RSV and NIV) over "I"

(NASB). Israel has rejected any partnership with the Lord. The yoke was a familiar harnessing device to link two animals for work such as pulling a plow. Israel has reneged on her side of the partnership, *I will not serve* (work). Her action has illustrated her word, for on hilltops, the usual places for Baal altars (1 Kings 14:23; Jer. 3:6, 13), she sprawls (literally) in harlotry. Since sexual actions were part of Baal rituals (Hos. 4:11-14), the harlotry can be understood both as immorality and as spiritual unfaithfulness to the Lord.

Two metaphors elaborate the theme of Israel's evil. Using an image from agriculture, God describes his work of planting Israel as a choice vine of good reliable (lit., "true") stock (v. 2). Any future failure could hardly be blamed on God (cf. vv. 5-6). Still Israel has become degenerate. "But what a foul-smelling thing you've become" (Bright: 11). Israel is elsewhere likened to a vine (Ps. 80:8; Isa. 5:1-6), but the point here is the detestable plant that she has become. A second picture, now from a household setting, is of Israel's evil, so black and bad that even the strongest detergent (made of potash and alkali) will not remove it. Israel's behavior in the valley—a possible reference to child sacrifice in the Hinnom Valley—is evidence of her degeneracy. *[Topheth, p. 312.]*

Two more metaphors vividly picture both her restlessness and the sensual activity that characterizes Israel. The young camel is forever pacing about, apparently in enclosed areas, crisscrossing her ways, looking, one suspects, for adventure. The wild donkey, which by contrast is free, is also sniffing the wind, and in passionate desire wanders far and wide. There is no need to track her; male donkeys at least, have only to wait for her time of heat, when she will be readily at hand. Both allusions to animals point up Israel's "wild" nature, her running about. She offers herself to anyone who will have her.

Verse 25 adds an ironic twist. Israel is warned to put on shoes for all this running around, and provide something to drink since her great exertions will make her thirsty! Her response to such divine caution is, *It's no use!* The term expresses defiance and exasperation with the sense of "To hell with it" (Holladay, 1971: 126). *[Word/Deed, p. 313.]*

Her sinful conduct results in shame (v. 26). As in 2:8, four classes of leaders are cited in the promotion of false religion. Awkwardly these address a tree, symbol of a female deity in Baal worship, as "Father." Equally confusing, they speak to a stone, often in the form of a pillar, a symbol of a male deity, as the mother figure. So serious is the multiplication of deities that every town has its own brand of religion. Here, as in the preceding disputation, the root problem is: *they have turned their backs to me* (v. 27).

The variety of metaphors used to describe Israel's apostasy is not unlike the imagery of Hosea, who describes Israel's illicit passions as "an oven heated by the baker," and as a "cake not turned" (Hos. 7:4, 8).

## 2:29-37 Israel Has Forgotten the Lord

This disputation, like the one in 2:14, opens with a question. The courtroom atmosphere, set in 2:4ff., is continued with the word *charges* *(rib)*, except that it is Israel who is now taking the Lord to court (v. 29). But the tables are quickly turned, for the passage is filled with the Lord's accusations against her (vv. 29-30; 31-35b; 36cd). The announcement of God's action, implying a verdict of "guilty," is given midway in the list of accusations (v. 35c) and points to their exile (v. 37).

God basically charges that Israel has rebelled *(pesha‘)* against him (v. 29). The Hebrew term has its cradle in political language and refers to a breach, as in failure to observe treaty terms. Specific citations to buttress this generalization are given at once. Israel has not responded to chastening. *[Discipline, p. 295.]* Instead she has paraded her rebel spirit by putting God's prophets to death. King Jehoiakim's slaying of Uriah the prophet could be an example within Jeremiah's lifetime (26:20-23).

An appeal, together with a self-reflection, interrupts the list of charges. The tone of the appeal is one of impatience. "And this generation! You! Consider the word of the Lord" (v. 31). The Lord pauses for self-examination. Is the fault perhaps with him? Has he been a disappointment to his people, a *desert . . . or land of great darkness?* (cf. 2:5). God is puzzled over a people who in defiance assert their independence, *We are free;* and as a first act of that freedom decide, *We will come to you no more.*

The accusations continue. A generalized complaint, *my people have forgotten me,* is followed by specific examples. Israel is warned not to forget God (Deut. 4:19; 8:14), but her forgetfulness is part of the historical record (Judg. 3:7; Ps. 106:21; 78:7f.; Hos. 4:6; Jer. 3:21; 23:27). Forgetting God is most unnatural. This fact is emphasized by an allusion to a bride who is unlikely to forget her ornaments, especially those ornaments that will mark her as married.

The shift to further accusations is immediate. Israel is so adept at making love to false gods that she could teach the worst of women prostitutes a thing or two (v. 33). The breach of loyalty is vertical with God and horizontal with fellow human beings, for Israel has oppressively victimized the innocent poor even to the point of bloodshed. *[Oppression, p. 305.]* A thief caught in the act could be put to death and the killer would not incur guilt (Exod. 22:2), but these victims are not thieves. They are innocent. Israel is condemned by words from her own mouth. Her bold claim to innocence, *I have not sinned*, stated in the face of her actions, shows how insensitive, even self-deceived and corrupt, she is. The Lord's anger has momentarily been suspended, so Israel rationalizes this lack of swift action to mean that she is blameless.

The instability of Israel is hinted at throughout. This is summed up in the concluding question, "Why do you gad about changing your way?" (v. 36, RSV). Throughout the passage, questions set the mood: e.g., exasperation ("Why do you contend with me?" v. 29), reflection ("Why do my people say. . .?" v. 31), disbelief ("Can a virgin forget her ornaments. . .?" v. 32), and pathos ("Why do you gad about. . .?" v. 36). In addition, there is sarcasm and anger (vv. 33, 35).

The announcement of passing a court sentence (v. 35c) is made specific in verse 36c. Egypt will humiliate Israel as Assyria had done earlier (cf. 2 Chron. 28: 16-20). Incredibly, Israel trusts in both Assyria and Egypt (cf. 2:18), but God has rejected these powers; Israel will not have success with them. The expression that they go with hands on their heads indicates surrender and thus captivity.

Thematic notes from other prophets can be heard in this passage. The silencing of prophets—even if not through death—is mentioned by Amos (2:12; 7:12) and is an accusation leveled by Jesus against the religious leaders (Matt. 23:29ff.), where, as here, the announcement is one of coming desolation. Amos and Isaiah both accuse Israel of oppressive action against the poor (Amos 2:6; 8:6; Isa. 3:13-15). For the theme of God's self-examination, see Isaiah 5:7. In Isaiah, too, chastisement has not brought results (Isa. 1:5ff.).

### 3:1-5 Israel Presumes on the Lord

The disputation opens in the Hebrew text (but not in the Greek version) with "to say" and introduces a new round in the argument, as though the defendant had appealed the court decision. The hypothetical situation of a divorce brings into play certain laws found in Deuteronomy 24:1-4. A husband who had divorced his wife could not remarry her after another marriage even if that woman was widowed or divorced. The prohibition, it is thought, was intended to forestall initial divorces and also to safeguard the second marriage. It eliminated serial marriages and warned against superficial commitments.

The Jeremiah text implies that Israel, through her departure from the Lord (2:5) and her declarations (2:20, 31), is maritally severed from the Lord in a divorce. Yet, quite flippantly, she turns back to the Lord, (the KJV uses the imperative "turn!" which though grammatically possible, does not fit the context), as if God, without further ado, would take her back. The seriousness of her situation is demonstrated by "can you come back to me?" (v. 1).

Israel's separation from God is documented. She has been a prostitute spiritually with many lovers (v. 1). On the barren height, the customary place for Baal shrines, she has carried on a Canaanite worship. It is not that she has been overtaken by temptation, but like a nomad who plans to pounce on a desert caravan, so Israel has deliberately planned harlotry. Both physical and spiritual harlotry may be in view here (v. 2). Such unfaithfulness defiles the land even as taking back a divorced party after an intervening marriage and divorce defiles the land (v. 1; cf. Hos. 4:1ff.). Already the consequences of such moral action have affected the environment, for there is an absence of rain (v. 3; cf. 1 Kings 17-19; Amos 4:6ff.). However, Israel is not embarrassed, nor does she blush. She brazenly displays herself as a harlot, apparently by means of a telltale mark on the forehead.

The marriage metaphor already begun in 2:2 persists, despite Israel's use of "Father." It is followed by the phrase *my friend from my youth* (v. 4), which is appropriate to marriage partners. The address *Father* reveals Israel's childish immaturity that expects fatherly tolerance. But Israel presumes on the Lord by taking lightly his position on sin, as though like a grandfather he will wink at evil and his anger will be a passing thing (v. 5).

The marriage metaphor persists, but another theme dominates here as well as throughout. Israel's story has been rehearsed in terms of land. God enjoyed Israel's devotion in the wilderness (2:2). He brought her out of a land of drought and deep darkness (2:6) into a fruitful land, which Israel later defiled (2:7). Foreign countries made this land a waste (2:15). Harlotry will continue to defile the land, as also will failure to observe divorce regulations (3:1-2).

"You have spoken evil and done evil things" (v. 5, NASB). The word/action combination, used frequently in the longer passage, closes the entire unit. [*Word/Deed, p. 313.*] The words in the phrase 'You have had your way" (v. 5, NASB) appear also in Isaiah 16:2, where the sense is "to prevail." Israel has succeeded in going after evil, having "done all the evil that (she) could" (RSV). She has compounded her evil by supposing that without any ado God will have her back if such is her whim. The force of the allusion to the divorce law is that judicially speaking God cannot have Israel back, without adding to the evil. At this point Israel is all but married to other gods: according to the law, she may not be able to return to the Lord, even if she would. Or is the divorce already a reality? If so, succeeding appeals by the Lord (4:1) do actually—and here is the marvel—invite Israel to return to the lover she had first known (2:1).

## THE TEXT IN BIBLICAL CONTEXT

*The Marriage Metaphor.* In Israel's earlier history, covenant discussion was along the line of political treaties with their stipulations, blessings, and curses (cf. Deut.). Hosea, 150 years before Jeremiah, was the first to illustrate God's relationship to Israel in a marriage metaphor (Hos. 2:14-15). Hosea's marriage to the prostitute Gomer set the backdrop for that book (Hos. 1:2; 3:1).

Just as in Hosea the marriage metaphor was the nucleus from which the rest of the book grew, so in Jeremiah 2:1-3 is the "seed oracle" for chapters 2 and 3; and these in turn are the "seed oracle" for the entire book (Holladay, 1976: 31).

Subsequent to Jeremiah, Ezekiel made extensive use of the courtship/marriage theme to discuss God's relationship with Israel (Ezek. 16:8-59; 23). Such portraits of intimacy cast in the language of marriage are striking. It is daring even, because Israel's apostasy consisted in going after the Baal religion, which was a sex- and fertility-oriented religion. Baal worship was dominated by rites of a sexual nature. Jeremiah does not discard such language; he uses the marriage vocabulary but redirects its meaning.

Paul capitalizes on this method of speaking of a close relationship when he describes the church, God's people, as the bride of Christ (Eph. 5:25-33). The church at Ephesus is later described as having lost her first love (Rev. 2:4-5), perhaps an allusion to Jeremiah 2:2. The marriage metaphor is used of the new Jerusalem "made ready as a bride adorned for her husband" (Rev. 21:2).

*The Lawsuit.* The lawsuit speech is used in Hosea (4:1ff.) and in Micah (6:1ff.). The lawsuit both formalizes God's case against Israel and shows that the coming punishment for Israel's evil is not capricious but just and for a reasonable cause. In Micah, as in Jeremiah 2, the action of God in bringing his people from Egypt is the background against which the accusations appear especially stark. Several of the epistles, such as Ephesians, exhibit a similar movement by discussing the Christian's behavior (latter chapters) in the light of God's actions in Christ (earlier chapters).

*Divine Persuasion.* Although in the form of a lawsuit, the divine word is not a precipitous accusation in which God seeks an early conviction of guilt. God reasons with his people patiently. The seriousness of the lawsuit is the occasion for asking Israel to "consider" (2:19, 23, 31). Similarly in Hosea God pleads with a backsliding, spiritually apathetic, and perverse people (Hos. 11:1-9; 14:1-7). God reasons with a wayward people, whether it be Israel (Isa. 1:18) or the local church (Rev. 3:14-21).

## THE TEXT IN THE LIFE OF THE CHURCH

*A Caring God, a Caring Church.* God does not take lightly the defection of his people nor does he quickly write them off when they prove stubborn. God's pleading with them has all the pain and urgency of an injured husband reasoning in the divorce court with the wife he still loves. The rift between God and people, like that between husband and wife, does not spring up overnight. There are signals of increasing strain along the way: the dissatisfied partner fails to give attention to the other (2:4-8), looks elsewhere for satisfaction (2:13-19), chafes under the demands of the covenant (2:20), swings free to make other alliances (2:23-28), and finally takes leave of the partner (2:31). Counsel, patient reasoning, efforts to win back love, or the sternest admonition seem to have no effect. In fact, the departing one may claim to be innocent! The church would do well to check its own attitudes—to assess what real attention it is giving to God, what other satisfactions and alliances it is seeking.

A caring church will also take seriously the wandering away of those who because of sin foolishly complicate their lives. The church will not ignore them, or hastily dismiss them, wash its hands of them, or shrug off the evil; but will in a tenacity born of compassion seek their spiritual restoration.

Jeremiah 3:6 – 4:4

# Appeals to Two
# "Ever-Turning" Sisters

PREVIEW

The key word here is "turn," which for Jeremiah means a redirection either toward God or away from him. In its various forms the word occurs 16 times in this section. In all of Jeremiah it is found 90 times. Verse 22 captures the mood, which is one of God's earnest pleading, "Turn, ever-turning children, and I will heal your turnings-about." There will follow hard words of judgment (4:5) but here, as in Jeremiah 30 and 31, the graciousness of the Almighty shines with striking brilliance. A likely date for this passage and the one which follows it is 626-622 B.C.

Israel, the kingdom to the north of Judah, had been disowned by God because of her spiritual unfaithfulness. "Adultery" was the word used to describe Israel's awful behavior. Because of it the Assyrians had overrun the Northern Kingdom (732-722). One would expect that Judah, a witness to these events, would learn the seriousness of spiritual adultery. The charge is that Judah has not learned. Of the two sisters, Israel, despite her worship of Baal, was more righteous than Judah.

The passage is punctuated with the summons to repentance (3:12-13; 14-22; 4:1f.; 4:3f.). Persuasive arguments for a "turning," a repentance, are offered at length, first to Israel (3:12—4:2) and then more briefly to her sister state Judah (4:3-4). [Summons to Repentance, p. 310.]

## OUTLINE

Comparison of the Two Sisters, Israel and Judah, 3:6-10

God's Appeal to Israel to Repent, 3:11— 4:2
  3:11-13    God's First Appeal to "Defecting" Israel
  3:14-22a    God's Second Appeal to "Ever-turning" Israel
  3:22b—4:2  Israel's Confession and God's Reaction

God's Appeal to Judah to Repent, 4:3-4

## EXPLANATORY NOTES

### Comparison of the Two Sisters, Israel and Judah  3:6-10

The force of the comparison between the two kingdoms lies in what had happened historically. Ever since King Solomon's time (922) the nation had been divided into the ten tribes of Israel in the north and the two tribes of Judah in the south. In 722 the Assyrians, the powerful enemy from the east, had captured Samaria, Israel's capital, and a large part of the Israelite population had been deported northward to the Habor River and to Assyria. To forestall rebel activity, peoples from the Assyrian-occupied countries had been imported to Israelite territory (2 Kings 17:23-24). If Jeremiah was in Jerusalem, as is most likely, one must remember that the Assyrian-occupied territory was less than 25 miles away. Judah was living with the object lesson of God's punishment of Israel constantly before her.

The eighth-century prophets Amos and Hosea had given reasons for such a devastation of Israel: spiritual unfaithfulness to God through the worship of other gods as well as indulgence in many social injustices. Punishment came because Israel had "committed adultery." The term "adultery" carries a double meaning: (1) husband-wife unfaithfulness within Israelite families, and (2) the nation's spiritual unfaithfulness to God. To go to *every high hill* and to spreading trees is colorful language for Baal worship. *[Baal, p. 291.]* Canaanite shrines and altars were conveniently and conspicuously located on high terrain.

Jeremiah drew on Hosea to picture God's relationship to Israel as a marriage. God's response to Israel's flirtation with pagan deities was to give her a certificate of divorce (cf. Deut. 24:1-3). The marriage relationship was terminated; the bond of covenant was broken (cf. Jer. 11:10). In fact, God sent her away, even to exile.

Throughout this comparison Israel is described as "faithless," literally "turnable" or "defecting." The adjective for Judah is different: "unfaithful" (cf. "treacherous," NASB). Judah has deliberately played false. "Judah does not blunder into evil; she plans it" (Boadt: 34). The comparison between the two sisters is shown in the chart.

|  | Israel 3:12 – 4:2 | Judah 4:3-4 |
|---|---|---|
| Description | turning, defecting | brazenly faithless, treacherous |
| Accusation | adultery on hill, etc. | adultery with stone and wood |
| Attitude | no interest in turning to the Lord | no fear<br>no turning to God<br>any turning was fake |
| Result | God divorced her | (unspecified) |
| God's response | pleas for return | pleas for return |

The chart shows that it is Judah's brazen attitude that makes her action of adultery even more hideous. Her sin is more grave since she has failed to learn from the example of another (cf. Jer. 7:12). One now expects a judgment word on Judah. That comes later (4:5ff.). First the defecting sister (also known as the Lord's wife, v. 14, and once as sons, v. 19) is summoned in God's grace to change, to turn.

## God's Appeal to Israel to Repent 3:11 – 4:2

The Hebrew has no word for "return"; it is simply "turn" or "turn around" (shub). Since Israel had turned away from God, the summons is clearly to "return." Often the word is used in its covenantal sense. That is, a person turns away in one's affection from a covenant partner; or, one may turn toward the covenant partner, signifying a stronger relationship. To turn back or return when earlier one has "turned away" is the Old Testament way of speaking of repentance. In Hebrew thought, to repent is to make an about-face turn. This entire passage turns on the word "turn," as does Jeremiah 31:15-20. [Repentance, p. 306.]

### 3:11-13 God's First Appeal to "Defecting" Israel

In the first appeal "defecting" Israel is persuaded to return by the argument that God is merciful, gracious (hesed). Hesed, which is often used in covenant discussions, signifies covenant loyalty (cf. Exod. 34:6;

Deut. 7:9; Neh. 1:5). God reaches out to his covenant partner and is totally reliable. Moreover, God promises not to retain anger.

### 3:14-22a God's Second Appeal to "Ever-Turning" Israel

In the second appeal the adjective is "ever-turning," and the designation is not feminine, as in 3:12, but masculine. The reasons urged for Israel to repent are more elaborate here than in the first appeal. Note the more intimate self-presentation: 'I am your husband (lit., ba'al), meaning "lord" (v. 14). God holds out an array of benefits—all nudges toward repentance.

1. A return from exile, even if only by a decimated remnant (v. 14).
2. Godly leaders, shepherds (v. 15).
3. A new experience of divine presence (vv. 16-17).
4. A transformed heart (v. 17c).
5. A united people (v. 18), already anticipated with the mention of Jerusalem and Zion in vv. 14-17.

The mention of the *ark of the covenant* recalls the fortunes of the ark, first in the wilderness (Exod. 25), then in Shiloh (1 Sam. 4:3), then in Kiriath-jearim (1 Sam. 7:2), and finally in the Solomonic temple (1 Kings 8:6). It was probably taken to Babylon in 586. The ark was venerated as the place where, symbolically at least, the Lord was enthroned. Jeremiah's audience must have been shocked at his "disregard" for this sacred object (cf. 26:9).

For all the reverence given to the ark in the past, Jeremiah announces, it will not even receive mention in the future because the presence of God will be so much greater and more overpowering. His throne in Jerusalem will be like a magnet to which nations will come. The presence of God will not be symbolized by the ark, hidden in the holy of holies, access to which is by the high priest alone. No, God's presence will now be symbolized by the entire city, openly accessible to all.

Three additional considerations are urged as reasons for repentance. First, God's heartbeat is heard in verse 19. God wants to give Israel the best of lands (lit., "beauty of beauties"); he wants an intimate father-son relationship (cf. 3:4; 31:9; Hos. 11:1ff.). Second, the people's disappointing, grossly affronting action is described, to their shame (v. 20). Third, Israel's present situation is depicted as one of misery (v. 21) because she has forgotten God (cf. 13:25; 18:15; and 23:27). Let them turn from their disregard for God which brought them misfortune, and their situation will be reversed! God will heal their sickness of forever turning (v. 22). The second appeal concludes as it began,

"Turn, ever-turning sons" (vv. 14 and 22). God has reason to abandon them—instead God's grace pursues them.

### 3:22b—4:2 Israel's Confession and God's Reaction

The persuasions of the Almighty are effective. One interpretation is that verses 22b-25 are the people's response of confession, and that God's welcome is in Jeremiah 4:1. Another is that as in Hosea 14:2, God is placing words in their mouths to show what "turning" would mean: these are the words they *should* say. A third interpretation is that these are insincere mouthings of repentance, and that 4:1 is essentially a rejection. In any event, the two parts, Israel's confession and the Lord's response, spell out the elements of repentance.

These elements include:

> 1. An affirmation of God's claim to be God, together with a recognition that salvation is in God and not elsewhere (vv. 22b, 23b).
> 2. An admission of the pointlessness and also the deceptive folly of their sinful actions (vv. 23a; 24). The mountain orgies with their hubbub were noisy affairs. The *shameful* thing is an alternative word for Baal (cf. Hos. 9:10).
> 3. An acknowledgement of sin and consequent disgrace by saying what are perhaps the hardest words to say, "We (I) have sinned."

With these statements the people turn away from their attachments.

But the turn is still only partial. The turn must be toward a new attachment. As explained in the Lord's response (4:1-2), the turning further involves:

> 4. Abandoning the idols and the ways of the past (4:1b).
> 5. Adopting a new orientation, one which focuses on ways which are truthful and just.
> 6. Asserting that the Lord lives; to swear by him implies a faith in him.

Then God can make good the blessings promised in the earlier statements to Abraham (Gen. 12:3; 18:18; 22:18; 26:4). Therein lies the final argument for repentance.

## God's Appeal to Judah to Repent  4:3-4

From the appeal to Israel in the north (3:12), Jeremiah turns to his immediate audience, those in Jerusalem and Judah. The appeal for a softening of attitude is shorter but also sterner. Judah has been accused of taking her relationship to God lightly and of brazenly going after other gods (3:9).

This crustiness of attitude is illustrated by two metaphors. The first image comes from agriculture. Breaking up *unplowed ground* is clearly more difficult than plowing previously cultivated soil; but the process of breaking up dare not be bypassed, otherwise even the input of the good is like sowing among thorns. Circumcision of the heart, a metaphor from physiology, recalls the covenant sign and points figuratively to the removal of obstructions (cf. Deut. 10:16). The heart in Israelite thought is not the seat of emotions, but the organ for thinking, planning, and deciding. Basic, life-changing decisions are called for.

The appeal is accompanied, not by wooing words and gracious promises, as for sister Israel, but by a threat. Failure to soften up spiritually toward the Lord will bring God's fitting, fiery, unquenchable wrath. God's response toward *evil* is anger. God urges a brazenly evil Judah to action, lest ominous judgment fall. *[Wrath, p. 313.]*

## THE TEXT IN BIBLICAL CONTEXT

*Repentance.* The elaborate appeal for repentance is an echo from Hosea, who used adultery language to describe Israel's faithlessness. Hosea confronted the northern tribes with their turning (backsliding), prompted them by wording a prayer of repentance for them, and declared that God would then heal their turnings about: "I will . . . love them freely" (Hos. 14:1-4). God's readiness to embrace a repentant person or people is nothing short of remarkable. (For other calls to repentance, see Matt. 3:2ff.; 4:17; Acts 2:38; Rev. 2:16, 21; 3:3). Jesus spoke about repentance, making a comparison between cities rather than "sisters" (Matt. 11:20-24). (For a further parallel on the meaning of repentance, see Luke 15:11-32 and 1 Thess. 1:9.) *[Summons to Repentance, p. 310.]*

*A God of Grace.* God's statement "I am gracious" (3:12) is illustrated in God's warm appeal to a people who have set him aside as their God. It is the very God who promises them so much good. Grace is demonstrated in Genesis 1—11 where, despite threats of punishment for sin, there is a "saving factor" (e.g., in the flood Noah's family is saved; following the dispersion at Babel, Abraham is called to carry on God's plan). God's good is routinely offered to rebels (e.g., Israel as a flighty wife in Hosea, the Ninevites preached to by Jonah, the "non-receivers" of Jesus in John 1:11). Because of God's great generosity (Exod. 34:6), people keep receiving "grace upon grace" (John 1:16).

## THE TEXT IN THE LIFE OF THE CHURCH

*Learning to Repent.* God's judgment of Judah took into account the fact that Judah had the advantage of being eyewitness to the fate of her disobedient sister-state, Israel. Judah had even less excuse than Israel to leave God; her judgment therefore was the more severe. The church today has hundreds of years of history and no lack of examples and warnings. Has the church paid attention? What has it learned? Has it taken warning from the hazards of triumphalism which came when Constantine made the Christian religion a state religion? Has it seen sufficiently clearly the perils of institutionalism as represented in a hierarchical church structure? Has it taken note of the consequences of drifting into secularism, of making alliance with political powers, of ignoring the ominous trend of events outside its safe sanctuaries? What excuses can the church give for failure? In Hermann Hartfeld's novel about Russia, a character cries out against the faithless segment of the church, "But where were you, o church, when I was gunning down the innocent? Why did you remain silent then, and why are you silent now?" (p. 179).

Menno Simons, one of the sixteenth-century reformers, pleaded with his listeners. "Dear sirs, repent. The Lawbook of Christ is entirely lost to you. Christ and His truth, sacraments, Spirit, and life, you have never known, much less possessed. You serve strange gods. You hear, follow, and use the doctrine, sacraments, ordinances, and commandments of Antichrist; you lead an unclean, ungodly, and carnal life. Ah, sirs, take warning, your sins have reached to heaven!" (p. 361).

Repentance is not an easy matter, either for church or nation. It is like plowing unbroken ground, or raising a crop among thorns. Yet repentance must be urged. What would a corporate liturgy of repentance for the church look like? What actions would it stress?

Defectors are welcome to return to God's family. Those individuals and churches who do repent will find that God is gracious; they will be offered acceptance and restoration. Entry into the parlor of God's grace is through the hallway of repentance.

*Circumcision and Baptism.* In the sixteenth century, the mainline Reformed churches based their practice of infant baptism on Old Testament circumcision; whereas Anabaptists like Michael Sattler used Jeremiah 4:3-4 to argue that "circumcision is an example and figure of the purification of the heart" (Yoder: 167).

Jeremiah 4:5 – 6:30

# Calamity and Collapse for a Sinning Society

## PREVIEW

Israelites did not need to gaze into crystal balls to discover the future—they had the Lord's prophets. Jeremiah tells his audience, their future involves an invasion by a foreign power. In chapters 4—6 military language dominates and not marriage language, as in chapters 2 and 3. God has declared war! Be ready to flee to the fortified cities! Invaders are coming! The word from the Almighty is followed by the prophet's response, much like an editorial comment. That dialogical feature also distinguishes this passage from chapters 2 and 3 which are one-way oracles from God.

We see the prophet as if he is standing on a Jerusalem wall. He looks outward and becomes panic-stricken as he sees the enemy advance. In agony he turns to look within the city where evil abounds. He looks up and trembles to hear God's judgment oracles. One helpful entry into the section is to search out and classify the passages according to these three perspectives.

The mood is intense. The accusations are punctuated by, *Should I not punish them for this?* The announcements about the invasion of an unnamed enemy come like trip-hammer blows. The prophet himself is torn up by the message and figuratively bends over, holding his stomach and exclaiming, literally, "Oh my guts!"

59

This long passage is in two parallel parts, each introduced by, "Announce [declare] in . . ." (4:5; 5:20). The first part which spells disaster upon disaster is addressed to Judah and Jerusalem (4:5—5:19). The second part has for its theme "Their evil deeds have no limit" and is addressed to Jacob and Judah (5:20—6:30). The parallelism of theme in the two parts is shown in the following itemization (not strictly an outline). The parallelism clarifies and reviews the flow of ideas and so compounds the impact of the message.

|  | Part A: 4:5 – 5:19 | Part B: 5:20 – 6:30 |
|---|---|---|
| Address | Judah, Jerusalem (4:5) this people (4:11) | Jacob and Judah (5:20) people of Benjamin (6:1) |
| Accusation | rebellion (4:17) refusal to repent (5:3) swearing falsely (5:21) adultery (5:7-8, etc.) | stubborn rebellions (5:23) disobedience (6:19) failure to defend the unprotected (5:26-27) prophets speak lies (5:31,etc.) |
| Announcement | I am bringing disaster (4:6) preparation urged (4:5-6) an army is coming (4:16) | disaster looms in the north (6:1) preparation urged (6:1-2) an army is coming (6:22) |
| Instructions | put on sackcloth (4:8) wash the evil away (4:14) | put on sackcloth (6:26) walk in the good way (6:16) |
| Jeremiah's Response | *"Oh, my anguish"* (4:19) *"You adorn yourself in vain"* (4:30) | *"Anguish has gripped us"* (6:24) *"I am full of the wrath of the Lord"* (6:11) |

The vocabulary for the accusations is rich and varied: a harlot's cosmetics, lusty stallions, cages of birds, and wells of gushing water. Sins by leaders are especially noted in Part B. The citations of the people's words are frequent and striking.

Preparations for war are everywhere urged, first in Jerusalem (4:5), then in Dan (4:15). Soon the shouts of the enemy's captain himself are heard (6:4-5). The devastation is total, so it appears, except for the ray of hope, "I will not destroy you completely" (4:27; 5:10, 18). To see how it all turned out, we must jump to Jeremiah 39.

Scholars hold that some of this material predates the reformation which began in 621. Parts of it may come from late in Josiah's reign or early in Jehoiachin's reign (i.e., 612-608). It therefore precedes the actual Babylonian invasion by one or two decades.

EXPLANATORY NOTES

## Announcements to Judah and Jerusalem  4:5 – 5:19

*"Disaster Follows Disaster"* Jeremiah's responses, which alternate with the word from God, provide an individual personal touch in what would otherwise be a series of blasts against the nation generally. At first Jeremiah reproaches God (4:10), but later he becomes a co-prosecutor (5:3-5).

### 4:5-9  An Alarm, "The Enemy Is on His Way"

The prophets are elsewhere described as watchmen—persons who were stationed on the city walls scanning the horizon for a sign of disturbance (1:11-12; Ezek. 33:7). Signals, perhaps crude signs pointing to shelters, or more likely a series of fire signals transmitting the news, were part of the emergency measures. Now a threat is imminent. A trumpet sound from the watchmen, like a modern city alarm siren, alerts the people in the fields and unwalled villages to scurry to the walled cities. The threat is an unnamed enemy from the north. To leave the threat unspecified is to call to mind the horrors associated traditionally with disaster from the north. Some have suggested the Scythians on the basis of a comment by the Greek historian Herodotus. But the description of an enduring nation (5:15) and an excellent army does not fit the Scythians. The coming army, as will be disclosed later, is Babylon. Though Babylon was east of Palestine, its westward move would follow the Euphrates and entry into Palestine would be from the north. *[Babylon, p. 291.]*

### 4:10  Jeremiah's Protest

Jeremiah reacts spontaneously. He protests by saying in effect, "It's unfair." Compare the same response in 1:6; 4:10; 14:13 and 32:17: "You promised peace, and a sword is at our throat." Peace and safety had indeed been promised to Jerusalem a century earlier by Isaiah when the Assyrians were advancing toward Jerusalem (Isa. 37:33-35). Perhaps on that basis, prophets contemporary with Jeremiah preach peace. The situation now, however, is different from that in Isaiah's time. Even so, Jeremiah at first argues with God about the threat of war. He employs strong language. *Deceived* is the same term used in the serpent's beguiling act (Gen.3:13). Later Jeremiah aligns himself with God, recognizing that judgment is deserved (16:10-11).

### 4:11-18  An Interpretation as the Enemy Nears

Initially compared to a lion, the speed of the oncoming army is now compared to a scorching wind (4:11). Gentle breezes blow in Palestine from the northwest, but sometimes a wind known as a sirocco sweeps in from the east, fierce with sandstorms. Too strong for winnowing, it carries away both the grain and the chaff, the good and the bad.

The watchman is not now in Jerusalem, but in Dan, the frontier border city in the north. *[Map, p. 316.]* Messengers might carry the news, but the prophets tell what's behind the news, namely Judah's sinful conduct. *Conduct* (lit., "way," v. 18), a much-used term in this passage refers to "lifestyle" (cf. 5:4, 5; 6:16, 25, 27). There is a last-minute call for Judah to clean up her act: *Wash . . . and be saved* (v. 14).

## 4:19-22  Agonizing Responses

That which is announced as future is as vivid as if already present. The trumpet alarm and the battle standards bring on a cold sweat. Jeremiah's heart pounds. "My anguish!" ("my soul," NASB; "my pain," GNB; lit., "my guts," the inward parts). The Hebrews located strong emotion in the viscera. The prophet is disturbed by wrenching pain as he sees the disaster brought on by sin. God also agonizes because of the folly of sin itself (v. 22). God specifies emphatically, "Me they do not know" (4:22; cf. Isa. 1:2-3).

## 4:23-28  A Look at the Appalling Ruin

The coming ruin is described as having already happened. In highly moving poetry Jeremiah describes the approaching devastation. The earth is now a formless void, an expression that harks back to Genesis 1:2. The earth has been uncreated. The disturbances are cosmic, touching sun and moon. They are terrestial, affecting city and field. The cosmos is undone. "Four times the verses begin with 'I looked.' Looked at what? At four visions of non-life (earth, heavens, mountains, hills), and at four visions of life (man, birds, fruitful land, cities)" (Holladay, 1974: 52).

Disorder and chaos are everywhere. Cities have been blasted away because of God's wrath. The creation order (lights, heavens . . . birds, man) is familiar, but instead of the final Sabbath rest, there is searing wrath. Have modern statements and films depicting the destruction following nuclear war said it any more powerfully?

The description of mountains shaking and the world becoming dark belongs to early war poetry (Num. 10:34-36; Judg. 5:4-5; Deut. 33:2-3; cf. Hab. 3:3-6). Though the term "day of the Lord" does not appear here, the language is day-of-the-Lord terminology (Isa. 13:1-10; Ezek. 30:1-3; Joel 2:30-31).

Verses 27-28 are a short divine oracle, inserted here for antiphonal effect. Stress is on the disastrous effects of God's wrath. The oracle recasts but essentially repeats the scenario of destruction. At first reading the statement *"though I will not destroy it completely"* contradicts the description of utter devastation (vv. 23-26). Some scholars, changing "not" *(lo')* to "her" *(lah)* read, "I will make her a total destruction." But devastation and annihilation are two different things (cf. 5:18). Jeremiah saw some grace even in judgment, for God stopped short of annihilation. *[Wrath, p. 313.]*

### 4:29-31 Jeremiah's Commentary

The unbelievably nonchalant attitude of Judah is set next to this terrifying word from the Lord and the people's scurrying for shelter. The prophet stands by incredulously. Judah is fixing to go to a party! She is like one standing on dynamite, about to be blown up, yet concerned about cosmetics! What a misreading of the situation! Wrinkled and worn through years of sinning and harlotry, she still intends to charm her invaders sexually. Made up with eye shadow, she is flirting with the nations that will do her in. Jeremiah sees it clearly: here is not a jeweled partygoer, but a woman in anguish as in childbirth. She is throwing her favors to oncoming enemy "lovers" who want her blood, murderers who are holding a knife to her throat (cf. 4:10).

### 5:1-2 The Lord's Dare

Like Abraham and God conversing about Sodom and Gomorrah (Gen. 18:23ff.), Jeremiah and God discuss the moral situation in Jerusalem. The city squares correspond to modern city malls. Like an ancient Diogenes, God challenges everyone (the verb is plural) to find in the city a single one who "does justice" *(mishpat)*, "deals honestly" (NIV). Is there even one whose oath is honest evidence of belief in the Lord? Adherence to one's commitment is to be expected of one who is faithful to the Lord (cf. Ezek. 17:15-20). It is in social and business spheres that God looks for uprightness. God is ready to forgive the entire city should there be even one. The Hebrew word for forgive, a pivot word here, is used in the Old Testament exclusively for God's forgiveness (v. 7). *[Justice, p. 299; Swearing, p. 311.]*

### 5:3-6 Jeremiah's Researched Report

Jeremiah goes first among the poor, normally a designation for the economically deprived. But in the context these are the information-poor. Moreover, contrasted with the next class, the "great," the higher-ups, the word "poor" specifies the ordinary citizens of Jerusalem. *The way of the Lord* is in parallel position with *requirements* ("ordinance," NASB; "law," RSV; lit., *mishpat*). The ordinary people do not have a sense of the order by which God intended them to live. *[Justice, p. 299.]*

In his public opinion poll Jeremiah discovers that the leaders, men of high station and culture, fare no better than the ordinary citizen. Though they knew the law of God, to a man they broke it. Historically, would this indictment come prior to Josiah's reformation? Or was the reformation short-lived, and is the passage to be dated later? A firm answer is not possible.

With "breaking of the yoke," a reference to the covenant by which God and people were joined, one expects the covenant curses to go into effect (Deut. 28:15-46; cf. Lev. 26:22). A seventh-century treaty between Esarhaddon and the ruler of Tyre reads, "May Bethel and Anath Bethel put you at the mercy of a devouring lion" (Hillers: 133). The *lion, wolf,* and the *leopard* may refer to actual animals, but, given the equation of a lion with the "northern army" (4:7), it is more likely that enemy peoples are intended. The unstated conclusion is that in Jerusalem there is not a single doer of justice. *[Covenant, p. 294.]*

### 5:7-19 God's Retort: You Force My Hand

God's oracle, which begins abruptly, consists of an accusation (vv. 7-13) followed by an announcement (vv. 14-19). The accusation already anticipates a judgment announcement (v. 10); similarly the announcement incorporates an accusation (v. 14). *[Judgment Oracle, p. 299.]* In effect God's retort is, You leave me no choice.

The sins of Judah are gross. The leaders (great ones) and the people generally have forsaken God (v. 7). They have substituted so-called gods for the true God and sworn by them (cf. 2:11, 12, 17). *[Swearing, p. 311.]* They have responded to God's gifts of abundance by living immorally (cf. Amos 2:6-15 for similar argumentation). Note the graphic language: each is a lusty stallion whinnying after the neighbor's wife (v. 8). Prosperity has led to luxury, which has led to preoccupation with sexual liberties and physical acts of immorality. Adultery, the breaking of the marriage covenant, apparently was regarded as more serious (it was punishable by death), than was fornication (sexual relations between unmarried men and women).

Their "ripened depravity" has reached its height in a refusal to take prophetic warnings seriously (vv. 12-13). When messengers of warning are repulsed, a people's fate is sealed (cf. the refusal to hear Amos and the consequences, Amos 7:12-13; 8:1-2). The people toss off any messages with "Not he" (literally). By this expression they call into question either the Lord's existence or his retaliation. The latter is more likely, given the context and also the fact that "he" can mean "it." Thus, "It is not" = "Not so" (Sutcliffe: 287-90). But the false prophets will be shown to be windbags. Since the word *ruah* means both wind and spirit, there is here an ironical twist, for prophets should be filled with the Spirit (Micah 3:8; Isa. 61:1).

The severe tone of this oracle is heightened with language about pruning vine branches (5:10) and burning wood (5:14). As fire devours wood (v. 14), so will the oncoming nation ravage and devour harvests, food, families, flocks, fruit, and fortified cities (v. 17). Quivers *like an open grave* is a roundabout way of suggesting that enemy arrows are deadly, or that as the grave craves for victims, so the quivers of the bowmen crave for more victims. Four times the word *consume* (lit., "eat up") is drilled home (v. 17). The enemy will destroy. But it is everywhere clear that it is God who orders the enemy (Babylon) into Judah.

## Announcements to Jacob and to Judah  5:20 – 6:30

*"Their Evil Deeds Have No Limit."* The themes from Part A (4:5—5:19) are repeated here, but greater stress is laid on Judah's evils, which are the reason for the oncoming disaster. The section contains two judgment speeches (5:20—6:9; 6:11b-23). Each is followed by a statement from Jeremiah (6:10-11a and 6:24-26). At the end, God speaks a private word to Jeremiah.

### 5:20 – 6:9  God's Citations and the Coming Siege

This divine oracle is composed of an accusation (5:20-31) and an announcement (6:1-9). *[Judgment Oracle, p. 299.]* The speech opens with an address to the house of Jacob = Israel. So, while targeting Judah, it also has the now-dispersed northern peoples in view. Their *eyes do not see* the situation nor God correctly. Their ears are closed (6:10; cf. Isa. 6:9-10; Matt. 13:14-15).

First God rebukes his people for their lack of reverence (vv. 20-31). The fear of God is shorthand for that reverence, humility, and obedience that describes a faithful Israelite (cf. 32:40; Prov. 1:7). Irreverence is a gross evil because God is Creator (5:20-25). God keeps the mighty ocean in check and does so by tiny particles of sand. God has set bounds for the sea, but Israel's sin in violating covenant boundaries is boundless. God's gift of the rains which make possible the regular week of harvest (the seven weeks between the Feast of Passover and the Feast of Weeks,

Lev. 23:15-16) is not received with gratitude and reverence. The sins of the people have literally stretched the seasons out of shape.

Second, specific accusations are directed against the rich, quite possibly the civil rulers (vv. 27-30), and the prophets and priests (v. 31). For a similar grouping see Micah 3:9-11. These folk are not overcome by temptation—they seek out sin (vv. 26-27). Like bird catchers, the rich in their greed bring home ill-gotten gains and make themselves fat (cf. Ps. 73:4, 12).

The sin of stubbornness is aggravated since it is the Creator himself whom these people have been resisting. Restraint and order, both themes from the creation, surface with the mention of keeping the sea in check and guaranteeing the seasons. God's prerogative is to set boundaries and also to reinforce them (v. 24). Should God's provident hand be withdrawn, chaos and havoc would result. Yet, for all this awesome power, these people do not fear or reverence God.

*Their evil deeds have no limit* (v. 28) could also be rendered, "Deeds of wickedness pass beyond some limit" or even "They overlook (excuse) evil." Given the two social strata of the well-to-do on the one hand and the oppressed on the other, God is on the side of the poor. Jeremiah confronts kings and those in power because they are in a position to take up the cause of the poor, yet have not done so because of vested interests. [*Oppression, p. 305.*]

The people affirm and support their morally twisted religious leaders, the conniving and power plays of the prophets and priests (v. 31). They bask in the positive thinking propounded by the prophets. But Jeremiah repeatedly lays charges against the compromising prophets (6:13; 23:9-40), and without flinching takes on the priests as well.

The announcement portion of the judgment oracle (6:1-9) repeats the watchman's cry (cf. 4:5) except that now the call is not to flee to Jerusalem, but to flee from it. The enemy is near, having reached the tribe of Benjamin (from which Jeremiah came) immediately north of Jerusalem. *Beth-Hakkerem* (lit., "house of the vineyard"), mentioned elsewhere only in Nehemiah 3:14, is perhaps to be identified with Ramat Rachel, a village south of Jerusalem. Tekoa, the home of Amos, is the last town in Judah at the edge of the desert, 12 miles south of Jerusalem. [*Map, p. 316.*]

*The north* was the mythical gathering place of the gods and represented "a kind of never-never land" (Holladay, 1974: 49). The word "comely" (RSV) can also mean "pasture." *Shepherds* is a metaphor for kings. From the time of Hammurabi of Babylon in the eighteenth century B.C., rulers were thought of as shepherds; peoples were their flock. Nebuchadnezzar's "flock" is about to denude the lush meadows. Each army division munches desirable portions of Jerusalem.

The commotion of war may be heard in the barking of a captain's orders (v. 4). Following hasty consultations, the enemy stages surprise attacks. God is now on the side of the enemy, leading the assault (cf. Jer. 21:4). God instructs siege ramps to be laid against Jerusalem (v. 6). Cut trees could provide towers for the archers, or be used for mobile battering rams or even firewood. Earlier God had summoned the enemy to go against Judah by going into the vineyard (5:10). Now God directs the battle. The instruction *pass your hand over the branches* is directed, judging by the singular "your," to Babylon and signifies an order to strip Judah bare. Judah is ranged in a fight ultimately against God. The rapid change of figures of speech adds to the feeling of upset and commotion.

## 6:10-11a Jeremiah's Exasperation

The previous judgment oracle, so relentless in pressing the message of disaster, calls for response. The prophet gets into action. He warns, but no one listens! Earlier the people have tuned out God's word (5:12-13); now they resent, loathe and despise it (6:10). Such encrusted wickedness brings Jeremiah's emotions to a boil. To be *"full of the wrath of the Lord"* is an appropriate response to entrenched evil ways.

## 6:11b-23 God's Orders: "Pour It On"

God is the speaker in verse 11b. The Lord directs the prophet not to withhold the message or the anger but to "pour it on" his audience. All levels of society share in the guilt (cf. 2:1-8, 29-32; 5:1-3, 20-29). That which is *poured out* is essentially God's wrath. The word *wrath* does not appear; but the idiom is unmistakable, and appears frequently in exilic writings (Lam. 2:4; 4:11; Ezek. 9:8; 20:8, 33; 30:15; Jer. 10:25; cf. Rev. 16:1). The word "poured" is used in verse 6 for pouring the siege ramps. By using the same word, Jeremiah underlines, as he has done all along, that it is God who is moving in punishment behind the military advances of the northern foe. Israel's failure even to blush at her sin (v. 15) plus the leader's greed (v. 13) and the prophets' irresponsible counseling (v. 14) make for an ugly package of evil.

The indictment is now fashioned from the very words of the people. Counseled to return to the old ways, the people declare, *"We will not walk in them"* (6:16; cf. 5:12-13). Urged to take seriously the trumpet call of warning, the people respond, *We will not listen*. Such deliberate obstinacy precipitates divinely-brought disasters (v. 19ff.; 22-23).

Sacrifices mean nothing if they are accompanied by an obstinate attitude, (v. 20). Costly incense came perhaps from Sheba, southwest of Arabia, and cane or calamus was imported perhaps from India. But when people are disobedient outward extravagance and ostentatious worship mean nothing. A similar point is made in Cain's offering (Gen. 4); it is underscored by Isaiah (1:1-13), Amos (5:21-27), Hosea (6:6), Micah (6:6-8), and again by Jeremiah (7:21-23).

The Lord's final word repeats the earlier message that the army is on its way (vv. 22-23; 4:7, 16; 5:15). Verses 22-23 are reused in 50:42 to describe, not Babylon, but the enemy attacking Babylon.

## 6:24-26  Jeremiah's Counsel

Jeremiah speaks for the people in identifying the frustration and anguish which will seize them when the destroyer comes. Whereas modern hospitals isolate the woman giving birth, Hebrew listeners would have been familiar with the cries and shrieks of women in labor. Jerusalem, who is called "Daughter Zion," is in travail. People are limp. *There is terror on every side*—a favorite expression (v. 25; cf. 20:4, 10; 46:5). Jeremiah counsels the people to remain in the city during siege. The call to *put on sackcloth* is a call not to repentance but to go into mourning rites. As upon the death of an only son, there were no future descendants in sight—a terrible catastrophe in that culture (Amos 8:10; Zech. 12:10).

## 6:27-30  Once More: Testing, Testing

God assigns Jeremiah to work like a tester, or assayer of metals. It is his calling to move in among the people to conduct his own investigation (cf. 5:1ff.). This testing activity may be intended to convince Jeremiah himself of the desperate situation which requires a desperate action. Or it may serve to add a human witness and so double-check God's indictment. The research is thorough. He concludes: these are "rebels of rebels" (lit., v. 28), corrupt to a man.

Furthermore, so runs the filed report, the refining processes are useless. Ore is put into a hot furnace. The searing heat is to melt the ore so that the silver will stand free. Copper and iron will become attached to lead which has oxidized. But after all this work, there is still no silver. The bellows, which intensify the heat by blowing air, are pumping ("snorting") at full blast. But the wickedness is too great—the lead does not carry off the alloy. With some changes in what is a difficult Hebrew text, Thompson translates: "The bellows puff, the fire is ready, lead, copper, iron. . . . In vain does the refiner smelt (them), and the ore is not separated out" (Thompson: 265). The silver which appears is spurious and must be rejected, not because God has not tried to purify a people, but because they are inordinately and incorrigibly stubborn.

This passage brings to an end the first major poetic collection of Jeremiah's words (chapters 2—6). It is characterized by intense warnings, earnest appeals to repentance, and dire threats. But the defiance of a stubborn people remains. There is no trace of genuine metal.

## THE TEXT IN BIBLICAL CONTEXT

*Identifying the Shape of Evil.* Prophets were to identify the shape of evil in their society (Lam. 2:14). Jeremiah railed against religious perversion and social malpractices (Jer. 7; 8:6-9; 11:9-10; 16:10-12). This confrontational ministry is what is meant by "to uproot and tear down" (1:10). The four eighth-century prophets each identified the oppression of the lower classes by the upper classes with "spiritual" defection (Isa. 1:21-23). Amos and Micah stressed injustices in business and law (Amos 5:11-24; Mic. 3:1-4). Hosea said less on this point but hit hard at Baal worship and spiritual adultery (Hos. 2).

*God's Agents.* God uses nations such as the eagle-swift and lion-powerful Babylonians, similarly described by Habakkuk, Jeremiah's contemporary (Babylonians = Chaldeans). Drought is also his agent for discipline (Jer. 14:1-12). So is a locust plague (Joel 1—2).

*God as the Enemy.* The idea of God making war against the people is shocking, but it is not unique to Jeremiah (cf. 21:4). Three other examples, as here, each involve a key city. God brought on Israel's defeat at Kadesh-Barnea (Num. 13:26—14:45). Similarly at Ai, God fought not for Israel but against her (Josh. 7:1-5). At Aphek even the ark of the covenant did not guarantee military victory because God fought against Israel (1 Sam. 4:1ff.). When Israel grieved God's Holy Spirit, "he turned and became their enemy and he himself fought against them" (Isa. 63:10; cf. Jer. 21:4).

## THE TEXT IN THE LIFE OF THE CHURCH

*Warnings of Doom.* Many a prophet has felt the frustration of warning against disaster he so clearly sees approaching, yet not being believed. He can do nothing but repeat his warnings with heightened language, more vehement words, and more vivid descriptions of the disaster ahead.

Jeremiah's vivid metaphors demanded that his listeners pay attention. He spoke about horses in the barnyard, wells supplying bad water,

gleaners in a vineyard, bird catchers, the forge of a smelter, men guard-
ing a field, women in childbirth pain, and the cosmetics of a prostitute.
He spoke about quaking mountains. His bold language is astonishingly
appropriate to a modern troubled world.

Eli Wiesel, a Jewish novelist, writes: "Quaking mountains? What did
Jeremiah mean to convey? I never understood the meaning of these
words until I visited Babi-Yar. Eyewitnesses had told me that, in Septem-
ber 1941, when the German invaders massacred some 80,000 Jews . . .
and buried them in the ravine, near the center of Kiev, the ground was
shaking for weeks on end. The mountains of corpses made the earth
quake. . . . And I understood Jeremiah" (Wiesel, 1981: 125-6.)

Jeremiah's warnings are paralleled by modern descriptions of nuclear war. A good exercise is to reread the sections describing the coming invasion (4:5-8, 11-31; 5:15-17; 6:1-8, 22-26); to imagine the sights
and sounds, then compare this description with those of nuclear war. In
both descriptions the earth becomes "formless and empty" (4:23),
mountains shift, fertile soils are poisoned, creatures disappear in the fiery
blast. Few people remain, and those are crippled, deformed. "Certainly
the possible disasters of the 1980s, for which the prophets of the
American churches should be preparing their people, already murmur
or shout their onslaught. . . ." (Shriver: 405).

Modern prophets have not left us in doubt about the immense
havoc which would be wrought by nuclear war. Biologists at a closed
session of the American Academy of Arts and Sciences in 1983, discussing nuclear winter, concluded dryly, "The possibility of the extinction of
Homo sapiens cannot be excluded." Novelist Gunter Grass writes, "The
fate of the human race now hangs on a slender thread." One wonders
whether the warnings are being heeded. The world continues to manu-
facture deadly weapons at a furious pace, or go to its parties; some
simply sit in silent fear.

The proper response to warnings is neither fear nor denial, but a
change of lifestyle. Jeremiah listed as evils, not minor violations of
cultural codes, but widespread economic and judicial perversion. The
charges are familiar. In the colonial period Europeans seized lands
under the guise of development in order to enrich themselves. During
two wars millions of people were executed without trial because of their
race or their religion. And today? Oppression? Of whom, by whom? The
nations cannot escape their fate, so Jeremiah's message goes, unless
they reverse themselves to follow righteousness.

God's people need to be on the side of Jeremiah. The church must
be the go-between between God and a corrupt society, alerting that so-

ciety, pleading with it (4:14), counseling it (6:16), and summoning it to repentance (6:26). How is this message best conveyed? Through example? Through rhetoric? Through media? Through political activism? Through all of these? The church needs to use the language of our day—computers, space shuttles, real estate, megatrends, nuclear fusion, oil gluts, famine relief—to capture its audience. Above all, the church needs to live its message, in opposition to kings and rulers if need be.

Jeremiah 7:1 – 8:3

# Straight Talk About Worship

## PREVIEW

A people's destiny may be more bound up with its pulpits than its parliaments. So said a British pastor. Before us in this text is the justly famous temple sermon (7:1-15). The sermon is followed by two elaborations. The first deals with evils in conjunction with worship (vv. 16-26). The second depicts wholesesale punishment (7:27—8:3). The subject of false worship, introduced in 7:2 and concluded in 8:2, brackets the entire passage. The Hebrew word "place" *(maqom)* occurs eight times (7:3, 6, 7, 12, 14, 20, 31; 8:3).

Jeremiah 26 is almost certainly a report of the same sermon in a condensed version. From it we learn that the sermon was preached early in the reign of Jehoiakim (ca. 609-605). The sermon startled, inflamed, even enraged the audience. Prophets and priests rallied the crowd by calling to Jeremiah, "You must die." A lynching was forestalled only by the conciliatory words of some elders and a certain Ahikam, son of Shaphan (26:17-24).

An earlier "sermon" (chapter 2) was followed by the announcement of a coming siege (4:5—6:30). This sermon also precedes a further set of announcements about disaster (8:4—10:25). For a chart describing the relationship of sermons to announcements of disaster, see p. 40.

OUTLINE

The Temple Sermon, 7:1-15
    7:1-2a        Instruction to Jeremiah
    7:2b-15     A Word to the People

Perversions and Precepts Involving Worship, 7:16-26
    7:16-20    Instruction to Jeremiah
    7:21-26    A Word to the People

Carcasses Everywhere, 7:27—8:3
    7:27-28a   Instruction to Jeremiah
    7:28b—8:3  A Word to the People

    Striking in this outline is a series of God's private communications with Jeremiah, who converses with his unseen partner as if using a walkie-talkie. We get a glimpse here of what Jeremiah means when he states elsewhere that prophets stand in the council chambers of God (Jer. 23:18). As for the sermon, it can be compared with other "sermons" in Jeremiah (11:1-17; 17:19-27; 34:8-22) and elsewhere (Matt. 5—7; Acts 2:14-36; 17:22-31). The increasing seriousness of Judah's situation is evident when God, in conversation with Jeremiah, prohibits Jeremiah from making intercession (7:16).

EXPLANATORY NOTES

The Temple Sermon  7:1-15

The sermon is given in the name of the *Lord Almighty*. [*Lord of Hosts, p. 304.*] The crowd is milling about. Solomon's temple, still standing after some 300 years, is everyone's pride. Religious traffic is brisk.

    The sermon has a double theme, stated clearly up front as an admonition. One, conduct: *Reform your ways and actions* (v. 3a). Two, belief: *Do not trust in deceptive words* (v. 4). "[The sermon] echoes both of the major themes of justice and idolatry that make up the meat and potatoes of the prophet's preaching" (Boadt: 59). The following list shows how the admonitions were aimed at specific practices.

    The main admonitions are elaborated. First, "Reform your ways!" That means, practice justice (v. 5). Once more the legal and economic concern for society's disadvantaged—the stranger, the fatherless, and the widow—is put forward (5:28). These are the powerless. The shedding of *innocent blood* is a reference to violence which involves killings; or possibly judicial corruption whereby innocent persons are executed (cf. 19:4; 1 Kings 21). Beyond these social correctives, the reform calls for a change in worship. No longer may other gods be followed. The ultimatum is crisp: continued possession of the land is contingent upon reform. *[Justice, p. 299; Oppression, p. 305; Word/Deed, p. 313.]*

Second, "Do not be seduced by deceptive words!" says Jeremiah. "Do not trust in the temple!" Most pious words they are: *This is the temple of the Lord* thrice chanted. The chant underscores God's protection. Has not God chosen Jerusalem as his city and especially his temple as a place to dwell (Ps. 132:13, 14; 11:4)? Did not Samaria fall because that city had no temple? Had not God miraculously shielded the temple and the city from danger 100 years earlier when Sennacherib's forces descended on the city (2 Kings 19)? Will not God, so the argument runs, protect the temple under any circumstances? In this pious faith, grounded in tradition, lurks deception.

True, God's presence in the temple had once been a pledge for the people's safety. But conditions have changed. The people are now disregarding the commandment (cf. v. 9 with Exod. 20). They worship not God but Baal, yet have the audacity to hang their hopes on the temple. Moreover, despite their gross evil they enter the temple with the doctrine of (eternal) security saying, "We are safe!"

Judged historically, the people's claim for security was hollow. Under the judges Shiloh was the place of the ark, and thus the dwelling place of God from which he revealed himself (1 Sam. 3:21). But even so, Shiloh was not invulnerable nor invincible (Ps. 76:60). It fell, Jeremiah reminded his audience (v. 12). According to Danish archaeologists, Shiloh likely fell to the Philistines in 1054 (cf. 1 Sam. 4:10). Shiloh, 18 miles north of Jerusalem, was not far from Shechem in the territory of Ephraim. *[Map, p. 316.]*

| Jeremiah's Admonitions | Judah's Practice |
|---|---|
| *Behavior* | |
| 1. Deal justly | |
| 2. Don't oppress the alien, fatherless, widow (6a) | They stole, committed adultery and perjury(NIV) (9a) |
| 3. Don't shed innocent blood (6b) | They murdered (9a) |
| 4. Don't walk after other gods (6c) | They burned incense to Baal and followed other gods (9b) |
| *Belief* | |
| Don't trust in the temple (4) | Criminals hide in the temple saying, "We are safe" (10) |

A second historical example of God's punishment despite the people's claims to God's presence was the defeat of Samaria (Ephraim) only 100 years earlier in 722 (v. 15).

## Perversions and Precepts Involving Worship  7:16-26

Prophets are not only proclaimers. Often overlooked is their service of intercession. The prophet Samuel, something of a granddaddy of the prophets, was an intercessor (1 Sam. 7:9; cf. Moses, Exod. 32:11-13, 30-32; Num. 14:13-25; Isaiah, 2 Kings 19:3f.; Amos, Amos 7:1-6). The power of intercession is obvious from God's action to forbid it, lest intercession halt his follow-through of the judgment (11:14; 14:11; cf. 15:1). It is now too late for prayers to avail.

In conversational style God points Jeremiah to the perverted practices of the common people. The entire family was involved in these exercises of devotion. Food in the form of cakes, round and flat like the moon or perhaps star-shaped, along with drink, was carefully prepared for the Queen of Heaven, Ishtar, the Babylonian fertility goddess. The Hebrews now credited this female deity with responding to cries for help (44:17). [Asherah, p. 291.]

Verse 21 hints at another perversion. The meat of some offerings was to be eaten (Lev. 3; 7:11-18), but burnt offerings were to be offered in their entirety, meat and fat, to the Lord (Lev. 1). Ironically God says in effect, "Go ahead, overstep the regulations and eat all the meat yourselves." For a similar sarcastic statement see Jeremiah 25:27. Perhaps the cakes for Ishtar were easier to come by than meat for Yahweh.

The instruction is not to be read as though God did not command sacrifice. He did, as the legislation in the Pentatuech documents. Rather, it is the Hebrew idiom or style to make comparisons between the less important and the more important in this blunt fashion. We may compare the statement, "Jacob have I loved and Esau have I hated" (Mal. 1:2f.). So here. By comparison, obedience was far more critical than the mundane offering of sacrifices (v. 23; cf. 1 Sam. 15:22). Or the sense might be, *For when I brought your forefathers out of Egypt and spoke to them, I did not just give them commands about burnt offerings . . . (v. 22).*

Despite the prophets God sent, the people *did not listen* (vv. 24, 26). Despite the incentive that to walk in God's way would bring well-being, they refused compliance (v. 23b). Despite God's appealing offer of an intimate relationship, *I will be your God and you will be my people,* they reneged (v. 23). [Covenant Formula, p. 294.]

## Carcasses Everywhere, 7:27 – 8:3

Judah's response is predictable. They will not listen. The Lord characterizes them as unresponsive to correction. Moreoever, they lack integrity, for they speak lies. True and honest speech is gone (v. 28; cf. 5:1, 3). Their worship now, as during Manasseh's rule (2 Kings 21:5-6; 23:10), defies rather than honors God (v. 30).

Verse 29 anticipates the judgment speech that follows and calls for a funeral lament. In grief mourners would cut their hair and go about bald (Mic. 1:16). The lament by a people overcome with grief would continue in the deserted places, the barren heights (cf. 9:17-22).

The judgment speech proper (7:30—8:3) begins with an accusation (vv. 30-31) which specifies (1) idolatry (a flashback to 7:9) and (2) child sacrifices (an elaboration of 7:21-26). The Ben Hinnom Valley, or Topheth, the site of these idolatrous acts ("Gehenna" in New Testament times) lies south of old Jerusalem. *[Topheth, p. 312.]*

The announcement is in keeping with the accusation: for dead bodies God will give more dead bodies. Cemetery space will be unavailable except for the area around the reserved place, Topheth. The carcasses will be exposed to vultures and beasts. Sometimes when graves were vandalized for plunder, dogs would drag out the bones. Invaders would also insult the populace by opening graves and scattering bones about. At the least, the afterlife rest, important to an Israelite (cf. 2 Kings 23:17-18) will be rudely disturbed. Worst of all the heavenly host of sun, moon and stars, so eagerly served, loved, and worshiped, will look on coldly (8:2)

We may observe the downward spiral of improper worship. For each step listed, note an announcement of judgment (cf. Isbell/Jackson).

| Misplaced Worship | Corresponding Divine Action |
|---|---|
| 1. The temple (7:4) | *"I will thrust you from my presence"* (7:15) |
| 2. The Queen of Heaven (7:18) | *"My anger . . . will be poured out"* (7:20) |
| 3. Sacrifices and Offerings (7:21-22) | *"The Lord has rejected . . . this generation"* (7:29) |
| 4. Child sacrifices (7:31) | *"The land will become desolate"* (7:34) |
| 5. Creature worship (8:1-3) | *"They will not be . . . buried"* (8:2) |

## THE TEXT IN BIBLICAL CONTEXT

*Corrupt Theology.* Characteristically Jeremiah was on a collision course with corrupt theology. The temple sermon described a perverted way of religious thinking, for the temple was illusory security. The prophets demolished such false securities. Isaiah, like Jeremiah, rebuked excessive regard for the temple and veneration of buildings, insisting that God was not confined there (Isa. 66:1-2). Like Jeremiah, Jesus accused the Jewish leaders who gloried in the temple of making it a den of thieves (Mark 11:17; Luke 19:46). When Stephen challenged temple doctrine, people's emotions were quickly raised to a boil (Acts 7); his sermon cost him his life. A once-good theology can, like the doctrine of the temple, become stale if not false.

*Acceptable Worship.* Obedience and moral rectitude exceed in importance any ritual acts of sacrifice. Jeremiah was simply reinforcing what Samuel (1 Sam. 15:22), Amos (5:21-25), Isaiah (1:10-17), and Micah (6:1-8) had said. Preoccupation with the external rituals was the subject also of Jesus' preaching (Matt. 5:23-24; Luke 18:9-14). Obedience, compliance with God's demand for just dealing, matters supremely. Worship is not acceptable without just and upright conduct, including fair payment of wages by employers (Isa. 58:3). God's assessment of worship is based upon what happens in the marketplace.

## THE TEXT IN THE LIFE OF THE CHURCH

*Religious Clichés.* Pious mouthing of tradition-worn clichés can be deceptive. When people tout being "born-again" as a cliché without a genuine experience of a spiritual turnaround together with appropriate actions, they are like the Jerusalem worshipers announcing their orthodoxy, *"This is the temple. . . ."* Those who insist they are "baptized church members" and therefore safe, but whose behavior is unholy, scandalize God. Those who parade their faith in the inspired, inerrant Word of God but order their lives by the values of the TV screen, scandalize God. Behind what other theological shibboleths (clichés) do people take shelter today? We may hide behind some doctrinal cliché because we are afraid to face a holy God outright; but God sees through our defenses.

*Children in Society.* One gauge of a society is the value it places on its children. The people of Jeremiah's day, caught up with idol worship, sacrificed their children into the arms of the image of Molech. Western culture on the one hand nurtures and protects children; on the other hand it terminates lives through abortion, and sacrifices young men and women to the military machine. More horrifying still is the growing exploitation of children in pornography to satisfy the lusts of adults. A society that no longer safeguards its children has reached ultimate depravity.

*Sermonizing.* Evaluate the "sermon on a sermon" with the outline:

## Moving Against the Stream

I. Jeremiah's Challenge to the People's Action
   A. The Call: "Change your ways"
   B. The Corrective: "Practice justice";
      "Do not oppress the disadvantaged"
   C. The Consequence: "So you may dwell here"

II. Jeremiah's Challenge to Popular Theology
   A. The Cliché: "This is the temple of the Lord."
   B. The Challenge: Inconsistency, insult
   C. The Clincher: A lesson from history

**Diagram** (see page 79, bottom)

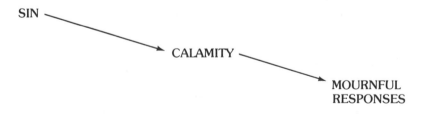

SIN

CALAMITY

MOURNFUL
RESPONSES

## Jeremiah 8:4 – 10:25

# A People's Sins, an Enemy's Siege, and a Prophet's Sorrow

### PREVIEW

The themes of sin and of coming judgment of earlier chapters (4:5—6:30) appear here again but, as in a symphony, the accents differ. As before, the prophet bears down on the sins of the people. As before, too, there looms the foe from the north. New here is the greater space given to mournful responses. There is some analysis. There is satire. But overall, one meets a bleary-eyed prophet.

These materials, their datings left unspecified, may well come from different times. The argument against idols (10:1-16) fits the Josianic reform of 621, though some scholars assign it an exilic date. The mention of a present siege (10:17; 8:14) would suit 598, the time of the first Babylonian siege of Jerusalem.

The three chapters are said by some to be a miscellaneous collection, but there is a definite theme and a certain rhythm. One can think of a long beat (list of sins), a short beat (siege), and a medium long beat (mournful responses). This sequence of three beats occurs three times as though in three rounds, as the diagram on page 78 shows and as the outline on page 80 details more exactly.

OUTLINE

Round I:  Sin, Siege, and Sorrow, 8:4—9:2b
  A. *"No one repents,"* 8:4-13
  B. The sound of snorting horses, 8:14-17
  C. Everyone's hurting, 8:18 —9:2b

Round II:  Sin, Siege, and Sorrow, 9:2c-25
  A. *"No one speaks the truth,"* 9:2c-9
  B. Bitter food and poisoned drink, 9:10-16
  C. A summons to the wailing women, 9:17-22
  D. Interlude: The Lord's hall of fame and ill-fame, 9:23-25

Round III:  Sin, Siege, and Sorrow, 10:1-25
  A. A tirade on idols and a doxology to the Lord, 10:1-16
  B. Hurled from the land, 10:17-18
  C. A city sighs; a prophet prays, 10:19-25

Each of the three "A" sections treats Judah's or Israel's evil. The first contains a trash barrel of general evils (8:4-13). The second is primarily concerned with lying and other sins of the tongue (9:2c-9). The third is a satirical blast at idolatry (10:1-16), made the more heinous by a contrast with the living God. Each of the "B" sections alludes to an enemy invasion or siege. Each of the "C" sections offers a sad, mournful minor-key response. In them one feels pain, particularly the pain of a prophet who grieves over his erring people.

EXPLANATORY NOTES

Round I: Sin, Siege, and Sorrow 8:4 – 9:2b

*8:4-13 "No One Repents"*

The elements of a classical judgment speech are transparent in this passage with its accusations (8:5c-7, 9, 10c-11) and announcements (10a+b, 12d-13). But there is also disputation or argumentation. The opening questions (e.g., *When men fall down, do they not get up?)* elicit the consent of the listener/reader: "Of course they do!" A man who stumbles will usually pick himself up. Normally, people correct their mistakes. Similarly, if one finds himself on the wrong road, his normal action is to turn around.

Such common-sense responses sharpen the oddity of Judah's behavior. Shown that she is on a wayward path, Judah does not turn! Note the wordplay on "turn," five times repeated in verses 4-5 (cf. 3:10-14; 3:22—4:1). A patient God has listened attentively for any indication of turning (i.e., repenting) but has found none. All *pursue* (lit., *turn)* their own way (cf. Isa. 53:6 where the analogy is with sheep; here it is with a horse in battle and then with birds, v. 7; cf. Isa.1:3). *[Repentance, p. 306.]*

Moreover, the scribes are boasting that they possess God's law (e.g., Deuteronomy) (v. 8) much as the people boast of the temple (7:4). A *lying pen* has nothing to do with deliberate miscopying of the law or a distortion of it for their own ends (though the RSV gives that impression). Scribes were expositors or teachers as well as copyists. They handle the law falsely when their expositions do not challenge a complacent nation with God's demands. Likely they endorse the status quo, like the prophets and the priests who cry, *"Peace . . . when there is no peace"* (8:11). Both the prophets and the scribes perpetuate a stale orthodoxy and are insensitive to their nation's crisis. They do not rightly divide the word of truth (2 Tim. 2:15). Sadly, one can be occupied with the Word of God, yet reject it and remain unwise.

The section 8:10c-12 is found also in 6:13-15. *[Doublets, p. 296.]*To it is added the announcement that the harvest will be taken away (v. 13; cf. v. 10 for the removal of wives and fields). The difficult Hebrew could be rendered, 'Ah, but I'll harvest them" (Bright: 67). Vineyard imagery is found also in 2:21 and 6:9. The last line in verse 13 is difficult. The sense may be as in NIV, *"What I have given them will be taken from them."*

### 8:14-17 The Sound of Snorting Horses

The invasion has brought the foreign enemy with its *snorting horses* to Dan, just inside the northern border of the land. *[Map, p. 316.]* The northern foe (Babylon) which is in view here, has come to occupy *(devour)* the land. The people rally. Inside the fortified city the refugees from the countryside face another hazard: poisoned water supplies. It is only when the punishment is underway that they acknowledge, *We have sinned* (v. 14). As often in human affairs, they hope till the last moment that good will come and danger will be averted (v. 15). The Lord's speech about snakes and vipers recalls the wilderness experience (v. 17; Num. 21:6) and perhaps some proverbs ( Eccl. 10:11; Ps. 58:4-5).

### 8:18—9:2b Everyone's Hurting

Picturing the outcome of the siege, namely the devastation of the city and the removal of the population to a foreign land, the prophet breaks out, "My grief is beyond healing" (v. 18, RSV, following the Greek version). Another translation option is to regard the problem Hebrew word as a noun: *"O my Comforter"* (NIV) or, by dividing the word and attaching it to the preceding verse, "without recovery." That is, the serpent's bite will be fatal (Bright: 62). The question *"Is the Lord not in Zion?"* recalls Israel's persistent notion that Jerusalem is invulnerable because God's presence at the temple is assured (7:4). Jeremiah is hurting (v. 18).

Because God's people are crushed, the prophet himself is crushed (v. 21). So completely has Jeremiah identified with his people! Five times in 6 verses the affectionate name, "O daughter, my people" (rendered blandly as *my people,* NIV) is used. Jeremiah, the "weeping prophet," wonders why there is no physician, and why the spiritual pharmacy is empty. Resin, used as a salve or balm, came from the storax tree grown in Gilead (vv. 22; cf. Gen. 37:25). *[Map, p. 316.]*

Like Jesus, the greater prophet, Jeremiah weeps over the city (9:1, 10; 14:17-18; cf. Matt. 23:37). He has another reaction: disgust. He would like to get away from it all (9:2). The reason is not so much that he feels tired, but that he feels soiled. He is repulsed by the sin all around him.

If Jeremiah is pained, so is God (v. 19d). As if interrupting the people's speech, whose next question will likely be, "Why then has he not heard?" God inquires, *"Why have they provoked me to anger with their images . . . ?"* Idolatry, not mentioned in the trash barrel of evils (8:4-11), will be the subject in 10:1-16.

The people also are hurting, for it is they who speak (v. 20; cf. vv. 14-16). The harvest of grain in Palestine comes in May-June. Summer fruits ripen in September-October. Both harvests are over. Earlier Jewish commentators refer *the harvest is past* to Judah's hope to get help from Egypt, but Egypt's harvest was already over, and still the expected military help had not come. Or the notion might be: "As a man counts on the harvest to repay him for all his toil, we counted on deliverance and we are disappointed" (quoted in Freehof: 69). In short, all is lost.

## Round II: Sin, Siege and Sorrow, 9:2c-25

### 9:2c-9 "No One Speaks the Truth"

The second round with its themes of sin, siege, and sorrow opens with a general characterization of the people as adulterous and unfaithful, and continues with a frontal exposé of the sin of lying. Our translations suggest that the tongue is a bow, but in verse 8 the tongue is the arrow. More accurately, therefore, "They stretch their tongue, their bow is a lie." "The 'lie' is the bow that shoots the tongue (like an arrow) out to do its damage . . ." (Holladay, 1974: 57).

Falsehood yields distrust even among brothers and friends (vv. 4, 8). In a striking phrase harking back to Jacob as deceiver (Gen. 27:36; 31; cf. Hos. 12:2-4) the prophet charges, "Every man deceives (lit., 'Jacob's') his brother" (v. 4). Corruption is everywhere, and "you live in the middle of deceit," says the Lord, addressing Jeremiah (v. 6; cf. Isa. 6:5). Lying, slander, deceit, and falsehood come easily when people do not know (i.e., acknowledge) God (vv. 3, 6). *[Falsehood, p. 296.]*

God's response is to *refine and test* them to see if there is even one who seeks the truth (v. 7; cf. 5:1). God's integrity, and perhaps also his reluctance to move in punishment results in an inward struggle: *"Should I not punish them for this?"* (v. 9; cf. 5:9, 29). It is as though God is inviting someone to show cause why he should not punish.

## 9:10-16  Bitter Food and Poisoned Drink

First Jeremiah refers in a lament to the devastation brought on by the enemy siege (v. 10; cf. 4:23-25). God intensifies the picture of desolation (v. 11; cf. 10, 22). Biblical covenants contained curses upon the covenant-breaker, such as cities becoming wastelands and people perishing of poison. Ancient curses by neighboring nations pictured animals inhabiting ruins. An eighth-century Sefire treaty between two Syrian kings reads: "May Arpad become a mound for . . . gazelle and fox and hare and wildcat and owl" (Boadt: 81).

## 9:17-22  A Summons to the Wailing Women

In the previous round, it was Jeremiah who responded in sorrow and weeping (8:18—9:2b). Here a call is issued for professional mourners, women skilled *(wise)* in the art of prompting others in an outpouring of grief. Wailing women customarily shrieked and tore at their clothes with dust in their hair. The people are saying as they leave Zion and the land, "We are devastated" (v. 19; cf. 8:19). The Lord's word is echoed by the prophet, who urges that the wailing women teach their daughters to wail and so increase the number of mourners (v. 20). Death is near, if it has not already come.

The siege has brought death to families, children, and young men within the city (v. 21), while outside in the fields corpses lie like dung. *Death has climbed in through our windows* may refer to plagues, or as in Akkadian literature, to a demonlike personification of death called Lamastu. The prophet appeals to the visual—corpses—but also to the auditory—the sound of women wailing—to make vivid the coming destruction.

## 9:23-26  The Lord's Hall of Fame and Ill-fame

These verses are a departure from the "Sin, Siege, Sorrow" cycles—
a wisdom piece breaks into the pattern. The connection of these verses
with those immediately preceding is at first unclear. One may see these
verses as a rebuttal and summary of the larger section (8:4—9:22) where
people boasted in their wisdom (8:8), were greedy for riches (8:10) and
generally independent (8:6). Especially strong is the theme of "knowing"
and "wisdom" (8:8-9, 12b; 9:12; 10:23-24). Perhaps the background
question is, "What is worthwhile knowing"?

The values held by nations or individuals are disclosed by their
priorities. Jeremiah may be taking on the entire value system of royalty.
Solomon is the prototype of someone who had riches, wisdom, and
might. This triad characterized the royal establishment (e.g., wisdom,
1 Kings 3:4-15; riches, 1 Kings 3:11, 13; 10:23; might, 2 Sam. 10:7; 16:6;
20:7). Wisdom may mean culture, science, or technical know-how. King
Jehoiakim, Jeremiah's contemporary, gloried in riches. The word to him
was "woe," but of Josiah, who wished to "know God," it was said, "Then
it was well" (22:13-16). Verses 23-24 are a strong critique of the way of
kings (David-royal) and an affirmation of the commoner's way (Mosaic-
covenantal).

To glory in the things in which God delights is to glory in loving-kindness, justice, and righteousness—another triad. God *"practices steadfast
love"* (RSV). In lyrical but generally accurate fashion, Morgan writes,
"Loving-kindness is the stoop which is prompted by love. It is the bending down, and the bending over, which is love-inspired. . . . It is love in
action" (Morgan: 68). The love that acts is binding covenant love. Or, as
some define the word, love is voluntary help given to those in need.

*Justice* is fair dealing in honorable relationships. *[Justice, p. 299.]*
*Righteousness* is the inner disposition of integrity and uprightness that
prompts just action (v. 24). Right governance was expected of a king (Ps.
72:1-2). God ruled as the righteous one (Ps. 7:10; 11:7; 119:137; Isa.
45:24) and so the term "righteousness" came also to mean salvation
(Ps. 24; Isa. 45:8; 46:13; 51:5-6). This second triad compares with
Micah's and Isaiah's preachments (Mic. 6:8; Isa. 5:7). If God delights in
these qualities, his displeasure at their absence should be no surprise.

Abruptly Jeremiah is onto the topic of circumcision (v. 25f.). Others
beside Israel practiced circumcision, for circumcision was not the exclusive rite of the Hebrews (cf. Ishmael in Gen. 17:23). These nations—
Egypt, Edom, Moab, Ammon, and certain desert groups with peculiar
customs—were quite possibly in a military alliance against Babylon.
*[Map, p. 317.]* Israel had the practice of circumcision in common with

them, but she was also one of them in having an uncircumcised heart. *Uncircumcised in heart* refers to an unyielding stubbornness (cf. 4:4). Jeremiah, a radical to be sure, has called into question the values of ark (3:16), temple (7:4), sacrifice (7:21), and now circumcision (9:25).

## Round III: Sin, Siege, and Sorrow  10:1-25
### 10:1-16  A Tirade on Idols and a Doxology to the Lord

The third and last round in this sin-siege-sorrow sequence opens with a warning against astrology and continues with one of the most blistering exposés of idolatry in the Bible. The obnoxious sin of idolatry, already mentioned in 8:19c, is here ridiculed. The message is directed to the *house of Israel*, likely an umbrella term for God's people, who were often tempted to idolatry. The designation could be the northern tribes taken into foreign territories in 722, or Judah in Babylonian exile. The latter is not unlikely. Jeremiah later wrote to the exiles (29:1ff.). "Fear" before idols could be a normal response of the newly exiled people in Babylon. But, as the chapter now stands, verse 17 with its references to siege would suggest an audience contemporary with Jeremiah. Verses 12-16 are duplicated in 51:15-19. [*Doublets, p. 296.*]

The section alternates between a mocking poem to false gods and a doxology to the Lord. Perhaps two choirs sang the parts antiphonally.

> A mocking poem about false gods (vv. 2-5).
> A doxology praising the Lord (vv. 6-7).
> A mocking poem about false gods (vv. 8-9).
> A doxology praising the Lord (vv. 10-12).
> A mocking poem about idols (vv. 14-15).
> A doxology to God Almighty (v. 16).

The mocking poem, full of satire, describes the making of an idol. A tree is cut and a craftsman's chisel shapes the figure. The piece is overlaid with silver from Tarshish (southern Spain) and gold from Uphaz (possibly Arabia) (v. 9). It is then dressed in royal colors of blue and purple (v. 9), but not before it has been fastened down with hammer and nails so it does not wobble. The idols are as mute as a scarecrow in a vegetable garden. They can't stir a step (v. 5)! Their "teaching" is foolish (cf. Hab. 2:19). Their impact is nil. Of people who worship them the prophet says with gusto,

> They are fools and blockheads one and all,
> learning the nonsense from a block of wood (v. 8, NEB).

The comparison between idols and the Lord of the universe (v. 16) makes ridiculous the idols while highlighting the Lord's greatness. For another ludicrous description see Isaiah 44:9-20 (cf. Isa. 40:19; 41:6f.; 46:5f.). The following comparison shows how completely unlike idols and God are.

| idols | God |
| --- | --- |
| fashioned by man (v. 3) | unique (vv. 6-7) |
| created (v. 3) | Creator (vv. 12, 16) |
| helpless (v. 5) | mighty in power (v. 6) |
| speechless (v. 5) | wise (v. 12) |
| contemptible, impotent (v. 5) | worthy of reverence (v. 7) |
| inanimate (v. 5) | living (v. 10) |
| ineffective (v. 5) | powerful (vv. 10-11) |
| perishable (v. 5) | enduring |
| wooden, emptiness (v. 8) | King, Lord Almighty (vv. 7, 10, 16) |
| fear is inappropriate (v. 5) | fear is quite appropriate (v. 7) |

The doxology especially points to God's incomparability (v. 16). *No one is like you* (vv. 6a, 7c) is a protest against equating God Almighty with other gods. [*Inclusio, p. 298.*]. A related question "Who is like you?" means not only that God is the greatest when compared to other gods, but that God is utterly different from all other gods and idols and is in a class by himself (Labuschagne). The Lord's incomparability is linked to the creation and, as elsewhere, to his miraculous intervention in history whereby he redeemed a people for himself (v. 16; cf. Deut. 4:34). The *Portion of Jacob* with its sense of family is an old theme which contrasts God's lively interest in people with the metallic lifelessness of idols (Deut. 32:9; Ps. 16:5; 73:26; 119:57).

Verse 11 stands apart, both since it is in prose and since it is not written in Hebrew but in Aramaic. Scholars have suggested that a scribe—noting down the meaning of the preceding verses—placed this sentence in the margin; later copyists copied it as part of the text. But the strangeness of another language and the shock technique fit Jeremiah's style. There are extended scholarly debates about the unity and authorship of 10:1-16. Those who deny Jeremianic authorship point to an exilic setting. Some who affirm Jeremiah as the author note the orderly composition as well as a similar theme elsewhere (2:8-13, 26-28; 3:1-5; 5:20-25).

## 10:17-18  Hurled from the Land

A short reference to the consequences of invasion and siege is made

here. The prophet instructs others to gather their belongings in preparation for departure from the land. God declares that he will *hurl* (the term
is used for slinging stones, Judg. 20:16) his people out of the land. Beyond the terrible conditions of siege depicted in the previous rounds
(8:14-17; 9:10-16) lies the prospect of deportation into exile.

## 10:19-25  A City Sighs; a Prophet Prays

The speaker in verses 19-22 is the city Jerusalem or the land Israel
rather than the prophet. References to the sons who *are no more* and to
the destroyed tents (buildings) would argue for the city as speaker. The
shepherds ( = civil leaders) in their stupidity fail to seek God, and hence
the city's citizens because of God's judgment have been scattered. The
scene depicts the aftermath of the onslaught of the foe from the north (v.
22), whose coming has been in view throughout (8:4—10:22).
Jerusalem will be very severely damaged.

Set in this corporate complaint by the city is a personal outburst of
anguish by the prophet: *I said to myself, "This is my sickness, and I must
endure it"* (v. 19). One might expect a sweet satisfaction in that the
people's sins, so revolting to the prophet (9:2), would at last be dealt
with. Instead, Jeremiah grieves over the fate of his people. The image of
sickness and wounding is a favorite with Jeremiah (30:12, 17).

The prophet's prayer (vv. 23-25) includes a confession and two petitions. The confession is an acknowledgment of general human weakness, an inability to chart the proper course in life. Contrast Proverbs
16:9 (cf. Prov. 19:21; 21:2; 16:2; 20:24). If the confession is in behalf of
the people, it represents a frustration over the helplessness of the
populace to make good decisions. If it is personal, it may represent
Jeremiah's quandary in not knowing what moves to make next, given
leaders who refuse to inquire of the Lord (v. 21). The two petitions are
made in the light of the preceding announcements of coming judgment.
Jeremiah himself is not exempt from evil. He opens himself to God's
correction (cf. 15:19). But here too one could leave open the possibility
that the "me" may be collective with the people speaking corporately.

Jeremiah's petition (or perhaps the people's quotation of Ps. 79:6-7)
is for God to *pour out your wrath on the nations* (v. 25). Compare the
so-called imprecatory psalms (cf. Ps. 109, 137). Before such a prayer is
dismissed as sub-Christian, one should note that it accords with the principle, "Vengeance is mine, I will repay." Moreover, it is a prayer indicat-
ing the zeal of a prophet for the honor of God's name. At the same time
one can understand the prophet's inward pain at the prospect of his
people's destruction and his desire for the removal of the spoilers.

## THE TEXT IN BIBLICAL CONTEXT

The lead ideas in the three rounds—a people's sin, an enemy siege, and a prophet's sorrow—bring theological insights about sin, God, and the prophetic ministry.

*An Understanding of Sin.* Telescope the three passages on sin (8:4-13; 9:3-9; 10:1-16) into a consolidated piece, and observe the range of human experience which these exposés of sin address. Idolatry (10:1-16) is disregard for the first and second of the Ten Commandments (Exod. 20:3-4). Falsehood (9:3-9) breaks the ninth commandment (Exod. 20:16). Sins of greed, deceit, disobedience, and refusal to honor God (8:4-13) are transgressions of others of the Ten Commandments (Exod. 20:17), but especially of the covenant relationship generally.

*(1) Idolatry.* God's total "otherness" gainsays any attempt to worship him alongside other gods, and his uniqueness precludes fashioning substitute gods. Exasperation with idols (cf. Moses and the golden calf, Exod. 32:15-21), sarcasm against those who make gods in their own image (Isa. 44:9ff), arguments against the validity of idols (1 Cor. 8:4), and prohibition of substitute deities (1 John 5:21) are all methods of combating this evil. *(2) Falsehood.* The sin of lying is the direct opposite of what characterizes God, namely truth. Truthfulness is important to God (Eph. 4:25, 29, 31; Col. 3:9). Lying and deception bring God's displeasure and wrath (cf. Ananias and Sapphira, Acts 5; Rev. 21:8). *(3) Sin.* Sin is essentially a breach in relationships between a person(s), God and others. Basic to the intended relationship of God and the people is intimacy. Absence of intimacy or even interest in intimacy *("my people do not know the requirements of the Lord"* 8:8; cf. 9:3, 6) is not only evil but as the root evil accounts for other evils.

*An Understanding of God.* In justice and power and in many other ways God is superior to human power (Jer. 49:18), to idols (Ps. 89:9; 115:1-7), to rival deities (Ps. 18:31 = 2 Sam. 22:32), and to the entourage of heavenly beings (Ps. 89:7). That God is King is indisputable according to the Scriptures (8:19; 10:10; 1 Sam. 12:12; Ps. 10:16; 84:3; 95:3; cf. Isa. 33:22; 43:15; 44:6; Zeph. 3:15).

A righteous God cannot allow evil to go unchecked. Sin is dealt with through direct punishment (cf. David and Bathsheba, 2 Sam. 11 and 12; Israel's wilderness wanderings, Num. 14:26-35) or through the absorbing of the punishment by a substitute (Isa. 53:6). Roy Clements said, "The Son of man casts no rebel into hell for whom he has not wept."

*Understanding the Ministry.* Jeremiah announces judgment, but not dispassionately; he is emotionally involved with his people to the point of interceding for them. Prophetic ministry involves speech; it also entails caring. Messages of judgment necessarily have a hard edge to them. But the one sounding the judgment need not be hard; instead, he or she must be compassionate. Jesus denounced the sins of a city and its leaders but wept over the city (Matt. 23:37). Paul berated the Jews for disbelief, but his spirit of concern showed: *I have great sorrow and unceasing anguish in my heart* (Rom. 9:2). Such expressions do not dilute the harsh message but rather give it credibility, for God's messengers are emissaries of a God who is not aloof from our misery. God does not wear an eternal distant plastic grin, but comes among us.

## THE TEXT IN THE LIFE OF THE CHURCH

*Identifying the Shape of Evil.* How does one respond to the charge, "The 'system' is making crooks of us businessmen?" The preacher needs to speak to the sins of the "system." "Megatrends of sin" might be corporate misrepresentation; double-tongued diplomacy; deceit, cheating, and petty thievery in business; excessive competition; the hoarding of power; conspicuous consumerism; excessive concern for advancement and self-fulfillment. Often low in priority are opposite values: compassion for others, concern for building of community, unselfishness and self-sacrifice. So subtly do shifts occur that even sociologists and psychologists find themselves asking, "Whatever became of sin?"

Have the prime values of wisdom (education, culture, and technical know-how), might (military power), and riches (investments) become substitute gods? If so, the preacher will point to the consequences. Solzhenitsyn, the Russian novelist, in warning the Western world of its present evils commented, "We offer you the experience of our suffering."

*Soul Sickness.* William Cowper, British poet of the eighteenth century, captures some of the revulsion that godly persons feel when inundated by the constant reports of evil:

Oh for a lodge in some vast wilderness,
Some boundless contiguity of shade,
Where rumour of oppression and deceit,
Of unsuccessful or successful war,
Might never reach me more! My ear is pained,
My soul is sick, with every day's report
Of wrong and outrage with which earth is filled.
—"The Time Piece," Book Two of *The Task*
(quoted in Nicholson, 1973:92).

The emotional wrenchings which come to a minister when the congregation or its individual members go astray are only pale reflections of God's anguish.

Part 3

---

# Stories About Wrestling with Both People and God

# Jeremiah 11 – 20

Jeremiah was unique among the prophets in that he expressed how he felt. He wept, argued, cried out. His feelings were strong because his involvement, both with people of Judah and with God, was intense. He was caught as between two grindstones, the middleman between an indignant God and the disobedient people. From God the unwilling prophet received a stern commission to preach judgment. At the hands of the people he received scorn, rejection, violent opposition. His suffering was acute. Seeking to serve God in the midst of widespread spiritual barrenness, he had no one to turn to. Even God was no refuge—in fact, God had become part of the problem. Hence the sensitive prophet's bitter laments.

Through this window into Jeremiah's life we can see his personal struggles. But more than that, we get in touch here with covenant, compassion, persistence, pain, and divine discipline—God's larger agenda.

With Jeremiah 11 we enter a ten-chapter section of poetry intermixed with prose. These chapters differ from chapters 2—10 in that here the messages are clustered around personal experiences. We learn about a plot to take Jeremiah's life, a hide-and-find experience with a linen girdle, a drought, a directive for Jeremiah to remain unmarried, a visit to a potter's workshop, a pottery-smashing demonstration, and an imprisonment. Threats of personal injury both open and close this block of materials (cf. 11:18; 20:1-6). Six prayers, sometimes called "laments" or "confessions," are found in these chapters (11:18ff.; 12:1-6; 15:10-11, 15-20; 17:14-18; 18:18-23 and 20:7-11). Former chapters have put us in touch with God's message; these chapters acquaint us with the messenger as well.

Jeremiah 11:1 – 12:17

# Preaching to the People and Protesting Before God

## PREVIEW

Some sermons go nowhere; others, pointed and direct, stir people to action, sometimes even to an attack on the preacher. When Jeremiah's audience heard about covenant-breaking and about God's plan to uproot the nation, men from Jeremiah's home village hatched a plot to do away with the prophet—as though that would resolve the issue!

The sermon itself is summarized in 11:1-17. Several questions arise from it. Jeremiah's shocking statement that the covenant is broken brings up the problem of what happens when covenant breaks down. What *is* covenant? The assassination plot raises perplexing questions about justice for Jeremiah personally (12:1-17). God answers both questions in the context of his larger agenda.

Scholars have often pointed to the similarities of style between parts of Jeremiah and the so-called Deuteronomic materials, especially the book of Deuteronomy. This chapter is a prime example of this affinity, for here is a wordy, repetitive style. [*Style, p. 309.*]

OUTLINE

Covenant Talk, 11:1-17
   11:2-8      Admonitions
   11:9-13     Accusations
   11:14-17    A Prohibition and Announcements

A Plot Against Jeremiah, 11:18-23

Jousting in Jordan's Jungles, 12:1-17
   12:1-4      Jeremiah's Case
   12:5-17     God's Reply

EXPLANATORY NOTES

## Covenant Talk  11:1-17

Covenant language—blessings, curses, broken covenants—underlies this section. Covenant was the basic arrangement between God and Israel.

Verses 2-13 are sometimes described as a sermon. That is a fair label, except that the biblical text identifies three (actually four if one includes v. 14) private messages to the prophet (vv. 2b-5, 6-8, 9-13). Since these are headlined by the command in the plural, "Listen to the terms . . . ," the "private" messages to the prophet were no doubt conveyed by way of sermon to the people. Judah and Jerusalem, the target audiences, are mentioned in each of the three "private" oracles. Other words which punctuate the subsections are *covenant, listen,* and *forefathers.*

### 11:2-8 Admonitions

A sermon may instruct but more frequently admonishes. Here, in two admonitions (vv. 2-5; 6-8), the centerpiece is *obey me.* The same word translated in English as *listen* or *obey* occurs eight times in the sermon (vv. 2, 3, 4, 6, 7, 8, 10, 11). It occurs more times in Jeremiah than in any other book. *[Obey/Listen, p. 305.]*

While both admonitions mention a curse, each has a different emphasis. The first urges obedience by offering positive incentives: fulfillment of God's promise, a *land flowing with milk and honey;* and thankfulness for the past favor of release from the *iron-smelting furnace* (vv. 2-5). The second admonition (vv. 6-8) majors on another kind of incentive: threat. People are urged to "listen up." They are reminded of the stubbornness of the forefathers and of how God implemented the covenant curses. These curses are detailed in Deuteronomy 27:15-26 (cf. Lev. 26:14-39), where following each curse Israel responded, as does Jeremiah here, with an *"Amen"* ("so be it," RSV).

In the ancient Near East curses were customary in political treaties, which in form are close to covenants. A Sefire treaty involving Syrian kings reads: "Whoever will not observe the words of the inscription . . . may the gods overturn that man and his house and all that is in it; and may they make its lower part its upper part!" (Fitzmyer: 21).

Jeremiah is talking about the Mosaic covenant at Sinai (Exod. 19— 24) rather than the one which Josiah made following the discovery of the book of the law (2 Kings 23:1-3). *This covenant* is connected with the deliverance from Egypt, and the covenant formula used at the Exodus is also used here: *You will be my people, and I will be your God"* (cf. Exod. 6:7). *[Covenant, p. 294.]*

## 11:9-13 Accusations

Following the two admonitions, both of which look to the past experiences of the forefathers, the preacher now directs two accusations to the hearers themselves (vv. 9-13): they have refused to listen to God's words (cf. 6:17); they are serving other gods, especially Baal, here "uglified" by the designation "the shameful thing" (v. 13, NASB). *[Baal, p. 291; Judgment Oracle, p. 299.]*

Covenants are not like contracts, for contracts involve itemized duties and are task-oriented. Covenants are arrangements between parties which aim toward personal closeness. The basic "item" is loyalty. That loyalty may be spelled out by some details, but a failure to observe the detail does not mean, as in a contract, that the arrangment as such is off. Still, a covenant can also be broken when the failure to be loyal is not sporadic, but becomes chronic. The motive of the covenant partner, if defiant, also represents disloyalty. Then the relationship is bankrupt. Loyalty to the Lord, for Israel, involved singleness of affection to him. The first commandment spelled it out: "You shall have no other gods before me." The persistence of Baal worship makes it clear that Israel's loyalties are now elsewhere. The covenant is dissolved, annulled. Jeremiah is the prophet who puts it baldly and unmistakably: Israel and Judah *have broken the covenant* (cf. 31:32).

## 11:14-17 A Prohibition and Announcements

So irreparably broken, in fact, is the covenant that God again prohibits Jeremiah from praying (v. 14; cf. 7:16; 14:11). Given her divided loyalties, sacrifices will not avert disaster (v. 15), for sacrifices do not automatically take away sin (1 Sam. 3:14). Jeremiah echoes the Lord's announcement of disaster in a poetic restatement. He compares Judah to an olive tree, a symbol used by Hosea (14:6). This tree, though planted by the Lord of hosts (covenant blessing), will be destroyed by a lightning fire (covenant curses) (v. 16).

## THE TEXT IN BIBLICAL CONTEXT

*Covenant Demands.* A covenant relationship includes demands. In times of spiritual smugness when people revelled in the promise that God was on their side, prophets emphasized the covenant demands and urged obedience. The message of the eighth-century prophets, Amos and Isaiah, brought to the fore the covenant requirements of just dealing, sensitivity to the unfortunate, and integrity of word and deed. A century later, Jeremiah likewise highlights the requirements of covenant, specifically exclusive devotion to God and righteous behavior toward one's fellow human beings (7:3ff.; 11:6f.). Similarly Jesus points the self-congratulating Pharisees to God's requirements (Matt. 23:23).

*Covenant Promises.* In covenant God offered benefits (11:4f.; cf. Gen. 12:3; 2 Sam. 7:9ff.). When a nation was broken and crushed, as pictured in the last half of Isaiah's book, then the promise side of the covenant was underlined (Isa. 41:10; cf. Ezek. 37:11-14). Similarly in Jeremiah's "Book of Comfort" a devastated people is reassured (30:8-11; 31:1). Paul's letters display that remarkable balance between promise and demand represented by the covenant formula, "I will be your God, and you shall be my people." Often in the first half of a letter he expounds the work and promise of God; in the second half he presses home the duties involved in covenantal relationships.

## THE TEXT IN THE LIFE OF THE CHURCH

*Covenant and Obedience.* Historically, that balance between covenant promises and covenant demands has been hard to achieve. In Reformation times, Luther and Calvin were marvelous spokesmen for the great salvation work of God: the power and grace of God were stressed at the expense, so at least the radical Anabaptists thought, of the demands of the gospel.

The Anabaptists would have chorused an "Amen" to the message, *"Obey me."* Their understanding of the Christian life was that to believe in Christ was to take seriously the requirements of living a Christlike life.

Their term, *Nachfolge Jesu* (following after Jesus), was succinctly put by Hans Denck: "No one can truly know Jesus unless he follows him in his life." Earlier Peter Waldo had determined to "follow nakedly a naked Jesus." Obedience ranked high, if not highest, in Anabaptist priorities.

A twentieth-century Quaker, T. Canby Jones, stressed that obedience is a grateful response to God's gracious covenant expressed in the formula, "I will walk among you, and will be your God, and you shall be my people . . . I have broken the bars of your yoke and made you walk erect" (Lev. 26:11-13; cf. Jer. 11:4). For Jones, the "only conceivable response to such love is obedience, total obedience, holy obedience, grateful obedience. Out of gratitude arises the will to obey and keep his statutes, commandments, and ordinances" (Durnbaugh: 212).

## A Plot Against Jeremiah 11:18-23

The men of Anathoth, Jeremiah's hometown people, plot to kill the prophet (cf. 18:22b-23a). If they, like Jeremiah, were priests (1 Kings 2:26) they might have been incensed by jealousy, by his invocation of covenant curses, or by his disturbing speeches generally. After all, to pronounce the covenant with God dissolved was to cut the main nerve of Israel's religion! When the message cuts deep, angry listeners, rather than repent, sometimes do away with the messenger (cf. Jesus, John 19; Stephen, Acts 7), or at least try to silence him by forbidding him to preach (v. 21; cf. Amos 2:12; 7:12).

Here we meet the first of the so-called "confessions." *[Lament, p 301.]* In bold and bitter language Jeremiah unburdens himself before God. Jeremiah's prayer is a defense of his own integrity (cf. 12:3a; 15:11, 15; 17:16b; 18:20). For him, prayer was something like addressing a court with a presiding judge, who tested the *heart and mind* (lit., "kidneys" and "heart"—the Hebrews regarded the kidneys as the seat of emotions, NASB "feelings," and the heart as the organ of thought).

This prayer for vengeance at first seems to betray furious resentment instead of saintly piety (v. 30). In Jeremiah's defense, we may note that since the plotters forbade him to speak in the Lord's name, the vengeance is in the interest of the Lord's honor. Moreover, our word "vengeance" hints strongly at vendetta, but the Hebrew word has the meaning of "legitimate power" or "sovereignty." "Jeremiah is asking that God show himself *as God* with these people" (Holladay, 1974: p. 91). The punishment is pronounced in the form of a judgment speech with its customary reason and announcement (vv. 22-23). *[Lament, p. 301; Vengeance, p. 312; Judgment Oracle, p. 299]*

## Jousting in Jordan's Jungles 12:1-17

In one of the boldest speeches in the entire Bible, the overwrought prophet complains to God about unfairness. The chapter is in two parts. God, it must be inferred, is the speaker in the second part (vv. 5-17).

### 12:1-4 Jeremiah's Case

The three stanzas corresponding to the three verses (12:1-3) are in a wrap up or chiastic arrangement with the companion poem of 11:18-20. Note the words *know, sheep, righteous, kill, justice, fruit, cause (case)* in both. (Lundbom: 100-101). [*Chiasmus, p. 292.*]

In these opening verses Jeremiah presents his case to God the Judge (vv. 1-4). The word *case* has definite legal and court overtones (Isa. 50:8-9a). The subject is justice, right dealing. The polite *Yet would I speak with you about your justice* can also be rendered more boldly, "Yet I would pass judgment upon you." Jeremiah wishes to have his day in court with God, even though he knows that God will come through as *righteous* (or innocent). If God can sue Judah for breach of covenant, then so can Jeremiah sue God for "failures." Jeremiah's two questions are: (1) Why do the wicked (men of Anathoth? the Babylonians? others?) prosper? and (2) How long will Judah's countryside suffer drought? (v. 4; cf. 14:2-6). [*Justice, p. 299.*]

Jeremiah is also angry because his prophecies of judgment have not come true and he is being mocked by his kinfolk (v. 6). Jeremiah had indeed prophesied that evildoers would not escape judgment. But God has taken no action. Instead, God has planted the wicked, that is, he tends them, even though they are double-tongued (v. 2). The problem is not only personal. It is the question of how social power is arranged. Jeremiah's harsh request for revenge in verse 3b echoes 11:20.

### 12:5-17 God's Reply

God replies to Jeremiah's *case* by appealing to the "from the less to the greater" principle. The lesser demand is to race on foot with others and/or to manage on safe (level, open) country. The greater demand is to compete with horses, and/or to "make it" in heights of the jungle thickets of the Jordan Valley, known to be inhabited by wild animals (cf. 49:19; 50:44). The word *batah* has two quite separate meanings, "trust" and "fall," making for translation options such as, "If you trust in a land of safety" or "if thou fallest flat on thy belly in a land of peace" (v. 5b) (Driver: 59).

If Jeremiah barely manages in the footrace in the open country, so

God argues, how will he do when racing with horses or jousting in Jordan's jungle? In other words, if a small problem knocks him flat, how would he withstand a blockbuster? By these questions God does not explain how it is the wicked prosper. By them God sets up Jeremiah to see that whatever intellectual difficulties he has, he hasn't seen anything yet! There are harder things to explain. He is "still only at the threshold of his trials" (von Rad: 203).

Verse 6, with its reference to the plot of the men of Anathoth, justifies our linking of chapters 11—12. The treacherous plot against Jeremiah is the lesser of the difficulties—like running in open country. The greater difficulty is the problem of God's overturning his very own people, abandoning them, even hating them (v. 7f) and ensuring their destruction. Some translations render a past tense, "I have forsaken my house" (v. 7, NASB, RSV). The historic incident in view could be the assault of invading bands of Moabites and Ammonites in 602 (2 Kings 24:2), but the devastation pictured here is most severe. Others quite permissibly translate the Hebrew verb in the future tense, *"I will forsake my house"* (vv. 7-13). The gist of these verses, namely destruction item by item, is clear from the diagram. Note the personal pronoun "my" suggesting great affection.

| my house (v.7) (cf. Joel 2:17) | my inheritance (v. 8) (cf. Ps. 78:7) | my vineyard (v. 10) (cf. Hos. 10:1) | my field (v. 10) |
|---|---|---|---|
| abandoned to enemies | beasts will devour | ruined and trampled | laid waste |

Or one might consider the suggestion of a Jewish commentator, "Your townspeople had conspired against you and yet you knew nothing of it. Now if you could not read the minds of your fellow townsmen, how do you expect to understand my purposes?" (Freehof: 89).

Some further notes: *Inheritance* is distinctly a reference to the tribe of Israel (vv. 7, 8, 9, 15). The word occurs in parallel with *Portion of Jacob* (10:16). The term occurs often in Leviticus, Joshua, and Ezekiel where it primarily denotes family or even tribal land portions (e.g., Lev. 36:2-12; Josh. 15:20; Ezek. 45:1) and in Psalms and Jeremiah where its predominant meaning is Israel as God's portion (e.g., Ps. 78:71). The *roar* as of a lion (v. 8) is the cry of the violence of Jerusalem, which like the cry of the city of Sodom was great (Gen. 18:20). The *shepherds* (v.

10) are not tenders of animals but civil and possibly religious leaders (cf. 6:3; 23:2) who have ruled roughshod over the people. The word *forsake* is often used for the people's lapse in keeping covenant (1 Sam. 8:8; Deut. 28:20; Jer. 2:17-18). Here God rejects the people (cf. Jer. 7:29; 14:19), a step opposite to election and one that paves the way for destruction.

Thus far the Lord's answer has only complicated the question, just as it did for Habakkuk, who asked a similar question (Hab. 1:3). In the final verses the answer is more reassuring. Those who have been planted (compare Jeremiah's charge, 12:2) will be *uprooted*, whether nations or Judah itself (v. 14). The clue to the question of God's justice lies in the future when a repentant Israel (and not the wicked) will be planted in the land (vv. 16f; cf. 32:41).

But surprising and hard to deal with, like a jungle thicket, is the Lord's claim that he will restore each of the wicked nations, following punishment, to their own country. That sort of justice (or is it better *compassion?* v. 15) is exceedingly difficult to comprehend. God will have compassion on Moab and Amon (cf. 48:47; 49:6). God will bless Egypt (Isa. 19:24). Apparently God has "missionary" intentions for these wicked nations, provided they swear by the name of the Lord—a way of saying that the Lord God is their ultimate value. [*Swearing, p. 311.*]

Jeremiah asks about justice. God answers him by complicating the question and then by changing the agenda to a discussion of compassion. He assures Jeremiah, however, that in the meantime evildoers will certainly be punished.


## THE TEXT IN BIBLICAL CONTEXT

*Theodicy.* Theodicy is a term given to the rule of God in which evil is allowed to flourish. Questions of theodicy have only partial answers. The issue has been posed: if God is good and intends good, why is evil present? If God is powerful, why is evil permitted? From the presence of evil some people draw the conclusion that God is neither good nor powerful. But the Scriptures claim that God is both. And more: God is just.

The classical discussion of evil and suffering is found in the wisdom materials of Proverbs and Job. The straightforward teaching in much of Proverbs is that doing good will be rewarded and evil persons will be punished. But in life, as the psalmist observed, evildoers prosper (Ps. 37, 49, 73). The book of Job and to a lesser degree the book of Habakkuk address the problem. From Job the answer in part is that God chooses not to disclose the answer. God himself, rather than an intellectual answer, is sufficient. Habakkuk's answer, while reaffirming that the evildoers will be punished (2:5ff.) calls for the just to live by faith, namely the faith that God will really do right by all (2:4ff.). From Jeremiah 12 the answer, while also pointing to the eventual uprooting of the evildoers, is more patronizing, as if to say, "There are even more difficult questions."

## THE TEXT IN THE LIFE OF THE CHURCH

*"It's unfair!"* There are times when Christians feel they have gotten the short end of the stick. Like Jeremiah they have submitted their motives to God for careful testing. But others prosper—those with less conscience, or professed Christians who live hypocritical lives, who spout pious clichés yet are quite out of touch with God. Things go well for them but not for the faithful.

When we come upon such times, we can take a clue from Jeremiah.

1. We may voice our complaint. We can present our case to God. It is proper and acceptable to raise questions.

2. We should not expect coddling. Comparison with others, especially those who prosper, can bring a surge of self-commiseration. It is not likely, however, that God will pamper us. We may expect, instead, some bracing questions such as, "If you are paralyzed by personal rebuffs and disappointments, how will you manage when the going gets really rough?"

3. We should listen for an answer. God has a word for us. We inquire about justice and fairness. God may wish to speak with us about compassion. God may call us to courage rather than to sort out a mystery, for ultimately there remains a mystery.

Jeremiah 13

# A Ruined Girdle, Smashed Wine Jars, and an Awful Pride

## PREVIEW

Arrogance is the temptation of those who "have made it." Arrogant people not only sideline God; they become self-sufficient, even to the point of making their own rules. Jeremiah insisted that pride precipitates God's punishment, for it frustrates God's intentions.

Chapter 13 concludes a thematic cycle. The theme of the foe from the north has been building since chapter 4. In chapters 4—6 the foe was announced as on his way. Chapters 8—10 focused in large measure on the siege. In chapters 12—13 the unnamed enemy from the north (Babylon, as will be clear later) is pictured as carrying all of Judah into exile. The reason for this judgment is sin of various kinds, but pride is now in the spotlight. An action having to do with a new garment introduces the theme.

## OUTLINE

A Symbolic Action: The Linen Girdle, 13:1-11

A Proverb: Smashed Wine Jars, 13:12-14

A Warning: Pride Is Harmful, 13:15-27

Here is the first of several sign-acts or symbolic actions in the book. Others include the breaking of a pot (19:1ff.) and the wearing of oxen yokes (27:1ff.). *[Symbolic Actions, p. 311.]* The poetic portion of the chapter is in two parts: Jeremiah pleads for the people not to be arrogant (vv. 15-23), and the Lord announces judgment (vv. 24-27).

## EXPLANATORY NOTES

### A Symbolic Action: The Linen Girdle  13:1-11

For twelve chapters, so to speak, God has been sending urgent messages, but the people have played deaf. What then will catch their attention? In the next chapters God commands a series of object lessons—some of them very striking indeed.

God sends Jeremiah shopping. He is to buy a linen *'ezor*, which is not so much a belt (NIV) or a waistband (NASB), but a clothing piece hugging the hips and reaching down toward the knees. Then God sends the prophet traveling. The Hebrew *Perathah* is usually understood to be the Euphrates River in Mesopotamia—a 700-mile round trip. (That the word refers to a stream near Anathoth, Jeremiah's birthplace, is less likely.) The prophet is to bury his *'ezor* in the riverbank. A return to the Euphrates, 60 days away, would make the sign act all the more striking.

Jeremiah did as he was commanded. Moisture, dirt, and insects had, no doubt, spoiled the girdle. It was *completely useless*. The interpretation, even by Calvin, that this was a vision can be dismissed not only because the prophet reports obedience, but because the force of the symbolic action lay in its performance. *[Symbolic Actions, p. 311.]*

And useless also, so stresses the divinely given interpretation, are God's people because of their pride (vv. 8-11). It is noted three times that Jeremiah was to wear the skirt around his waist. Similarly, God intended to bind Israel and Judah tightly to him (v. 11). Just as a brightly colored, carefully made skirt adorns the wearer, so God intended Israel and Judah as a people to be his attractive ornament, a good reputation (name, renown) bringing honor to the Lord (Exod. 19:6; Isa. 43:7; Rev. 4:11). Israel was to be bound close to God. But too proud to listen to God, Israel had become, like the linen girdle, *completely useless*.

### A Proverb: Smashed Wine Jars  13:12-14

Wine jugs (not *wineskins* which can't be smashed, v. 14, NIV) would inadvertently be toppled by the clumsy feet of those drunken at parties.

Or perhaps clay jugs would be deliberately smashed, just as today drinkers hurl wine glasses at the fireplace. Jeremiah indicates that God will break up the whole structure. The point is made from a lighthearted jest, a witticism thrown about, we may imagine, at banquets or perhaps drinking parties. Jokingly the wine bibbers josh about every person, themselves included, filled like jars with wine.

Jeremiah seizes on their joke but turns it into a judgment. By God's order all will be drunken and literally smashed. The notion of drunkenness, total bewilderment, resulting from drinking God's cup of wrath, is a familiar one (25:15-16). The paragraph points to the ruin which God will let come on arrogant people.

## A Warning: Pride Is Harmful  13:15-27

The prophet next issues a warning about pride (vv. 15-19). The Lord is the likely speaker beginning with verse 20. Some versions supply Lord (v. 21, NIV), but the subject could also be "they" (=foreigners, RSV).

A prescription offered by the prophet for those with exaggerated estimates of their own importance is to give glory to God. Proud persons give glory to themselves. But God deals with pride: proud persons will stumble in the darkness (v. 16). For Judah, pride will bring a disastrous fall in the form of enemy subjugation.

This message is something of a final plea, and the prophet weeps as he realizes the people will not humble themselves (cf. 4:19-20; 8:18-19; 9:1). The foe from the north, which as it turns out is Babylon, will reach and blockade, shut up the Negev, that is, the cities in the south (v. 19), and so the entire country will be in enemy control. The king, possibly Jehoiachin who ruled for three months, together with his mother, the queen of the late Josiah (d. 609), will be deposed and their crowns will be removed. The story is told in 2 Kings 24:8ff.

The prophet addresses Zion with a series of rhetorical questions (vv. 20-23). The verbs are feminine, and some ancient versions include the name of the city. The meaning of verse 21 can be paraphrased: How will you feel when foreigners, the very Babylonians whose friendship you tried to enlist, shall be in command over you? This proud people, Judah, is in for a major surprise, indeed a devastating humiliation.

Some would see verses 20-27 as a detached oracle, since pride is not mentioned. But in this speech the Lord spells out the consequences of pride for Judah. Given the spin-off sins of pride, such as stubbornness and unwillingness to listen, the sins of adultery may be but an extension of the arrogance. God's charge is that so ingrained is evil in the people that it is as much a part of them as their own skin color: they can change neither the one nor the other.

Two figures of speech suggest how God will bring the proud down. The proud will be whipped about like chaff (vv. 24-25). Second, like a woman, prideful Jerusalem, the Lord's *daughter*, will be ravished, raped, and humiliated (v. 26). To *pull the skirts over the face* is to expose the nakedness of the body to view, a great disgrace and humiliation. The phrase may be a euphemism for sexual advances (Lev. 18:6-19; 20:17). *Your body mistreated* translates literally "treating the heel violently," or in English idiom, "stripped naked from head to toe" (v. 22). Because of indecent exposure, Jerusalem will suffer great outrage.


## THE TEXT IN BIBLICAL CONTEXT

*Pride.* The Hebrew words for pride in this chapter are three. One, translated *"pride"* (v. 9), means "height," "eminence," or "majesty" (Job 40:10; Isa. 24:14) and in a derogatory sense, "pomp" (Isa. 14:11; Ezek. 30:18). Just as here the pride of Israel is identifed, so elsehwere one reads of the pride of Sodom (Ezek. 16:49), of Moab (Jer. 48:29), of the Philistines (Zech. 9:6), and of the Assyrians (Zech. 10:11). A second term, sometimes translated as *"haughty,"* occurs in verse 15. It means "to be high" or "lifted up." A most fascinating yet scathing tirade on the pride or haughtiness of women is found in Isaiah 3:16-18. Those "high of eyes" (Ps. 101:5) will not endure; God detests those proud (high) in heart (Prov. 16:5). An example of pride can be cited from Judah's history. When King Uzziah became powerful he also became proud and assumed prerogatives which did not belong to him (2 Chron. 26:16). For Hezekiah's pride see 2 Chronicles 32:24-26. A third term, also meaning *"pride"* (v. 17) and found only four times in the Old Testament, is used in conjunction with Nebuchadnezzar (Dan. 4:37).

Ultimately pride leads to self-exaltation and substitution of other gods for God (cf. the prince of Tyre, Ezek. 28:1-19). Pride and idolatry are therefore linked. Moreover, pride corrodes covenant. In the day of the Lord, a day monopolized by God, God will ruthlessly dismantle all that is prideful (Isa. 2:12-18; 13:11). God detests pride (Prov. 8:13) and judges it (Ezek. 17:24; Hos. 5:5, 7; Amos 8:7).

In the New Testament the virtue of humility is exemplified in Jesus (Phil. 2:4-11). Proud and self-sufficient people will not make it into the kingdom (Rom. 1:30). James cautions against pride (4:6, 16). John declares that "pride of life," namely lust for advantage and status, is "of the world" (1 John 2:15ff.).

## THE TEXT IN THE LIFE OF THE CHURCH

*Pride/Humility.* Augustine, a major theologian of the fourth century, confessed concerning his past, "yea my pride-swollen face closed up my eyes." To St. Bernard are attributed these words: "It is no great thing to be humble when you are brought low. But to be humble when you are praised is a rare and great attainment." Pride was identified as one of the seven deadly sins in the Middle Ages; others were envy, wrath, covetousness, gluttony, lechery, and sloth.

Sir Thomas More, a Catholic, was beheaded in 1535 by King Henry VIII in one of England's most notorious executions. He had refused to take the oath to support the Act of Succession and Supremacy. Sir Thomas, a lawyer and a writer, maintained that the ideal society would already have come "if that one monster pride" did not forbid it. In his *Utopia* (1516) he wrote: "Pride is the infernal serpent that steals into the hearts of men, thwarting and holding them back from choosing the better way of life."

Twentieth-century novelist Gunter Grass remarked, "It is the hubris in our human thinking that has brought us to the edge of chaos." Hubris is excessive or over-reaching pride of the sort first seen at Babel.

Jeremiah 14—15

# Drought, the Lord's Double "No," and a Prophet's Anguish

## PREVIEW

When economic setbacks bring people up short, they may in desperation cry to God for help. What if God's answer is "No"? God's people in Jeremiah's day experienced drought and famine. This time prayer to God did not spell relief. And they learned why.

The drought likely came early in Jeremiah's career, although the date of 601 has been put forward. The two chapters are dominated by prayers, both by the people as a response to the drought, and by Jeremiah who is caught up in a personal crisis. The Lord answers the people's pleas twice with a "No." He reassures the prophet, but not apart from a chastening rebuke. The chapters are part of the larger cluster (11—20) in which incidents from Jeremiah's personal life are in focus.

## OUTLINE

The two chapters fall symmetrically into neatly paired sections. We choose, however, not to follow the text sequence but rather combine similar sections for comment. That the two larger parallel sections (14:2-16 and 14:17—15:9) should be seen together is evident from several inclusio features, most notably the Hebrew word "languish" (14:2; 15:9). [Inclusio, p. 298.]

107

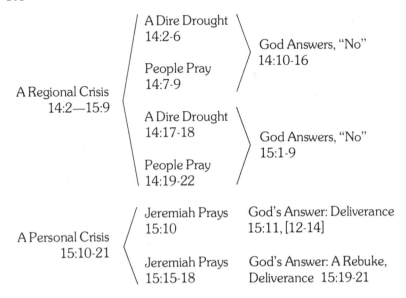

A Regional Crisis
14:2—15:9

A Dire Drought
14:2-6

People Pray
14:7-9

God Answers, "No"
14:10-16

A Dire Drought
14:17-18

People Pray
14:19-22

God Answers, "No"
15:1-9

A Personal Crisis
15:10-21

Jeremiah Prays
15:10

God's Answer: Deliverance
15:11, [12-14]

Jeremiah Prays
15:15-18

God's Answer: A Rebuke,
Deliverance 15:19-21

## EXPLANATORY NOTES

### A Dire Drought 14:2-6, 17-18

Basic to a standard lament is a complaint and a prayer. In the two largely parallel laments (vv. 2-9; 17-21) the complaint consists essentially of eyewitness descriptions: the rains have failed, the cisterns are empty, people and animals are suffering. The description of the drought, as of the grasshopper plague (Joel 1:5-12), shows how certain select groups are affected. (1) The people mourn in the city gates, an assembly point comparable to today's shopping malls: "They bow down in black unto the ground" (v. 2, JPS). (2) Nobles and farmers alike can't find water. (3) The deer behave unnaturally and the donkeys' eyes are glazed. A graphic prose account of famine is found in 2 Kings 6:25-29. An Assyrian inscription during Ashurbanipal's rule (669-627) recounts how famine broke out and the curses of the oath were fulfilled: "The young of camels sucked at seven udders ... and could not satisfy their bellies with milk" (Luckenbill: 318).

The second description, beginning with *Say to them*, is not an oracle of revelation but Jeremiah's public declaration of what he feels and sees (14:18-19). In the fields he sees those pierced with a sword. Some think a military defeat is in view, but animals could have been mercifully put out of their misery. In the city he witnesses, no doubt, crying youngsters,

bloated stomachs of malnourished babes, and the "diseases of the
famine" (NASB). His colleagues have left the stricken country to "ply
their trade in a [foreign] land."

## People Pray 14:7-9, 19-22

This dire situation drives the people to prayer. Two prayers have been
recorded (vv. 7-9,19-21). Both have similar elements but not in identical
order: a petition, an acknowledgment of sin, plaintive questions, and
assertions of confidence. In both prayers the petition turns on the Lord's
name (vv. 7, 9, 21). In the first the preoccupation with the name opens
and concludes the prayer. [Inclusio, p. 298.] Beyond the inclusio there is
a chiasm (Beuken/van Grol) [Chiasm, p. 292.]

> 7a your name
> 8a name of God: Savior
> 8b reproach: God at a distance
> 9a reproach: God cannot save
> 9b name of God: God's presence
> 9c your name

The argument for God to act for the sake of his name is found
elsewhere and is used by God himself (Ps. 25:11; 106:8; 143:11; Ezek.
20:9, 14, 22, 44). The people also appeal to the covenant (v. 21; cf. we
bear your name, v. 9). Their special relationship to God is used as le-
verage.

The people acknowledge their sin in each of the two prayers, saying,
We have sinned against you. To this basic admission of sin they add language about backsliding (v. 7) and guilt of the forefathers (v. 20). They
ask several plaintive questions. In the first prayer they inquire about
God's temporary interest (like a traveler who stays only a night) and his
ability ("like a soldier who fails in the pinch") (Bright: 98).

In the second prayer their anxiety is more acute. They ask, Has God
totally rejected the people? (v. 19; cf. Ps. 74). Rejection by God would be
intolerable; it would mean the end of election status, cancellation of
God's personal relationship with Judah, apathy or even hostility toward
Zion, and abolition of the covenant (cf. 7:14-15, 29; 12:7). God's rejection of the people would be a prelude to punishment.

But Judah, so often delivered in a crisis, sees it as improbable that
God should cast off the people. The people insist, You are among us (v.
9; cf. the temple sermon, 7:4 and Amos 5:14). Statements of confidence
are more profuse in the second prayer than in the first: hope for an

answer (in this case rain showers) is in *you, O Lord our God* (v. 22).

These are wonderful prayers. One scholar calls this passage "one of the finest prayers in the Bible." The prayers are surely deserving of gracious answers. But God's reply to them both is "No." Why?

## God's Answer, Twice "NO" 14:10-16; 15:1-9

In the first of the two answers, the reply is abrupt: *So the Lord does not accept them* ( v. 10). The "No" is not only abrupt; it has a finality to it. The reason is that despite their confession of sin, the people *love to wander* (v. 10). They continue in their evil. Consequently, the fine prayer notwithstanding, God will *punish them for their sins.* (For unacceptable sacrifices, see 6:20; 7:21-26.) The overall reply here is cryptic following the sequence: situation (10a+b), God's stance (10e), and sequel (10f.).

So indignant is God that even the prophet's prayer, which could conceivably be effective, is forbidden (v. 11; cf. 7:16; 11:14). Even fasting, often practiced in emergencies, will do no good (cf. Isa. 48:3-11; Joel 1:13-14; 2:15-17; Zech. 7:4-8). This is a blow, since fasting had always been a last resort. So specialized and extensive had fasting become that the Jewish Talmud devotes an entire treatise, *Taanit,* to the subject. Not only will God not send rain, he will intensify their trouble by sending sword, famine, and plague. These three agents of punishment often appear in trio form in Jeremiah (e.g., 21:7; 24:10; 27:8; 32:24).

Jeremiah remonstrates with God, asking in effect if it would not suffice if the false prophets were to perish (v. 12). False prophets were a constant menace (23:9-32; 27—29). The Lord's answer is "No". In a judgment oracle God details the sins of the false prophets: they resort to lies, proceed as prophets though unauthorized by the Lord, and rely on "false visions, worthless augury and their own deluding fancies" (v. 14, NEB). The calamity of sword and famine is coming, both for people and for prophets (vv. 15-16). *[Judgment Oracle, p. 299.]*

In his further reply (15:1-9) to the people's second prayer (14:19-23), God again rejects the possibility of prophetic intercession. God is exasperated! Earlier Moses and Samuel, noted as effective intercessors (Exod. 32:11-14; Num. 14:13-19; 1 Sam. 12:9-23; Ps. 99:6), had both secured answers from God in emergency situations: Moses brought water from a rock (Num. 20:1-11); Samuel's prayer in a national crisis brought thunderings, and presumably rain (1 Sam. 7:9-11). But now even were Moses and Samuel, these "greats" from the past, to intercede, God will not hear. A people's cry will indeed go unanswered (cf. 11:11).

The sins of Manasseh (15:4), easily Judah's most wicked king, are detailed in 2 Kings 21:1-8. Sixty years later the nation, by its own choice, was still in the grip of the idolatries which that king had introduced.

The lament-like speech by the Lord paints a dismal future (vv. 5-9). The stress is on bereavement. Widows will be numerous since husbands will die in battle. Women, even robust ones, *the mother of seven*, will weaken, languish, and die. *Her sun*, that is, her hope in her offspring, will set (v. 9). The *destroyer* is likely both famine and the warring foe. The Hebrew verbs are in the future tense (15:5-9 NIV, cf. 12:7-13), though most translations employ the past tense. The introductory questions, *Who will have pity on you?* (v. 5), as well as the *I will send . . .* of verse 3 could favor the future tense. So could the severity of the coming judgment. If the material all dates from before 601, then no such large-scale calamity had occurred in the people's recent past.

Generally in a lament the complaint and the prayer would be followed by a reassuring answer from the Lord. But while there is in the unit a carefully framed double lament (see outline), the divine answer is the opposite of that expected in a lament poem. We ask again, why? There is more than a hint of an answer. "You," says the Lord, addressing these people with their pious prayers, "have *rejected* me and continue to go away from me" (15:6). When actions fail to match words, even earnest prayers are pointless.

## THE TEXT IN BIBLICAL CONTEXT

*Calamity and God's Purpose.* Accounts of famine punctuate the biblical story. The stories of prominent persons are linked with drought: Abraham went to Egypt because of famine (Gen. 12:10); Joseph rose to power in Egypt during the crisis of a national famine (Gen. 41:1—43:1); and famine conditions were decisive in the stories of Ruth and Elijah (Book of Ruth and 1 Kings 17:1ff; 18:2). Famine was one of the punishment options offered to David (2 Sam. 24:3). Famine came in the time of the apostles (Acts 11:27-30). References to famine are very frequent in Jeremiah (11:22; 14:12; 15:1; 16:4; 18:21; 21:7, 9; 24:10; 27:8; 29:17; 32:24, 36; 34:17; 38:2; 44:12, 18, 27).

How is a calamity such as a drought to be assessed from a biblical viewpoint? Drought can come because of people's sins, e.g., drought in King Ahab's reign. Drought was threatened as a curse for disobedience to the covenant. But while sin precipitates a calamity, the reverse of the equation does not follow. Not all calamity is God's immediate punishment for sin. Drought in one part of the world, or even in immediate neighborhoods is not uniformly or necessarily God's judgment on sin.

## THE TEXT IN THE LIFE OF THE CHURCH

*When Saying "Sorry" Is Not Enough.* Much of the repentance talk in the home with children or with spouses, as well as in the church, is shallow, as though a flippant "Sorry" constituted repentance. "In our home," writes a teacher of pastoral care, going a step further, "we have a rule that whenever we say, 'I'm sorry,' we will specify exactly what we are sorry for."

But the acknowledgment "We have sinned" is hollow without some evidence of change. Augustine, who later became a North African bishop, reportedly prayed, "Lord, deliver me from lust but not yet." Such penitence, or grief over what sin has caused, differs from repentance, which is a decisive about-face.

*Responding to Disaster.* In the 1520s when the Turkish army, numbering in the thousands, was outside the gates of Vienna, Martin Luther detected two enemies approaching the Holy Roman Empire: one was Suleiman the Magificent; the other was God. This situation called for two types of defenses.

> "Since the Turk is the rod of the wrath of the Lord our God . . . the first thing to be done is to . . . take the rod out of God's hand, so that the Turk may be found only, in his own strength, all by himself . . . and without God's hand. . . . This fight must be begun with repentance, and we must reform our lives, or we shall fight in vain . . . for God is devising evil against us because of our wickedness. . . (Luther: 170-71).

## A Personal Crisis  15:10-21

Among the so-called "confessions" by the prophet, the confession of 15:15-21 is the most soul-stirring. The occasion for either of the two confessions or prayers is not specified. One can conjecture that the drought, the artificial repentance, and the Lord's "No" with its cold finality were enough for the prophet to throw up his hands and cry, "What's the use"? *[Lament, p. 301.]*

### 15:10-14  A Prayer of Complaint: "Everyone Curses Me"

The feelings voiced by the prophet are feelings of frustration and pain and a veiled wish not ever to have been born. Jeremiah sees himself in the middle of a gigantic struggle; everyone is arrayed against him. It is an uneven match: Jeremiah versus the world. As in other of the confessions, the prophet protests his innocence (12:3a). In merchandising, a lender may be angered by a client who is tardy in his payment; or a borrower may become hostile toward a lender who overcharges.

Though neither lender nor borrower, Jeremiah is still the object of the curse.

The Lord's reply is comforting. In the sense of setting Jeremiah free, the deliverance will be for a *good purpose*. The RSV unfortunately follows the Greek with "So be it" and a conjectural reading of the verb which yields, "So be it, O Lord, if I have not entreated thee for their good" (v. 11). But a divine reply is a common, though not inevitable, feature of the laments (cf. 11:21-23; 12:5ff. and 15:19). The verse is complicated by textual difficulties, but the meaning, following the Hebrew text, is perhaps best caught in NEB, which offers a sense roughly comparable to NIV:

> I will greatly strengthen you (NEB).
> *Surely I will deliver you for a good purpose* (NIV).·
>
> In time of distress and in time of disaster (NEB)
> *Surely I will make your enemies plead with you* (NIV)
>
> I will bring the enemy to your feet (NEB).
> *in times of disaster and times of distress* (NIV).

Yet another possibility is to see verses 11-14 as two statements by the Lord which Jeremiah quotes and which, because they are contradictory, he makes the heart of the complaint: (1) Jeremiah will have success, and (2) an enemy will wipe out Judah.

"Can iron break steel from the north?" (v. 12, NEB). This question is best understood in the sense, Can anything stop the mighty foe from the north from advancing? Verses 13-14 are found also in 17:3-4, where they more readily fit. See comment there. The certain announcement placed here that Judah's wealth would be plundered, her people would be enslaved—and all this because of God's anger against her sin— restates and reinforces the central message about which even the prophet may have himself come to have some doubts. *[Doublets, p. 296; Wrath, p. 313.]*

### 15:15-21 A Prayer of Complaint: "Why Is My Pain Unending?"

The second confession, like the first, is in two parts: Jeremiah's prayer (vv. 15-18) and the Lord's reply (vv. 19-21).

The prayer, while it begins with a petition, ends more like a bitter reproach. Jeremiah's request for vengeance has more to do with God showing himself sovereign and squaring accounts than with a personal vendetta (v. 15; cf. 12:3b; 20:12b). His petition for himself is that the Lord pay attention to him, take up his cause, and not allow him to die (v. 15). He argues for favorable attention to this request on the grounds of

who God is—an understanding and long-suffering God (Num. 14:18;
Exod. 34:6; and frequently in prayer, Neh. 9:17; Ps. 86:15)—and on the
grounds of his past ministry and his bearing of God's reproach (cf. esp.
Ps. 89:51).

His personal stress level becomes more intense as he voices his inward contradiction of feeling. On the one hand he knows some joys.
Perhaps "finding of your word" has in view the discovery of the book of
the law in the temple (v. 16; cf. 2 Kings 22:13; 23:2). Figuratively speaking, he devours the message with eagerness (cf. Ezek. 2:8—3:3; Rev. 10:9-
10). Moreover, he belongs to God: *Thou hast named me thine. [Lord of
Hosts, p. 304.]*

But he knows sorrow. There is no one with whom he can share his
joy. Those who revel are making merry on other grounds. Indeed, he
has been forbidden to celebrate at weddings or to party (16:1-9). He is
reduced to isolation because the word from the Lord is a message of un-                .
relieved judgment: Jeremiah cannot be occupied with this word without
himself becoming indignant with the people. The net effect is that he is
socially ostracized.

But his personal crisis goes deeper than social isolation. His quarrel
is with God. Although framed as a question, the bitterness and hurt are
hardly disguised. God has not come through for him. In the Judean hills
a thirsty traveler approaching a *wadi* or ravine will see a mirage of water,
but the stream bed will actually be dry. God is like that, Jeremiah complains, for he has held out promises, but in the time of stress, there is
nothing (v. 18).

The Lord's reply to this bitter outburst is reassuring, though not immediately so: "If you will turn back to me, I will take you back" (v. 19,
NEB). If the prophet will *turn* (it is the word used often in Jeremiah for
"repent"), then God will permit continued service. "To stand" (RSV,
NASB) is a synonym for "serve" since it can refer to a servant standing at
the ready to minister (Num. 16:9; 27:21; 1 Kings 12:8; Ps. 134:1; Zech.
3:1). Another interpretation holds that if Jeremiah will return to his task
instead of complaining, then God will restore him. This explanation is
the more satisfying since the "if" is expanded by the call to speak *worthy*
words. His self-pitying words are dubbed *worthless.* Following a change
in his attitude (not necessarily a repentance from sin), the prophet can
return to his speaking function and be God's spokesman (lit., mouth).
The personal pronouns "I," "me," and the like, are numerous.

The wordplay on "turn" in v. 19, now understood more physically,
makes the point: people may turn on you, but don't you take your cues
from them. Public opinion should not determine your lifestyle. Signifi-

cantly, God again uses the imagery of fortifying him as a *wall of bronze* employed earlier in Jeremiah's call (1:18-19). *"I am with you"* is a striking and powerful promise found in salvation oracles (Isa. 41:10; 43:2; Jer. 30:11) as well as in call commissions (Exod. 3:12; Jer. 1:8). *[Divine Assistance Formula, p. 295.]*

The reply which answers Jeremiah tit for tat does so in reverse order of Jeremiah's speech to make the pattern A:B:C/C:B:A. *[Chiasmus, p. 292.]*

> A Personal disquiet, verse 15
> B Social ostracism, verse 17
> C Reproach to God, verse 18
> C Change of attitude, verse 18a
> B You must not turn to them, verse 19b
> A I will fortify you, verse 20

The two laments could profitably be compared and contrasted with the two in Jeremiah 11:18-23; 12:1-6(13) by noting the two prayers and God's two replies. *[Lament, p. 301.]*

## THE TEXT IN BIBLICAL CONTEXT

*God's Freedom.* Prayer is dialogue with God, whose answers or responses are at times quite opposite to one's expectation. The reports on answers to Jeremiah's prayer (15:15-21) or the people's prayer (14:7-9; 19-21) say something about God's freedom.

People assault God's throne in the crisis of a famine, urging his promises, his covenant, his honor. They address him as the "hope of Israel" and even acknowledge their sin. But even confessions can be forms of spiritual bribery to get one's way. To be sure, God pities the helpless. But God preserves his independence, not to mention his integrity, and is not bound to grant every request. God dealt with his prophets' despondencies in different ways (12:1-17; cf. 1 Kings 19:1-18; Hab. 1:1—2:4).

Similarly, God is depicted in the scenario of Jeremiah's prayer as free to encourage, but also to rebuke. Self-pity does not twist the arm of God to come speedily to one's aid. The possible loss of a prophet, even one of the stature of Jeremiah, is not a threat to the Almighty.

At the same time, in spite of the fact that prayer is not an attempt to convince God, who acts in freedom, both the people and Jeremiah address God without hesitation. Note the arguments offered by the people (14:7-9, 19-21) and Jeremiah (15:15-18). Moses and Job had extensive arguments with God, as did Abraham when interceding for Sodom. The dialogical aspect of prayer underlines the freedom of both partners in a covenant.

## THE TEXT IN THE LIFE OF THE CHURCH

*Despondency.* Where is the believer who has not been on the outs with God? There is a place for the honest setting forth of one's feelings. Hiding them before an all-knowing God is pointless. Giving voice to them is itself a therapeutic relief. Our modern hymnbooks rarely contain laments. Should they? A good experience is to write a lament following the Hebrew lament form. For a modern lament, see the glossary entry "Lament," p. 301.

But prayer is not merely self-expression. There is in addition a listening God who, though he corrects, also counsels and comforts. The comfort with which God comforted Jeremiah remains available to us.

Raphael van den Valde was arrested in 1576 at Ghent, Flanders, for his faith and confined in a strong tower. After seven weeks, during which he was "dreadfully tormented," he was burnt alive. In a letter he writes, "Further, my dear wife, I cannot forbear . . . to comfort and rejoice your heart, and this by the Word of God, for this must now be all our comfort . . . as also the prophet Jeremiah says," and he quoted Jeremiah 15:15, 16 (van Braght: 1031).

Jeremiah 16 – 17

# Remain Single – Something Is Desperately Wrong!

## PREVIEW

How does one communicate persuasively? Jeremiah has already used his personal clothing as a sign-act (13:1ff.). Now not only his actions, but also his condition as an unmarried man is to become a message for the people.

The immediate interpretation of why Jeremiah was not to marry is followed by a puzzling patchwork of poetry, proverb, and "sermons" that is not built around any single theme, although the note, "Something is desperately wrong," shrill and ominous, sounds again and again. Ever ready with image and metaphor, Jeremiah speaks of fishers and hunters, of desert bush and streamside tree, of diamond-point pen and tablet, and even of partridges and a blazing fire. One may at first be distracted by this kaleidoscope of images, but one point will be clear: trouble is on the way.

## OUTLINE

Don't Marry, Don't Socialize, 16:1-13
Is It Salvation or Judgment? 16:14-18
A Medley of Poems: Arguing by Comparison, 16:19—17:13
"I'm in Trouble," 17:14-18
A Sermon on Sabbath-Keeping, 17:19-27

The Lord's prohibitions are given in prose (16:1-13), as are the two oracles (16:14-18) and the sermon (17:19-27). Sandwiched between the opening and the closing block of prose is material which can all be put in poetry (though 17:1-4 is given in prose in RSV). The poetry, which includes a proverb, is rich in comparisons.

## EXPLANATORY NOTES

### Don't Marry, Don't Socialize  16:1-13

Some prophets were married. Both Hosea's and Ezekiel's spouses became sign-acts (Hos. 1:2-8; Ezek. 24:15-27). In contrast to these prophets, Jeremiah was not to marry or have a family. Like Jesus and Paul, he was to remain celibate.

Jeremiah was given three instructions: not to marry, not to attend funerals, and not to frequent weddings. Each instruction was accompanied by an interpretation. The compliance is not reported here but can safely be assumed (cf. 15:17). In his first instruction God forbids marriage to Jeremiah and hence also the gift of children, so highly cherished in that culture (cf. Abraham, Gen. 15:1-4; and Boaz, Ruth 4:9-13), and in some cultures today. In twentieth-century Africa, for example, "To die without getting married and without children is to be completely cut off from the human society, to become disconnected, to become an outcast and to lose all links with mankind" (Mbiti: 134).

The reason for Jeremiah's not marrying, given also in modern times by couples in the face of nuclear war, is that there is no point in bearing children only to have them die. So ghastly will be the coming death wave that "unlamented and unburied, they will be like so much manure to fertilize the soil" (Bright: 107; cf. 9:22; 23:19 and the curse in Deut. 28:26).

Jeremiah is not to attend funerals. In the coming days of doom, deaths will be so numerous that there will not be time even to mourn the death of a parent (v. 7). Jeremiah is not to show sympathy even by shaking the head (so the Hebrew idiom), for to do so would compromise his message. God has withdrawn his blessing, and it is God who is sending the grave misfortune. God has broken ties with the people and so must the prophet.

In ancient times food was given to the bereaved because the home of the deceased was considered ceremonially unclean. The mention of "the cup of consolation" (drink, NIV) is a strong and sentimental touch. Cutting oneself and shaving the head were both pagan mourning practices forbidden to Israel (Lev. 19:28; Deut. 14:1) though apparently practiced by them (41:4-5). Jeremiah is forbidden to do all these funeral-associated things.

Jeremiah is also not to attend weddings, always a time of high joyousness (7:34; 25:10; 33:11). In this way he is to signal the end of happy times. Death-bringing agents—disease, sword, and famine—will come because the hearers and their forefathers have departed from the Lord (vv. 10-13). Questions similar to those in verse 10 are found elsewhere (5:19; 9:12b-16; 22:8-9; cf. Deut. 29:21-27). Society will crumble, and with it the conventions of weddings and funerals.

In summary, Jeremiah's behavior is a sign-act. [Symbolic Action, p. 311.] Elements of the judgment speech are also recognizable: announcements (vv. 3-9), accusations (vv. 10-12), and an announcement (v. 13). The accusations put us in familiar territory. Your fathers forsook me (v. 11; 1:16; 2:13; 5:7; see especially Deut. 29:21-27; 1 Kings 9:8-9). They followed other gods (v. 11; 11:10; 13:10). They did not keep my law. And the present generation is worse in comparison because the evil is more widespread and because of the stubbornness of [their] evil heart, a characteristic Jeremianic expression found eight times (3:17; 7:24; 9:14; 11:8; 13:10; 16:12; 18:12; 23:17). God is ready to hurl them out of the land ("hurl," RSV, NASB, is more apt than "throw out," NIV.) [Judgment Oracle, p. 299.]

## Is It Salvation or Judgment? 16:14-18

The mood switches abruptly from gloom to high promise. Israel's earlier deliverance from Egypt will pale in comparison with their coming glorious deliverance from Babylon. Here, without offering a reason, is the first of several announcements of a restoration from exile into the land (30:1ff; 31:8-9; 31:16-17). The oracle is introduced by an oath. [Swearing, p. 311.]

The net effect of placing this salvation oracle next to verse 13 is perhaps to explain that I will show you no favor is not intended as permanent. A similar side-by-side of opposite messages occurs in Hosea 1:9, 10. It is a way of qualifying what has been said. An explanation for this "contradiction" is offered in the text itself with the insertion of "first" in "I will first repay" (RSV, NASB) which NIV unfortunately eliminates, apparently following the Septuagint (v. 18). [Septuagint, p. 308.]

In a second abrupt switch, the thought of God's disfavor (v. 13) continues in the second oracle (vv. 16-18). Fishermen with their nets, so Jewish exegetes suggest, will catch the masses. In the same manner an army will capture the city. Hunters, in turn, will hunt down the single fugitives in the country. Fishing language is used especially in reference to the Babylonians in Habakkuk 1:14-17. This reference to marine and land food-gathering is a graphic way of saying that no one will escape (cf. Amos 9:1-4). It answers those optimists in every crowd who feel that even if misfortune strikes, they will be exempt. The *double* repayment for sin corresponds with Isaiah 40:2, though recent linguists are arguing that the word *double* here signifies *proportionate*.

The two oracles—verses 14-15 and 16-18—are opposite in their message and one is puzzled at their juxtaposition. The first oracle is a doublet from 23:7-8, where its position is clearer. [*Doublets, p. 296.*]

## A Medley of Poems: Arguing by Comparison 16:19 – 17:13

Judging from the way in which the poetry in these chapters is printed in some Bibles, the reader might mistakenly conclude that there is before him one poem with several stanzas. But the thoughts from stanza to stanza do not cohere. It is better to think of a situation in which poems written one to a page, as in modern books, suddenly appear in sequence without headings or demarcations. We must determine the beginnings and endings of the poems. Either by their composition or by their side-by-side placement, these poems in Jeremiah make a series of comparisons.

### 16:19-21 When Nations Are Converted

The first poem opens like a prayer with a warm relational address to God, *my strength . . . my fortress, my refuge in . . . distress*. The poem shifts abruptly and significantly from the personal to the widely international. From the ends of the earth will come peoples who have renounced their worthless idols as so many "empties" (literally). The mention of idols may be the reason for placing the poem here (v. 19; cf. v. 18). The poem's freshness and largeness of vision is overpowering. Beyond the disaster of Judah so much in view till now, there is a vision of triumph when all God-substitutes will be acknowledged for what they are, man-made and nonfunctioning!

God responds to this wholesale revival (v. 21). God will teach them (Isa. 2:1-5; Micah 4:1-4). He will make them know his power and his might by letting them experience it. *This time* is the moment of their turnabout from idols when they become teachable. A variation of *then they will know that my name is the Lord* appears with striking frequency in Ezekiel, the prophet of the exile (e.g., 36:37). The name *Lord* (YHWH in Hebrew) is given its meaning at the Exodus where as God's salvation name it stands for power and might (Exod. 6:3). *[Yahweh, p. 314.]*

Further comments are found in "The Text in Biblical Context, p. 125."

### 17:1-4 Sin Permanently Engraved

The poem about Judah is a biting accusation in the form of a judgment oracle. Judah's sin is as permanent as letters chiseled into a rock. It cannot be rubbed out. The day will come, however, when God's law will be written on the heart (31:33), but for now sin is deep-seated (cf. v. 9). Because of their insincere and ineffective sacrifices, their sins are for all intents and purposes still stuck on the horns of the altar—the stone projections to which the animal would be bound and where the blood was sprinkled. Moreover, they are worshiping false gods. Asherah, a goddess and wife/consort of the Canaanite Baal, was represented by wooden carvings to depict the female deity. Children were tutored in such worship or at least heavily exposed to this worship model (cf. 7:18). *[Asherah, p. 291; Judgment Oracle, p. 299.]*

The phrase "*on the mountains*" (3a) is best attached to verse 2 (RSV) rather than as in NASB and NIV to the announcement which follows (cf. the doublet, 15:13-14). The doublet in 15:13-14 uses a Hebrew word meaning "without charge," which RSV translates "high places" (17:3). The fuller meaning of 17:3-4 is rendered smoothly with *together with your high places, because of sin* (NIV). Verse 4 can be restated: You will lose your grip on your inheritance = *land.* The announcement then addresses the unhappy future of (1) the country's wealth, (2) the land, and (3) the people. As in 12:13, the poem ends with a note about God's anger. *[Wrath, p. 314.]*

The two poems (16:19-21; 17:1-4) set up a comparison. The impact of the poem about converted nations shows up Judah to great disadvantage. Nations from the ends of the earth are turning from idols to God. Judah is turning from God to idols.

### 17:5-8 A Desert Bush and Streamside Tree

Like the previous companion poems, this poem draws a contrast. The Egyptian *Instruction of Amenemope* gives a similar contrast between the passionate and the poised man:

> As for the heated man of the temple,
> He is like a tree growing in the open.
> In the completion of a moment (comes) its loss of foliage
> And its end is reached in the shipyards;

(Or) it is floated far from its place,
And the flame is its burial shroud.
(But) the truly silent man holds himself apart.
He is like a tree growing in a garden.
It flourishes and doubles its yield;
It (stands) before its lord.
Its fruit is sweet; its shade is pleasant;
And its end is reached in the garden. . . .
(Pritchard: 422)

The parallel lines of verses 5 and 7 (NIV) make the contrast within the poem unmistakable:

Cursed is the one who trusts in man. . . .
Blessed is the one who trusts in the Lord.

The person who turns from the Lord and relies exclusively on human ingenuity or power is like the desert bush (ʻarʻar). He will not see prosperity. There is no prospect for improvement (cf. Ps. 146:3f).

By contrast, the God-trusting person will be as in Psalm 1 like a stream-side tree. "To trust" (batah) is "to throw oneself forward." While most translations follow "He will not fear" when the heat is on, one may legitimately render, "He shall not see when heat comes" (JPS) to parallel the preceding stanza: "He will not see prosperity." In contrast to Psalm 1, "Here the fruitage (outcome) of a man's rootage (commitment) is more brilliantly stressed" (Kuist: 56).

Some question whether this poem is from Jeremiah, for had he believed it, he would not have wondered about the prosperity of the wicked (12:1-4). However, Jeremiah is not here talking about himself, but preaching. He is warning those who place their hope in the new king, Josiah, for example, or who are forging military alliances with Egypt.

## 17:9-10; 12-13  The Devious Heart

There are likely two poems here, one given to the topic of the heart, described as deceitful (vv. 9-10), and the other given to the folly and shame of those who turn from the Lord (vv. 12-13). Thus they can loosely be said to be expansions of the former poem, where the self-trusting person was described as one whose heart turns away from the Lord (v. 5). Sandwiched in between one finds a proverb (v. 11).

In the first poem, the human heart is declared to be deceitful and very corrupt (v. 9). Beyond cure (NIV) indicates that something is desperately wrong. The Hebrew word for "beyond cure" occurs eight times in the Old Testament, five times in Jeremiah (15:18; 17:9, 17; 30:12, 15). Sin is so deeply ingrained in human nature (v. 1) that no one

can fathom it except the Lord (v. 10). Note a similar statement from
Jesus (Mark 7:21). God tests both heart and emotions (lit., "kidneys";
see 12:3). Though God's rewards are for deeds and actions, they are
based also on the heart as the springboard for those deeds and actions.

The poem in verses 12-13 contrasts the security of those whose
hope is in God with the sad plight of those who turn from the Lord. They
will be put to shame (v. 13). Judging from its immediately preceding
parallel line, the phrase written in the dust means some disgrace. Or as
recently proposed, "dust" or "earth" can also mean the netherworld,
and so the meaning is that the apostates are "listed for death" (M. Dahood). By contrast, others rejoice in God's glorious longtime throne. The
Lord is their sanctuary, a place of safety from peril as well as a rest from
restlessness. Their delight is in God (v. 12). By inference these linger at
the springs of living waters which the devious ones have forsaken (v. 13,
another link with the poem of 17:6-8; cf. 2:13).

Throughout the medley of poems, then, there appears a contrast,
primarily a contrast between those who trust in the Lord and those who
forsake him.

### 17:11  A Fool and His Ill-Gotten Money Are Soon Parted

The instruction of wise men in Israel was often given in proverbs using vivid comparisons. The comparison already noted above is now
continued. The partridge or a species of bird similar to it (Hebrew: "a
calling bird") gathers the eggs of other birds, so it is said, and then
broods on them to hatch them. But no sooner are the birds hatched
than they disown their "mother." Similarly a man may gain riches by unjust means, as in Turgenev's story "The Inn," in which an ingratiating
man named Naum so deceives the innkeeper's wife that she lends him
their cash savings. He then buys the inn from under the luckless innkeeper and so becomes rich. The proverb maintains that for such a man
riches will fly away at midday, and he will be shown to be a fool. Another
interpretation of this proverb holds that the partridge does not gather
other birds' eggs, but that the point of the proverb is that the bird is
vulnerable to attack—so also the ill-gotten wealth can easily be taken.

## I'm in Trouble  17:14-18

That a prayer begins here is clear from the address O Lord. Jeremiah is
once more complaining to his God. His petition is for healing, for salvation. This is one of several "confessions" or laments. "To be saved" carries the sense of being brought out from a restricting, confining place

into the freedom of open spaces. The complaint, which quotes the trou-blemakers, has to do with unfulfilled predictions. Jeremiah complains that he has announced impending, imminent doom, a final judgment, but that the doom has not materialized. There has been no destruction, and in jest, even in scorn, people are inquiring, *"Where is the word of the Lord?" [Lament, p. 301.]*

As in other laments, Jeremiah makes the case for his innocence. He insists he does not deserve such treatment (cf. 12:3; 17:16; 18:20). The reading "I have not pressed thee to send evil" (v. 16, RSV; cf. NASB) is preferable to *I have not run away from being your shepherd* (NIV), for it parallels *I have not desired the day of despair.*

Jeremiah also makes the statement of confidence usual in laments: *You are my refuge in the day of disaster* (v. 17). The day is "incurable" (literally); the same word is used to describe "heart" in 17:9. Thus it is the day from which there shall be no recovery. The rest of the prayer is a petition for vengeance. Unlike Jesus and Stephen, Jeremiah prays that God will bring trouble on his enemies. For the request for God to bring terror on his persecutors, see 11:20 and 18:21, and especially the glossary, "Vengeance". Double destruction may refer to proportionate destruction (cf. 16:18).

## A Sermon on Sabbath-Keeping  17:19-27

As with some of the earlier sermons, Jeremiah is instructed to deliver this message at a designated place (cf. 7:2; 11:6). The reading "Benjamin gate" (17:19, RSV) is literally "gate of the sons of the people" or a public gate (NASB). The traffic here might well have included royalty and cer-tainly people of commerce since the gate for those times corresponded to our present-day city mall. It was here that Jeremiah called attention to the Mosaic instruction not to carry loads, tools, or merchandise on the Sabbath. None was to be brought into the city—there was to be no external trading. None was to be brought out of their houses (business establishments) in internal work or trading. The explicit prohibition is followed by the positive word: *Keep the Sabbath . . . holy* (v. 22; Exod. 20:8-11; 23:12; 34:21; Deut. 5:12-15). Amos also objected to Sabbath trading (8:5) and in post-exilic times Nehemiah addressed a similar prob-lem (Neh. 13:15ff.). Jeremiah brings forward several incentives to urge compliance with the law:

1. The fathers were given this law, but they were stubborn. They did not respond to *discipline* (v. 23). Unstated is the inference that it did not go well with them.

2. The benefits of observing the law will be several: prosperity, signified by royal stability; security; the survival of the city; and religious prestige.

3. The punishment for failing to observe the Sabbath law will be the breakout of God's fire (wrath) against the city.

Jeremiah had elsewhere upheld the law (7:6, 9; 11:3, 6). It is at first surprising that the prophet should make the very survival of a nation dependent upon so "inconsequential" a thing as the observance of the Sabbath. The externals, such as the temple and the sacrifice, had elsewhere been deemphasized (7:4, 21ff.; cf. Isa. 1:13). But it must also be remembered that (in the words of Calvin), "The gross impiety of the people was thereby easily detected, for they despised God in a matter that could easily be done" (Calvin: 380).

Moreover, the Sabbath was a sign of the covenant (Exod. 31:16-17). In effect, disrespect for the Sabbath was illustrated in setting aside a celebration that was intended to highlight, even renew, the covenant relationship. The matter was hardly inconsequential. Sabbath-keeping was a touchstone of obedience (Exod. 16:27-29); failure to observe it carried the death penalty (Exod. 31:12-17).

## THE TEXT IN BIBLICAL CONTEXT

The disjointed segments in this section make it unwise to attempt a theological summary; two emphases found here but not too often elsewhere are noted.

*God's Intention for the Nations.* Jeremiah takes his place among the major prophets in holding out a vision of the nations turning to God (16:19-21; cf. Isa. 45:22; 49:6; Ezek. 36:22-32). God's missionary intention, promising blessing in contrast to the escalating evil of Genesis 1— 11, is clear already from God's call to Abraham (Gen. 12:1-3). Solomon knows of God's missionary intention (1 Kings 8:42-43) and the Psalms bristle with such statements as "May God be gracious to us and bless us . . . may your ways be known on earth, your salvation among all nations" (Ps. 67:1-2). Indeed one may argue that Israel's geographic position was divinely designated for a missionary purpose (Deut. 32:8).

Of individuals renouncing their idolatries and in worship embracing God, we may cite as examples Ruth (Ruth 1:16) and Naaman (2 Kings 5:17). Of whole groupings of people we may cite the people of Nineveh (Jonah 3:6-9) and in the New Testament the Gentiles (1 Thess. 1:9). That which Jeremiah glimpsed briefly is pictured more fully in Revelation 5:9-14.

*Sabbath-Keeping.* The concern for proper observance of the Sabbath is stated in legal texts (Exod. 20:8ff.) and reiterated by the prophets (Isa. 58:13; Jer. 17:19-27; Ezek. 20). There were religious (vertical) and social (horizontal) reasons for its institution. The Sabbath harked back to a divine timetable from the creation. It was a sign of the covenant (Exod. 31:13, 16-17; Ezek. 20:12, 20). From the first it was also prompted by a social concern (Exod. 23:12). The Sabbath was a symbol of sanctification (Ezek. 20:12; cf. Exod. 31:13).

Jesus observed the Sabbath law but not the legal accretions (Mark 2:27). For early Christians the Sabbath with its covenant aspects had been taken up in Jesus. (For the Christian stance to Sabbath-keeping, cf. Carson and Swartley).

## THE TEXT IN THE LIFE OF THE CHURCH

*The Bigger Outlook.* The work of the church is guided by great visions, such as that of God on an exalted throne (17:12) and of victory in the lives of nations (16:19-21). Concern for the salvation of people has characterized such leaders as Menno Simons, a sixteenth-century reformer:

> We preach, as much as is possible, both by night and by day, in houses and in fields, before lords and princes, through mouth and pen, with possessions and blood, with life and death. For we feel his living fruit and moving power in our hearts . . . . We could wish that we might save all mankind from the chains of their sins. (Quoted by Alan Kreider in *Heritage of Freedom*, p. 55.)

The big outlook for the church in the twentieth century is worldwide mission. The communications revolution has made possible an unprecedented spread of the gospel.

*Persuasion Techniques.* Christians in every age face the task of persuading their contemporaries to turn to God. A difficult and therefore perhaps neglected tool is literary composition: poetry, essays, stories, and other forms which use language in metaphorical or artistic ways. Preach! was the command, and Jeremiah . . . wrote a poem. In fact Jeremiah used various literary genre: visions, poems, cleverly turned dialogues, and inclusios. His oracles about the nations, in particular chapters 48 and 50, are among the finest in prophetic writing.

Good language is both attractive and persuasive. A twentieth-century Christian writer records that she was first attracted to the Bible, not by the gospel message, but by the fascinating poetry in Ezekiel. A man high in government found himself persuaded by the essays of C. S.

Lewis—one of many, no doubt, to be convinced by that writer. A novel, a poem can reach an audience not found inside church buildings. Not that sermons cannot be of high literary quality. Charles Spurgeon was a preacher adept at metaphor: "The heart is very slippery. Yes! The heart is a fish that troubles all gospel fishermen to hold . . . slimy as an eel, it slippeth between your fingers" (Spurgeon: 123).

A second persuasion technique often used by Jeremiah was the sign-act. Those who do not read may be willing to watch. Demonstrations, sit-ins, and picketing are of course no novelty; people are willing to stand up in the marketplace for almost any cause. The church has relied mainly on preaching, but may want to consider symbolic actions as an alternative way to deliver its message.

It should also be said that probably the most important sign-acts Christians can perform are acts of genuine love. Members of an archaeological dig at Gezer, in Israel, were impressed by the Christians: not by their preaching, but by the fact that they wrote letters and were faithful to their wives.

## Jeremiah 18 – 20

# About Pottery Making, Pottery Smashing

## PREVIEW

We are invited to follow Jeremiah around. Our stopping places are a potter's workshop, a business outlet, the Valley of Ben-Hinnom, the temple court, and a prison at the Upper Gate of Benjamin in the temple. In another sense we may follow him as he leaves the Lord's presence, performs his sign-acts, interacts with the people, and returns before the Lord, dejected, upset, and angry.

The series of symbolic actions begun in chapter 13 concludes with two sign-acts involving pottery. As with other sign-acts, a divine message accompanies the action. The people's attitude, generally negative, is now hardened to the point of defiance. The message concentrates therefore on the irrational audience response and the certainty of disaster. Jeremiah, imprisoned, appears dejectedly before the Lord with a lament.

We will proceed topically rather than chronologically according to the outline on the next page.

Our chapter divisions obscure a pleasing parallel structure in which the second sequence is more elaborate than the first, especially in the last two sections. Not only does a symbolic action lead off the narrative in the two parallel accounts, but both are of a private or semiprivate nature (only selected leaders were invited to go with Jeremiah into the valley, chapter 19). Following both the potter's house visit and the tour in the

128

Ben-Hinnom Valley, God commands Jeremiah to address the public (18:11; 19:14). Both accounts open and close with the spotlight on the prophet. The structuring, even apart from the story, stresses the deep involvement of the prophet in what is happening. The doubling also adds emphasis as well as precision. The structure or scaffolding of the story has the reader asking, "If the defiance of the people so impacted the prophet, who is only God's messenger, what must God feel like to be so decidedly spurned?"

## OUTLINE

| | |
|---|---|
| **18:1-20** | **19:1 — 20:18** |
| A Lesson from Pottery Making | A Lesson from Pottery Smashing |
|    18:1-10 |    19:1-13 |
| "I Am Shaping Disaster" | "I Am Bringing Disaster" |
|    18:11-17 |    19:14-15 |
| "Let's Attack Him" | "Let's Lock Him Up" |
|    18:18 |    20:1-6 |
| "Lord, They Are After Me" | "Lord, It's Them . . . and You, Too" |
|    18:19-23 |    20:7-18 |

## EXPLANATORY NOTES

### Pottery Making and Pottery Smashing  18:1-10; 19:1-13

*18:1-10  A Lesson from Pottery Making*

In this famous passage Jeremiah goes down to the potter's house. This sign-act, like most others, has three parts: (1) instruction (v. 2), (2) report of compliance (vv. 3-4), and (3) interpretation (vv. 5-10). The potter's equipment consisted of two wheels (the Hebrew is in a dual form). A larger, lower horizontal wheel was spun by the feet, and the vertical axis above turned an upper smaller wheel on which the clay would be shaped. The potter's first attempt was unsuccessful: the vessel was flawed. The word *marred* (spoiled) is the same word used to describe the girdle (13:7). So the potter started again. Perhaps this Scripture passage needs to be experienced to be understood. The student who enrolled in a pottery class to prepare for teaching this passage was on the right track. *[Symbolic Action, p. 311.]*

The interpretation could now take several directions, if we had only the story. We could, for instance, derive the lesson that where there is failure, God as divine potter begins anew. That truth, though established, is not the one given in the interpretation. Rather, the interpretation underlines the sovereignty and the freedom of the divine potter in working with the clay. The clay is Israel and also the nations (vv. 6-7). (For different uses of the potter and the clay image, see Isa. 29:16; 45:9; 64:8; and Rom. 9:21.)

Jeremiah announces that a change in the quality of the people will bring a change in God's plan. The word "repent" (vv. 8, 10, RSV) is misleading. "Relent" and "reconsider," or even "modify," are more accurate. Jeremiah further explains God's freedom. The Lord's intention to prosper a nation can be undone or modified if the people do evil. The entire interpretation could be reason for hope, maybe, or reason for anxiety. It all depends.... God is bound to consistency more than to predictions. The immediate conclusion for Judah would be that even were God announcing disaster, they by their repentance could reverse that judgment.

### 19:1-13  A Lesson from Pottery Smashing

Jeremiah stops at a shop to purchase a pot; then he goes with the elders to the Valley of Ben-Hinnom. The instruction portion of this sign-act has two crisp directives: buy a clay jar; together with some elders go out to the valley. To this is added a third and longer directive: say, This is what the Lord says.

The jar was Jeremiah's second purchase at the command of the Lord. The other was a girdle (chapter 13); and there was to be a third, a field (chapter 32). The flask (RSV, and more accurate) is a narrow-necked decanter called a baqbuq, perhaps because it makes a gurgling noise when the liquid is poured. The valley of Ben-Hinnom belonged at one point to the family of Hinnom. The Potsherd gate was littered with pottery rejects. [Topheth, p. 312.]

The lengthy instruction about the message content prior to the command to break the flask is already something of an interpretation. Its arrangement is (1) announcement (v. 3), (2) accusation (vv. 4-5), and (3) announcement (vv. 6-9). The general accusation is: They have forsaken me (v. 4). The specific accusation is that (1) this place, namely Jerusalem and more specifically the temple, has been exposed to alien religious influences, especially Baal worship; and (2) innocent blood, likely that of children offered in sacrifices, has been shed (cf. 7:31 and the comment there). [Judgment Oracle, p. 299; Baal, p. 291.]

The announcement, like the accusation, is first given in broad terms: I am going to bring a disaster. The tingling in the ears refers to a reverberation, like a catchy tune ringing in the mind. Verse 7 contains a wordplay on the name of the flask *(baqbuq)*: "In this place I will shatter *(baqqoti)* the plans of Judah and Jerusalem as a jar *(baqbuq)* is shattered." *[Wordplay, p. 313.]*

The specific announcements relate to war (vv. 7-9): *corpses* (for birds and animals devouring carcasses, cf. 7:33; 16:4); *pillage* of the city, such that people will hiss (moderns would whistle); and *famine* which will issue in cannibalism. (The fulfillment is described in Lamentations 4:10.) Massive burials will take place in the very valley where the group is standing. In ancient times roofs of houses were used for a variety of purposes (Judg. 16:27; 1 Sam. 9:26; 2 Sam. 11:2; Neh. 8:16; Matt. 10:27; Acts 10:9). They were used by this apostate people to sacrifice to starry hosts, a practice that was introduced by Manasseh (2 Kings 21:3; cf. Jer. 8:2).

Jeremiah is next instructed to smash the flask and then take a walking tour to the Hinnom Valley. The interpretation revolves around those two actions. For this reason one can discount those scholars who see the discussion about the valley as editorial additions. Just as the pot is smashed, so God will smash the nation, and like Humpty-Dumpty, it will not be "put together again." The reason is right before their eyes: the altars to Baal in the valley.

As for pottery smashing, one is reminded of Egyptian execration texts of the second millennium B.C. Names of enemies would be written on potsherds, which were then smashed. This would magically set a destructive power in motion which would defeat the enemy. As then, so here, the smashing of pottery would be high drama.

## THE TEXT IN BIBLICAL CONTEXT

*Prophecy and Prediction.* The second sign-act is forthright: God will smash the nation like a clay pot! But the first sign-act, which precedes it, qualifies that announcement. There is an "iffiness" about it. Some predictions which deal with God's initiative in the salvation plan, such as the coming of the Messiah or the Holy Spirit, are without a "rider" or condition. Other statements about the future (e.g., chapters 46—51), many of these considered "prophecy," are governed by the principle of condition spelled out at the potter's shed.

God is free to change the course of history, depending on the changed quality of a people, as in the story of Jonah and Nineveh (Jon. 3:4, 10). Most of what is said about future calendering in faddish books and in sermons, often with catchy titles, must be severely qualified (even discounted) because of this principle of divine sovereignty *and* divine freedom. God is free to shape the future in response to the human condition.

## THE TEXT IN THE LIFE OF THE CHURCH

*Freedom of Choice.* It is wrong to hold that since in God's knowledge all is known, the individual is bound to fate and is a victim to what has been ordained. It is wrong because while God as all-knowing knows the future, his knowledge of that future does not determine it. It is wrong because in the small things, such as which clothes to wear, we are conscious of choice. It is wrong because the principles of accountability and judgment rest on the fact that choice is possible.

Denominations have been polarized by emphases on either God's sovereignty or human free will. The Reformed and Presbyterian churches, largely following Calvin, have traditionally stressed God's sovereignty. Methodist and Nazarene churches, somewhat after the theologian Arminius, have been known so to stress human choice, that even the continuance of personal salvation becomes dependent on continuing godly choices.

The Anabaptists and Mennonites have been middle-of-the-road "Calminians" who, without harmonizing all biblical material, have asserted both God's sovereignty and human freedom.

## Forecast: Disaster  18:11-18; 19:14—20:6

### 18:11-18 "I Am Shaping Disaster"

After Jeremiah's visit to the potter's house, where he has a private session listening to God's message, he is instructed to preach to the public. He proceeds, we may infer, to the temple area with an address to *Judah and those living in Jerusalem.* Of the options for action given in the sign-act (18:1-10), God now announces the plan to shape disaster. The phrase "I am shaping evil" (v. 11, RSV) is preferable to *preparing disaster* (NIV) since the word for shaping pottery (v. 1) is here used. This announcement, given the principle of 18:7f., should stir Judah into repentance. *[Summons to Repentance, p. 310.]*

The reason for the coming judgment is given in the poem in verses 13-17 with its centerpiece, *Yet my people have forgotten me* (v. 15; cf. 3:21; 13:25). People must worship something, and Judah has turned to idols (lit., worthlessness) which *made them stumble* (better than "they stumbled," RSV). Quite in the nature of things, as though God need not even take a hand in the matter, their waywardness has made their land a horror (v. 16), so that others will hiss at it in scorn (cf. the English idiom, "whistle in disbelief").

That Judah should react so callously to God's powerful threat is incredible, irrational, and certainly unnatural. One can find nothing like it among the nations (v. 13; cf. 2:10). Verse 14, which makes this point, is a problem verse. The Hebrew is strange. Sirion (RSV for "fields," or *rocky slopes*, NIV) is a name for Mt. Hermon in the north, the snow-capped 9000-foot peak.

The gist of the verse is that pebbles (a preferred alternate understanding for "rock") will not depart from the fields, nor will snow melt from Lebanon, nor will people forget the whereabouts of cool streams, yet ironically God's people have forgotten God!

### 19:14-15 "I Am Bringing Disaster"

A message to the populace follows after the second sign-act of pottery smashing, as it did after the first. Returning from Topheth, Jeremiah preaches a judgment oracle in the temple court, as he had once before (7:1ff.). His message, simply put, is: disaster will strike because you are stiffnecked.

When the response is one of determined defiance, extreme measures may be called for. Examples of appeals in Jeremiah 18—19 are: (1) a rational appeal demonstrating the irrationality of a non-response (18:13ff.), (2) graphic outlines of the consequences of rejection (19:7ff.), and (3) engagement in some action that will compel attention and possible reconsideration (18:1-10; 19:10).

### Assailing the Prophet  18:18; 20:1-6

### 18:18 "Let's Attack Him"

The reaction of the people (18:18) is already anticipated in verse 12, where it is given in two parts, corresponding to verse 11 with its two parts. To God's threat of disaster, they say, to put it crassly, "To hell with it!" (v. 12; cf. 2:25, Holladay, 1971: 126). To the appeal to repent, they respond, "We will follow our own plans" (v. 12, RSV). The people's actual reaction, especially that of the plotting leaders, is described in verse 18 (cf. 11:18-23). Their plans include verbally beating Jeremiah with slander. Pashhur was later to lash him by beating (same word, 20:2). They reason that Jeremiah is not the only leader; if they ignore him there still will be other leaders. Their reasoning is similar to that of people who, disliking the message heard in their church, leave it to attend a church more to their liking. (The teaching function of priests is specified in Malachi 2:7.)

## 20:1-6 "Let's Lock Him Up"

The lightning of Jeremiah's electrifying words against the city (19:15) is followed by a rumble of thunder. Pashhur, a priest himself and a chief officer in the temple with the assignment to maintain order (cf. Luke 22:52), arrests the prophet, has him beaten, possibly with forty stripes, and locked up in stocks in the prison at the Upper Gate of Benjamin. His release of the prophet the next morning does not exempt Pashhur from hearing further fiery language. His name—Pashhur—will become Magor-Missabib, "terror on every side."

It has been suggested that this name is a reversal of the meaning of "Pashhur" which, though it is an Egyptian name, can be heard or twisted in Aramaic to mean "fruitful on every side." Name changes are not uncommon: Abram-Abraham, Jacob-Israel, and Peter-Cephas. In the coming siege, Pashhur and his family will be a showpiece, a target of vicious enemy attacks from every direction. By the time Jeremiah wrote his letter to the exiles, Pashhur's office was held by another (Jer. 29:24-26). (For a similar devastating oracle addressed to an individual, though not a fellow prophet, see 28:15-16.)

Symbolic actions, including verbal fireworks such as those addressed to Pashhur, were more than clever or entertaining visual aids. Sign-acts, it was believed, already initiated the action by letting loose a power to fulfill the prediction. Disaster, like a hurricane wind, was ominously near.


## THE TEXT IN BIBLICAL CONTEXT

*Obstinacy and Defiance.* There are stages of non-response. One may hear the Word of God but not heed it. Even if one ignores it, or sets it aside, there is at least the possibility of openness to another appeal. But a new stage has been reached when the failure to respond is willful and deliberate: *We will continue with our own plans* (18:12); *We will pay no attention* (18:18; cf. 6:17; cf. 22:21). It is by the words of one's mouth that one is judged. Worse than obstinacy is defiant aggression. Jeremiah is imprisoned (20:1-6). The scroll is cut and burned (36:20-26). Stephen is stoned (Acts 7). Jesus is crucified. And in each of these four instances, the message, though hard medicine, was intended ultimately to heal. Surely Jeremiah is right: the heart is deceitful and incurably corrupt (17:9). In the words of an old Roman proverb: In the evil society, the good man is the criminal.

## THE TEXT IN THE LIFE OF THE CHURCH

*Appeals to the Ear and the Eye.* How can a spiritual message be made understandable? What is the place of symbol in Christian God-talk? The Bible's messengers used all kinds of visual and narrative aids. Instead of a philosophical essay on God, sovereignty, and human free will, Jeremiah reported how the potter works. Instead of giving involved explanations about the kingdom of God, Jesus told parables and instituted the ordinances of baptism and the Lord's Supper. The early church used the egg at Easter to depict how life can break out of what appears lifeless. Modern audiences are accustomed to the eye appeal of television and film. What is the legitimate place for visual depiction of the biblical message? In place of the organ prelude in a worship service, should a potter be put to work on the platform?

## "Lord, People Are After Me . . . and You?" 18:19-23; 20:7-18

We choose to telescope two separate laments of Jeremiah (18:19-23; 20:7-13) and treat them in a block. A third piece, more like a curse, follows (20:14-18). *[Lament, p. 301.]*

### 18:19-23 "Lord, They Are After Me"

While isolated for discussion, the lament should be seen in context. Following the disclosure of the people's evil plan (v. 18; cf. 11:18-23; 12:1-6), Jeremiah comes before God with yet another complaint. The elements of the prayer are four. (1) The personal petitition asks for God to give heed to him, even though people do not (v. 19; cf. v. 18). (2) The complaint centers around the hearers' intention to do him in (vv. 20, 23a). The question *Should good be repaid with evil?* (v. 20a) could be Jeremiah's question, or it could be a quotation from Jeremiah's opponents. (3) The statement of innocence or self-justification puts before God Jeremiah's work as intercessor (v. 20b). Jeremiah interceded to secure the people's good (NIV omits "good"). Is maltreatment at their hands to be his reward? (4) The petition for vengeance is the longest and most biting of any laments. It seems cruel. It calls for terrible things to happen to children, to women, and to youths (vv. 21-22a). Worst of all, Jeremiah demands of God that he not extend forgiveness.

How can this prayer be explained? As a window into the soul of a prophet who, though God's messenger, is very human? Perhaps. As an emotional over-reaction to possible personal injury? Perhaps. As a momentary reversal in a life of intercession? Perhaps. After all, he had earlier spoken precisely to avert God's wrath. Should he now pray to invoke it? As a legitimate response to threats and enemies? No! The pattern taught by Jesus and exemplified by him is to pray, quite opposite to Jeremiah's prayer, "Father, forgive them." *[Lament, p. 301; Vengeance, p. 312.]*

### 20:7-13 "It's Them . . . and You, Too"

The lament could conceivably have been composed in prison (vv. 1-6), though it may be a general reaction to Jeremiah's troubles. Enthusiasm for ministry was definitely at low ebb! In this lament one finds a loud complaint, a cry of protest, a "blast of unreasoned anger." If there is a standard form to laments, then this one conforms most closely. *[Lament, p. 301.]*

(1) The **complaint** (vv. 7-10) consists of a reproach to God and a description of his troubles with his *friends*. He finds fault with God's methods. The Hebrew word for *deceived (patah)* is the same word used to urge Delilah's scheming on Samson (Judg. 14:15), and also of sexual seduction (Exod. 22:16). One writer paraphrases and comments: " 'I was a virgin and you raped me.' Thus reverently Jeremiah describes his call to the ministry" (Blackwood: 161). But this is an over-translation. The word more generally means "to persuade" ( 1 Kings 22:20, 21, 22; Prov. 24:28) but with a sinister or at least questionable purpose. "O Lord, thou hast duped me. . . . Thou hast outwitted me and hast prevailed" (v. 7, NEB; cf. 15:18). The Hebrew of "prevail," variously translated, is found four times (vv. 7, 9, 10, 11) and graphically suggests how much Jeremiah felt himself overpowered. In the scramble, he was at the bottom. The words "deceive" and "prevail" in v. 10 are a recapitulation of verse 7. *[Inclusio, p. 298.]*

Moreover, Jeremiah is experiencing the compulsion from within that, when he tries to curb it, only tortures him. God's word, which he likens elsewhere to a hammer (23:14) has become like a fire. Since *cry out* (v. 8) is a technical term for "a cry of appeal made by an innocent sufferer against an unjust oppressor," Jeremiah may be pressing his case against God harder than at first appears. He was damned if he refused to speak God's word and he was damned if he spoke it! When he did speak, he was the object of ridicule (v. 7) and gossip (v. 10); for he preached violence, namely the coming disaster, but disaster did not come and the people mocked.

The name he had given Pashhur, Magor-Missabib (v. 3; cf. 6:25; 46:5; 49:29) has been turned back on himself in gossip as a nickname (v. 10). One might imagine the people commenting, " 'Terror-on-every-side' is on the streets preaching again." His "friends," perhaps his family at Anathoth (12:6) or his priestly colleagues, were waiting for him to make a bad move. Friends is literally "persons of peace." Since peace (shalom) means well-being, one scholar colorfully renders it "my ~·~~ort system." Indeed the double complaint, one about God (l̩a⌐ ' ˙na u̩e other about people (label B), alternate throughout the ˙s follows (Clines/Gunn: 26):

| 7a | 7b | 8a | 8b | 9 | 10 |
|----|----|----|----|----|----|
| A  | B  | A  | B  | A  | B  |

(2) The **statement of confidence** (v. 11) while clear in itself, makes dramatic the tension in which the prophet is immersed. God is his problem but must in the end also be his solution (cf. Ps. 13:5; 22:3-5). Jeremiah recalls God's promise, made at the time of his call, to be with him (1:19). God as a mighty warrior is language from Exodus 15 (cf. Judg. 5; Hab. 3).

(3) The **petition** is found in verse 12. As in 12:3a, God is acknowledged as one who assesses the mind (lit., heart, the center of a person) and the emotions (lit., kidneys, the seat of feeling). The request for vengeance is found in 11:18-23; 12:1-6(13); 17:14-18; and 18:19-23. (See comment there.) [Vengeance, p. 312.]

(4) **Praise** (v. 13) is placed next to the prayer for vengeance. That appears like a poor fit. Either the answer to a prayer, or an oracle in the temple giving assurance of an answer, or a change of circumstances almost certainly preceded the call to praise (cf. Ps. 6:8). Interestingly, of the approximately fifty laments in the Psalms, almost all include a note of praise.

## 20:14-18 "Cursed be . . . "

With verse 14 there begins a piece distinct from the preceding lament. It is not strictly a lament, though it is sometimes classed with the confessions. It is a poem of cursing. The prophet curses (1) a time period, namely the day of his birth, which in one sense was his call to ministry (1:3; cf. Job 3:2-10), and (2) a family friend. Both are clearly innocent of any wrongdoing but serve as scapegoats for a man who is dissatisfied with life and has a need to lash out at something. After all, it was forbidden to curse one's parents (Exod. 21:17). The towns of verse 16 are Sodom and Gomorrah (Gen. 19:24-28).

He wishes for his own birth to have been a still birth, a death in the womb, or in modern language, an abortion, rather than to live and face so much trouble. The report of Jeremiah's suicide wish does not imply that suicide is proper or acceptable.

It may be, however, as has been suggested, that this is not Jeremiah's personal statement at all but rather a standardized outcry at some terrible calamity. The setting then would be the public's response to Jeremiah's own prediction of a Babylonian invasion described in what immediately follows (Jer. 21:1ff.).

## THE TEXT IN BIBLICAL CONTEXT

*Spiritual Struggles in the Ministry.* Jeremiah's laments illustrate that those who are called to serve God may have to wrestle with God. God may become the problem rather than the solution. To be God's servant is to be in God's grip; one cannot wiggle out from the Lord's grasp. God's call means that an inescapable divine compulsion is laid on the individual (Amos 3:8; 1 Cor. 9:16). While this ministry at God's summons is a privilege (15:16), it is also a burden. The message is not always pleasant and acceptable, but one has not the luxury to call it quits (20:8, 9). Instead of God's presence there is an experience of his absence (15:18). David (Ps. 22) and Jesus (Matt. 27:46) knew this tension. The tensions, often intense, are nevertheless in the end eased by God who, as always, is vindicated (12:1).

## THE TEXT IN THE LIFE OF THE CHURCH

*Responding to Enemies.* Jeremiah's prayer to God to harm those who make his life difficult raises the question about a Christian response to enemies. Insults and injuries, when severe, evoke anger and hostility. One should note:

> 1. There is a language of anger. Exaggerations usual within a culture need to be taken into account, as when a mother addresses her misbehaving child with "I could kill you."
> 2. The "enemies" for Jeremiah were essentially God's enemies. Jeremiah was totally identified with God's cause. Their intent to silence Jeremiah was at bottom an attempt to shut God out.
> 3. Jeremiah handed over his case to God. He did not take vengeance into his own hand but followed Scripture: "To you I have committed my cause" (11:20; 20:12; cf. Lev. 19:18; Deut. 32:35).

Still, his action cannot be totally approved in the light of the entire Scripture, for that Scripture which says not to seek personal revenge also says, "Love your neighbor as yourself" (Lev. 19:18). Indeed, Jeremiah himself counseled prayer for the exiles' enemies (29:7). The way of Jesus is to love one's enemies, contrary to natural impulse as that may seem.

In the history of the church Stephen illustrates love for enemies (Acts 7:60). So have many others. In 1569 Dirk Willems, a Christian fleeing for his life, successfully scrambled across thin ice, only to notice that the man who was pursuing him had broken through the ice and was pleading for help. Dirk pulled him to safety. However, the man's superior insisted on arresting Dirk. Shortly thereafter, following torture by means of a "lingering fire," Dirk was executed.

Part 4

# Disputations with Kings and Prophets

# Jeremiah 21–29

If there is disaster coming, who is responsible? Jeremiah's answer is: the leaders. The common people are by no means guiltless, but leaders, both kings and prophets, carry a large proportion of the blame.

In these chapters, much more than in the preceding ones, we meet kings and prophets by name. The first audience group is a set of kings—the last four kings of Judah: Jehoahaz, Jehoiakim, Jehoiachin, and Zedekiah. They are measured against the demanding standard set by God as constituting just and godly rule.

We also meet prophets: Hananiah, Ahab, Zedekiah, and Shemaiah. The issue is one of authority: who has the true word from the Lord?

The book began with sermons and continued with sign-acts. In these chapters the message of judgment is woven into debate and disputation. In contrast to earlier chapters, we will find several historically dated incidents. The material is not arranged chronologically, however (cf. 21:1 and 25:1), but topically, with the material grouped according to different target audiences, primarily kings on their throne and prophets at the temple.

A flow chart of the content can be graphed as follows:

Kings ———————➤ Prophets ———➤ Kings ————➤ Judah/Nations
(21:1—23:8)        (23:9-40)       (24:1-10)      (25:1-38)

Prophets ◄————— Kings/Priests ◄——— Officials/Priests/Prophets ◄
(chapters 28—29)    (27:1-22)        (26:1-24)

Jeremiah 21:1 – 23:8

# Kings Weighed in the Balances

## PREVIEW

Jeremiah took dead aim at royal policies. An urgent appeal to Jeremiah from Zedekiah, the last of Judah's rulers, set the stage for some blistering remarks. After Jeremiah outlines the standards by which monarchs should rule, the kings are paraded, so to speak. Each king is assessed and a fitting pronouncement given. The messages to the various kings may well have been given at various times, possibly during the course of their rule, but they are brought together here and arranged chronologically.

The unit closes by depicting the ideal king who meets the standards of righteous and just rule given at the beginning of the section. The passage opens with a threat of judgment on the king and people, but closes with the opposite, a promise of a new king and a restored people. The mood, at first sinister and ominous, is hopeful and positive at the end.

## OUTLINE

An Address to Royalty, 21:1—22:9
    21:1-10    God's Fight Is Against Zedekiah
    21:11—22:9    Basics for Good Government

A Parade of Royal Failures, 22:10-30
    22:10-12   Verdict on Jehoahaz
    22:13-23   Verdict on Jehoiakim
    22:24-30   Verdict on Jehoiachin

Introducing a New Phase and a New King 23:1-8

The standards for godly rule listed here can be compared to bookends which hold up a row of kings set between them for perusal. None measure up except Josiah.

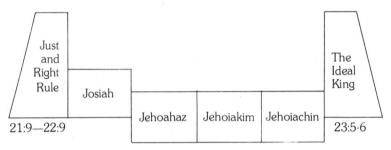

## An Address to Royalty  21:1 – 22:9

*21:1-10  God's Fight Is Against Zedekiah*

King Zedekiah, fated to be Judah's last king (597-587), faces huge armies of attacking Babylonians. The date is likely 589. After years of submission to Nebuchadnezzar, Zedekiah has rebelled, only to face the threat of swift action by irresistible forces. *[Kings of Judah, p. 300; Nebuchadnezzar, p. 304.]*

The situation is desperate. Zedekiah turns at last to God for help. Zedekiah consults Jeremiah four times. Two consultations are private (37:17-21; 38:14-28), and twice he sends a delegation. Zephaniah, a priest of considerable stature, is in the delegation both times (37:3-10, 21:1-2; cf. 29:24-32). Pashhur, a member of the king's inner circle (not the priest who imprisoned Jeremiah, 20:1-6), was also in the first delegation. Later he will call for Jeremiah's death (38:1-6).

The royal embassy, like the embassy that was sent to Hezekiah in the previous century, asks the prophet to intercede. Indeed, the delegation hopes that as in Hezekiah's day a miracle might be the answer to their difficulty (2 Kings 19:1-35). Or the *wonders . . . in times past* may refer to God's intervention at the Exodus.

Jeremiah stands up to this royal delegation and speaks a most disconcerting message. First, he makes clear God's stance: *I . . . will fight against you* (vv. 5, 13). God does take a position **against** people as well as for people (23:30; Ezek. 35:3). The language of an outstretched hand and a mighty arm is holy-war language and for Israel usually meant that God would work in her behalf (Exod. 6:6; Deut. 1:30; Josh. 23:10; Isa. 30:32). But not now! The Almighty could and did turn against the people in war (Isa. 63:10).

Second, Jeremiah clarifies how God will fight against Zedekiah (vv. 4-6a). *To turn . . . weapons of war* has formerly been interpreted simply as troops retreating. But recently a similar phrase has been discovered both in a thirteenth-century Hittite king's treaty as well as in a seventh-century Babylonian treaty. In each case the god is the subject of "to turn weapons." The phrase describes a military retreat amidst confusion and internal mutual destruction (cf. Judg. 7:22). "Verse 7 reaches a crescendo like cymbals in the final movement of a symphony. Every sector is repeated three times: the king, his officials, and the people; the pestilence, the sword, and the famine; Nebuchadrezzar, their enemies, and those who seek their life; he shall not pity them, spare them, nor have compassion" (Boadt: 161).

Third, turning to the people, Jeremiah issues as it were one last opportunity for change by setting out options of death and life (cf. Deut. 30:15, 19). He counsels surrender to the enemy. It is his oft-repeated advice and understandably evokes the charges of "traitor" and "treason" (27:1-15). Jeremiah is not pro-Babylonian, however. When the siege comes he does not desert to Babylon but stays in the land (40:1-6; 42:7-22). Understood as a political statement only, his advice appears as treason; understood as a word from God, it is a summons to submit to God's judgment. To have one's life as booty is to return home from war, without plunder—but at least to return alive.

## 21:11—22:9 Basics for Good Government

In concept these two passages are parallel, even though one is poetry and the other prose. In both, directives for ruling well (21:12a-c; 22:3) are followed by threats and/or promises (21:12d-14; 22:4-8)—mostly threats.

The word from the prophet of God to Judah's king on his throne, given at the palace, is crystal clear: *Do what is just and right* (22:3; cf. 21:12). Justice, a pivotal word in the Old Testament, especially for the prophets, means to act honorably, in accordance with the demands of the relationship. Righteousness, used frequently in parallel with justice and often as a synonym, differs in that it refers to both the action and the motive, and so means "uprightness," "integrity." God's call for rulers to govern with honor and sensitivity, with uprightness and integrity, is embedded in the law (Deut. 17:18-20), stressed in Israel's poetry (Ps. 72:1-3), and trumpeted by the prophets (Micah 3:1-4). [Justice, p. 299.]

Justice goes beyond being fair in legal decisions. It deals with helping those who are victims of oppression, people cheated from their land or wages by large landowners or employers. It also means not taking advantage of people who are easily exploited or mistreated: aliens, orphans, and widows (22:3; cf. Exod. 22:21-26; Lev. 19:33-34; Deut. 10:18-19).

The promise and the threat make clear the absolute importance of this call for justice upon those who govern. Blessings include a secure kingship (22:4; cf. 17:25). Threats include the outbreak of God's wrath (21:12d) which will burn the city, Jerusalem (v. 13). The proper name "Jerusalem" does not appear in the text, but the verb is feminine. Cities, viewed as mothers with their daughter villages, were addressed as feminine. Failure to rule with justice will bring the ruin of "this house" (RSV), the royal palace (22:5), where Jeremiah stands and gives his speech. [Wrath, p. 313.]

Even if the royal house (palace or also dynasty) is as impressive as Gilead and Lebanon are for their forests, God will unhesitatingly devastate such resources and such beauty if justice is not practiced. Gilead, a region east of the Jordan bordering the Sea of Galilee, had been destroyed more than a century earlier by Tiglath-pileser (2 Kings 15:29). Lebanon, north of Palestine, was renowned for cypress groves (1 Kings 5:8).

God's agents or destroyers will rip up the palace cedar beams for burning (cf. "fire" in 21:14)! The frequent scenario of questions from passersby (5:19; 9:12-16; 16:10-13) clinches the point that God will not exempt the people from punishment when they sin. Moreover, even in its destruction Israel will be a revelation to the nations.

## A Parade of Royal Failures  22:10-30

### 22:10-12  Verdict on Jehoahaz (Shallum)

The first of several kings listed for assessment and verdict is Jehoahaz, whose personal name was Shallum. The instruction Do not weep is likely said with King Josiah in view. His tragic death at Meggido in 609 was greatly mourned.

His son, Shallum, who ruled for three months, was taken captive by Pharaoh Neco, first to Riblah, north of Palestine and then to Egypt, where he died (2 Kings 23:31-34). To die in a place other than one's native land was unthinkable. (Jeremiah was destined also to die outside Judah in Egypt.) The verdict on Shallum: "It's all over; he will not return to his homeland. He's through." *[Kings of Judah, p. 300.]*

## 22:13-23  Verdict on Jehoiakim

The assessment of Jehoiakim is the longest of the three. This text is a classic one on the exercise of royal power. Jehoiakim comes under scathing criticism for his pretentious palace ("house," RSV) with its terraces (NAB) and its upper rooms with ornate paneled cedar and fancy windows (v. 14). It is tempting to equate an elaborate complex of buildings found by archaeologists south of Jerusalem with Jehoiakim's "palace." The imposing wide house with large chambers was surrounded by a citadel extending over five acres.

The Lord criticizes (1) Jehoiakim's disregard for proper wages, (2) his competitiveness with other kings, his showiness (v. 15), (3) his greed and oppression (v. 17), and (4) his priorities. *[Oppression, p. 305; Kings of Judah, p. 300.]*

A king's priority is to govern in righteousness and justice (v. 15; 21:11-12). Not satisfied merely to live well, having food and drink like his father, Jehoiakim reversed priorities and lived sumptuously, perhaps in imitation of King Solomon. Heavy taxation, due to the Egyptian Pharaoh's imposed tribute (2 Kings 23:33-35), burdened the people, but Jehoiakim, small-minded man that he was, built himself a palace. Woe!

The contrast between Jehoiakim and Josiah is striking:

| | | | |
|---|---|---|---|
| **Jehoiakim** | Riches<br>Might | Palace<br>Cedar<br>Vermillion | Woe |
| **Josiah** | Knowing God | Justice<br>Righteousness | Well-being |

For Jeremiah and Hosea, "knowing God" is the highest priority (Jer. 9:24; Hos. 4:6; 6:6). Such knowledge is not so much information as it is experience. Indeed, caring for the disadvantaged is what it means to *know me* (God). Knowing God, while it includes a private grasp of data about God, is here not private, but public.

The future for King Jehoiakim and also for Jerusalem, which shares in Jehoiakim's wicked ways, is detailed in verses 18-23. For all the king's attempts to be "somebody," he will not so much as have mourning rites

at his funeral (cf. 16:5-7). *Alas, my sister* is the way mourners will address
each other in view of the loss. Worse still, there will be no burial; but like
an animal, he will be dumped outside the city. It cannot be determined if
this actually happened, because 2 Kings 24:6 may simply be a "frozen
formula" to say that he died. For King Zedekiah, Jeremiah could at least
predict public mourning (34:5).

Jehoiakim is in view in verse 23. Here *Lebanon* refers, not to the territory north of Palestine (vv. 6,20), but to Jehoiakim's palace called by
that name (1 Kings 7:2-5; Isa. 22:8). The pain of coming desolation, says
Jeremiah, will be like the shrieks of a pregnant woman in labor—more of
an everyday family experience before the days of hospitals and
anesthesia (v. 23; cf. 13:21; 30:4-6). Although obscured by the English
"you," several statements in the announcement are addressed in the
feminine form and refer to the city Jerusalem. Jerusalem's cry of distress
is to be heard at distant places: *Lebanon* in the north; *Bashan*, east of
Jordan; and *Abarim*, a mountainous range with Mt. Nebo its highest
peak, also east of Jordan but south near the Dead Sea (v. 20). Judah's
"lovers" (vv. 20, 22, RSV) is a term for her allies. They are crushed; consequently, Judah doesn't have a chance (v. 22).

The hot desert *wind*, picturesque speech for the invading
Babylonians, will sweep (lit., "shepherd") away the *shepherds*, a standard name for kings (23:1; Ezek. 34:1ff.). *[Wordplay, p. 313.]*The reason
for such devastation is Jerusalem's defiance, "*I will not listen*"(v. 21; cf.
6:17; 18:12). To this defiance her leaders have contributed, for mistakes
of leaders such as Jehoiakim's are hardly private matters. The verdict on
Jehoiakim: a huge failure.

### 22:24-30 Verdict on Jehoiachin (Coniah)

Coniah (his personal name) or Jehoiachin (his regal name) was the
18-year-old son of Jehoiakim who ruled for three months, 598-597. Like
his father, he did evil (2 Kings 24:9). The signet ring was used in making
impressions on soft clay to identify correspondence and was a sign of
royalty. Haggai calls Jehoiachin's grandson Zerubbabel a "signet ring to
the Lord" (Haggai 2:23). From an archaeological excavation at Samaria
we have the signet ring of one "Shema, servant of Jeroboam."

Coniah's dreadful future is given in no uncertain terms. The queen
mother, Nehushta (2 Kings 24:8), will be hurled from the land. So will
the king, his children (v. 28), and the citizenry generally (cf. 10:18).
Coniah, like Shallum (his uncle), will die in a foreign land. So it happened. Jehoiachin was taken into Babylon by King Nebuchadnezzar
(2 Kings 24:15). *[Kings of Judah, p. 300.]*

The word for *pot* is a term for a degraded quality of jar, and the question *Is this man . . . a . . . broken pot?* is therefore a sinister jab at the king. The threefold address to *land*, like the three-fold cry "holy" (Isa. 6:3), intensifies the call. As in the days of Jehoiakim, when the city suffered, so now too the entire country will be affected. Like the desert bush, Jehoiachin will not prosper (v. 30; cf. 17:6).

Since Jehoiachin had seven sons (1 Chron. 3:17-19; cf. v. 28), it is not that Jehoiachin will be recorded *childless*, that is without descendants, but rather there will be no successor from his family on the throne. He will be "stripped of all honor" (NEB). The announcement is particularly sad, because with Jehoiachin, there ended (apart from Zedekiah) more than 350 years of Davidic dynasty rule. It is a dismal obituary to end a series of depressing obituaries. The verdict on Jehoiachin: a useless pot.

## Introducing a New Phase and a New King  23:1-8

The discussion of kings from the previous chapter continues under the figure of shepherds, a common term in the Near East for civil rulers at least from the days of the early Babylonian ruler, Hammurabi, eighteenth century B.C. (cf. Ezek. 34 for a parallel and more elaborate statement). Again, attention is called to the king's responsibility to care for the poor (cf. 22:15f.). Eventually, however, the *flock*, the king's subjects, dispersed and uncared for, will be gathered from the far countries and returned to the land. Here at last is a promise of hope, set within the grim predictions of doom like a diamond sparkling in a heap of cast-offs.

These themes will be taken up later by Jeremiah and especially by Ezekiel: regathering (30:2; 31:9-10; Ezek. 11:17), resettlement (32:42; Ezek. 20:42), repopulation (33:10; Ezek. 37:26), prosperity (33:6-9; Ezek. 36:30), new leadership (33:14-27; Ezek. 37:24), and security (Ezek. 36:33-38). Several of these themes appear immediately in the succeeding oracle.

The poetic oracle of verses 5 and 6 is one of the few messianic announcements in Jeremiah (cf. 33:15-17). The *Branch* follows the imagery of Isaiah, who pictured the pride of nations, including Israel's, cut down like trees. From one stump, however, there was to sprout a "Branch" (Isa. 10:33—11:4; cf. 4:2). As in Isaiah, so here this branch is characterized as *righteous . . . wise . . . just.* That is, the divine demand on kings to administer justice, given at the outset of the review of the kings (21:12), is not only repeated here, but emphasized. Unlike Jehoiakim, the coming king from David's line will do justly. Justice is a key feature also in Isaiah's portrait of the servant (Isa. 42:1-4). *[Justice, p. 299.]*

Indeed, the name of the forthcoming king will be *The Lord Our Righteousness*. As God's presence is made unforgettable in the very name of the new city, "The Lord is there" (Ezek. 48:35), so the concern for righteousness will be made memorable in the very name of the king. Just as unrighteousness on the part of Judah's kings resulted in the people's destruction (21:11-14; 2:20-23), so the installation of the coming king will result in the people's salvation (23:6).

It has been customary to hold that King Zedekiah (597-587) is in view here, since his name means "the Lord is righteous." If so, then all the kings ruling in Jeremiah's lifetime receive mention in the kings' review. Incidentally, even the name" Yahweh-tsidqenu, "the Lord our righteousness," is essentially "Zedekiah" *(tsidqiyahu)*, written with the two parts of the name reversed. The wordplay on King Zedekiah's name could be a not-so-veiled rebuke and admonition to him. But the expression "the Lord is righteous" specifies a king who appears in future days, especially after the judgment and the dispersion. Indeed, the ideal king will be quite the opposite of the wicked Judean kings. *[Wordplay, p. 313.]*

The coming new phase in Judah's and Israel's united history will outdo in splendor the magnificent deliverance from Egypt, which was clearly the politically shaping experience in her past (v. 7f.). *Israelites* refers to the northern tribes scattered in 722 B.C. The return to the land for both Israel and Judah is elaborated upon in Jeremiah 30-31. Verses 7-8, which also appear in 16:14-15, more readily fit here, where they serve to announce a new phase of history in addition to the announcement of a new king. A god-sized problem, it has been said, was given a God-sized cure. Though a partial fulfillment of the prediction of resettlement came in 538, fulfillment of the king oracle came with Jesus. *[Land, p. 303.]*


## THE TEXT IN BIBLICAL CONTEXT

*The Practice of Justice.* The message to royalty is: kings are accountable before God who measures them on the basis of their practice of justice.

It goes without saying that kings and governments have power. The question is, to what purpose is the power put? The story of Israel's kings, and those of the world, for that matter, shows that the temptation is to use power for self-serving ends. However, God places value, not on achievements of conquest, but on acts of compassion. Do kings redress the inequities among their people? Do they come to the aid of society's marginal people, the lame Mephibosheths? Do they set in force an equitable judicial system? More is at stake than the enforcement of laws. It is easily possible to proceed legally but still, in the biblical definition of justice, unjustly. *[Justice, p. 299.]*

In striking contrast to unjust rulership there is pictured ever more clearly a king whose trademark will be justice. The hope for such a king is fueled at each royal installation (Ps. 72; 132). The prophets not only underscore God's delight in just behavior (Amos 5:24; Micah 6:8), but specifically announce this quality of justice as a mark of the ideal king (Isa. 9; Jer. 23:5-6). To see a just king in action, we turn to the life of King Jesus in the Gospels: he employs power on behalf of the blind, the lame, and the emotionally disturbed, and exercises his power by a voluntary surrender of that power on the cross.

*The Davidic Covenant.* The covenant with David in 2 Samuel 7 is erroneously said to be unconditional. A basic understanding of covenant was loyalty. The promised permanence of the Davidic throne was affected by the loyalty of the monarch (Ps. 132:11-12). In his address to the royal dynasty, Jeremiah makes the continuation of the Davidic succession dependent upon carrying out God's commandment (22:4). The Sinaitic and the Davidic covenants, then, are not two different kinds of covenant, one conditional and the other unconditional. Both are conditional. God's promises, while sure, paradoxically are affected by people's behavior (Jer. 18). *[Covenant, p. 294.]*

## THE TEXT IN THE LIFE OF THE CHURCH

Evaluate the following statements. Are they correct? Do they need qualification?

1. Elaborate homes for those who can afford them are appropriate to God's people provided the owners show concern for the disadvantaged (cf. Amos 6:4-7).

2. "He who is on the side of the poor is always on the side of the right" (R. C. Maritain).

3. When a godly king like Josiah has sons like Jehoiakim who are self-serving, the blame must be laid to the shortcomings of the father.

4. Responsibility must be assumed by governments and businesses when people suffer hardship because of their policies.

5. Attention to spirituality, especially to knowing God, is best done privately through Bible reading and prayer.

6. It is the church's duty not to lobby for special interests, but to address governments, insisting on the practice of justice in national policy.

7. "Your task [kings and rulers of the land] is to do justice between a man and his neighbor, to deliver the oppressed out of the hand of the oppressor; also to restrain by reasonable means, that is, without tyranny and bloodshed, manifest deceivers who so miserably lead poor helpless souls by hundreds of thousands into destruction. Whether the deceivers are priests, monks, preachers, baptized or unbaptized, it is your task to restrain them so that they may no longer detract from the power of the almighty majesty of God . . ." (Menno Simons: 193).

8. "True peace is not through kings with armies, but through the Messiah who is a different kind of king" (Martin: 51).

9. The gospel is never static. The Exodus is a great miracle, but it is not the last.

*Christians and the Poor.* Aristides, the Athenian philosopher, was deeply impressed by the care and concern of the apostolic church. A Christian, he said, "gives to him who has not, ungrudgingly and without boasting. When the Christians find a stranger, they bring him to their homes and rejoice over him as a true brother. If they find poverty in their midst, and they do not have spare food, they fast two or three days in order that the needy might be supplied with the necessities."

# Jeremiah 23:9-40

# Taking on the Prophets

## PREVIEW

The subject for this section reads like the heading of an essay: "Concerning the Prophets." The passage follows another essay, or rather "oracle," about kings (21:1—23:8). Jeremiah himself was at war with groups of prophets who, like him, claimed to speak in the name of God but with a different message. The story of one of them, Hananiah, is told in chapter 28. Contradictory messages from the one God, everyone knew, were impossible. Jeremiah stalks boldly into the forest where "the deer and the hypocrites roam." Someone is lying. Jeremiah brands the opponents as false and tells why.

## OUTLINE

Setting the Tone, 23:9-10

These Prophets Are Unqualified, 23:11-15

These Prophets Are Unauthorized, 23:16-40
    23:16-22    Bogus Prophets
    23:23-32    Dreamers!
    23:33-40    Sued for False Advertising

153

The literary forms accord with the content. The section about un-qualified prophets consists of two judgment oracles; the section about unauthorized prophets begins with a disputation, a feature of which is ci-tations of the opponents' words.

## EXPLANATORY NOTES

### Setting the Tone 23:9-10

It is not with arrogance that Jeremiah takes on his colleagues, but with brokenness. He does not relish exposing his opponents. He is disturbed in mind, generally shaken if not shocked, and even appalled! And the reason? God has met him and overpowered him! God's word has come to him—and it concerns his colleagues! If the strongly worded oracles against the people were difficult, this assignment is even more difficult.

Jeremiah is also emotionally in turmoil because of the evil all about him. *Adulterers* may refer both to spiritual two-timing, carryings-on at the same time with Baal and the Lord (v. 10; cf. 3:6-10), and to marital un-faithfulness (cf. 5:5-8). There was also cursing. However, for "cursing" some manuscripts read, "Because of these [i.e., adulterers], the land mourns" (v. 10). In any case, their immoral behavior affects the environ-ment (cf. Hos 4:1-4). *Prophets* is inserted (v. 10, RSV) but "they" who *follow an evil course* and "gather strength for evil purposes" are better understood as the adulterers and cursers.

### These Prophets Are Unqualified 23:11-15

Two crisp judgment speeches both make the point that the character and lifestyle of these *prophets* are not becoming to God's messengers. In the first, the charge is wicked practice in the temple, details of which may be found in Ezekiel 8:6-18 (vv. 11-12; cf. 2 Kings 23:7). In the second, their way of life in society is primarily in focus (v. 13f.). In the Northern Kingdom and in Samaria (its capital), prophets had bought into Baal worship. But Judah is worse than Samaria, as Jeremiah has said elsewhere (3:6-10). Adultery among the clergy! (cf. 29:20ff.). Deliberate support for schemers! Wickedness like the sins of Sodom and Gomor-rah! (cf. 49:18; Isa. 1:9). [*Judgment Oracle, p. 299; Baal, p. 291.*]

Moreover, by what they said, the prophets lent their influence and support to evildoers. The term *ungodliness* or "pollution" wraps the two oracles in an inclusio (vv. 15, 11; cf. 3:1, 2, 9). [*Inclusio, p. 298.*] A cor-rupted character disqualifies these prophets. Their hypocrisy needs to be unmasked. [*Prophets, p. 306.*]

Each oracle also has an announcement, one about slippery paths and darkness (v. 12; cf. Micah 3:5-7), and the other about *bitter food* and *poisoned water* (v. 15; cf. 8:14). Their destiny is darkness. "In that terrible day of Judah's final decay the prophets were characterized by the loss of that aloofness of character which creates power to touch national life healingly" (Morgan: 131).

## These Prophets Are Unauthorized  23:16-40

### *23:16-22  Bogus Prophets*

In this disputation-like speech the focus is on what prophets say, rather than on what they do. They say the standard things, *You will have peace*; but they say them to the wrong people, namely those who *despise me* (v. 17; the RSV, following the Septuagint, reads "those who despise the word of the Lord"). Presumptuous optimists, they give people what they want to hear—comfortable homilies. Their message is too predictable; it lacks a cutting edge. They also speak self-originated messages, *visions from their own minds* (v. 16). By contrast, authorized prophets are carriers of God's message which they have received in the circle of God's intimates, in his *council* (v. 18: cf. 1 Kings 22:19-23). The message from that *council* for this time in Judah's history is that God's anger is breaking loose (23:20; cf. 30:23-24). [*Doublets, p. 296; Septuagint, p. 308.*]

That anger is almost personified. Like a deputy it is sent out to accomplish a mission and will return only when that mission has been fulfilled. The swirling hurricane of God's anger is descending! But the prophets prophesy, "Peace." Nothing shows more clearly that the false prophets are totally out of touch with God who had not sent them! Moreover, true prophets are distinguished by turning people *from their evil ways* (v. 22); they do not confirm people in their evil (v. 17; cf. Lam. 2:14).

### *23:23-32  Dreamers!*

The presumption of these persons who *prophesy lies in my name* (v. 25) and say, *The Lord declares* (v. 31), is frightening, given God's presence everywhere (omnipresence) and total knowledge (omniscience) (v. 23f.). The question, *Am I only a God nearby?* may not however be a reference to God being everywhere present so much as it is a rebuke to the false prophets, for whom God was near and therefore easily manageable. Verse 26 is not smooth grammatically and thereby suggests the speaker's exasperation. The sense is, How long will there be in the heart of these prophets the prophesying of false things? The Talmud mentions "stealing" oracles, which may refer to taking a message from an earlier time and applying it to a situation no longer valid. Did Hananiah, the false prophet, "steal" the expression "breaking the bow" of Elam (49:35) from Jeremiah (28:4)? Alas, false prophets are borrowers.

The excitement of the false prophets over dreams is misguided. The dreams are self-induced, not God-given. Preoccupation with them has led the people to follow another agenda, and really to forget God. That God speaks through dreams is not denied (cf. Jeremiah himself 31:26), but surely a prophet should be able to distinguish between his dream (straw) and a God-given dream (grain). And the difference? God's message is not entertaining like a colorful dream, delightful and fluffy, which is eagerly related to one's fellows (v. 27). God's word is a force, a pounding, a fire, a jackhammer! "False dreamers" and "prophets of God" are two quite different people. God is dead set against certain people including dreamers (v. 32: cf. 21:5; Ezek. 35:3). They are anything but harmless; they do great damage.

## 23:33-40  Sued for False Advertising

Another set of explosive indictments against the false prophets is now taken up, but in prose rather than poetry. The wordplay on a Hebrew word, massa', which means both "oracle" and "burden," is evident from English translations: What is the oracle of the Lord? (v. 33); "What is the burden of the Lord?" (RSV). A word from God was a weighty matter, to be shifted, like a burden, by the prophet onto designated audiences, e.g., Babylon (Isa. 13:1) Nineveh (Nah. 1:1). The double talk in this passage, centering on the word massa', is entertaining, for it portrays the total confusion that people feel upon hearing opposite messages. Reading massa' as "oracle" (NIV and NASB in v. 33) gives the sense that there is already an oracle, namely, I will forsake you. For the people to ask for further oracles is pointless. However, reading massa' as "burden" (v. 33, RSV following the Septuagint, which also divides the letters differently to make two words rather than three), the reply is, "You are the burden." Either way, the people's hankering for additional "prophecies" is rebuked. [Wordplay, p. 313.]

The remaining verses single out the improper usage of the trademark formula used by the prophets, This is the oracle ("burden," RSV) of the Lord. The use of this formula is to be restricted to the authentic prophets. "That is reserved for the man to whom he entrusts his message" (v. 36, NEB). God will sue and punish anyone who abuses this trademark by falsely appropriating it, or even someone who asks for it. God's punishment for those who peddle poison under a trusted label will be to *forget you and cast you out* . . . (v. 39; cf. RSV, which again following the Septuagint continues the wordplay on *massa'*. Since *massa'* can also mean "to lift up," RSV reads, "I will lift you up and cast you away . . ."). In either case, the outcome is disastrous and distressing.

## THE TEXT IN BIBLICAL CONTEXT

*God's Word: Sweet and/or Explosive.* God's word is by definition a word from God. That message, depending on the circumstances, is at times reassuring and sweet (15:16; cf. Ps. 19:10, Ezek. 3:3, 14). But God's word in other circumstances explodes like dynamite! It is a fire that scorches and consumes, a hammer that smashes the hardest rock! (23:29). The New Testament describes it as a two-edged sword (Heb. 4:12). Receiving the Lord's message is anything but a trivial matter. Jeremiah was shaken by it (23:9). Ezekiel went limp (3:15).

*True and False Prophets.* How can one distinguish false prophets from true? A helpful exercise is to list the marks of false prophets from 23:9-40 in one column and in a second list the marks of true prophets. Two major criteria are set out in Jeremiah 23. (1) The character and way of life of the prophets will reveal their identity: false prophets live a lie, strengthen hands of evildoers, and live immorally (23:14). (2) The message will be God-originated (23:18); it will interrogate the conscience and not confirm people in their present ways. Dietrich Philip, an Anabaptist bishop in the sixteenth century, described false preachers as those who "lay pillows under the people's arms and cushions under their heads and shoulders" (p. 186; cf. Ezek. 13:18-22). False prophets speak self-originated messages, though—and here is the confusion—they announce them as God's word.

To these criteria are to be added two more. (3) The message will be in keeping with past messages: only false prophets speak good things in evil times (28:8). (4) The message, if it is a prediction, will come to pass (Jer. 28:9; cf. Deut. 18:22).

Israel needed to discriminate between true and false prophecy (26— 28; Mic. 3:5-7). So did the early church (1 Thess. 5:20). Jesus said, "Beware of false prophets" (Matt. 7:15; cf. John 10:12). As surely as counterfeit currency will appear to rival minted coinage, so counterfeit prophecy will appear where true prophecy is given. True prophets know the ways of God, analyze the shape of evil in their society, and bring the appropriate word to bear on the situation.

## THE TEXT IN THE LIFE OF THE CHURCH

*A Right Message for a Wrong Audience.* There is no easy way to spot bogus preachers, especially if the issue is a misplaced emphasis. The message about peace (23:17) is in itself part of the Old Testament message, but in Jeremiah's day, given the audience, it was inappropriate. "It is the historical context which makes an otherwise unobjectionable message false" (Overholt: 42).

Each of the Reformers in the 16th century fended off preachers and teachers who were false. Menno Simons, after whom the Mennonites are named, wrote a tract in 1535, "The Blasphemy of John of Leiden." He exposed the error of the Muensterites who wanted to establish the kingdom of God by force of armies. Menno wrote:

> This is the true nature of all false teachers. They desert the pure doctrine of Christ and begin to traffic in strange doctrine. . . . So all false teachers forget the covenant of God whereby they are bound to Him, as, O God, many do at present who have forgotten all that upon which they were baptized, namely, the cross, and would recommend and make use of the sword. . . . The Almighty God shall raise a Jeremiah to reprove the deceiver of the people, who shall speak nothing but that which God commands him to speak, and the Lord must place His Word in the mouth of this Jeremiah as a fire, and all false teachers as stubble (pp. 33-34).

*The Use and Abuse of God-Talk.* The Bible does not systematize doctrine, not even the doctrine of God. Rather, the nature of God is brought to bear on situations in life. It is in the dispute with the false prophets that Jeremiah spells out God's transcendence (distance) and his immanence (nearness) (23:23-24).

Religious language can deteriorate into meaningless clichés. It happened in Jeremiah's day with the expression, *This is the oracle of the Lord.* Since it meant everything, even one's own ideas, the expression was emptied of meaning. It is a serious thing to bandy about, as some do, the assertion "Thus says the Lord." In North America the phrase "born again" has been virtually emptied of meaning—it has even been applied to new paint jobs on cars. Used flippantly, "Praise the Lord" is an empty phrase. Can such language be rehabilitated?

One pastor told his congregation, on the basis of Jeremiah 23, "When I stand in this pulpit, I want you to know that at least *I* think God has given me something to say. And I make this covenant with you: 'If he doesn't speak—I won't!' "

Jeremiah 24 — 25

# Two Baskets of Figs and a Cup of Wine

## PREVIEW

Three newspaper banner headlines summarize chapters 24—25: BIG FIX MIX-UP, JUDAH DECLARED DEAF, and GOD ROARS AGAINST NATIONS.

First, the confusion regarding the good and bad figs. The vision report of baskets of figs touches on three groups: (1) those taken into exile, (2) those remaining in the land, and (3) the Babylonians. In these two chapters the future of each of these is announced. The exiles will see "good." Those remaining face destruction. Babylon, which will last for 70 years, will drink of the cup of the wrath of God, as will all nations. The material is not in chronological sequence. The basket vision in chapter 24 occurs after 598-597 B.C. during Zedekiah's reign. The message of chapter 25 is dated earlier, namely during Jehoiakim's reign in 605. The two chapters belong together in that they announce the future for the people of Judah, both the exiles and the homeland population, as well as of Babylon and nations generally.

These two visions, the vision of the basket and the cup, are, apart from the two visions of an almond branch and a boiling pot (chapter 1) with which they are in some sense parallel, the only visions in the book of Jeremiah. Several allusions (e.g., "build and plant," "the thirteenth year of Josiah") return us to chapter 1. These visions placed first and last have the effect of bracketing chapters 1—25 as one large unity. Looking at it another way, the vision of the basket of figs, placed almost at the middle of the book, signals a major shift from the judgment speech to deliverance speeches.

## OUTLINE

Figs: Some Good, Some Rotten, 24:1-10

Twenty-three Years of Nonlistening, 25:1-11 (14)

The Cup of God's Wrath, 25:15-38
    25:15-29 Nations Drink the Cup
    25:30-38 Nations Experience God's Wrath

## EXPLANATORY NOTES

### Figs: Some Good, Some Rotten  24:1-10

The chapter is in two parts. The report of the vision, together with the detail and dialogue, is given in 24:1-3. Its interpretation, in two parts corresponding to the kinds of figs, follows in verses 4-10.

### 24:1-3  The Vision of Two Baskets

The date for the vision is 598-597. In this year Nebuchadnezzar laid siege to Jerusalem, deported the city's upper crust of society, and set Zedekiah on the throne (2 Kings 24:10-16). The Babylonians chronicled their history on clay tablets inscribed in wedge-shaped combinations of impressions called cuneiform. Several tablets unearthed by archaeologists describe political and military developments in the years 616-595. Publication of these in 1956 made available to us this remarkable report from the "enemy's" viewpoint:

> In the seventh year [of] the month Kislev the king of Akkad mustered his troops, marched to the Hatti-land, and encamped against the city of Judah and on the second day of the month Adar he seized the city and captured the king. He appointed there a king of his own choice (lit., heart), Zedekiah, received its heavy tribute and sent (them) to Babylon (quoted in Green: 58).

The month of Kislev is comparable to December 18-January 15; the seventh year is 598-597. The king of Akkad is Nebuchadnezzar. The city of Judah is Jerusalem, its king Jehoiachin. The second day of the month, Adar, is March 16. Thus we know to the day when Jerusalem fell. *[Nebuchadnezzar, p. 304.]*

The seizure of Jerusalem by the Babylonians and the resulting "new situation" was given various interpretations in Judah. One was that it was those deserving of God's punishment who had been exiled. Those remaining in the land, now highly optimistic, continued to claim Abraham's promise and disparaged the exiles (Ezek. 11:14-15; 33:23-24; cf. Jer. 28). The question was, If God continued with his people, with which of the groups would it be? A second interpretation was that the siege "fulfilled" and exhausted Jeremiah's foreboding prophecies. Both notions were wrong, as the vision makes clear.

Figs, like the proverbial vines, were basic to Israel's life (e.g., Joel 1:7, 12). The mark of prosperity was for every man to "sit under his own vine and fig tree" (Mic. 4:4). Several centuries after Jeremiah, figs were so important to the general economy that the Greeks made special laws to regulate their export. The figs in front of the temple were perhaps brought as the firstfruits at the Feast of Weeks (Deut. 16:9-12; 26:2-11). The question to Jeremiah, What do you see? can be compared to questions in other visions (1:11, 13; Amos 8:2, a fruit basket!). The question makes for a pause in the story and prepares for what is essential in it.

### 24:4-10  The Vision's Meaning

A divine umpire calls it quite different from the way people see it. The people hold that the desirable figs correspond to the people remaining in Jerusalem. Not so, says the umpire. It is the exiles, even though not "good" in themselves, who will be the object of God's favor. God now takes initiative in redemption. In detail this means restoration to the land and security in it (v. 6; cf. 1:10; 30:3). Physical restoration will be accompanied by spiritual restoration. The history of Israel and Judah had made it obvious that the failure to obey was a recurring and deep-seated problem. Israel repeatedly was unwilling to follow God's ways. Was she even able?

Both Jeremiah and Ezekiel give hope for a new heart and so go to the core of the problem (Jer. 31:33; 32:39; Ezek. 11:19; 36:26). The new experiences will include the acknowledgment *that I am the Lord* (v. 7). The translation "for I am the Lord" (NASB) is not apt since the reason for the dramatic change is given only at the end of verse 7, *they will return to me. . . ."* The covenant formula, *"They will be my people, and I will be their God,"* found nowhere more often than in the book of Jeremiah, is a shorthand way of saying it all: God and people in intimate relationship. The hopeful word which is now given comes only after Judah has experienced God's punishment. *[Knowing God, p. 301; Covenant Formula, p. 294.]*

The rotten figs "not fit to eat" (NEB) stand for the survivors who continued in Palestine and others who sought refuge in Egypt. Some may have gone with King Jehoahaz in 609 (2 Kings 23:34). A colony of Jewish people flourished at Elephantine in south Egypt from 520-400. Aramaic documents from its library are still available. Just as spoiled figs would be thrown out, so will these "survivors" be eliminated through *sword, famine and plague* (v. 10; cf. 14:12; 21:7). The vision leaves no doubt as to who is in charge. It is the *God of Israel* who operates decisively in both groups. In both instances the *land* figures as symbol of God's promise, blessing, and presence.


## THE TEXT IN BIBLICAL CONTEXT

*Moving from Judgment to Grace.* The first part of the book of Jeremiah repeatedly announces, "I will bring sword, famine and pestilence." And now that it has come? Beyond judgment lies salvation! God takes the initiative, and apart from any merit on their part, surprises these hard-hit exiles with grace: "I will do you good!" So Jeremiah will announce repeatedly (29:11; 30—31).

Isaiah also calls out the assurance of God's gracious comfort to those who have endured the Lord's discipline (Isa. 40:1-31). The world's evil is dealt with by the Son of God, who absorbs the punishment on the cross. It is in consequence of the cross that the salvation offer is made. Believers exclaim, "By grace we are saved."


## THE TEXT IN THE LIFE OF THE CHURCH

*When Obvious Conclusions Are Wrong Conclusions.* The conclusion that God's favor was withdrawn from those who were deported to Babylon was a logical one in the light of Jeremiah's numerous announcements. But it was wrong. Similarly the opinion that the servant was "stricken by God, and afflicted" did not take account of a larger purpose (Isa. 53:4). When Samuel, standing with Jesse, calculated that Eliab, who was tall and good looking, was God's choice for a king, he was wrong (1 Sam. 16:7). Those who concluded on surface evidence that the crucified, dying Jesus was only a criminal were completely in error. Not infrequently our conclusions, though they appear warranted, are wrong.

# Twenty-three Years of Nonlistening  25:1-11[14]

The date is 605, the year in which the Babylonians clashed with the Egyptians at Carchemish (46:2). That year, following Nabopolassar's death, Nebuchadnezzar became king. At his palace, Jehoiakim displayed contempt for God's word by burning Jeremiah's scroll piece by piece (chapter 36). [Nebuchadnezzar, p. 304; Kings of Judah, p. 300.]

The literary segment is in two parts: an accusation (vv. 3-7) and an announcement (vv. 8-14). [Judgment Oracle, p. 299.]

## 25:3-7 Accusation

The accusation, repeated four times, is that Judah and Jerusalem did not listen (vv. 3-4, 7-8). This sin of nonlistening is aggravated by repeated prophetic calls to turn. To speak again and again (vv. 3-4) or "persistently and without interruption" (Bright: 156), translates a Hebrew idiom about early rising. It means, "speaking early and often," or "taking pains to speak" (NEB) (7:13; 11:7; 32:33) and sometimes "sending early and often" (7:25; 25:4; 26:5; 29:19; 35:15). The nonlistening (nonobedience) incurs the more guilt because of the number and nature of spokespersons mentioned in the order: (1) Jeremiah, (2) prophets from the past, and through them (3) the Lord (vv. 5-6). To each of them God's people responded with a nonlistening ear (cf. 6:17; 18:12). The message of the prophets was a call for people to redirect their course (cf. 23:22). [Summons to Repentance, p. 310.]

The same word in the Hebrew (shema') means both "to listen" and "to obey." In Jeremiah the charge is made more than 30 times that "you (they) have not listened (obeyed)" (e.g., 7:13, 24, 26, 28; 13:11; 35:14). The verbal form occurs 44 times in five chapters (7, 11, 26, 35, 42). The summons to listen is found in Jeremiah more than 30 times, though not all are addressed to Judah. In the New Testament, Jesus speaks of hearing and doing (Matt. 7:24, 26), of doing the will of God (Mark 3:35; John 7:17), of hearing the Word of God and obeying it (Luke 11:28). The importance of listening/obedience is illustrated in the parable of the two sons (Matt. 21:28-32). [Obey/Listen, p. 305.]

## 25:8-11[14] Announcement

The "enemy from the north," so often in view in chapters 2-20, is explicitly named as Nebuchadnezzar of Babylon. Since his army consisted of a conglomerate of peoples, the expression "all the tribes of the north" (v. 9, RSV) is appropriate. The mention of surrounding nations (v. 9) is to the point because Israel sought out allies to meet the threatened invasion (27:3).

While destruction had earlier been announced, the use of the word
*destroy (herem)*, "utterly destroy," would send chills down the spines of
the listeners. The word recalled the practice of a Yahweh war. One of the
guidelines for such a war was to burn structures and kill all things living,
person or beast, and devote these irrevocably *(herem)* as a massive
sacrifice to the Lord (cf. Josh. 6:21; 11:20). The coming ruin will bring an
end to all social life (bride/bridegroom); all commercial activity *(sound of
millstones)* and any form of domestic life *(the light of the lamp).*

Servitude to the king of Babylon will extend for 70 years. At the end
of 70 years, Babylon, whose king has just been described as *my servant*
(25:9), will be judged for its *guilt* (v. 12). Oddly, like the Assyrians who
occupied Israel a century earlier, nations are agents in God's purpose
("Assyria is the rod of the Lord's anger") and also the object of the
Lord's anger (Isa. 10:5). Assyria overreached her limit. The guilt of
Babylon is her arrogance (50:31). *[Seventy Years, p. 308.]*

It is at verse 13 that the Greek translation of the book inserts the
oracles against Babylon and the rest of the nations (46—51). It seems
clear that there is some literary bridging in verses 13-14—from the
reference to Jeremiah in the third person in verse 13 and in the first
person in verse 15. *[Formation of Book, p. 296; Septuagint, p. 308.]*

## The Cup of God's Wrath  25:15-38

Although not introduced formally as a vision, the report about the cup of
God's wrath can hardly be anything but a vision (cf. 24:1). It is not a sign-
act, for literally administering a cup for nations to drink is unlikely, if not
impossible. Like a sign-act, however, the "vision" is in three parts: (1) a
directive, verses 15-16; 27-28, (2) a report of compliance, verses 17-26,
and (3) an interpretation which is first given succinctly, verse 29, and
then elaborated, verses 30-38.

### 25:15-29  Nations Drink the Cup

The graphic picture of a cup filled with the wine of God's wrath is
frequent in literature focusing on the exile. In a woe oracle about those
who made others drunken with wine, Habakkuk announces that a cup
will be handed round in turn to the supplier of the drink (Hab. 2:16).
Jerusalem is to drink it, and did (Ezek. 23:32; Lam. 4:21). Isaiah, looking
to the end of the exile, rallies those who have drunk from the cup of
God's wrath, "who have drained to its dregs the goblet that makes men
stagger," with the assurance that the cup will be passed on to the tor-
mentors (Isa. 51:17-23).

In Jeremiah, the first to drink the cup and so experience the force of God's anger is Jerusalem and its environs. Essentially, wine, blood-red, intoxicates, and like anger, causes unusual actions. Nations who are made to drink of God's anger will be disoriented, overpowered, and quite at a loss what next to do. Or, as one scholar argues, the point of the cup is not intoxication but poison, and hence, death (McKane: 490f.).

Jeremiah now fulfills his calling as a prophet to the nations (1:10). Detailed messages to most of the nations listed are given in chapters 46—51. He passes the cup by turn to nations large and small, beginning with Egypt to the south. The listing is like a geography lesson. Uz, the land of Job (1:1), is at the eastern fringes of the Jordan, and may refer to the territory at the edge of the desert at the border of the regularly watered region. The Philistines along the Mediterranean, just south of Jerusalem, had five key cities, four of which are mentioned (cf. 47:1ff.). Edom, Moab and Ammon are countries lying east and south of the Dead Sea (cf. 48:1—49:22). Tyre and Sidon, (located in what was known in ancient times as Phoenicia and now as Lebanon) are on the coast north of Israel. Dedan, Tema, and Buz are in the Arabian Desert (49:28-33). Zimri is unknown. [Map, p. 317.]

Beginning with Arabia, the list includes nations increasingly distant from Israel to the east, with Elam and Media east of the Euphrates (cf. 49:34), and concludes with virtually all the kingdoms on the face of the earth (v. 26). Still, special mention is made of Babylon (cf. 50—51). Sheshach is a cryptogram for Babel—the word is formed by numbering the letters of the alphabet beginning with the last letter, and then substituting the letters that correspond in a forward numbering. Thus B-B-L = SH-SH-CH. The list begins and ends with the two world powers of the time, Egypt to the south and Babylon to the east.

There is no escape from the sword since the Lord Almighty is sending it. Though the departure point for passsing the cup is Jerusalem, in the end it will be a global drinking party. [Lord of Hosts, p. 304.]

## 25:30-38 Nations Experience God's Wrath

The single-sentence interpretation of verse 29 is elaborated, first by a divine oracle (vv. 30-32), and then by the prophet's echoing commentary (vv. 33-38). The destruction is not in cold blood, but comes after the judge's weighing of the charges against the nations. It comes, however, from one infuriated. The roar is the powerful voice of an incensed deity ; it reverberates to the ends of the earth (cf. Isa. 63:1-6; Amos 1:2). The shout is like the combined shouts of a company of people who together are treading grapes in a winepress. [Wrath, p. 313.]

The prophet echoes and expands several themes (vv. 33-38). The dead will be everywhere (cf. 7:32; 16:4). Those addressed as *kings* in the former announcement (vv. 17-26) are now addressed as *shepherds*, a common term for civil rulers. That term propels the poet toward *flock* (people) and to *pastures* and *meadows* and to the lionlike *destroyer*. The final line, *because of the Lord's fierce anger*, is an echo of the Lord's roar (v. 30) and is an inclusio when taken with the opening statement, *cup filled with the wine of my wrath* (v. 15). *[Inclusio, p. 298.]*

## THE TEXT IN BIBLICAL CONTEXT

*The Teaching About God's Wrath.* A Jewish scholar writes, "Our embarrassment in reading the harsh expressions of divine wrath is also due to the general disposition of man. We have no sense of spiritual grandeur. Spiritual to us means ethereal, calm, moderate, slight, imperceptible. . . . Those of us to whom the crimes of the world are mere incidents, and the agony of the poor is one of the many facts of life, may be inclined to describe the God of the prophets as stern, arbitrary, inscrutable, even unaccountable. But the thought of God and indifference to other people's suffering are mutually exclusive" (Heschel: 296). *[Wrath, p. 313.]*

## THE TEXT IN THE LIFE OF THE CHURCH

*The Widening Swath of Judgment.* God's harsh words against Israel are unrelenting because of their nonlistening. If his judgment with the "household of God" is severe, what shall the outcome be for the nations? Where shall the ungodly stand?

The roll call of nations, all candidates for God's wrath, is a forceful reminder that the world's nations are in the end accountable to God. For their anti-God actions, they will receive the cup of his wrath. The world of peoples was destroyed at the time of Noah, and God did not spare Sodom and Gomorrah. Peter's argument is compelling and sobering: if God did not spare angels who sinned nor the ancient world, then what judgment must await those in more recent times who have far greater enlightenment (and hence greater accountability)? (2 Pet. 2:4ff.).

For the church there are two lights of brightness in these grim assessments. In the Flood of the ancient world God preserved Noah; for as the apostle underscores, "The Lord knows how to rescue the godly" (2 Pet. 2:9). In the meanwhile, the cup of the Lord's salvation through the atonement in Christ is held out to the nations.

Jeremiah 26 – 29

# Deciding About Prophetic Voices

PREVIEW

In these four chapters one finds a sermon, two symbolic actions, and a letter. Common to each is the agenda of deciding who has the true word from the Lord. Jeremiah's sermon lands him in a court trial, but the verdict is, *"He has spoken to us in the name of the Lord"* (26:16). The wearing of an oxen yoke is accompanied by the message, "Do not listen to (your) prophets" (27:9, 14, 17). The prophet Hananiah also engages in symbolic action and offers a word from the Lord—different, however, from that of Jeremiah (chapter 28). And so do three other prophets, Ahab, Zedekiah, and Shemaiah (29:21, 24). Amidst many and strong contrary voices, Jeremiah is fighting to gain a hearing. He is at the temple, in the street, and at his home dictating letters. He addresses politicians, priests, prophets, and people in an accelerating drama.

These chapters are vignettes from Jeremiah's personal life. In them one may see a shift of interest from the prophetic message to the prophetic messenger. The incidents date from the reigns of Jehoiakim (609-598) and Zedekiah (597-587) and are in chronological order. Quite possibly these chapters are mainly the writings of Baruch. Note, for instance, the insertion of the account of Uriah's fate (26:20-23).

167

## OUTLINE

| Genre | Place | Date | Subject |
|-------|-------|------|---------|
| A Sermon (26:1ff.) | Temple | 609 | "Repent or Perish" |
| | | | Trial of Jeremiah |
| Symbolic Actions | Embassy | 594 | The Babylonians |
| (chapters 27—28) | Temple | | —submission to |
| | | | —release from |
| A Letter (29:1ff.) | Home | 594 | The Exiles' Concerns |
| | | | —their conduct and |
| | | | future |
| | | | —their homeland |
| | | | —their leaders |

## EXPLANATORY NOTES

### A Sermon: Preaching for a Turn-around 26:1-24

#### 26:1-6 The Sermon

The date for this passionate sermon is approximately 609 B.C., the year when Jehoiakim became king. Some have suggested that the sermon was preached at the king's coronation, but there is no evidence for such a view. Actually, a summary is given here, and not the sermon itself, which is found in chapter 7. The reason the sermon sequel is not given in Jeremiah 7 may be that there, in the collection of sermons, the content is of prime interest; here, in the narrative from Jeremiah's life, the trial holds greater interest. [Kings of Judah, p. 300.]

Compared with the fuller account (7:1-15), the summary (26:1-6) differs in several ways: the Lord is prepared to relent should they repent; there is reference to the former prophets and to the law generally. There is also a more threatening tone—God commands not to *omit a word*. The subject of repentance dominates. [Summons to Repentance, p. 310.]

#### 26:7-16 Jeremiah's Arrest and Trial

In their fury, members of the religious establishment, priests and prophets, seize Jeremiah. Both the priests and prophets gained their livelihood in the temple. The offense of the sermon is the threat that the temple will be destroyed like Shiloh (cf. 1 Sam. 1—4; see comment at 7:1-15). The audience apparently did not hear the chief point of the sermon: a call for repentance and contrition. The leaders reason that to speak in the Lord's name (that Lord whose covenant was with David and by extension with the temple, God's dwelling place, 2 Sam. 7; Ps.

132:13), and at the same time threaten the temple's destruction is in-congruous and contradictory. In their reasoning, therefore, Jeremiah is a false prophet, who deserves the death penalty (cf. Deut. 18:20).

Also, the political establishment was drawn into the fracas. Details about the *New Gate* are not available, except that it was in the Upper Court (36:10; cf. 2 Kings 15:35). The people's charge before the *officials* (princes, RSV) is not theological but political: *he has prophesied against the city.* Jeremiah's defense is bold and tactful. He appeals once more for a spiritual turnaround: "Make well your ways and doings! Make them sound, make them healthy, make them beautiful" (Morgan: 141). The Lord will then *relent* (more apt than "repent," cf. "change His mind," NASB). Jeremiah puts concern for city and people ahead of his own safety. He stresses that *in truth the Lord has sent me* (vv. 12, 15; cf. 28:9; 23:28). One may contrast these claims with the eight occurrences of "I [the Lord] have not sent them [false prophets]."

## 26:17-24  Recalling History: Micah and Uriah

Perhaps the verdict by the officials has been challenged. In any case, certain elders lend their support by offering an insight from history. A century earlier, Micah, a recognized prophet, prophesied during the reigns of Jotham (742-735), Ahaz (735-715), and Hezekiah (715-687). Like Jeremiah, Micah threatened both temple and Jerusalem "in the severest threat against Jerusalem ever found in the whole Bible" (Wolff: 43).

This text quoted verbatim from Micah 3:12 is one of the relatively few instances in the Old Testament of quotations of other "Scripture" (cf. Dan. 9:2). Micah's home was in Moresh-Gath, 35 miles from Jerusalem. This Israelite village was a satellite of Gath, the Philistine city. Micah's prophecy was not fulfilled because of Hezekiah's acts of reform, reported in 2 Kings 18:3ff. Indeed, God relented then, and the city was miraculously spared (Isa. 36—37).

The elders' illustration from history also sets up a sharp contrast between the responses of kings Hezekiah and Jehoiakim (vv. 20-23; cf. 22:15-16; 36:1ff.). The additional help Jeremiah received from Ahikam was not the only help he received from this official's family, nor from other high-placed officials (cf. 38:7-13). *Elnathan,* an official, was later sympathetic to Jeremiah (36:12, 25). He was the son of Acbor, an of-ficial under Josiah (2 Kings 22:12, 14), and has been identified as the father of Nehushta, mother of Jehoiachin (2 Kings 24:8). *[Shaphan, p. 309.]*

Baruch, the reporter, adds the story of Uriah to this illustration from history, apparently to show how precarious Jeremiah's position was. (Calvin, however, suggests that verses 20-23 are not the words of Baruch, but of Jeremiah's opponents.) Nothing more is known about Jeremiah's contemporary, Uriah, than is stated here. His hometown, one of four Gibeonite cities, was eight miles northwest of Jerusalem; its name means "town of forest thickets."

The story about Uriah shows the contrast between Jeremiah, who fearlessly stood up to political authorities, and Uriah, who fled for his life (cf. Elijah, who also fled, 1 Kings 19:3). Uriah is one of two prophets mentioned in the Old Testament as being executed (cf. 2 Chron. 24:20-22; Matt. 23:37). Uriah was not even accorded a decent burial but was thrown in a trench in the Kidron Valley, where the bodies of stateless persons were cast (2 Kings 23:6). All three prophets—Jeremiah, Micah, and Uriah—were village persons from outside Jerusalem, and each spoke against the temple.

## THE TEXT IN BIBLICAL CONTEXT

*The Correspondence Theory of History.* It has been claimed that whereas pagan views of history are cyclical, biblical history is linear. Not altogether. From the Bible it is clear that some events, though centuries apart, correspond remarkably to each other, yielding a view of history which can be diagrammed as both cyclical and yet linear as follows:

Jeremiah                    Jesus

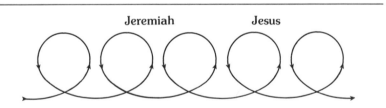

Between Jeremiah and Jesus there is close correspondence. Each was a very public figure who preached repentance and challenged the traditions. Each was arrested by the "religious establishment" and was tried in the political process. Each also had friends in the upper leadership circle (e.g., Ahikam, Joseph of Arimathea). Each had a contemporary spokesperson—the one, Uriah, and the other, John the Baptist. Both were put to death by kings. For other pairing of events, compare Isaiah 7:14 and Matthew 1:22f.; Hosea 11:1 and Matthew 2:15.

## THE TEXT IN THE LIFE OF THE CHURCH

*Courage.* Throughout the church's history men and women have stood courageously before civil authorities: Peter and Paul in the first century, Martin Luther King in the twentieth-century. Less spectacular but equally important is the courage to witness for Christ and for faith in situations of apathy; or the boldness, when in delicate circumstances, to state one's convictions without fudging; or the resolution of mind to rebuke evil fearlessly, whether in church or society.

Sören Kierkegaard, a nineteenth-century Danish thinker, began his criticism of the church with an attack upon Bishop Mynster, who had confirmed him and whom the state had appointed to the office of church president. Mynster had Denmark's leading citizens as his audience. In this Kierkegaard saw a compromise between Christianity and worldly interests, and wrote, "Instead of leading the people to stand before God and Christ, the clerics encouraged them to 'listen with their hands on their stomachs, directing a sleepy upward look.' " People responded to Kierkegaard's writings in mockery and hailed him in the streets as "Old man either/or" (the title of one of his books) and "The great philosopoher with uneven pant legs" (one of his legs was shorter than the other). (Olan: 23f.)

## Symbolic Action: Persuading Politicians and Priests 27:1-22

The following stories suggest the question "Should today's Christians meddle in politics?"

The making and the breaking of a yoke as symbolic actions is the story framework for Jeremiah 27—28. The actions are coupled with corresponding messages about the duration of Babylonian rule. Chapter 27 represents Jeremiah's speech to three groups: to foreign envoys, to Zedekiah, and to priests. Common to each, and also striking, is a double exhortation: (1) submit to the Babylonians, and (2) do not listen to (your) prophets.

The dates for the events related in the two chapters are close; some suggest they took place on the same day. The major Hebrew text of 27:1 gives the date as in the reign of Jehoiakim, but many translations (NIV, RSV, NASB) rightly follow manuscripts, both Hebrew and Syriac, which read "Zedekiah." Reasons for this are: Zedekiah is addressed in verse 12 (cf. v. 3); the date for the Hananiah incident is given as the "fourth year of Zedekiah" (28:1); Nebuchadnezzar, mentioned in verse 6, was not in power till after 605; and the move toward a coalition of nations resisting Nebuchadnezzar came in 594.

*27:1-11  A Double Message to Visiting Envoys*

A meeting similar to a foreign ministers' conference was being held in Jerusalem. Once more Jeremiah engaged in symbolic action—wearing a yoke. The yoke was a crossbar placed on the necks of animals (such as oxen), enabling them to be hitched for plowing. Straps, either of rope or leather, were used for reins and also to secure the bar either to the horns or to the animal's body. By wearing such a yoke, Jeremiah sent messages to the countries surrounding Israel to the south and to the north. Envoys of these countries were in Jerusalem, possibly at King Zedekiah's invitation, to plan strategy concerning a resistance movement against the Babylonians, to whom Zedekiah, at least, was a vassal. *[Symbolic Action, p. 311; Map, p. 317.]*

All of these nations now had a common enemy, for by 594 their territories were in Nebuchadnezzar's grip. Nebuchanezzar was troubled by internal ferment at home. It seemed politically reasonable to form a coalition. (Nothing ever came of it.)

Jeremiah sent a message from the *Lord Almighty. [Lord of Hosts, p. 304.]* This title, suggesting supremacy, and especially the designation of God as Creator of the earth and all its content, was a rebuke to the plurality of pagan deities. An Israelite hearing such an introduction would call to mind a God of power and sovereignty and would feel hope in a difficult situation. These titles announced to all that God was higher than Nebuchadnezzar, who presently filled the horizon—indeed that Nebuchadnezzar, though not a Yahweh worshiper, was nevertheless God's servant (v. 6). God was fully in charge and would have the last word, even to the point of assigning animals their master (v. 5).

The summons is twofold. The first summons is to submit to Nebuchadnezzar, and to *bow . . . under his yoke,* for his rule will not be short-lived, but extend over three generations. *His son and his grandson* is not to be taken literally but as three generations. Submission to Babylon—certainly a painful and politically reprehensible act—is urged for the following reasons: (1) the Creator God has given Nebuchadnezzar control; (2) failure to bow to his yoke will mean destruction; and (3) compliance with the order will mean continued possession of the land (cf. 7:3). *[Babylon/Babylonians, p. 291; Seventy Years, p. 308.]*

The second half of Jeremiah's message is an appeal to disregard prophets with a different message. Israelite kings consulted prophets about military undertakings (1 Kings 22). So did the kings of other nations, as documents from Mari on the Euphrates show. Nebuchadnezzar himself consulted omens via diviners of livers (Ezek. 21:21). But neighboring kings are now urged not to listen to such *diviners,* nor to *sorcerers* or *mediums,* who would cast charms, perhaps to undo Jeremiah's dark predictions. Nor are they to listen to *interpreters of dreams,* possibly women (so say some versions).

### 27:12-15  A Double Message to Zedekiah

Zedekiah, Judah's king, seems to have been torn during most of his reign between the pro-Egyptian and the pro-Babylonian parties. Jeremiah has two pieces of advice: submit to Nebuchadnezzar; don't listen to opposite counsel. However, the king is being urged by his political counselors to mount a resistance movement against Nebuchadnezzar, who has installed him to be a puppet king (2 Kings 24:15-20). The advice from Jeremiah to submit means to capitulate. This is not the way of kings: they counter force with force, not with pacifistic surrender.

Submission to Nebuchadnezzar is the more difficult because of prophetic voices such as Hananiah's, who supported the political counselors by predicting a short-lived Babylonian supremacy (28:1ff.). Jeremiah's constant insistence on not heeding other prophets (vv. 14-15; cf. 14:14-16; 23:16-40; 29:8) shows how unacceptable and unpalatable his advice was for king and people. But tragically the king, who heard Jeremiah's advice on other occasions (cf. 38:14-23), does not submit and loses everything (52:4-11). *[Falsehood, p. 296.]*

### 27:16-22  A Double Message to Priests and People

The same messages, namely "surrender to Babylon" and "do not listen to them (prophets)," are now carried to the priests. If political rulers worried about land, priests worried about the temple and its furnishings, for in these they had a vested interest. For the priests to "give in" to Babylon would be to lose their livelihood. To the contrary, Jeremiah claimed, in what must have seemed an unbelievable word, *"Serve [Nebuchadnezzar] and you will live."*

Some prophets, with Hananiah as a prime example (28:2), had proclaimed an optimistic message about an early return—as soon as two years—for the temple furnishings which Nebuchadnezzar had removed in the siege of 598-597. Jeremiah rebukes the smooth-talking prophets by reminding them of the intercessory functions of true prophets (v. 18; cf. Amos 7:1-6). To each group (foreign dignitaries, Zedekiah, and the priests) the message is, *"Don't listen to . . . [your] prophets"* (vv. 9, 14, 16). Three times also the same reason is given: *"They are prophesying lies"* (vv. 10, 14, 16).

More than just branding their words as lies, Jeremiah specifies what will become of Solomon's showcase splendor at the temple (cf. 1 Kings

7:15-37). The free-standing, 27-foot-high pillars called Boaz and Jakin were valuable for their bronze, "more than could be weighed," as was the molten over-sized laver, or *sea.* The movable stands or "trolleys" (NEB), ornately made of wood and highly prized metal, will be transported to Babylon, says Jeremiah. (See 2 Kings 25:13-17.) While some pieces will be taken with the intention that the metals will be melted down and reused—miracle of miracles—there will be a restoration of these to Jerusalem! Eventually. Not soon. That note of hope suggests at a minimum that Jeremiah was not a sour prune who delighted in evil. Much more, such words held hope that judgment, however severe and excruciatingly painful, would issue in redemptive acts by God on Israel's behalf.

(For guidelines on authentic prophecy see "Prophetic Word Versus Prophetic Word," p. 179.)

## Symbolic Action: Tangling with the Prophet Hananiah  28:1-17

In this chapter and the next the false prophets have "faces," or at least names: Hananiah, Ahab, Zedekiah, and Shemaiah. The symbolic actions of the ox yoke carries on from chapter 27 into chapter 28, as does the concern about temple furnishings.

The chapter is a study in conflict. Sociologists would see it as a struggle for influence. They point to modern societies in which shamans (intermediaries between people and gods) are caught in controversy. In one instance the Zezuru people of southern Rhodesia heard the claim of one called Wild Man to be a medium for the spirit Chaminuka. Muchatera, who made the same claim but objected that it was impossible for two people to acts as hosts for the same spirit, challenged Wild Man at a public meeting to make rain. Wild Man climbed on a rock, waved his arms, and rain clouds appeared. Supporters of Wild Man forced Muchatera to leave in disgrace. Such reports lend a certain "immediacy" to our chapter (Fry: 43f.).

### 28:1-11  Breaking the Wooden Yoke

The date for the dramatic context which pitted prophet against prophet is August 594. Each is designated by the term "prophet." Each claims to speak in the name of the Lord of hosts. Each engages in symbolic action. In the year 594 King Zedekiah, a puppet ruler appointed by Nebuchadnezzar, went to Babylon, perhaps to pay tribute or even to affirm his loyalty (!) (51:59). But in that year also there was a ferment brewing, apparently both in Palestine and among the exiles in Babylon, to throw off the Babylonian yoke and be independent. The people, the priests, and the prophets had a lively interest in the matter. [Kings of Judah, p. 300.]

Hananiah, whose name means "Yahweh has been gracious," was a prophet from Gibeon, a town six miles northwest of Jerusalem, famous as the place from which Joshua called the sun to stand still. His message, given publicly at the temple, is that God will break Nebuchadnezzar's hold on the peoples. Consequently, the articles absent from the temple since the siege of 597—a concern to the priests in the audience—will be returned from Babylon soon. And so will the exiled peoples and King Jehoiachin return soon—within two years! (cf. 27:9). Jeremiah by contrast claimed that the Babylonian hold would extend for three generations (27:7). Not only would the temple articles not be returned immediately; additional ones would be removed (27:19ff.). Since Jeremiah also spoke about a restoration (27:22), the issues involved timing.

Jeremiah's reply to this bold, authoritative, highly optimistic and appealing announcement by his professional colleague is surprisingly conciliatory and tactful. Or is there a trace of sarcasm? A harsh message need not be accompanied by harsh demeanor. He had earlier said "Amen" to the curse (11:5). Essentially he puts forward two tests by which both Hananiah and he himself may be judged: (1) Does the message accord with the message of former prophets? (2) Will the prediction come to pass? (cf. Deut. 18:21ff.). Former prophets who under similar circumstances predicted disaster were Amos (2:4), Hosea (4:6), and Isaiah (3:13-15). (This test does not exclude words of hope, else Jeremiah himself would be suspect.) Is Jeremiah perhaps proposing, "I have the great prophets on my side?"

Hananiah adamantly reaffirms his message by dramatically removing the wooden yoke from Jeremiah and breaking it. Such action, while a visual aid of sorts, was also more than that, since it was believed that with the action itself forces were set loose to bring the message to pass. With masterful restraint Jeremiah walks off. The people's dilemma in deciding whom to believe is unresolved. Clearly, Hananiah will be the more popular. The suspense continues. [Symbolic Action, p. 311.]

## 28:12-17 A Message About an Iron Yoke

The interval underscores that Jeremiah's words were not self-originated, as were those of the false prophets (23:16). Whether Jeremiah appeared with an iron yoke is not stated, but to do so would be in keeping with his sign-acts. His message was in the name of the Lord

*Almighty. [Lord of Hosts, p. 304.]* Control over *wild animals* already assumes absolute control over the domestic economy (cf. 27:6).

The judgment speech directed to Hananiah is one of the few directed to an individual as contrasted with those to nations. Jeremiah states the double accusation, *The Lord has not sent you, yet you have persuaded the nation to trust in lies;* and with a characteristic *therefore* he introduces the announcement, "I am going to 'send' you—right off the face of the earth" (v. 15, Bright: 199). The word for *rebellion* occurs only two other times, but in each instance it refers to a false prophet (Deut. 13:5; Jer. 29:32). Upon Hananiah's death two months later, the people were handed some evidence on testing a true prophet's message. *[Judgment Oracle, p. 299.]*

(Further comments on true prophecy are given on p. 179, "Prophetic Word Versus Prophetic Word.")

## A Letter: Counseling Exiles and Countering Bad Leadership  29:1-32

In this chapter we dip into Jeremiah's correspondence file. Here is a pastoral letter not unlike Paul's letters to New Testament churches. The letter is from Jeremiah of Jerusalem, and sent to the exiles in Babylon 700 miles away. In it Jeremiah seeks to head off an insurrection (vv. 1-23). A second note, if not a letter, concerns Shemaiah (vv. 24-32).

### 29:1-3 The Historical Setting

The lengthy letter, though undated, was written after 598-597. That was the date Nebuchadnezzar carried off to Babylon King Jeconiah, another name for Jehoiachin. A likely date for the letter is four years later, in 594, for in that year there was ferment among vassal nations about an uprising against Babylon. Among the exiles such talk was inflamed by the rhetoric of the prophets Ahab and Zedekiah (vv. 20-23). The letter is sent by Elasah, a member of Shaphan's family, whose family was friendly to Jeremiah (36:10-12; 39:14; 40:5). Their errand may have been to present Judah's tribute monies. *[Nebuchadnezzar, p. 304; Kings of Judah, p. 300; Chronology, p. 293; Shaphan, p. 309.]*

### 29:4-9 Counseling Exiles About Their Lifestyle

From: The Lord
To: The Exiles

The letter begins, as do other letters from that time, like an inter-office memo, but the usual greeting of peace *(shalom)* is deferred to verse

7, a procedure the exiles must have considered rude. It is partly from Jeremiah's advice that we reconstruct the situation now faced by the exiles.

If the smooth-talking prophets are right in that the exile will be short (cf. Hananiah in Jerusalem, 28:2-4), then the reluctance of the exiles to settle down in a foreign country is understandable. But Jeremiah, insisting that the exile will be long, sweeps away all hopes for an early return. Already Jeremiah has appealed to the people at home to tune out such prophets (27:14, 16-17; cf. 23:16; 14:14).

His advice to *build houses* and to *plant gardens* presupposes that the Judeans, though captive, have considerable freedom. Apparently they were settled in colonies (Ezek. 3:15). The Jews followed Jeremiah's advice—we can document this from the archaeological finds at Nippur of 700 inscribed tablets, known as the Murashu Archives. These record contracts and loan certificates of a Jewish family of the fifth century B.C.

Certainly the counsel to work for the welfare of the city—the city in which they were held hostage—and to *pray to the Lord for it* is revolutionary. The **lex talionis**, "an eye for an eye," is here superseded by a quite different directive—prayerful concern. Such radical counsel about treatment of enemies anticipates Jesus' words: "Love your enemies, and pray for those who persecute you" (Matt. 5:44).

### 29:10-14 Counseling Exiles About Their Future

The counsel to exiles about settling down permanently in Babylon— as unnatural for homesick captives as submission to the enemy was for people back home—is given a basis in a salvation oracle. In it one can distinguish statements about God's initiative (e.g., *I will come to you)*, and statements about the consequences of this intervention (e.g., *Then you will call upon me). I will come* translates a verb often rendered as "visit." It means to pay attention. In a military context it means, "to muster, to superintend." The 70-year span, while affecting the length of the exile, is strictly a time period specified *for Babylon. [Seventy Years, p. 308.]*

The salvation oracle both opens and closes with the hope-inspiring promise, *I will . . . bring you back to this place.* The return, mentioned sparingly in the book till now, will be center stage in the "Book of Consolation" (30-31; cf. 24:4-7). The basis for the return is in God's gracious plan. Forthright statements in the Old Testament of God's plan are relatively few (cf. Isa. 14:27; 46:10; Ps. 33:11; Prov. 19:21; Jer. 32:19). Here the plans, mentioned three times, are introduced with an emphatic *"I know ..."* (v. 11). *[Inclusio, p. 298.]*

The plans are for good (lit., *shalom*). *Shalom* embraces all that belongs to the good and satisfying life. It means "peace," understood as "well-being, wholeness, unimpaired relationships, and harmony." It is the opposite to fragmentation, conflict, and alienation. The discomfort of the long exile is intended to issue in good, namely a close relationship with God. The human basis for the restoration is a new heart which seeks after God (cf. 24:7; 31:33; Ezek. 36:26ff.). God is immediately available to the seeker (Deut. 4:29). Physical restoration to the land is connected with spiritual restoration to God (cf. 31:16-20). *[Shalom, p. 308.]*

The main parts of a "pronouncement of salvation" oracle stand out: (1) the difficult situation, verse 10; (2) the Lord's stance, verse 11; and (3) the announcements, verses 12-14a. *[Deliverance Oracles, p. 295.]*

The restoration announcement is carefully phrased, first with an overarching statement: "I will restore your fortunes" (not as in NIV, *"I ... will bring you back from ... exile,"* v. 14). Beyond the general statement are two specifics: (1) regathering of the people and (2) their return to the land. While the major deportation was to Babylon, other Israelites had sought refuge elsewhere as in Egypt (43:4-7). Their physical return to their land was made possible in 539 by Cyrus the Persian (Ezra 1:2-4). *[Restoration Formula, p. 307.]*

## 29:15-19  Counseling Exiles About Their Homeland

Since they have relatives in Judea, plus the fact that they are emotionally attached to the homeland generally, the exiles are anxious about the fate of Jerusalem. Jeremiah's message, a repeat of earlier statements (e.g., 16:1-4), is essentially that this siege and deportation are not yet the total of the disaster. Nor is the word about the king different from what had been told to Zedekiah (27:3-15). *Like poor figs,* whose fate was to be thrown out, recalls the vision of Jeremiah 24 . The oracle has the familiar two parts: announcement and accusation. The accusation is short: they have not listened (cf. 25:1-11 and comment there). The disturbed logic and grammar in verses 14-17 might be attributed to the agitation of the letter writer, or to an ellipsis—that is, without quoting the false prophets, Jeremiah is already answering them. *[Judgment Oracle, p. 299.]*

## 29:20-23  Countering the False Prophets, Ahab and Zedekiah

These two prophets belong with Hananiah (chapter 28) to the category of prophets who speak lies. We know nothing about them other than what is stated here, though they are suspected of instigating an abortive revolt. As in 23:9-40, these false prophets are identified by their evil lifestyle (here *adultery* and *outrageous things*) and their unauthorized speech. The punishment for false prophecy, as it was for adultery, was death (Deut. 18:20; 21:22). *[Falsehood, p. 296.]*

If the last line in verse 23 is translated, as has recently been proposed, "I myself know the word and the witness," it would be a fitting summary of the subject of false prophets, stressing God's knowledge of both the message and the character of the prophets (Dahood: 483). But from letters brought to light through archaeology, we know that *"witness"* meant "countersigned." Thus the letter ends: "countersigned: the Lord."

### 29:24-32  Countering a False Prophet, Shemaiah

The passage appears confused because within the announcement there is a throwback to an event. But good sense is obtained if it is understood as the report of a scribe who was charged by Jeremiah, "To Shemaiah . . . you shall say" (RSV), as though the prophet gave the gist but did not bother to reply personally. The letter begins, "With reference to what you have sent (as a message). . . ." Shemaiah's letter is then quoted, a custom common in the ancient Near East. Then, after the telling of the event, the real "letter" follows (v. 31). Such an interpretation, recently proposed by a scholar, involves the omission, as in the Septuagint, of *This is what the Lord says* (v. 25a).

Shemaiah, angry with Jeremiah for his advice based on a long exile, maneuvers via letter for Jeremiah's removal. Jehoiada apparently succeeded Pashhur as security officer in the temple (cf. 20:1). Shemaiah, in a unilateral action, deposes Jehoiada and installs a new security officer, Zephaniah, whom he charges to deal with *madmen* like Jeremiah. Either because of naïvete or because he sympathizes with Jeremiah, Zephaniah, reads Shemaiah's letter to Jeremiah. For Jeremiah's word to Shemaiah, compare 28:15-16. From the standpoint of a neutral observer, Shemaiah's writing of letters and meddling in the affairs of Jerusalem was no different from Jeremiah's writing of letters meddling in the exile. Both were operating from their respective power bases.

### THE TEXT IN BIBLICAL CONTEXT

*Prophetic Word Versus Prophetic Word.* The problem of false prophets is a long-standing one. Elijah does verbal battle with the prophets of Baal. Within Israel Micaiah is opposed by Zedekiah and 400

court prophets (1 Kings 22) and Jeremiah by Hananiah, Ahab, Zedekiah, and Shemaiah (Jer. 28—29). In the early church, Paul was opposed by Judaizers. "We can always believe a prophet is a prophet when
he has been dead long enough! The difficulty is to recognize him and
believe him in the day of his living message" (Morgan: 154). Both Testa-
ments make clear that it is the people who must distinguish between true
and false prophets. God's people have need of training to learn to make
the distinction. Help can come from the following guidelines.

1. Divine authentication through a call. Prophets and apostles relate
their experiences of call to show that they are divinely sent, and not merely
to give a "testimony."

2. Scrutiny of personal character. Jeremiah advances this criterion, as
does Jesus (Matt. 7:16). Sincerity is not the only mark of integrity, but it is
essential; false prophets are in it for the money (Mic. 3:5-8).

3. Attention to activity. True prophets demonstrate concern to turn
people into God's ways (23:22); intercession is a test of true prophecy (cf.
14:13; 37:3; 42:2). False prophets speak with a brash and bombastic
certainty (cf. Zedekiah, 1 Kings 22). True prophets wait for God's word
and sometimes pass through times of uncertainty.

4. Examination of the message. "False prophets like to humor
people" (Wolff: 71). The message must be in accord with "what has been
delivered." To hold a recognized position is not itself evidence one way or
the other.

5. Test of fulfillment. Nonfulfillment of a predictive word obviously
denotes a false message. However, a predicted sign or a wonder by itself is
no guarantee of an authentic message (Deut. 13:1ff.).

## THE TEXT IN THE LIFE OF THE CHURCH

*Religion and Politics.* In Israel, prophets addressed civil rulers. Elijah
rebuked King Ahab, and Isaiah advised King Ahaz about foreign policy
(Isa. 7). Jeremiah advised not only an Israelite king but also the kings of
neighboring nations. The church is not like Israel, which was both a nation and the "people of God." This fact has led to the conclusion that the
church has no business getting involved in political questions. But is the
church really immune from responsibility to government? If it does have
a responsibility to address civil rulers, what is the basis for that responsibility? Does it include "meddling" in political processes? Even if one dis-
counts the prophets to Israel as a model for the church because of Israel's unique political/religious situation, what does Jeremiah's message
to the non-Israelite kings mean? Is his action peculiar to one situation, or
might it be normative and pacesetting?

*Adopting a Debating Style.* It is accepted by many Christians that the witness to one's faith is made unobtrusively, and that to stir a ripple in the sea of public opinion is to be too forward. Jeremiah's preaching was of the argumentative variety. He was locked in serious verbal and belief battles with false prophets and spared no energy in public debate, exhortation, and letter writing. Jesus often debated sharply with his opponents. Paul argued a good deal, employing logic, personal experience, and historical example. The progress of the Christian faith is made in the public arena.

Individual Christians would do well to come out of their shells and interact more vociferously with those who disagree. While in some countries evangelical Christian people argue for the biblical faith via debates, books, and telecasts, in other lands Christians have kept to their sacred huddles, denouncing opponents but from safe distances. Hard-line engagement and the presentation of evidence has too often been minimal.

*What Should You Do?* Of the many links to present-day church life that come from these chapters, here are a sample few:

> 1. About timing. False prophets wanted to "speed up the divine purposes." What other biblical examples are there of such "speeding up" actions? Even if a planned action is right and proper, what attention should be given to its timing?
> 2. About the doctrine of creation. In this passage the teaching of God as Creator is incorporated into a message to non-Israelites (27:3). Elsewhere it functions to refute idolatry (10:12-13) and is invoked in prayer when facing a strange decision (32: 17). How does the doctrine of creation impact one's belief and action?
> 3. About God's guidance. False prophets did not distinguish between God's message and their own wishful thinking. When one so much desires a certain result, how can one remain sufficiently detached to hear from God?
> 4. About treatment of enemies. What happens to emotions when one prays for enemies? How does the power of prayer compare in effectiveness to other power leverages?
> 5. About corruption. Do you agree that "debased spiritual authority is far more evil in national life than debased civil authority?" (Morgan: 139). Which is the more important to combat?
> 6. About prayer. The promise for God to answer those who search for him with all their heart is not a promise limited to the exiles. Charles Finney, a 29-year old lawyer, was converted to Christ out in the woods near the village of Adams, New York, on October 10, 1821, when in spiritual misery he seized on the words of Jeremiah 29:12-13. The text was vindicated for him and, incidentally, also for the group of church young people who had prayed for Finney. In that group was Lydia Andrews, who later became Finney's wife.

# PART 5

# The Book of Consolation

# Jeremiah 30 – 33

Dark has been the prospect; the outlook gloomy on every side. Without letup, Jeremiah has preached coming ruin.

But now, light! Ruin will not be the last word! God will make possible recovery of what was lost!

The "book," known as the "Book of Consolation," is one of hope— hope for return to the land and hope for a spiritual renewal. God and the people will be knit together as God intended from the first. In brief, the first two chapters of poetry contain a collage of oracles announcing a future deliverance. This poetic outburst is followed by two chapters of prose, a narrative of a sign-act, and a description of what it will be like when God brings salvation to a people who have been judged and exiled.

The subject is mostly Israel; less is said specifically of Judah. Israel, the Northern Kingdom, experienced an Assyrian assault in 734 B.C. and exile in 722 to the region of the Habor River (2 Kings 15:29; 17:6). These oracles were written for the benefit of the northern exiles, and can be compared to the letter of chapter 29, which was addressed to the southern exiles.

Proposals for the date of the poetry portion have varied from 612-609, just after the fall of Nineveh, to a time just prior to Jerusalem's fall (587), to a date in the exile. The prose of chapter 32 is dated to 587. It is possible that the oracles which were directed to Israel came early in Jeremiah's ministry, and that those addressed to Judah in this section were later added in.

The hope oracles of these four chapters are preceded by announcements of judgments and followed by warnings. That the material should be so arranged carries a message in itself: the good word of comfort must not be misused by pulling it out of context. That ordering also shows that promise was a part of God's design from the outset.

Jeremiah 30 – 31

# Recovery of What Was Lost – and More!

## PREVIEW

Here comes the good news!

Most of the material to this point has been of the gloom-and-doom variety with only an occasional ray of brightness (e.g., 12:14-16; 24:4-7). But now there is a burst of light and hope. The poetry is lyrical and upbeat. The images are mostly bright and hope-filled. The past is not forgotten—the hurts have been too deep, but beyond them is new life! Like all true art, this poem, at first catches attention with a pleasing general impression, but yields its full contents more slowly.

The subject is restoration of people to their land (30:1ff.), and of people to their God (31:1ff.). The snapping of the enemy's hold is the basis for hope in the first poem. A divine work of grace in the human heart becomes the basis for the second promise. One might well read these chapters against the background of some questions: What accounts for God's favorable consideration of his people, the shift from judgment to salvation? What grounds are given for the promise of restoration? Why was a return to the land desirable or even essential?

OUTLINE (Schematic)

## The Recovery of the Land 30:1-24

| The Situation | The Action (The Lord's Stance) | The Outcome |
|---|---|---|
| yoked, vv. 1-9 | "I will break the yoke" | release |
| fearful, vv. 10-11 | "I will surely save you" | peace, security |
| wounded, vv. 12-17a | "I will restore to health" | enemies eliminated |
| reproached, vv. 17b-24 | "I will bring them honor" | a joyous society |

## The Recovery of a Relationship 31:1-40

God's Love v. 3 [1-6]
- Israel's Father—protection, vv. 1-9
- Israel's Shepherd—provider, vv. 10-14
- Israel's "Mother"—comforter, vv. 15-26
- Israel's Covenant-maker—people-former, vv. 27-40

The message of judgment was cast into an oracle of judgment which had two chief parts: an accusation and an announcement. The new message is presented in a new speech-form, "oracles of deliverance," of which there are four kinds. Elements found in them are: an allusion to lament, a word of consolation, statements defining the Lord's stance and intervention, and announced consequences. [Deliverance Oracles, p. 295.]

## EXPLANATORY NOTES

The discussion that follows employs an expanded version of the outline given above.

## The Recovery of the Land Jeremiah 30:1-24

### 30:1-3 "Write a Scroll"

Jeremiah has finally made it as a theologian: he is asked to write a book! As a rule, oracles by prophets were spoken. Later they were collected, sometimes by disciples, and recorded (Isa. 8:16; Amos 1:1; Jer. 36:4). Writing figures prominently in Jeremiah; Baruch was the scribe. Here Jeremiah can be compared with Moses: Moses recorded the book of the law; Jeremiah recorded the Book of Consolation. [Baruch, p. 292.]

The book follows a popular modern genre: it is about the future:

*"Days are coming."* But unlike current books of this kind, it brings hopeful news. The book is divided into fourteen oracles.

God will "restore the fortunes" of his people. This catch phrase, found especially in the Book of Consolation (e.g., 30:18; 32:44), signifies a general recovery of what has been lost. The rendering in NIV, *bring my people . . . from captivity*, obscures an important distinction between the general announcement of hope, "restore the fortunes" (RSV), and the specifics, one of which was *restore them to the land.* Recovery of the land is the chief emphasis of chapter 30. The recovery of a relationship with God, earlier broken, is the subject of chapter 31. *[Future-time Formulae, p. 298; Restoration Formula, p. 307.]*

The book is about the future of two groups, Israel and Judah. Israel, strictly defined as the northern 10 tribes with Samaria as the capital, had been brought to an end by the Assyrian takeover in 721. *[Map, p. 317.]* In this chapter Israel is also called Jacob, Rachel, and Ephraim. Judah will be restored as well (31:23-24; 38-40). Both groups are included in the new covenant (31:31-34).

In chapter 30 the oracles build on images of breaking a yoke, healing a wound, and removing reproach.

## 30:4-9 *"I Will Break the Yoke"*

First comes the good news about deliverance from enemy bondage—after pain comes freedom! This deliverance oracle has these parts: (1) a description of a stressful situation, (vv. 5-7); (2) a straightforward announcement of the Lord's action (v. 8a+b); and (3) a brief mention of the sequel or outcome (v. 9). The tone, set by the question, *Ask and see . . .* is somewhat argumentative. The oracle is the "pronouncement of salvation" type. *[Deliverance Oracles, p. 295.]*

The identity of the *we* in "we have heard" is not clear (v. 5, RSV). The NASB, to correspond with verse 6, reads "I." The "we" is best retained, however, to introduce a quotation by the people. Such quotations as lead-ins to a salvation oracle are found elsewhere (31:17b-21; Ezek. 37:11ff.). Following this quotation by the people, the Lord speaks. He depicts Israel's dire situation: she is in intense agony, writhing in extreme pain like a woman giving birth—a vivid image to people accustomed to witnessing births in homes.

The *time of trouble for Jacob* is elsewhere described as the "day of the Lord" (Amos 5:18; Isa. 2:12-21; Joel 1). It is the day monopolized by the Lord, a day when he visibly dominates the stage. One aspect of this *day* is the judgment of evil, whether of Israel or the nations.

Here judgment and salvation, the one following so soon on the other like bad and good news on the same day, are in tension (cf. Dan. 12:1). Whereas judgment oracles supply a careful rationale, the salvation announcement is presented without explanation other than God's decision (v. 8). As sometimes is done in the Hebrew, the pronouns are not consistent throughout; hence the variety in translations. The sense is that God will break the yoke by which nations (Assyria, Babylon) hold Israel and Judah in servitude. Verses 8-9 are helpfully rendered in poetry in NIV, rather than prose (NASB, RSV).

On that wonderful day the people will at last serve the Lord—in sharp contrast to their former service to foreign gods (v. 9; cf. 13:10; 16:11). New leadership from the family of David will be raised up (cf. v. 31). References to David and the messianic ideal are relatively few in Jeremiah (cf. 23:5-6; 33:14-16, 17-26; Ezek. 34:23-24; 37:24-25).

And what is the time of "Jacob's trouble" and Israel's deliverance? Jewish rabbis identified these as the pre-messianic days. Some Christians have placed these far forward to an end-time tribulation period. Its calendering cannot be pinpointed. Its message to the people of the sixth century, as to people in trouble in any age, is that God can seize the initiative, and will.

### 30:10-11 "I Am with You and Will Save You"

Another deliverance oracle tumbles into view. This oracle is addressed to *Jacob*, meaning all of Israel and Judah. The word of consolation, *Do not fear*, is typical of the "assurance oracle" and is found in Isaiah 43:1, 5. *I am with you* is found in Jeremiah's call (1:8, 19). [*Deliverance Oracles, p. 295; Divine Assistance Formula, p. 295.*]

God declares he will save the nation, though he will first discipline it. Yet even the discipline will be in justice, so that Ephraim will acknowledge, "You disciplined me like an unruly calf" (31:18). It is training that corrects but does not overcorrect (cf. 10:24). The language is reminiscent of Hosea, from whom Jeremiah seems to draw frequently (cf. Hos. 7:12, 15; 10:10). The promise *I will . . . save you* suggests entry into a wide spaciousnessness—the opposite of *distress*, which is restriction and confinement (v. 7). "Saving" is return of the exiles to their homeland. The indestructibility of God's people is a part of the overall comfort (v. 11; cf. 31:35-37). This oracle reappears in 46:27-28. [*Discipline, p. 295; Doublets, p. 296.*]

### 30:12-17a "I Will Restore You to Health"

Still another deliverance oracle follows, this time around the image of healing. Israel is pictured as a physical body in pain. A key word is "struck," translated as *injury* (v. 12), and *wounds* (v. 17). The hurt is not that of sickness but of inflicted strokes resulting in brokenness, "hurt" (v. 12, RSV), for which there is no healing. Verse 14 is literally, "I have struck with the striking of an enemy." Isaiah uses an image similar to this in 1:5-6.

In the middle of talk about wounds is courtroom language: *There is no one to plead your cause.* This phrase seems to mix the metaphors but is actually a clue to the meaning of the oracle. The Jewish rendering is, "None deemeth of thy wound that it may be bound up" (v. 13 JPS; cf. "No salve for your sore," Bright: 271). It is not a bodily injury but politically devastating blows to a society that are in view. The "lovers" are Israel's allies, Egypt, or perhaps neighboring nations (v. 14; cf. 27:1ff.). God has precipitated the blows. The reason is twice stated: *because of your great guilt* and "your sins are flagrant" (RSV).

The same God who injures also promises *I will restore you to health*—a preliminary step which means dealing effectively with the enemies (v. 16). This is once more a political note and one found in all the salvation oracles in this chapter (vv. 8, 11, 20). With its remonstrating question (v. 15), the speech form can be classed as a "pronouncement of salvation." *[Deliverance Oracles, p. 295.]*

### 30:17b-22 "I Will Bring Them Honor"

Once more the imagery changes. Now the poet speaks about sheep shelters and tents. Attention to speech forms as well as context shows that verse 17b belongs to a new oracle. Here is an allusion to a lament, as is fitting for the "announcement of salvation." *Zion* is problematic and apparently represents some textual confusion for *tso'n* (flock), so that a better rendering would be: "Indeed, 'driven-off,' they designate you, 'She is a flock none seeks.' " But the Lord's position is to reverse that nasty situation. *[Deliverance Oracles, p. 295; Restoration Formula, p. 307.]*

*Jacob's tents* refers to dwellings as well as to the occupants, "Jacob's clans" (NEB; cf. "tents of Joseph," Ps. 78:67; "tents of Edom," Ps. 83:6). God's compassion results in a reconstruction program both of buildings and of a solid society. Note the alteration of intervention, *I will add . . . bring . . . honor*, with the resulting consequences, *they will not be decreased . . . not be disdained* (vv. 19-21). Bestowal of honor and "home rule" counters the opening dismal scene of a dispersed and despised "flock." God will redress the situation in which people are derided.

The theme of the restoration of fortunes is repeated in a warmly human image, "Their sons will be what they once were" (v. 20, NEB). In all, there is recovery of (1) dwellings, (2) a sizable and solid society, (3) a reputation, and (4) leadership. The leader will not be some puppet appointee, like Zedekiah (the current king), but priestlike. The future leader will rule at the Lord's invitation; he will be intimate with God. Verse 21 has the sense of who of himself or of his own accord would pledge himself to be near to God, except that God put it in his heart? An alternative but less acceptable interpretation is, it is deadly to appear before God without being summoned (cf. Lev. 16:1ff.). The oracle builds toward a climax, namely the goal of a people in covenant with God—a goal long ago envisioned (Exod. 6:7). [Covenant Formula, p. 294.]

### 30:23-24 Guaranteed!

Should there still be doubt about deliverance despite the repeated oracles, Jeremiah adds a final refrain. Was it perhaps a well-known refrain? It appears as a doublet also in the harangue against the false prophets (23:19-20). The wrath against the wicked must be understood as against Israel's enemies, who have been mentioned in each of the four preceding oracles (vv. 8, 11, 16, 20). Seen here in each oracle as freedom to return to the homeland, Israel's deliverance is possible only when those who hold her down have been subdued. That victory is guaranteed but will become reality only later, that is, following the judgment, which at the time of the oracle is still future. [Doublets, p. 296; Wrath, p. 313.]

(For reflections see pp. 197-199.)


## The Recovery of a Relationship  31:1-40

So the good news is that the hold of the enemy will be broken—there will be release from captivity and recovery of a normal life in the homeland (30:1ff.). There is to be even better news! The people will be spiritually restored into right-relatedness with God! (31:1ff.). It was the absence of that relationship which had brought the loss of land and their captivity in the first place.

### 31:1-9 "I Am Israel's Father"

In chapter 31 the images change to describe God: as father, shepherd, mother, covenant-maker.

At that time resumes the theme of "days are coming" when God will restore the fortunes (30:3). Beginning with 31:1 the spotlight is on the recovery of a people's relationship to God. [Restoration Formula, p. 307; Covenant Formula, p. 294.]

As in other announcement-of-salvation oracles, this oracle (vv. 2-6) opens with a sketch of a pathetic situation—refugees in the desert (cf. 30:17b). The refugees could be those of the Exodus (cf. Hos. 2:14ff.) but more likely include those of both catastrophes—in 721 and in 586— since the address is to *all the clans of Israel.* These survivors, especially of the 586 deportation, had lost virtually everything—home, temple, and land; and were perhaps not sure of God. Into this bleakness God appeared "from a distance" ( RSV, NASB) or *in the past* (NIV). *[Deliverance Oracles, p. 295.]*

Only here in Jeremiah is there mention of love with God as subject. *"Loving-kindness"* is too anemic for the Hebrew term *(ḥesed),* which occurs 245 times in the Old Testament and means "covenant love, covenant loyalty" (see Exod. 34:6; Ps. 136). In a direct, personable way the Lord gives of himself to his people, for their well-being is his concern. Augustine, the fourth-century theologian, said that God loves each one of us as if there were only one of us to love.

Three successive Hebrew lines of poetry open with *Again* (vv. 4f.). Again there will be happiness in social life *(dance),* in physical work (harvest), and in worship (going to Zion). How so? God will bring it about. In a parallel triad God says, *"I have loved you," "I have drawn you," "I will build you up."* *Ephraim* is a name for Israel often used in Hosea (cf. 31:18; Hos. 5:3-14). *Zion* is Jerusalem. This is a vision of Israel united in worship.

This salvation oracle (vv. 7-9) reminds one of the Lord's war in which victory shouts preceded the military engagement (Josh. 6:20). Praise for the Lord's help is given even as that help is asked: "The Lord has saved his people" (v. 7, RSV, following the Septuagint).

This is a picture of an exodus, not now from Egypt but from the north country (cf. 23:7-8; Isa. 51:9-11). God's tender watch-care in looking after the blind and lame and others without strength is like that of a father (cf. Hos. 11:1ff.; Deut. 32:6). On their part, the exiles' weeping is either for their sin which occasioned the exile, or for their uncontrollable joy in their release. God's love in verse 3 and his fatherlike care in verse 9 hold the intervening material together like brackets.

## 31:10-14 *"Like a Shepherd the Lord Will Watch over His Flock"*

This oracle continues the portrait of God as a saving God. The summons here is to *nations,* who are to be informed of God's deliverance and recognize that the very same God who judges, disciplines, and scatters a people is also the one who regathers—a theme in Ezekiel (Ezek. 36:16-23). The God who inflicted injurious blows will heal (30:14, 17).

This oracle describes the provision of God, not as a father as in verses 7-9, but as a shepherd. *Ransom* and *redeem* are strong theological words used in the Exodus story (Exod. 4:23; Deut. 7:8; 15:15), and also in legislation about a substitute "buying out" the firstborn who belonged to the Lord (Exod. 13; 34:20). The basic idea of *ransom* comes from commercial law and refers to the transfer of ownership achieved through a purchase price. The Hebrew word for *redeem* does not have a commercial but a family setting: redemption from difficulty or danger was the privilege and duty of a near relative.

The result of God's work will be joy—rejoicing in fruitfulness of field and flock, celebration and worship. This great exchange of comfort for sorrow is elaborated in Isaiah 61:2-3.

### 31:15-22 "I Have Great Compassion for . . . Rachel, for Ephraim, and for Virgin Israel"

After the climax of joy, the poet starts once more with the problem: a people languishing in exile. This oracle is a triple exposure, showing first two persons, Rachel (the mother) and Ephraim (the son), each in tears. Next, God bends over each to comfort. Another snapshot on the same frame shows the daughter, Virgin Israel, as she could be. The word "turn" or "return" figures prominently, and that in the double sense of coming back to God and coming home to the land.

The opening scene of a woman weeping uncontrollably arouses sympathy. Rachel, the second of Jacob's two wives, was the mother of Joseph and Benjamin (Gen. 30:24; 35:18), and so the grandmother of Ephraim and Manasseh. These two tribes occupied the largest territories to the north, and so the northern ten tribes were referred in shorthand as Ephraim. *Ramah*, five miles north of Jerusalem on the boundary between Judah and Israel, was near the burial site of Rachel (1 Sam. 10:2ff.). Ramah was the place where Jeremiah was released into freedom (40:6). *[Map, p. 316.]*

Rachel's children [who] *are no more* (i.e., with her in the land) are the ten tribes, large numbers of whom had been taken into exile by Assyria in 721. The *work* of weeping will be rewarded by the return of the exiles to the homeland. No motivation or reason is given for such a promise. Rachel, it seems, must cling to the bald statement: *There is hope for your future* (cf. Jer. 29:10-14).

A dialogue between Ephraim and the Lord follows (v. 18ff.). Ephraim is shown in repentant position, acknowledging God's discipline or chastening, which consists of instruction, rebuke, and correction. Ephraim, "rocking in his grief," says, "I have come to myself" (v. 19, NEB).

The past is reviewed under the figure of straying like an unruly calf. There are language similarities here to Hosea (Hos. 10:10-11; 11:2ff.; 14:2). Sorrow for the wrong is captured in *I beat my breast,* literally "thighs," a gesture of remorse (Ezek. 21:17). *[Discipline, p. 295.]*

The verb "turn" is used five times in verses 15-22. It refers both to coming home to the land and coming home to God. Without excuse or blame-passing, Ephraim says, *"I was ashamed and humiliated."* Gone is the arrogance. Ephraim prays, totally cast upon God, *"Restore me,"* (lit., "turn") *"and I will return."* God is embraced anew: *you are the Lord my God* (v. 18). The vocabulary is like that of the repentance prayer prescribed in 3:22-25, with which this confession should be compared (cf. also 14:7-9, 20-22). Repentance is seen as a turning, first from disgraceful ways, and then to God, without reservation. *[Repentance, p. 306.]*

God replies that he not only owns this son, but owns him as a favored son (v. 20). I "remember him vividly." Though *I often speak against him* is a reference to admonitions and warnings found profusely in Jeremiah. One might also render simply, "As oft as I mention his name. . . ." (Bright: 275).

God is speaking here as mother. The Hebrew word for *compassion* has the same root as "womb." Compare Joseph yearning for his brother (Gen. 43:30) or more aptly, the woman whose "compassion grew warm" (1 Kings 3:26). God unhesitantly declares, "I will truly show motherly compassion upon him." God and Ephraim have found each other. That is really why Rachel can hope.

In verses 21-22 the commands are in feminine gender. A daughter, *Virgin Israel* is now addressed. The switch from masculine to feminine for the same subject is also found in Jeremiah 3:12f., 19f. As earlier, the summons to *return* implies both a "returning to the land" and "returning to God." *Road signs* envision physical travel (v. 21). *How long will you wander,* turnable daughter? supports a moral and spiritual interpretation of the word "turn" (v. 22; cf. 3:12).

Verse 22 has been described as the most difficult verse in Jeremiah. The words are straighforward, but even so the sense is blurred. Jerome in the fourth century interpreted *a woman will surround a man* as the virginal conception of Christ. The *new thing* God creates may be a reversal of roles, such that in war or in sex, women become aggressive. Still another interpretation is literary. The two poems, one about the woman *Rachel* (v. 15), and the other of the *Virgin Israel* (vv. 21-22), *surround* the poem about the male *Ephraim.* Or, we may have here a common proverb whose sense is lost to us but which might depict an upside-down state of affairs.

Any interpretation must come to terms with the *new thing*, which, like the "new covenant" (v. 31), God will *create*—a word used only with God as subject. Formerly God encompassed the woman Israel. In the new situation the Virgin Israel, a woman, will embrace a man (lit., "strong man"), here intended as God. Following the prayer, *"Restore me, and I will return,"* and anticipating the new covenant, this pithy comment underlines the radical nature of the new situation which God will bring about. Now it is clearer why Rachel can be comforted. God will intervene and spring a surprise.

### 31:23-26 "I Will Refresh the Weary"

So far much has been said about Israel, the northern tribes, and the good news for them. This short "portrayal of salvation" is restricted to Judah (vv. 23-24). It opens with a promise of recovery of what has been lost (cf. 30:3, 18). The formula translated *bring them back from captivity* includes more than physical restoration (cf. comment at 30:1). The restored people will be enthusiastic about worship at the temple hill, God's *righteous dwelling*. Farmers and shepherds—two groups who often clashed—will peacefully coexist; and God, always with an eye out to the weak among the group, will refresh and sustain those who are weak (Isa. 40:31). *[Restoration Formula, p. 307; Deliverance Oracle, p. 295.]*

The unexpected comment about awaking from sleep may mean, "This is like a dream, too good to be true!" Earlier messages were bitter because of sin and punishment; this word was pleasant.

### 31:27-30 In Coming Days: A Solid Society

The three remaining oracles are uniformly introduced with *days are coming*. The first uses the language of Jeremiah's call—*build and plant, uproot and overthrow*—together with the important word *watch* (1:10, 12). The replenishment of the population is a vital post-deportation concern (31:17; Ezek. 36:10). The proverb about grapes makes the point that though the fathers have sinned, *eaten sour grapes*, it is not the fathers but their children who bear the consequences, *whose teeth are set on edge* or blunted. The proverb overstates the principle in order to emphasize inequity. The principle of group solidarity and group responsibility, illustrated in the Achan story, remains (Josh. 7). The full explanation about individual responsibility is given in Ezekiel 18:1-29. True, Jeremiah challenged collective responsibility, but Kuist's comment goes too far in seeing the stress on individual responsibility as Jeremiah's "most significant single teaching" (Kuist: 23). *[Future-time Formulae, p. 298.]*

## 31:31-34  In Coming Days: A New Covenant

In modern Ethiopian culture, the word "covenant" is seldom used because it is such a strong word. One of the strongest statements about that potent word is made in this oracle. The new covenant picks up a relationship after the old one is broken.

In some ways this passage is the apex of Old Testament salvation history. It has been described as "one of the profoundest and most moving passages in the entire Bible" (Bright: 287). It looks back to the covenant at Sinai, and forward to the the work of the Messiah. Quoted in full in Hebrews 8:7-12, this is the longest Old Testament passage repeated in the New Testament. In fact, it is from the mention of "new covenant" in this passage that we get the designation, the NEW TESTA-MENT, first given by Origen, an early church father.

The oracle does not fully conform to any of the four salvation oracles. Stripped of all else it has the basics: God will intervene; a new situation will result. The acts of intervention clearly predominate, as shown in the "I will" assertions and the four statements *declares the Lord.* Perhaps the oracle was initially addressed only to Israel, as has been suggested on the basis of verse 33. Then, following the Judah disaster, Judah was incorporated also. In New Testament times the promise incorporated Gentiles, for the discussion in Hebrews about the encompassing work of Christ begins and ends with reference to Jeremiah's new covenant (Heb. 8:8-12; 10:16, 17). The covenant of a deity with a people, as of God with Israel at Sinai, is singular in world religions. *[Covenant, p. 294; Deliverance Oracles, p. 295.]*

The Sinai covenant (Exod. 19:5-6) has been broken, says Jeremiah, and therefore terminated, dissolved, voided, and annulled, not first by God's action but by the action of the people (cf. 11:10). The foundation element of loyalty has been flagrantly violated through Israel's disobedience and so the relationship hangs in tatters. " . . . the old covenant is broken, and in Jeremiah's view Israel is altogether without one" (von Rad: 212). The statement with an emphatic first person, *I, I was a husband* to them, shows how reprehensible was Israel's action in breaking with him, for the Hebrew term *(ba'al)* can mean both "husband" as in a marriage relationship, or "lord" (cf. 3:14). As "lord," God is in a position, however, to frame a new covenant with new terms.

The Sinai law was written on tablets of stone. Formerly the law was "set before the people" (Jer. 9:12; Deut. 4:8; 11:32). That is, it was not in their hearts. Jeremiah repeatedly emphasizes the evil in human hearts (3:17; 7:24; 9:14; 11:8; 17:1). Now God's *law* (better, "instruction") will be put in the inner being (Ezek. 11:19; 36:26; Deut. 6:6, 20). The priests, scribes, and prophets until now have been mediators of knowledge; but their services will no longer be needed since each person will *know*, in the sense of "experience," God individually. Since different "teachings" make for rivalry, the dispensing with teachers could imply the end of rivalry. *From the least . . . to the greatest* suggests also that elitism will be gone. The particular verb for *forgive* throughout the Old Testament always has God for its subject (e.g. Isa. 55:7; cf. Num. 14:17-20; Ps. 103:3). *[Knowing God, p. 301.]*

The covenant objective, *"I will be their God, and they will be my people,* remains in force (31:1; 30:22; *[Covenant Formula, p. 294.]).* The new covenant is like the old in that:

1. God (the same God) takes the initiative.
2. The covenant is based on God's law (the same law).
3. The goal of the covenant (the same goal) is an intimate relationship: "I will be their God, and they will be my people."

The new covenant is "new" in that:

1. The demands of the covenant will be met through a God-given internalized provision.
2. The experience of God will be direct and unmediated.
3. Forgiveness is the new covenant's cornerstone. "It draws a definite, final line under all of our past life" (Wolff: 61).

The "newness" is more a newness of emphasis, for the old Sinaitic covenant did hint at inwardness. The law was to be internalized in the heart (Deut. 30:6; Ps. 37:31). Forgiveness too was incorporated in the old covenant (Exod. 34:6; Lev. 4:31, 35). Now forgiveness becomes a cornerstone of the relationship. Jeremiah's covenant was new in that it followed the collapse of the old covenant and was addressed to a people who were without covenant. It was new, as we now know, in that it centered in the God-man, Jesus; for in the fullest sense, this prophecy was fulfilled only through the work of Christ (Luke 2:20; 1 Cor. 11:24; Heb. 8:7-13).

## 31:35-37 Guaranteed by Oath!

Just as the section on the recovery of land concluded with a guarantee (30:22-24), so the oracles about the recovery of a close relationship to God conclude with a guarantee—a double guarantee in the form of an oath.

The message is that Israel will not be annihilated even though she will be decimated. Israel is indestructible. Of that fact we today are witnesses. For the creation motif in Jeremiah, see 10:12-13; 27:5; 32:17; 33:3. [Lord of Hosts, p. 304.]

### 31:38-40  In Coming Days: A Rebuilt City

Like the oracle of 31:23-26, this oracle has Judah in focus, specifically Jerusalem. The city, devastated by the Babylonians in 587 (an event now past), will be rebuilt. The *Tower of Hananel* was located in Jerusalem's northern wall (Neh. 3:1; 12:39; Zech. 14:10). *The Corner Gate* in the northwest of the city was first built by Uzziah, 783-742 (2 Chron. 26:9). *The hills of Gareb and . . . Goah* mentioned only here, are believed to have been located respectively in the southwest and southeast of the city.

Rebuilding of the city was the major undertaking of Nehemiah when he returned from the exile about 445 (Neh. 2:11-18; 6:15). Preoccupation with the *measuring line* characterizes the description of the future temple (Ezek. 40—48; Zech. 2). Understandably, the rebuilding of Jerusalem was of great concern to everyone, not only because politically and economically it stood at the heart of their country, but also because religiously it was the place where God dwelt.

### THE TEXT IN BIBLICAL CONTEXT

*The Communal Nature of God's People.* The frequency of "I will be their God, and they shall be my people" emphasizes God's intention to form a people. Indeed the determination to do so is the more pronounced in that, with the disruption caused by the exile about to be a reality, God's purpose is not only often repeated, but provision for it is made in the birthing of the new covenant. Centuries later, a nucleus of disciples becomes the core for an enlarged peoplehood at Pentecost. This community is not some miscellaneous collection of individuals, but a "charter group" committed to Christ and his kingdom. God's people are kingdom people.

*The New Testament's Use of the Old Testament.* Our chapters contain two texts which are quoted in the New Testament and which offer examples of the meaning of the word 'fulfillment." The statement about Rachel weeping in Ramah is a description of the loss experienced with the exiles in 587. Matthew cites this Jeremiah text as being "fulfilled" in Herod's slaughter of the infants (Matt. 2:17-18). However, Jeremiah's statement is not a prediction, but a fact of past history. "Fulfilled" means "corresponds with."

The promise of a new covenant, on the other hand, is in the nature of a prediction. It is given specifically to Jews, the house of Israel and Judah; but the fulfillment is in Jesus (Heb. 8:7-16), through whom the target group becomes enlarged to embrace Gentiles. In both these instances, the New Testament writers were not afraid to give expanded meanings to Old Testament statements.

## THE TEXT IN THE LIFE OF THE CHURCH

*The New Covenant: A Large Promise.* In the new covenant there is pictured a new day, the birth of a new order. The word of hope in this promise is most reassuring, for it takes into account the fundamental reason for past failures: a faltering will and an inability to follow God.

One may track the fulfillment of the new covenant in the church, beginning with Jesus. He brought the promise of the new covenant to mind with the Last Supper (Matt. 26:28; Mark 14:24; Luke 22:20; cf. 1 Cor. 11:25). Writing to the early church, Paul referred to the "ministers of the new covenant" and the future experience for Israel of forgiveness (2 Cor. 3:6; Rom. 11:27). The author of Hebrews quoted the Jeremiah covenant passage in full, stressing that Jesus Christ was a fulfillment of the promise of new covenant (Heb. 8:7ff.; cf. 9:15, 10:16, and 12:24).

There are several ways to think about fulfillment of prophecy. One way is to jot in the margin beside every announcement a date for its fulfillment. For example, Israel's captors were subdued in 539 (promised in 30:8). The people, at least some, did return (Ezra 8:1ff., promised in 31:17). The city of Jerusalem was rebuilt (Neh. 1—6, promised in 31:38). The new covenant promised in 31:31 was put into force with the work of Christ (Heb. 8:7ff.).

But these announcements have an ongoing character about them which such calendaring obscures. A single fulfillment does not exhaust the promise: the future remains open. For example, the restoration to the land fell short in the long run of the beautiful description in 31:11-14. The new covenant is in one sense fulfilled, for a new heart, a new willingness to do God's law, has come; but teaching and catechism are still necessary. This is the nature of biblical promise. Though realized in part, there is often a remaining element that continues to carry the hope for a still better day. It is not that the announcements are untrue; rather, they are true in so rich a sense that pinpointing a "fulfillment" does not exhaust them. They live on.

So Jeremiah's programmatic word finds a new fulfillment in the new community which Jesus brings about. In this community one finds people with a new heart; there is also forgiveness. But even there fulfillment is not final, for teaching is still necessary in the home, in the Sunday school, and in the seminary: "Know the Lord." God showed Jeremiah a distant future when all would know the Lord directly and without instruction. "It means the final end of the teaching profession" (Wolff: 51). In that sense the hope of the new covenant is still future.

Incidentally, the state of Israel still affirms hope for future possession of the land, as voiced in its national anthem:

> . . . our hope is not yet lost,
> the hope of two thousand years
> to be a free people in our land,
> in the land of Zion and Jerusalem.

*God as Father . . . and Mother?* Our chapter has an explicit statement about God as father (31:9), and an implicit statement about God with qualities of compassion (womb) associated with mother (31:20). Elsewhere God is depicted as travailing like a mother (Isa. 42:14; cf. 66:13). However, nowhere in the Old Testament is God designated as feminine, or addressed as mother. In this way, Old Testament belief contrasts strikingly with the female deities of the Canaanite religions.

Elizabeth Achtemeier, an Old Testament scholar, writes, "In the Old Testament, Israel is surrounded by peoples who worship goddesses such as the baalistic Canaanite Astarte and Asherah, known through fertility cults. Unfortunately, female terminology for God does not stand alone. It participates in a metaphor system that includes fertility, sexuality and birth. But the biblical God is not known through fertility cults, and Yahweh is totally different from the deities of baal religion. The Old Testament wants no confusion about this" *(The Presbyterian Outlook,* Nov. 14, 1983).

The complete absence of mother God language and the perversions which have been associated with female deities have been cited as reasons for avoiding talk about God our mother. God is neither male nor female but is beyond sexual designations.

Jeremiah 32 – 33

# Reversing a People's Fortunes

**PREVIEW**

Restoration is ahead! How will it happen? These chapters zoom into focus on Jerusalem. The Babylonian siege is under way; it will last one and a half years. According to Jeremiah's word, the city will be burned. And is the final destiny of the city to be ashes? In these chapters the answer is NO! God takes the burned-up and burned-out city and reverses its fate—it will be built up and glorious.

The last two chapters of the Book of Consolation are in prose, in contrast to the poetry of 30—31. These two chapters of the Book of Consolation take up the themes of the two former chapters, such as the regathering of a people, the return of a people, commercial revitalization, worship, spiritual renewal, and provisions for leadership. A symbolic business transaction launches the hope-filled oracles.

**OUTLINE (Condensed)**

About Repopulation and Rulers, 33:1-26
  33:1-13      The Resettlement of Jerusalem
  33:14-26     The Reinstatement of Leaders

## EXPLANATORY NOTES

### About Real Estate and Renewal 32:1-44

The chapter tells of a land purchase, reports a prophet's prayer, and makes a series of predictions about Jerusalem. For once a symbolic action conveys good news.

### 32:1-15 A Prisoner's Purchase

Zedekiah was Judah's last king. His tenth year—the date for the real-estate purchase—is 588/587. Nebuchadnezzar became the ruler of the Babylonians, also called "Chaldeans," following the battle at Carchemish in 605. The Babylonian siege is described in chapter 39, which means that here again the arrangement of the material is not chronological, but topical. The siege is a significant setting for what follows, since it makes the real-estate purchase by the prophet so odd, even preposterous. [Kings of Judah, p. 300; Nebuchadnezzar, p. 304.]

The guardhouse, where Jeremiah was held in custody, was in the palace area and allowed the prophet some freedom of movement. Later he was put in a cistern (38:6). Zedekiah had reasons for keeping him under surveillance. The prophet's message was demoralizing to the war effort, and was also most unflattering to the king, if not a personal affront (cf. 21:3-8; 27:12-15). Any resistance to Babylon, Jeremiah was saying, would be pointless because God was fighting against Judah.

Anathoth, two miles from Jerusalem, was the prophet's home. Hanamel, Jeremiah's cousin, urged Jeremiah to purchase his property according to the provision of Leviticus 25:25-28. This law held that if a man was in danger of losing his property for reasons of poverty or debt, a family member, the nearest relative, was to buy it. The first right of possession was both a privilege and a duty. Nearer relatives may have declined the purchase because of the siege conditions. One may infer from "Then I knew . . ." (v. 8, RSV) that Jeremiah was at first uncertain about the origin of this message.

Jeremiah had made other purchases (13:1; 19:1). Land transactions are also found elsewhere in the Old Testament (Gen. 23; Ruth 4:7), but nowhere is the procedure of sale so detailed. In ancient times silver shekels were of various sizes; hence the use of scales (cf. Gen. 23:16). Only later were these considered coins. Shekels weighed two fifths of an ounce (= 11.5 grams). If so, the price was just under seven ounces of silver.

One copy of the deed was signed by the purchaser and sealed. To it was attached a rolled-up but unsealed copy so that the contents of the deed, together with instructions of sale, could be reviewed without breaking the seal. Such copies are known both from Elephantine in Egypt and from mid-twentieth century excavations in the Judean desert. Baruch, Jeremiah's scribe, mentioned here for the first time, becomes custodian of the documents, which are placed in jars, the safety vaults of the times. Similar jars were found in the 1947 discoveries at Qumran near the Dead Sea. *[Baruch, p. 292.]*

The entire incident is more than a report of an investment; it is a symbolic action. A financial transaction is surely not the usual setting for the word from the Lord! The interpretation, given succinctly in verse 15 and elaborated in verses 36-44, contains hope beyond the present tragedy. *[Symbolic Action, p. 311.]*

## 32:16-25 It Doesn't Add Up—a Prayer

The absurdity of a land purchase during a military siege in which, according to the prophet's own word, the enemy would win, brings Jeremiah to second thoughts and drives him to prayer. After 40 years of ineffective preaching to an increasingly degraded society, he has scarce grounds for hope.

A recalling of creation is found elsewhere in Jeremiah (10:12-13; 27:5; 33:2) and in prayers in stressful times (Isa. 37:16; Acts 4:24). After a historical review of God's acts, the point of the prayer is reached in verse 25. To Jeremiah it must have seemed that all the former oracles of judgment were canceled out. He appears profoundly puzzled. The build-up of his prayer, which turns around the Hebrew words "make" ('asah, variously translated) and "power" can be shown in the following.

| God In | Making ('asah) | Addressed As | Characterized As |
|---|---|---|---|
| Creation v. 17 | "heaven and earth" | Lord God Sovereign Lord | powerful with outstretched arm |
| Early human history v. 19 | steadfast love, v. 18 | Lord of hosts "Lord Almighty" | great and powerful doing signs and wonders |
| Israelite history, vv. 20b-23 | yourself a name, renown | | strong hand, outstretched arm, signs and wonders |

## 32:26-35   Jerusalem Will Burn!

The Lord's answer to Jeremiah's prayer begins with a self-identification not unlike God's "I AM" to Moses (Exod. 3:14). An understanding of who God is puts this crushing situation of the moment in new perspective. *Is anything too hard for me?* is a repeat of Jeremiah's own confession of faith which he had voiced, but the implications of which he had not grasped (v. 17; cf. Gen. 18:14; Eph. 3:20). The symmetry of structure of verses 26-35 and 36-41 should not be missed.

---

**Proposition: Nothing is too hard for me.**

| | |
|---|---|
| Therefore, v. 28 | Therefore, v. 36 (omitted in NIV) |
| re. immediate situation, v. 28 | re. immediate situation, v. 36 |
| fiery destruction, v. 29 | intervention for deliverance, vv. 37-40 |
| (because of) their evil, vv. 30-35 | (because) I choose to do them good, v. 41 |

---

The *burning* of Jerusalem, ironically, is the response to the housetop *burning* of incense (cf. 7:17-19; 19:13). Jerusalem was an old city; it is mentioned in the *Egyptian Execrations Texts* early in the second millennium. It became a Hebrew city when David's men took it from the Jebusites in the tenth century (2 Sam. 5:6ff.). It is also, Jeremiah charges, a wicked city. Israel's history is entirely shot through by evil (v. 30; compare the striking historical review in Ezekiel 20:4-26.) The offensive evil of the city resides first in its leaders (v. 32). *They would not listen* occurs with nauseating frequency. It was Manasseh, a century earlier, who placed an idol in the temple (2 Kings 21:4-5). Human sacrifices for pagan gods, Baal and Molech, are noted by both the prophet (7:31) and the historian (2 Kings 21:6). With a judgment oracle like this Jeremiah is thoroughly familiar. *[Obey/Listen, p. 305; Baal, p. 291; Tophet, p. 312.]*

## 32:36-44   Jerusalem Will Flourish!

But the salvation note, familiar to us and indeed almost expected, was then new and quite contrary to the judgment oracles. The salvation word is addressed head on into the stressful situation of the moment (v. 36). The link with Jeremiah's prayer is in *sword, famine, plague* (cf. v. 24). The themes of this "portrayal of salvation" are familiar from the previous two chapters: regathering and security (30:8, 10; 31:8ff.; cf. Deut. 30:1-5); restoration of covenantal intimacy (30:22; 31:1, 33); a heart transplant (31:33); and a physical replanting in the land together with showers of God's goodness (30:18-21; 31:3-6, 10-14, and especially 27f.). (See commentary in chapters 30—31.)

The restatement here of the new covenant fits with the style of this book, in which poetically-given announcements are repeated for an "echo" effect (v. 38ff.; 31:31-33). Parallelism is characteristic of Hebrew poetry. The reiterations, made for emphasis, are neither boring nor trite since fresh nuances are sometimes given in the echo section. Here, in a new twist, the covenant is hailed as *everlasting* (cf. Ezek. 37:26). The spring of action is God's goodness: *I will never stop doing good to them* (cf. 29:10-14). The consequence, also an addition to 31:31-34, is *I will inspire them to fear me*. Such fear is not fright, but the greatest of reverence which takes account of the enormous distance between the person and God.

Bustling commercial activity is now announced for Jerusalem and its satellite villages (vv. 42-44). Vigorous business life which was lost during Babylonian dominance will be restored. The borders of Benjamin are immediately north of Jerusalem. *The hill country* lies to the north; to the west are the coastal low hills, the Shephelah; and to the south lies the Negev, which includes Beersheba. *[Restoration Formula, p. 307; Map, p. 316.]*

## About Repopulation and Rulers  33:1-26

### 33:1-13  The Resettlement of Jerusalem

*Reaching for the Inaccessible, verses 1-3.* Jeremiah's circumstances remain unchanged; he is still in the *courtyard of the guard* (cf. 32:1-2). The language about creation invites comparison with 32:17 and other creation passages (10:12-13; 27:5). The "her" in the sentence *He who made the earth* (lit., "her"), might refer to "earth," but could equally well mean "city" or even "history" as such. *The Lord is his name* is a sign-off trademark found in hymnic pieces treating the creation (Amos 4:13; 5:8; 9:6). The announcement about the city, and about its leadership (vv. 19-26), is not wishful thinking but is grounded in nothing less than creation.

God dares Jeremiah to discover the totally unexpected (cf. Mal. 3:10). *Unsearchable* refers ordinarily to a well-fortified, virtually impregnable city (2 Kings 18:13). It is here used metaphorically to mean "inaccessible." (RSV, following another text, translates this "hidden.") God is ready to open the storehouses. He is not stingy with revelation to those who call.

*Jerusalem, the City with a Future, verses 4-9.* With startling effect, Jeremiah paints an optimistic picture about the future greatness of the city at this dismal time when the city is under siege! Beyond the military machine and the corpses, there is hope. Now there are broken-down houses and disfigured palaces! In the future, a city of renown! Now there are dead bodies everywhere, and God's face has turned away! In the future, there will be *health and healing,* with God's face turned toward the city, providing *abundant prosperity and peace! [Wrath, p. 313.]*

The themes echo the message of hope given in 30—31, punctuated, as there, with "I will restore the fortunes . . . ."(v. 7, cf. 30:3, 18). *I will cleanse them from all the sin* should be read against the catalog of sins listed in 32:30-35; 25:3-7; 7:17-26. (For the forgiveness of sins see 31:34.) Spiritual transformation, together with physical restoration, will result in the city bringing renown to God, which is God's purpose for all of Israel and Judah. This purpose has already been memorably stated in connection with the new girdle (13:10). The restoration of Israel is important for its impact on nations (v. 9, cf. 30:10ff.; Ezek. 36:16-23). We can see the elements of an "announcement of salvation": reference to a lament or plight (vv. 4-5); declaration of God's intervention (vv. 6-8) and goal (v. 9). *[Restoration Formula, p. 307; Deliverance Oracle, p. 295.]*

*Repopulating the City. verses 10-13.* The people's statement about *desolate waste, without men or animals* follows the fall of the city (cf. 32:43). God takes pains to make clear that precisely this hopeless situation will be turned about. Festivities and the normal happy activities, usually weddings (contrast 7:34; 16:9; 25:10), will return. Celebration is a hallmark of the coming age (30:19; 31:7). The worship scenes will involve thank offerings extolling God's goodness (cf. 31:6; 1 Chron. 16:34; Ezra 3:11). The pastoral scene includes shepherds at evening counting the incoming flock to ensure that none is missing.

The rhythmic repetition of themes in these adjoining passages is like a drumbeat announcing the good news of God's transformation. The chart shows both the themes and the essential repetition.

|                          | 32:26-44                   | 33:1-11                            |
| ------------------------ | -------------------------- | ---------------------------------- |
| **Description of God**   | "I am the Lord," 32:27     | God as Creator, 33:3               |
| **Situation of the city** | Babylonians attack, 32:29 | A fight with Babylonians, 33:5     |
|                          | "my anger," 32:29          | "my anger and wrath," 33:5         |
|                          | houses burned, 32:29       | houses torn down, 33:4             |
|                          | removal from God's sight, 32:31 | "I will hide my face," 33:5   |

| Promise of Deliverance regathering | "I will surely gather them," 32:37 | "I will restore the fortunes of . . ." 33:7 |
|---|---|---|
| renewal | "I will give them singleness of heart and action," 32:39 | "I will cleanse them from all the sin," 33:8 |
| joy | "I will rejoice in doing them good," 32:41 | "This city will bring me . . . joy," 33:9 |
| restoration | You say, "It is a desolate waste," 32:43 | You say: "It is a desolate waste, without . . . . 33:10 |
| | "I will restore the fortunes," 32:44 | "I will restore the fortunes," 33:11 |

## 33:14-26 The Reinstatement of Leaders

The gracious promise (lit., "good word") is that justice-bringing leadership will be reinstated. The name *The Lord Our Righteousness* is assigned to the future king in 23:6, but here to "her," namely the city Jerusalem, or perhaps Israel—both are regarded as feminine in Hebrew. Verse 17 reiterates a promise from the Davidic covenant (2 Sam. 7:13), fulfilled according to the New Testament in Jesus of the Davidic line. *[Justice, p. 299.]* (Compare comment on this doublet at 23:5-6.)

Levitical leadership, inaugurated with Aaron (Num. 8:19) and covenantally established with Phinehas, is reaffirmed (Num. 25:12-13; cf. Mal. 2:5). Both royal and religious leaders are held responsible for evil. Any hope then, must deal with royal and priestly leaders.

Both the Davidic and the Levitical covenant are made sure in an oathlike declaration that is anchored in creation (vv. 19-26). Here there is not, as in the Exodus incident, a story, part of the *Heilsgeschichte* as a setting for the covenant. Rather, here assurance is drawn from "behind the story of Israel," namely from creation—the basic order of existence on which rest the "irreducible attributes of deity."

Another oathlike statement combines the Davidic and the Abrahamic covenants. Here too for a second time, both are made sure, by tying them to the stability of creation, *day and night . . . heaven and earth* (vv. 23-26). The salvation oracle is in a response to a bad scene, specifically the mocking inference that the Lord has rejected the people (cf. v. 23; 33:10; 32:36; 32:43). Given the view that a god protects those who worship him, the conclusion of *these people*, namely other nations, is understandable. God refuses to let that conclusion stand (cf. Ezek. 36:17-23). The "two families" are Israel and Judah, though Rashi, a famous Jewish interpreter, took them to be the families of David and Aaron. The restoration formula, an inclusio, binds the entire Book of Consolation together (cf. 30:3). *[Restoration Formula, p. 307.]*

Verses 14-26 represent the largest continual section missing in the Septuagint. The concern is how to relate the various covenants—creation, Abrahamic, Levitical, Davidic—with the new covenant (31:31-34). These salvation oracles reaffirm each covenant to show that each continues in force. Essentially that means the continuance of Israel in human history. Israel will endure. So will the Levitical priesthood and the Davidic royalty. A similar conclusion is found in 31:36-38. *[Septuagint, p. 308].*

## THE TEXT IN BIBLICAL CONTEXT

*The Great Reversal.* Great cities in world history, such as London in the seventeenth century, have been destroyed by fire. A twentieth-century novelist in end-time mood writes about *The Burning of Los Angeles.* But people need to look beyond disaster. Like the myth of the phoenix bird resurrecting out of its ashes, this story tells of eternal hope.

How does one speak of the transforming work of God? Here it is pictured as the rebuilding of a city. Devastated Jerusalem is once more put on its spiritual and economic feet. Physically speaking, the rebuilding after the exile was not as spectacular as anticipated; yet in some ways, given the link of Jerusalem with Jesus, the city's renown exceeded what could have been imagined. The renovated city is described by the prophets (Isa. 65:17-19; Ezek. 48:30-35), and further anticipations of the "new" city, Jerusalem, are given in Hebrews (11:10) and Revelation (21).

*God's Goodness.* In chapter 33 God, his work, and his word are unequivocally declared to be good. The nature of God as good and his purposes as acts of goodness are affirmed throughout Scripture (e.g., Gen. 50:20; Ps. 106:1; Rom. 8:28). In this quality God is distinguished from capricious, often malevolent pagan deities, and also from the highly indifferent or quite unpredictable God of philosophy.

*Fitting the Covenants.* The new covenant of Jeremiah 31:31-34, with its echoes in 32:36-40 and 33:6-9, is the last of a series of Old Testament covenants: Noahic (Gen. 9:9), Abrahamic (Gen. 15:18), Sinaitic (Exod. 19:24), Levitical (Num. 25:12-13), and Davidic (2 Sam. 7:13). Some would list others.

Observations for further testing are:

1. Nowhere in Jeremiah or Ezekiel is the Abrahamic covenant invoked as a reason for Israel's return to the land. The land is described as given by God to the fathers, but the reasons for a return lie in another direction: (1) the unexplainable grace of God, (2) the honor of God's name, and (3) the means whereby nations would acknowledge God.

2. The new covenant is said specifically to supersede the Sinaitic covenant. Covenants with individuals, such as Abraham, Aaron, David, since they are not isolated from the people of Israel, are taken up in some sense into the new covenant. Thus the royal and priestly offices of the Davidic and Levitical covenants are caught up in the fulfillment of the new covenant in Christ. The hard-to-answer question is, Are the promises in these individual covenants thereby exhausted? That is, to cite an example, Is the promise of land which was made to Abraham still awaiting fulfillment?

## THE TEXT IN THE LIFE OF THE CHURCH

*The Creator's Invitation: Risk Great Things.* The prophet's purchase of property at a time of siege was a risk to his reputation as well as his finances. To reassure himself that all would be well, the prophet rehearsed some creation theology: "You have made the heavens and the earth. . . . Nothing is too hard for you." A review of God's acts in nature and history occurs frequently in Bible prayers (Neh. 9:6-37; Isa. 63:7—64:12; Dan. 9:4-19). Recalling God as Creator causes a new dimension to emerge in our praying. Our problems diminish, the resources grow.

To Jeremiah God replied that he, the Maker of the earth, would show to those who called upon him "great and mighty things" (33:3; cf. 29:10-14; Ps. 145:18; Isa. 58:9; Mark. 11:24; Matt. 7:7). That is, God's vast power as Creator is available to people. To move with God, often on the basis of his bare word, entails risk (cf. Abraham, Gen. 12:1; Gideon, Judg. 6—7). Yet to what extent is it really risk if we move in response to a God who is good? Is it not a far greater risk to "lean on our own understanding" and follow it rather than God? Said one pastor: "I know what *I* can do. I long to see what *God* can do. I'm for taking risks: if I'm to drown walking on water, I just as soon drown in deep water."

The birth of modern missions is traced to William Carey. On May 31, 1792, he preached from Jeremiah 33:3 with the appeal: "Expect great things from God; attempt great things for God." By June of the following year he was in India. Under his supervision Scripture was eventually translated into 35 languages and dialects.

Part 6

---

# Narratives About Wicked Leaders, a Suffering Prophet, and a Destroyed City

# Jeremiah 34—45

If the book were simply a story, then chapters 34—45 would be a climax. The warnings are not now as sharp as earlier, but the actual accounts of godlessness are appalling. God's judgment falls. Jerusalem is besieged, captured, and burned. The people, and Jeremiah especially, are subjected to great suffering. Since these are narratives about, rather than by, Jeremiah, it has been suggested, quite plausibly, that Baruch is the author. This section, then, could be designated "Baruch's narratives."

The disregard for God is illustrated by Zedekiah's unscrupulous treatment of the slaves and Jehoiakim's disdainful treatment of the scroll containing the Word of God. The disobedience of the people looks all the more appalling set over against the fierce loyalty of the Recabites.

God's act of punishment for such evils is in the form of an enemy invasion, and abruptly we are told of the Babylonian destruction of Jerusalem. Anguish, consternation, and confusion result when in the aftermath Gedaliah, the Babylon-appointed governor, is assassinated. A frightened remnant disregards Jeremiah's counsel and sets out for Egypt, Jeremiah among them.

The narrative is punctuated by the messages from God through Jeremiah to the kings Zedekiah and Jehoiakim, the people, Johanan the leader of the remnant, and to Baruch himself.

Jeremiah 34 – 36

# Repeat Message: Disobedience Dooms

## PREVIEW

Generalizations are necessary but seldom move people to action. Jeremiah has been confronting his audience with their failure to obey God. Now in these chapters specific—and major—incidents of such failure are described. Two incidents involve kings. These three chapters are arranged topically and not chronologically. For example, Zedekiah, the subject of chapter 34, succeeded Jehoiakim, mentioned in 35—36. [Kings of Judah, p. 300.] The overall structure of these three chapters is evident from the following chart.

## OUTLINE (Schematic)

| Chap. | Event | Addressee | Message |
|---|---|---|---|
| 34 | The freeing of the slaves; their reenslavement | Zedekiah | You have not obeyed me, v. 17 Disaster, vv. 18-22 |
| 35 | Offer of wine to the Recabites | Jerusalemites Judahites | Disaster, v. 17a They did not listen, v. 17b |

211

| 36 | Jehoiakim burns Jeremiah's scroll | Jehoiakim Jerusalemites Judahites | Disaster, v. 31 They did not listen, v. 31 |
|----|-----------------------------------|-----------------------------------|-------------------------------------------|

Of the three events, one involves the entire society, a second a family unit, and the third the personal action of a king. The same message emerges in each: disobedience to God brings doom.

## EXPLANATORY NOTES

### Going Back on One's Word 34:1-22

God's word to the prophet is about the everyday affairs of the people. Society had become layered: the have-nots were slaves to the haves. The first message, given specifically to Zedekiah, can be dated to 588 because the Babylonian siege is presented as in progress. The second message, about breaking a pact, follows the rescinding of liberty to the slaves, who had just been promised freedom.

### 34:1-7 Bad News and Good News for Zedekiah

The Babylonian army is laying siege to Jerusalem. The bad news is that they will win. The good news is that Zedekiah himself will not be killed in the fight. Zedekiah had heard about Jerusalem's fate and his own via messengers he had dispatched to the prophet (21:1-10). He now hears from Jeremiah personally. Jeremiah's "reward" is to be put into custody (32:3-5). The unwelcome news is that Zedekiah will be captured and will answer to Nebuchadnezzar for his conduct (i.e., his rebellion) and then be exiled. Verse 4 is best considered as a promise, conditional on the surrender by the king of the city to Babylon.

Provided he follows Jeremiah's counsel, Zedekiah will be spared a violent death, *You will not die by the sword.* "Yet you shall die in peace" (RSV) misses the force of a particle: "If only [you obey] you shall die in peace." The principle of conditional prophecy which applies here is laid out in Jeremiah 18:1-12. If Zedekiah meets the conditions, his funeral will be honorable, including a *funeral fire*, which according to some Jewish commentators involved a bonfire and the burning of the king's personal belongings; others hold that it was a matter of burning spices (RSV, NASB). A dignified burial for Zedekiah would contrast sharply with Jehoiakim's disgraceful one: a donkey's burial with absence of mourning, "Alas, O master" (22:18ff.). However, Zedekiah, under pressure from the "nationalist" party, disregards Jeremiah's counsel. As it turned out, he was captured and his eyes were gouged out (39:4-7;

52:7-11; 2 Kings 25:4-7). Zedekiah was an exhibit of one who could have made an about-turn, but did not.

Invaders of Palestine first subdued the towns of the coastal plain and then marched up east to Jerusalem. Jeremiah's message, urging surrender, was the more sobering since only two fortified cities, Lachish and Azekah, remained. Lachish, which has been identified with the modern Tell ed-Duweir, lay about 23 miles southwest of Jerusalem. At its peak it occupied 18 acres and would have been larger than Jerusalem. Azekah, 11 miles north of Lachish, was 18 miles from Jerusalem. *[Map, p. 316.]*

Archaeologists excavating Lachish (1935-38) found pottery sherds with written messages, known as "ostraca," in a room with ashes. The "letters" were messages sent from outpost observers to the garrison commander at Lachish. Letter 4 of the 21 ostraca reads: "And let (my lord) know that we are watching for the signals of Lachish, according to all the indications which my lord hath given, for we cannot see Azekah" (Pritchard: 322). Azekah had apparently fallen at the time the letter to Lachish was sent—a remarkable evidence for the accuracy of verse 7. Lachish was destroyed by fire about 587 (hence the ashes found with the ostraca). With the fall of Lachish, the way was cleared for the Babylonian military machine to advance to Jerusalem.

## 34:8-22  The Making and Breaking of a Pact

As the siege intensified, Zedekiah made a decision, in fact a solemn agreement before the Lord: everyone was to free his Hebrew slaves. Zedekiah was prompted in part by a desire to follow the Mosaic law, which called for the release of those who had become slaves because of debt. Both male and female slaves were to be released after a six-year period of service (Deut. 15:12-18; cf. Exod. 21:1-11). RSV follows the Septuagint and renders "six" rather than "seven" years (cf. Deut. 15:12).

The freedom-giving measure was quickly rescinded, suggesting that there were motives for the release of slaves other than conformity to the law. Under siege the release of slaves would simplify the food problem. It would also make additional defenders of the city available. It has even been suggested that this act had magical overtones; that is, in return for the release of slaves, God would release Jerusalem from Nebuchadnezzar's grip. The act looks like " 'fox-hole religion'—a kind of last-ditch measure in a time of peril" (Blank: 47).

Siege pressure eased, however, apparently because of the approach of the forces of Pharaoh Hophra of Egypt. Nebuchadnezzar temporarily left off the attack on Jerusalem to deal with the Egyptians (v. 22). With the emergency past, the landowners and slaveholders reneged on the commitment which they had solemnly made before God in the temple. The slaves find themselves back in servitude (v. 16). Freedom? No!

Such fickleness did not go unrebuked (v. 17). God's review of history makes the point that ethical requirements are based on an experience of salvation (cf. Exod. 20:1ff.). Covenant matters.

Indeed, there is a possibility that the release of the slaves took place in conjunction with a renewal of the covenant. This ceremony was Israel's affirmation of her covenant with God. If so, Zedekiah's flippant treatment of slaves was symptomatic of a spiritual flippancy. In an emphatic way, easily obscured by our translations, the Lord specifies that he too made a covenant which had to do with release from a slave condition (v. 13; cf. "bondage," RSV). One might ask, What if God had been as fickle as Zedekiah and his princes? God was faithful to the covenant; but Israel, like the present landowners, was not. The piercing, oft-repeated indictment, follows: *Your fathers, however, did not listen to me* (v. 14), and again, *You have not obeyed me* (v. 18; cf. 25:1-11). *[Obey/ Listen, p. 305.]*

The reenslavement signifies the disregard of the kings and slave-owners for their commitment. No, worse, it profanes the Lord's name! To *profane* is to rob something of its special character, to misuse it and treat it as ordinary, and so to desecrate that which is sacred. It is to free something from the sanctity it should have. Similarly Ezekiel speaks about profaning the Sabbaths (e.g., 20:13, 16, 21), the sanctuary (23:39), and God's name (20:39; 36:21; cf. Lev. 18:21). Such a willy-nilly attitude toward covenant will bring punishment.

God's response is emotional and vigorous (34:17-21). The announcement of disaster takes up two ideas from the public ceremony, "freedom" and "cut," and performs a wordplay on each. Have Zedekiah and his officials played loose with freedom? God's sword will now swing "free," and the people will be "free" to become victims of plague and famine.

As for "cut," this covenant was ratified, as covenants often were, by cutting an animal in half and laying the corresponding sections on the ground opposite each other (Gen. 15:9-17). One may also compare a seventeenth-century B.C. political arrangement between Abba-AN and Yarimlim: "Abba-AN swore to Yarimlim the oath of the gods, and furthermore he cut the throat of the sheep. (He swore:) I shall not take back what I gave you." (Wiseman: 124-129). Now, the Lord says, in effect, it is not the animal, but *you* who will be cut up and butchered. *[Wordplay, p. 313.]*

Just as Amos turned the "day of the Lord" on its head (5:18), so

Jeremiah turns covenant ratification on its head. The meaning of familiar words is changed. So much for the leaders of Judah and Jerusalem. As for Zedekiah, the Babylonians, who have temporarily interrupted their siege to deal with the Egyptians, will be back. God will cut off Zedekiah from his people and hand him over to the Babylonians.

Jeremiah's speech is in the form of a judgment oracle (vv. 13-22). The accusation (vv. 13-16) is introduced by a recapitulation of the divine command. [Judgment Oracle, p. 299.] The entire chapter is framed, first and last, by a threat to Zedekiah (vv. 2, 21). [Inclusio, p. 298.]

## THE TEXT IN BIBLICAL CONTEXT

Ethical Requirements. Significantly the demand to deal in a humanitarian way with slaves is set in the framework of covenant, which in turn is set in the framework of an act of deliverance (34:13-14). Ethical requirements, therefore, are not arbitrary or irrational. They arise out of a particular relationship between God and people. First God delivered his people; then he presented the Ten Words (Exod. 20:1ff.).

Law within covenant specifies how the relationship already established is to be maintained. By observance of the law, a covenant partner gives expression in gratitude to the covenant maker. It is on this principle that many of the epistles in the New Testament first give an explanation of God's salvation and the resulting covenant status; and then, but only then, set out the conduct that befits such a status.

Justice by Those in Power for Those in Their Power. Those in power have the duty to secure the rights of those in their power. In the New Testament, James, like Jeremiah, predicts misery for the rich, those with power—not because they are rich, but because as persons of power they have taken advantage of those in their power. "Look! The wages you failed to pay the workmen . . . are crying against you" (James 5:4). Cecil Rhodes in South Africa in the late nineteenth century, powerful colonial developer that he was, did not see to the human rights of the Matabele tribe but forcibly dispossessed them. A major modern outcry concerns the oppression of small, weak countries by the superpowers. Those in power should empower those in their power.

## THE TEXT IN THE LIFE OF THE CHURCH

Respect for Covenants. Arrangements such as treaties and covenants are not to be taken lightly. God announced judgment upon Tyre for "disregarding a [political] treaty of brotherhood" (Amos 1:9). Is the keeping of commitments to the United Nations, for example, a matter of indifference to God?

An example of covenant made before God "in the house that bears my name" is the marriage covenant. Like the ancient covenant, it is duly solemnized, though with different forms. Marriage is first a covenanted relationship. Mutual love makes the keeping of that covenant a joy. Inconvenience, or some "better" opportunity, was not in the Old Testament a reason for covenant breaking, nor is it now sufficient reason for going back on one's word.

*Hallowing God's Name Through Humanitarian Action.* If breaking faith with people profanes God's name, keeping one's word is one way of hallowing God's name.

> The man in the slum who was born with the language of vulgarity upon his lips is not profaning the name of God so terribly as the man in the sanctuary who prays and yet fails to understand that the hallowing of the name of God means the taking up of right attitudes toward his fellow men. To hallow the name is to reverence the character, to defend the honour, to obey authority; and the test of our hallowing of the Divine name is that of our attitude toward our fellow men. We hallow the name of God when we respect humanity (Morgan: 224-225).

On May 12, 1789, William Wilberforce in the British House of Commons moved twelve resolutions for the suppression of the slave trade. He considered it his Christian duty. In 1807 the Abolitionist Bill was passed—as Wilberforce said, to the "goodness and glory of Almighty God." Earlier, in 1688 an antislavery petition, which was authored by the Friends with some Mennonite influence, was submitted to the Philadelphia Congress (Swartley: 55).

## Testing for Obedience  35:1-19

Casual disregard for one's commitment is the problem addressed in the previous chapter. In striking contrast, the story of chapter 35 depicts integrity in commitment. The nomadic Recabite family does not deviate from a 250-year practice of abstinence, despite the invitation from a prophet in the temple to drink wine. Their unswerving loyalty makes the flagrant disloyalty of Israel look all the more appalling by contrast. The story, basically a report of a symbolic action, is placed here, not because it fits chronologically (between 601-598; cf. v. 11), but because of the common thread of the failure to obey.

## 35:1-11 A Family Obeys

The Recabites (also Rechabites) were a strict conservative sect, descendants of the Kenites, a people who had joined themselves to Israel (1 Chron. 2:55; Judg. 1:16). Jonadab, son of Recab, assisted Jehu in his bloody purge of the house of Ahab and the riddance of Baalism in 842 (2 Kings 10:15-28). He also established for his descendants a nomadic way of life, apparently intending by this simple lifestyle to emphasize the sojourning nature of their stay in the land (v. 7). Or his reasoning may have been that urban life corrupts, or that the Lord Yahweh was a "nomadic" type of god, whereas Baal was a "settled" god.

Nazirites were required to abstain from wine for 30 days (Num. 6:1-21). But the Recabites were pledged to perpetual abstinence. The Recabites may have refused wine also because wine typified the worst in Canaanite practice—in Canaanite mythology the gods were pictured as drunken at banquets. The Recabites have been labeled "ultraconservatives," "radicals," "reactionaries," and "fanatics." Whether Jeremiah approved or disapproved of their practices is not stated. In the end there was a "reward" for them (vv. 18-19).

The entire story is on the order of a symbolic action with its directive (v. 2), the report of compliance (vv. 3-11), and the interpretation (vv. 12-16). On the report of compliance, we may note how each of the three directives of verse 2 is matched precisely in verses 3-5. Similarly the Recabites obey their ancestor point by point. The message ("obey") is reinforced by the form in which it is recorded. [Symbolic Action, p. 311.]

An emergency, namely the invasion by Nebuchadnezzar, had caused them to yield temporarily and for physical safety's sake, and take up urban residence in Jerusalem (v. 11). Their tents within Jerusalem would have been the talk of the town.

The invitation to this family to drink wine is given in a special room in the temple. Solomon's temple had three stories of rooms adjoining both long walls of the temple. The room was occupied by the disciples (the meaning of sons in certain contexts), followers of Hanan, about whom nothing is known. Maaseiah was perhaps the father of Zephaniah (21:1). The doorkeepers were priests whose duty it was to admit persons according to temple rules (2 Kings 12:9; Jer. 52:24). The setting in the temple and the provision of wine, plus the invitation of a prophet as prestigious as Jeremiah, were strong inducements to the Recabites to break their commitment. But they did not.

## 35:12-16 A People Disobeys

The Recabites' rigorous obedience to their patriarchal ancestor contrasts ever so sharply with Judah's total lack of obedience to her God. A series of parallel statements give God's complaints: *"I have spoken to you again and again, yet you have not obeyed"* (14c); *"I sent . . . the prophets. . . . You have not paid attention"* (15a, c); *"I called to them, but they did not answer"* (17d). Should obedience be more readily rendered to a man than to God?

God's speaking *again and again* is an idiom which deals with early rising and is appropriately rendered "urgently and persistently" (cf. 7:13; 11:7; 25:3; 26:5; 32:33). The prophets' message for a turnaround echoes Jeremiah's own message (v. 15). *[Summons for Repentance, p. 310.]* Nor should one miss another layer of meaning: as the Recabites obeyed Jonadab, so Jeremiah obeyed God. *[Obey/Listen, p. 305.]*

### 35:17-19  To Each a "Reward"

The short judgment oracle against Judah follows the pattern of (1) announcement and (2) accusation. The latter becomes the reason for the former. For their obedience the Recabite family is promised not only survival in the coming disaster, but a perpetual ministry. One meaning of to *stand* is to be "at the ready" for service (e.g., Ps. 134:1; Zech. 3:1). We may compare this promise with the one given Baruch (45:5b) and Ebed-melech (39:17f.). After the exile, a Recabite descendant who had settled down in Beth-hakkerem (lit., "the house of the vineyard!") assisted with the building of the Dung Gate (Neh. 3:14). This person seems to have compromised his tradition on two counts: settling down and growing grapes!


## THE TEXT IN BIBLICAL CONTEXT

*Fickle or Faithful.* The story of Zedekiah's fickle ways in dealing with slaves is put back to back with the Recabites' unswerving faithfulness. In one story the granting of major human rights is decided on the basis of convenience; in the other, a dietary regulation is observed with the greatest strictness. For metaphors of fickleness see Hosea 4:4; 7:8. Likewise the Pharisees of Jesus' time paid great attention to dietary scruples but set aside larger questions of justice (Matt. 23:23).


## THE TEXT IN THE LIFE OF THE CHURCH

*The Service Rendered by "Purists."* No value judgment is placed on the principles espoused by the Recabites. If their intent was, as it appears, to safeguard a belief system from contamination through isolation, then they take their place in history with the Qumran community of the first century B.C. and the Amish of the Reformation and today. How indeed is a belief system or value system to be kept from distortion in subsequent generations? Is unquestioning adherence the answer? If the concern for "purity" is a correct one, do conservative groups render a service to the groups over against which they stand in protest?

*Faith Within Families.* The book of Jeremiah offers some windows on the perpetuation of religious faith in the context of families. Josiah was a godly king, but his sons—Jehoiakim, for example—were evil. Shaphan's family, on the other hand, seemed to be devoted to God's ways. There is something admirable in the firmness of conviction displayed by the Recabite family. By contrast, whole families participated in pagan worship (7:17-18; 44:15-18). One could compare Abraham's family (Gen. 12—50) or David's family (2 Sam. 13; 1 Kings 2). What are key elements for the nurture of faith in families? What place has authority or modeling?

*To Ponder.* The text, whose message about integrity is straightforward, nevertheless raises issues for reflection.

1. Sojourning: If believers are sojourners, how can the entanglements of a this-worldly mind-set be avoided? Is a simple lifestyle a solution?

2. Ethics: "In morals, as in everything, there are two opposite tendencies. The first is to say: 'Everything matters infinitely.' The second is to say: 'No doubt that is true. But mere sanity demands that we should not treat everything as mattering all that. Distinction is necessary . . . indifference is necessary. . . .' The Rigorous view is vital to sanctity; the Relaxed view is vital to sanity" (Williams: 31).

3. Traditions: Do they bind people, liberate them, or even do both at once?

## Rejecting the Word of God  36:1-32

This chapter, the last of the triad of chapters, tells about a third attempt by Jeremiah to get through to the king and people. He has spoken the word orally (chapter 34); he has engaged in symbolic action (chapter 35); and now he puts his message in writing. This chapter is unique in that it provides information on how prophetic books were written. Early in Jehoiakim's reign, perhaps at its outset, Jeremiah had preached the controversial sermon at the temple (7:1ff.; 26:1ff.). In the king's fourth year (605) the prophet summarized his message of over 20 years, urging repentance and threatening a 70-year servitude to Babylon (25:1-11). At about the same time, 605-604, a scroll was written and a strategy was devised. The scroll was read publicly on a fast day the following year—three times to three different audiences, including the king.

## 36:1-7  Preparing the Scroll

Jeremiah's writing project is a private project, but the goal is a public one: the spiritual reversal of a people. The motivation urged for this change of ways is first a threat, the *disaster I plan to inflict on them*, but also the appeal of a promise, *then I will forgive their . . . sin.* The Lord's passion and his earnest desire for a spiritual change are repeated (vv. 3, 7). In each instance the introductory *perhaps* is a foreboding word: the attempt to communicate is made on the chance that a conversion might happen at the last moment. *[Wrath, p. 313.]*

Baruch, Jeremiah's scribe, wrote on a scroll likely made of papyrus, though it may have been leather. Leather when burned, so some have noted, would give off a terrible smell! The contents of the scroll are similar to his summary of his 23-year service. [For *Josiah* and *Jehoiakim*, see *Kings of Judah, p. 300.]*

Jeremiah himself is restricted in his movement, a detail not explained. He is not in prison, for he is free to *go and hide* (v. 19). Possibly the temple authorities had banned him from the temple area following the controversial sermon there (chapters 7 and 26). Or it may have been the better part of wisdom to go underground. Restrictions do not keep him from devising ways to get his message out.

## 36:8-26  Reading the Scroll

The first reading from the scroll is by Baruch at the temple. The fast on that December day was likely called, not because of drought, but because of a military threat. In 605 Nebuchadnezzar defeated the Egyptians at Carchemish in the north and was poised to swoop down into Syria and Palestine. The next year, by December, he had taken Askelon on the coast some fifty miles from Jerusalem. Emergencies like these called for a fast (cf. Joel 1:13ff.; Jonah 3:6-9).

The scroll is read from the window of a second-story temple room that belongs to Gemariah of Shaphan's family. Shaphan had been supportive when the law was read in a similar situation under Josiah 20 years earlier (2 Kings 22:3-8). *Micaiah*, Shapan's grandson, now plays a key role in alerting his father, Gemariah, who with other officials is in session at the palace. *[Shaphan, p. 309.]*

A second reading by Baruch at the request of the officials, scribes and secretaries takes place in a chamber of the palace (vv. 11-19). His reading evokes fear. No wonder! Jeremiah's message for years has been that failure to turn to God would bring disaster in the form of a Babylonian invasion from which Jerusalem would not escape. The scroll says exactly the same thing (v. 29). And now Nebuchadnezzar is within miles of the city! The group makes two decisions: (1) the king is to be informed and (2) both Jeremiah and Baruch are to go into hiding. The suspense heightens.

A third reading is given at the state room in the palace, but not by Baruch (vv. 20-27). Upon receiving the report from his officials, King Jehoiakim dispatches Jehudi to bring the scroll and also to read it. Presumably the impressive palace with its paneled rooms—a building project to which Jeremiah objected (22:13-14)—was the setting for this winter day reading. Penknives were used by scribes to sharpen the reeds for pens and also to trim the papyrus. In theatrical style the king, using a penknife, slits the scroll after the reading of each three or four columns and tosses the pieces into the fire. Quite possibly such action, while registering contempt, was also meant in some magical way to nullify the message.

Among those who made an effort to dissuade the king from such effrontery was *Elnathan son of Acbor,* whom the king had enlisted to extradite the prophet Uriah from Egypt. (Jehoiakim had then killed Uriah, 26:22f.). One can speculate that Elnathan had had a change of heart and, instead of abetting the king, now tried to restrain him.

### 36:27-31  Judgment on Jehoiakim

For such disdainful disregard of his written message, God had a special word. How Jeremiah fulfilled God's command to get a message to King Jehoiakim is not stated. The message, in the form of a judgment oracle, cited Jehoiakim as one who had arrogantly set himself up as a censor. Behind Jehoiakim's comment is the assumption that the prophet had either no right to convey bad news or that the prophet should have checked signals with the king. But kings were accountable to prophets, not prophets to kings! In the coming disaster, says Jeremiah, the king's body will be thrown to the elements. There is a wordplay on *throw* and also on *frost/winter,* for which the same Hebrew word is used. Since the king's action epitomizes the people's response, it is upon the people that the disaster will come. The king had defiantly turned his back on the means of his rehabilitation. *[Wordplay, p. 313.]*

### 36:32  Rewriting the Scroll

The action of Jeremiah in response to God's command, *Take another scroll and write on it all the words that were on the first scroll* (v. 28) is given in verse 32. Characteristic of the accounts relating to Jeremiah and Baruch, the repetition emphasizes the careful listening/obedience which stands in such marked contrast to Jehoiakim's high-handed action of contempt. The second scroll, like the first, was to include a message about *Israel, Judah, and all the other nations* and was to be disaster-oriented (cf. v. 2). Such a description fits the contents of chapters 2 to 20. We may think of the message of the second scroll as embedded primarily in the early parts of chapters 2 to 20. *[Formation of Book, p. 296.]*

## THE TEXT IN BIBLICAL CONTEXT

*Similar Situations but Contrasting Responses: The Revival That Might Have Been!* The account of chapter 36 has many similarities to the reading of the law in Josiah's day 20 years earlier (2 Kings 22).

> In both of them we read of a scroll, in the one a scroll of the law and in the other a scroll of prophetic oracles. Jeremiah's scroll began its public history, so to speak, in the temple (2 Kings 22:8; Jer. 36:10). In both instances the scroll first comes into the hands of a state official (2 Kings 22:9f.; Jer. 36:10f.). Both narratives record the reaction of the king (2 Kings 22:11-13; Jer. 36:23-26) and both give a prominent place to a prophetic oracle which followed that reaction (2 Kings 22:15-20; Jer. 36:28-31). There appears to be a very deliberate contrast drawn between Josiah and Jehoiakim . . . . "When the king [Josiah] heard what was in the book of the law, *he rent his clothes"* [2 Kings 22:11], whilst Jer. 36:24 records, "Neither the king nor any of his courtiers who heard these words showed any fear or *rent their clothes"* (Nicholson: 110-111).

## THE TEXT IN THE LIFE OF THE CHURCH

*The Indestructible Word.* "The grass withers and the flowers fall, but the word of our God stands forever" (Isa. 40:8; cf. 1 Pet. 1:24-25). Just as there is a law of conservation of energy in the universe, so is there a divine law of the conservation of Scripture. Bible burnings by Jehoiakim and those of his mind-set since have not silenced the enduring Word. Nor will censorship in whatever form. Nor will the penknife of scientists, or the literary critics' excising of "nonauthentic" materials. In the end God will judge men and women, and not men and women the Word of God.

*On Writing Books in Prison.* More than ten years after the writing of the two scrolls, Jeremiah wrote another "book," the "Book of Consolation" (chapters 30—31[33]). The first two efforts were made from a place of hiding. Similarly, some of Paul's books, such as Philippians, were written in prison. John Bunyan's *Pilgrim's Progress* was written from a jail in Bedford, England. During World War II, Dietrich Bonhoeffer was thrown into the Tegel prison in Germany for speaking against the government and was later executed. From his jail cell he wrote the letters that were later published as *Prisoner for God, Letters and Papers from Prison.* That which would be interpreted from a human point of view as tragic and interruptive of a ministry was precisely that which expanded the ministry beyond expectation.

*Strategizing.* When normal communication channels for God's message are blocked, persistent persons will strategize, finding ways of entering the corridors of power so that their message may be heard. Strategists take pains, as did Jeremiah, to select the right medium, the right person and the most opportune moment. Christian radio broadcasters, for instance, beam the Christian message in many languages into areas inaccessible to missionaries.

But the best of strategizing fails in the face of defiance. In the series of steps that lead to spiritual callousness, a new level of hardness is reached when people defy the means for their wholeness. Thus the Jews in a defiant frame of mind did away with Jesus, their potential deliverer. Jesus himself warns against sinning against the Holy Spirit, for this is setting aside the last agent, God's ultimate strategy to bring conviction and enlightenment.

Jeremiah 37 – 39

# A Leader Falters,
# a City Falls

## PREVIEW

In Judah things are falling apart. After numerous warnings and threats reported in foregoing chapters, the events of Judah's final year, 588-587, are presented with dispatch. Three times Zedekiah seeks help from Jeremiah. Death hangs over the city; death at the hands of the officials hangs also over Jeremiah. The Babylonians (=Chaldeans) are successful: they take the city, pursue an escaping Zedekiah, capture him, try him, and gouge out his eyes. Jeremiah, by contrast, is treated with respect and remains with his people at the home of Gedaliah.

    This bare summary omits the emotional anxiety and physical pain which is inferred rather than learned from the text. The siege and fall of the city are also told elsewhere, but there Jeremiah is not mentioned (2 Kings 25:1-21; Jer. 52:3-27). Central in this account are Zedekiah, Jeremiah, and state officials. The story shifts back and forth between Zedekiah's search for help and Jeremiah's dangerous position. Much of the story goes beyond human entanglements to tell how God's word prevails.

OVERVIEW

A Royal Inquiry of Jeremiah
(37:1-10)

Officials Arrest and Beat the
Prophet (37:11-16)

Zedekiah's Personal Inquiry
of the Prophet (37:17-21)

Officials: "Death to the Prophet"
(38:1-13)

Zedekiah's Further Inquiry
of the Prophet (38:14-28)

Jerusalem Falls, (39:1-18)

There is more here than the telling of a story, for the way it is told, together with its tie to the scroll burning of chapter 36, carries a weighty message in itself, as shall be explained. Note the many speeches and the details, including names of people, from gate sentry to higher officials, both Judahite and Babylonian. What can be inferred about conditions within the city in its last year? More important, what do content and story structure convey as an abiding message?

## EXPLANATORY NOTES

### King and Prophet: Final Showdown 37—38

*37:1-10 A Royal Inquiry of Jeremiah*

Sometimes when things get really tough, help is sought from a "spiritual" person. The setting for the inquiry is given with two brief notes: one about the political state of affairs, a second about the spiritual state of affairs. Verse 2 summarizes the spiritual condition of king, officials, and people, characterized by disregard for the word and prophet of God. [*Kings of Judah, p. 300.*]

The king dispatched messengers to the prophet—the first in this final series of royal inquiries. Earlier in his reign Zedekiah had made a similar inquiry; then, as now, *the priest Zephaniah* had been in the delegation (21:1-7). *Jehucal* appears in the Hebrew as "Jucal" in 38:1. The reason for the inquiry now is a turn of events. It is the summer of 588. Pharaoh Hophra, who came to the throne earlier in the year, has marched his army out to aid Judah. The Babylonian ( = Chaldean) army has temporarily left off the siege at Jerusalem to intercept the Egyptians (cf. 34:21). The event has the makings of a deliverance for Judah similar to that in Hezekiah's day a century earlier (2 Kings 19:14-36). Prayer by a prophet should certainly help!

But Jeremiah told the delegation that the lifting of the blockade of

Jerusalem was temporary and that the Babylonians would return and capture and sack the city. With "rhetorical exaggeration" he added that even were the Babylonians to be routed, the wounded left along the way would be enough to bring about the city's defeat (cf. 2 Kings 19:35-37).

### 37:11-16  Officials Arrest and Beat the Prophet

The temporary lifting of the siege made it possible for people to leave the city. Jeremiah headed north through the *Benjamin Gate* in the city's north wall to his hometown Anathoth, in the territory of Benjamin. Jeremiah went there to see after some property or other business (v. 12). The reference to his "portion" (RSV) is sometimes linked with his land purchase (32:6-15), but this is unlikely, for Jeremiah had not yet been imprisoned, nor had the siege been renewed.

If he was a brother to *Jehucal,* one of the king's delegates, the sentry at the *Benjamin Gate* might well have been informed and also incensed over the prophet's answer to the king. His charge that Jeremiah was defecting to the Babylonians was realistic, for considerable numbers, perhaps in response to Jeremiah's counsel (21:8-10; 38:2), had gone over to the enemy (38:19; 52:15). Moreover, Jeremiah could be expected to follow his own counsel.

So Jeremiah was arrested by a gate sentry and flogged. The indignant *officials* ("princes," RSV) consigned the prophet to an underground *dungeon* located in a scribe's house. The place was used, perhaps, for maximum security reasons, or because other detention places were filled.

### 37:17-21  Zedekiah's Personal Inquiry of the Prophet

The king now personally meets with the prophet. In Jeremiah he has access to a "special intelligence agent." Perhaps Zedekiah was hoping for a change in the prophet's message. The encounter was dramatic: a 32-year-old king stands before a prophet aged sixty.

Jeremiah, however, was blunt, perhaps even curt. An extra sting was added to his answer with the question *Where are your prophets who prophesied* Babylon would not attack? Jeremiah has a psychological advantage and makes a request. He declares his innocence, as he had also done earlier (26:15). Zedekiah's favorable answer to Jeremiah's request for a transfer out of the dungeon suggests that Zedekiah was inclined at certain moments to believe Jeremiah (cf. 38:14-28). At least now, as again later, he acted to prevent the prophet's death (cf. 38:10).

Jeremiah was then moved to detention in the *courtyard of the guard*—an improved condition over the dungeon—and by royal order was given preference in what may well have been wartime food rations. Famine conditions were severe and in the end contributed to the city's collapse (2 Kings 25:3; Jer. 52:6). The visit of Jeremiah's cousin Hanamel may well have taken place when Jeremiah was confined to the guardhouse (32:6-15).

## 38:1-13  Officials: "Death to the Prophet"

How Jeremiah could be *telling all the people* is puzzling, except that people like Hanamel had access to him (cf. 36:6-15). The rumors originating with Jeremiah may well have circulated widely. In addition to that fact, others were aware of the city's predicted fate (37:3), including Jehucal (=Jucal), who was a member of Zedekiah's inquiry delegation, and also Pashhur, son of Malkijah, member of the earlier delegation (21:1). The message to defect to the Babylonians, given in the name of God, was clearly discouraging the war effort (lit., "weakening the hands of the soldiers"). In the Lachish ostraca unearthed in the 1930s, one of the "letters" makes the same charge against some of the princes in Jerusalem.

The officials continued to demand the death warrant on the grounds of treason. Ironically, the charge *This man is not seeking the good of these people* is totally untrue. For almost 40 years Jeremiah sought the good through a spiritual turnaround. Presumably these men, the pro-Egyptian party, were seeking *good* via military alliances. Pashhur, whose son was Gedaliah, is possibly the Passhur of 20:1.

The king's response—not totally honest—exposes how weak is his control of the internal situation (v. 5; cf. v. 10). He washes his hands of responsibility. The new "home" for the prophet is a waterless but muddy cistern which belonged to the king's son. (That son's fate would be execution at the hands of the Babylonians, 39:6.) "A typical cistern was dug out of limestone rock and consisted of a narrow neck perhaps three feet across and three or four feet in depth opening into a much longer bulbous cavity of varying depth" (Thompson: 638). The intent of the officials was not to detain Jeremiah, but to starve him to death away from public notice (v. 7ff.)

Had it not been for a foreigner, a Cushite (Ethiopian) official, the plot to kill Jeremiah would have succeeded. Ebed-Melech, whose name means "servant of the king," intercedes with the king at the Benjamin Gate, where the king may have been adjudicating court cases, as was the custom (2 Sam. 15:2-4). Or he may have been inspecting the city's defenses, since city gates were the most vulnerable.

The detail about *old rags and worn-out clothes* secured from "beneath the storerooms" (NASB), and the consideration shown in the rescue operation by padding the armpits, contrasts with the treatment given the prophet by the officials, whose action was almost certainly rude (v. 6). On the authority of one manuscript, RSV reads "three" instead of *thirty men*. Jeremiah is back in the guardhouse, thanks to the Cushite, whose reward for this kindly deed is revealed in 39:15-18.

### 38:14-28 Zedekiah's Further Inquiry of the Prophet

Again King Zedekiah sought out the prophet Jeremiah. Or did he? Some have thought that there was only one arrest and only one dungeon experience. In light of several similarities their reasoning is that the two personal interviews of Zedekiah with Jeremiah (37:17-21 and 38:14-26) are "two divergent accounts of one and the same course of events."

Specifically, the note about Jeremiah staying in the *courtyard of the guard*—presumably only until the bread supply was exhausted and thus the city captured—makes the second arrest contradictory. However, two different kinds of events precipitate the action; also, two different dungeons are named, and in only one account is a rescue related. Despite the difficulty of the amount of the bread supply (37:21), the present narrative stands as a description of the confusion of the final days of the siege.

Jeremiah's message is given only after an assurance on oath by the king. The message is surrender and live or resist and perish. Should Zedekiah defect to the Babylonians, his personal fears are allayed. The enemy will *not hand over* the king to Judahites who had already defected, and who might in blaming the monarch grossly maltreat him. [*Swearing, p. 311.*]

Like the two previous counsels of Jeremiah, this advice is underpinned by an additional consideration, namely a special revelation from the Lord (v. 21; cf. 37:9-10; 37:19). The victors will take the women of the royal court for themselves. The poem about betrayal recalls several psalms (Ps. 41:9; 69:14; cf. Obad. 7). *Your feet are sunk in the mud* is a flashback to Jeremiah who *sank down into the mud* (v. 6). Politically speaking, Zedekiah will end up stuck in the mud. This was the last encounter between Zedekiah and Jeremiah.

### Jerusalem Falls  39:1-18

The Babylonian ( = Chaldean) siege under the overall command of Nebuchadnezzar lasted from January 588 to July 587. The siege was Nebuchadnezzar's answer to Zedekiah's breaking of the loyalty oath and his attempted rebellion (2 Kings 25:1). An interlude came in the summer of 588 when the Egyptians moved in to help, but they then pulled back. In that interlude the incident of the freeing and the reenslaving of slaves took place (34:1ff.). Zedekiah found it necessary to use strategy, and so he also sent a delegation to Jeremiah (37:3-10).

The story of Jerusalem's fall is told in 2 Kings 25:1-12 (=Jer. 52:4-16). *Samgar* was a province in Babylon (v. 3). The names of the Babylonian officials who took over the *Middle Gate* as a sign of battle triumph are variously rendered in our translations, depending on which syllables are considered titular positions and which are names. The first, *Nergal-Sharezer*, is almost certainly the Neriglissar, who succeeded Nebuchadnezzar's son Amel-Marduk (562-560), to whom he was related as a brother-in-law. Here he is described as a "Rabmag," namely a high-ranking officer (v. 13).

The story is rapidly concluded. That which befell each one is quickly told.

1. *Zedekiah's* attempted escape was unsuccessful. The king's garden was in the Kidron Valley. The gate between the two walls was the city's southernmost gate (v. 4). Zedekiah may have planned to escape eastward beyond the Jordan Valley. *Riblah* was north of Palestine, the command post of Nebuchadnezzar and a decade earlier of Pharaoh Necho. It was here that Zedekiah answered to the great king concerning his breaking of the oath of loyalty (Ezek. 17:11-21). His life was spared, but his eyes were gouged out (2 Kings 25:7).

2. The *city* with its palace and the *houses of the people* was set ablaze (v. 8).

3. If they had defected or were city dignitaries, the *people* were carried off along with "the rest of the workmen" (NAB). Those without property and who remained—those not likely to cause trouble—were allocated fields for tilling.

4. *Jeremiah* was the object of the great king's personal concern (vv. 11-14). News about the prophet may have reached Nebuchadnezzar from defectors who volunteered or were coerced to give intelligence reports. After being escorted from the guardhouse, Jeremiah was given the option of leaving the country, or staying. He stayed. After incarcerations at (1) the dungeon in Jonathan's house (37:15-16), (2) the detention quarters of a guardhouse (37:21), (3) a muddy cistern belonging to the king's son (38:6), and (4) the guardhouse (38:13), Jeremiah's new home was with the friendly family of Shaphan (39:14). *[Shaphan, p. 309.]*

5. *Ebed-Melech,* the compassionate Cushite, was promised escape with his life because *you trusted in me)* (the Lord, v. 17f.).

## THE TEXT IN BIBLICAL CONTEXT

*Evidence That Demands a Sentencing.* That the several chapters are intended for more than historical information or as a resolution to a long conflict is best shown by the careful positioning of two parallel accounts (chapter 36 and chapters 37—38). In each, the political situation is a key point. In the first account, the Babylonians are taking Ashkelon (chapter 36); in the parallel account they are besieging Jerusalem (chapters 37—38). In both there is a hearing of God's Word: in the one, Jehoiakim hears the scroll read; in the other, Zedekiah is given the prophetic word face-to-face. The message for each king is that Babylon will overthrow Jerusalem (e.g., 36:29; 38:17f.). In each case that message is given three times. In the first case, Jeremiah devises a strategy to get a hearing; in the second, Jeremiah is sought out. In each, the officials of the king attempt to influence the king, though in opposite directions (36:25; 38:4). In each, the king says "No" to the divine word: Jehoiakim through burning the scroll, Zedekiah through a decision to defend the city. In one the attempt is to annihilate the message; in the second, to annihilate the messenger.

Such a structuring makes overwhelmingly clear

1. That God has given adequate notice of the coming judgment.
2. That God's message is defiantly refused by two monarchs who, as heads of state, implicate themselves and the people.
3. That the judgment is abundantly warranted: the evidence, as in a court, demands a severe sentencing.

*A God Who Is Long-Suffering.* It is the Bible's assertion that God is long-suffering and slow to anger, that he is patient, and that he tarries before executing judgment (e.g., Exod. 34:6; Nah. 1:3). The 120-year grace period in the time of Noah is an illustration of such long-suffering, and so also is the call to repentance extended by the prophets (25:4-6; 35:15), especially the 40-year preaching of Jeremiah (627-587). Even when the evidence is already conclusive, there is still an optimistic "perhaps" (36:3, 7). After Jehoiakim's defiant act, a second chance is given to Zedekiah (chapters 37—38). And before the ax falls, there are three assurances advising a course of action. Similarly in the New Testament era, two prophets, John the Baptist and Jesus, are sent to preach repentance. A further interval follows; and only then does Jerusalem fall to the Romans in A.D. 70. God is consistently long-suffering.

*Jeremiah and Jesus.* The torture and suffering of Jeremiah—a passion story of its own—invites comparison with that greater passion story of Jesus Christ in the New Testament (cf. Matt. 16:13f.). Both Jesus and Jeremiah made Jerusalem a teaching center. Each was opposed by religious leaders. Both Jeremiah and Jesus carried their messages before political magistrates. Both were tortured, for in each situation officials and dignitaries were aligned against God's messengers. While sympathetic to God's spokesman, Pilate, like Zedekiah, was caught between the innocent prisoner and the pressure of officials. A striking contrast is that while in Jeremiah's story the guilty are put to death and the innocent are vindicated, in the story of Jesus the innocent one is put to death so that the guilty might be vindicated (justified). Another contrast is Jeremiah's apparent readiness for vengeance and Jesus' lack of vindictiveness.

## THE TEXT IN THE LIFE OF THE CHURCH

*How Much Proof Is Enough?* Zedekiah can serve as a case study of one who, already partly persuaded by the evidence, continued pursuit for additional evidence. But in the end, by default, he decided against the evidence. Not infrequently those unwilling to obey insist on having more data. How much "evidence" is enough? Few decisions in life, and certainly not the decision to become a Christian, can escape the need for a "leap of faith."

*Whistle-Blowing.* Anger against whistle-blowers is no new thing: Jeremiah was thrown into a dungeon; John the Baptist lost his head. One would imagine that society would welcome those who expose and try to correct its evils. Not so. Institutions have strong interest in protecting their wealth, reputation, and other self-interests. Anyone who speaks against corruption in the system can almost certainly expect to be fired, demoted, exiled to a minor job in a far country, maligned, shunned, and otherwise attacked. So widespread is the practice of firing workers who expose wrongdoing, in fact, that many states in the United States have passed "whistle-blower" laws protecting employees (especially government employees) from retaliation for revealing damaging information.

The New Testament admonition to rebuke evil also runs counter to a strong social value: loyalty. We are taught early not to betray our associates; even children despise anyone who "rats." Christians therefore find themselves in conflict when they discover wrongdoing. Evil can be rebuked in various ways: through the personal confrontation process outlined by Jesus in Matthew 18:15-17, open preaching in the style of Jeremiah, work at the government level to change laws, and so on. The encouraging thing is that whistle-blowers sometimes win: people repent, and social evils are curbed.

Jeremiah 40 – 45

# After the Catastrophe

## PREVIEW

Living in the aftermath of God's judgment has its own set of problems. The preceding chapters have focused on Jerusalem's plight. That city has fallen, and attention now turns to those who have survived the catastrophe and remained in the homeland or in the nearby countries of Ammon, Edom, and Moab. Except for the opening incident recounting Jeremiah's release into freedom, the picture is bleak and sometimes grim.

The Babylonians appointed Gedaliah to be the governor, but he was soon assassinated. Fearing Babylonian reprisals, the remnant fled to Egypt, disregarding Jeremiah's advice. In Egypt the aging Jeremiah rebuked the community for their return to the worship of a pagan God. The prose section ends with a message to Baruch. Chronologically speaking, this message appears to be something of a misfit, but it rounds off the story.

That is the story line of these six chapters—the organization of which is shown in the following overview. The main interest is in the homeland community, but biographical details about the two individuals, Jeremiah and Baruch, begin and end this section.

OUTLINE (Schematic)

| Jeremiah | Surviving in Judah | Settling in Egypt | Baruch |
|---|---|---|---|
| personal note | | | personal note |
| 40:1-6 | | | 45:1-5 |
| | Gedaliah | Rescue and | Disobedience | Idolatry |
| | Assassinated | Regrouping | 42:1—43:13 | 44:1-30 |
| | 40:7—41:3 | 41:4-18 | | |

The intention of these chapters is clearly not to present a full historical account, for there are many gaps and unanswered questions. The aim is theological: we are to learn, not the blow-by-blow developments, but an understanding of God's ways in the face of persistent human evil—brutality, disobedience, and idolatry. The faithless remnant is disqualified, absolutely disqualified, to be the carriers of God's further work with his people. The future lies with the exiled group in Babylon (24:4-10; 29:16-20). Throughout these chapters there are repeated explanations of the great catastrophe.

## EXPLANATORY NOTES

### Tragedy Among the Survivors in Judah 40—41

The good news is that Jeremiah is freed. The tragic news is that a Hebrew governor is assassinated. How to survive in such politically unstable times is a key question.

### 40:1-6 Jeremiah Is Freed

The chapter opens with The word came to Jeremiah from the Lord. But no word from the prophet follows. Calvin says, "He [Jeremiah] seems throughout the chapter to have forgotten the introduction." One may assume that the compilers of the book used this common expression to indicate that what followed was a message from God. Or perhaps the "word" has been lost, or, as some suggest, it is found in the speech of Nebuzaradan (vv. 2-3). Or, most likely, a theological point is being made. God's word comes into a historical situation which must be understood. "And now" (But today, NIV, cf. 42:15) is often used to show that something has happened which gives a new turn to the situation. [Revelation Formulae, p. 307.]

Jeremiah had earlier been released to Gedaliah's house by Nebuzaradan (39:14). Some think that 40:1-6 is a more detailed account of the same incident. But the more likely explanation for the two release accounts is that in the roundup of persons to be exiled, by mistake Jeremiah had again been arrested and, along with others, brought to Ramah, a dispatching point for exiles. Ramah is about five miles north of Jerusalem. The commander of the imperial guard, Nebuzaradan, not only releases the prophet but gives him several options: going to Babylon, staying in the land, or returning to Gedaliah's home. In a speech he gives theological reasons for Jerusalem's capture. Did he know of Jeremiah's message? Possibly. Had he become a convert to Yahwism? Certainly his giving gifts to Jeremiah contrasts markedly with the surly treatment given the prophet by his countrymen.

That Jeremiah chose to remain with his people—the most difficult of the options—is evidence that he was not a traitor, who unpatriotically urged submission to the Babylonians. He went to one of his friends, Gedaliah. Mizpah was a town in the neighborhood of Ramah, seven or eight miles north of Jerusalem. It was the appointed governor's residence (2 Kings 25:23).

### 40:7-12 Gedaliah Begins as Governor

Trouble is in the offing. These verses set the stage for the tragedy about to be described (cf. 2 Kings 25:23-26 for a parallel account). A century earlier the Assyrian policy was to populate conquered territory with alien peoples. The Babylonians, however, ruled by appointing leaders from among the conquered. Gedaliah was Shaphan's grandson, and Shaphan's family was associated with the royal court. As one who was sympathetic to Jeremiah's message, he may have favored a policy of submission to the Babylonians and so was a reasonable choice. Gedaliah set up headquarters at Mizpah, only miles from the Babylonian command post at Ramah. [Shaphan, p. 309; Map, p. 316.]

Certain officers of the Hebrew army had escaped Babylonian arrest by taking refuge in the hills. Johanan emerged as leader. In 1932, at Tell en-Nasbeh (=Mizpah) archaeologists found a beautiful seal with the inscription "belonging to Jaazaniah (=Jezaniah), slave of the king," but identification with the officer of 40:8 cannot be established. Ishmael was a treacherous character (41:1-3).

These Hebrew guerrillas had some questions: Would Gedaliah work in behalf of the homeland community, or would he be a tool of the Babylonians? Gedaliah reassured them and urged them to return to peaceful farming pursuits. Gedaliah's conciliatory policy had the effect of inducing refugees from the nearby countries of Moab, Ammon, and Edom to return home. The outlook was for a settled, even prospering, community.

## 40:13—41:3  Gedaliah Is Assassinated

One of these wilderness chieftains, Johanan, warned Gedaliah of a murderous plot instigated by Baalis, king of the Ammonites, in collusion with Ishmael. Baalis may have wanted the Babylonians to deal more oppressively with Judah, or tried by this plot to forestall any consolidation by the survivors so that he could reach in for his own political advantage. Gedaliah had just entertained a delegation of which Ishmael was a member. Perhaps because of his good nature and his hope for peaceable reconstruction of the country, Gedaliah refused to believe Johanan's warning. (Cf. Paul's reponse to Agabus' warning, Acts 21:10ff.) In his desire to prevent trouble of any kind, he forbad Johanan to proceed with the scheme to destroy Ishmael. Johanan's proposal, however, showed how readily some were prepared to resort to violence, as though the end justified the means. [Vengeance, p. 312.]

Less than four months into his governorship, Gedaliah was assassinated by Ishmael (cf. 41:1; 39:2). Ishmael violated all rules of Oriental hospitality. No motives are given. One can speculate that since he was of royal blood, he resented Gedaliah's appointment. More likely he consented to be hired by Baalis, either for a promised personal advantage or in order to take vengeance on the Babylonians. In cold blood Ishmael murdered Gedaliah, his entourage, and also some Babylonian (Chaldean) soldiers. Some believe that Gedaliah governed more than four months, perhaps five years. They equate the carrying off of slaves in 582 with this incident, hence the five years (cf. 52:30).

## 41:4-10  Ishmael's Murder Rampage

To secure himself, Ishmael slaughtered people wholesale. The 80 men who were on their way to Jerusalem to present grain offerings and incense, despite the destroyed temple, were from Shechem, Shiloh, and Samaria, three northern cities once in the territory of Israel. Shaved beards, torn clothes, and gashed bodies were signs of mourning and penitence. Needlessly and savagely, Ishmael killed all but ten who succeeded in buying him off with food commodities, probably at a premium following siege-time famine conditions. The corpses were thrown into the cistern at Mizpah. It was built 300 years earlier by King Asa (1 Kings 15:22). In future generations a fast commemorated this tragedy (Zech. 8:19). [Map, p. 316.]

## 41:11-18  Johanan's Rescue Operation

Johanan emerged as a hero. He had taken captive those of Mizpah whom Ishmael had not killed. Johanan overtook Ishmael and the group he held hostage at Gibeon's *great pool*, three miles south-southwest of Mizpah. At Gibeon Johanan put Ishmael and eight of his desperadoes to flight and freed the prisoners. Archaeologists have found a large pit at Gibeon, 30 feet deep and measuring more than 30 feet across its mouth, dug in the Early Iron Age (about 1200). Steps were cut in its side leading to a water chamber.

Johanan continued southward, bringing the soldiers with him, and the hostages, including court officials ("eunuchs," RSV), and perhaps additional citizens from Mizpah. They stopped near Bethlehem, six miles south-southwest of Jerusalem at Geruth Kimham, or "Kimham's holding" (NEB). They were fleeing to Egypt because they feared Babylonian reprisals for Gedaliah's death—a reprisal that would implicate the innocent. Kimham had received a grant of land in response to the suggestion of Barzillai, whom David wished to honor (2 Sam. 19:31-40). The location is not known.

## THE TEXT IN BIBLICAL CONTEXT

*A Non-Israelite's Testimony.* Nebuzaradan sermonizes about Jerusalem's capture (40:2-3). Some hold that verses 2-3 are "most improbable on the lips of the Babylonian officer" (Hyatt: 1082) or would argue that later editors composed this speech and attributed it to Nebuzaradan. But assuming that the event was historical, it is ironic that a pagan Babylonian should understand the ways of God when God's own people refused to understand. Persons from other cultures who have made comparable acknowledgements are Pharaoh (Gen. 41:38), Nebuchadnezzar (Dan. 4:34-37), and the Roman centurion (Matt. 27:54).

## THE TEXT IN THE LIFE OF THE CHURCH

*Violence Begets Violence.* Was Gedaliah wise or naive in restraining Johanan from killing a man suspected of intending an assassination? (40:15-16). His own life might have been spared if had he allowed Johanan free rein, but who can say what intrigue, suspicion, and further violence might have followed? It is the testimony of the Scripture and history that violence begets violence. True, giving another the benefit of the doubt or refusing to reach for the sword may not guarantee personal safety, but can peaceful living be even a possibility when each man forges his way by force? Terrorism may be explained by sociologists as especially frequent for societies in transition, but theologically it is diametrically oppposed to God's ways.

## Decision-Making by the Remnant  42–43

Poised to go to Egypt, the leaders of this remnant group have second thoughts. They consult Jeremiah, but against his advice go after all.

### 42:1-6  The Remnant Seeks Counsel

Apparently, Jeremiah was released earlier to go to Gedaliah's house at Mizpah. In the interval he had moved into the Bethlehem area, or he may have been taken captive by Ishmael and released there by Johanan (41:10-15). Johanan and Jezaniah ("Azariah" in RSV, following the Septuagint and to correspond with 43:2), together with the entire group, seek out Jeremiah to ask him to pray for guidance (lit., "let fall our petition before you," also v. 9). They speak of themselves as the *remnant*, "the remainder," a frequent concept in these chapters. With an oathlike statement, they promise, *We will obey. [Obey/Listen, p. 305.]* Jeremiah, who had been told not to intercede, does so now (7:16; 11:14; cf. Amos 7:2, 5).

### 42:7-22  The Counsel: Don't Go to Egypt

The delay of 10 days before an answer was received throws light on the prophetic process (cf. 28:12). Whatever the prophet's immediate personal views on the question, they were not necessarily identical with God's word. Nor was the prophet in a position to secure from God at will a needed directive. Submissiveness, so much preached by the prophet, was also a requirement for him personally.

Jeremiah's reply is in two parts. Verses 9-18 report the message from God. Jeremiah's personal exhortation follows (vv. 19-22). The word from God revolves around the two options: to stay, or to leave for Egypt.

But God's promises are associated with the option of staying (vv. 9-12). *Build, plant, tear down, uproot* are words from Jeremiah's call and represent something of a judgment-and-salvation refrain throughout the book (e.g., 24:6-10; 31:28). The term for *grieve over* ("repent" RSV, or "relent" NASB) means "to breathe heavily, to sigh" and properly here "to grieve." "I am sorry about the hurt that I have had to inflict upon you" (Bright: 256).

What follows is a salvation oracle of the "assurance" type. The word of consolation, "Do not fear," is spoken twice, and so directly addresses their fearful condition (41:18). God promises salvation and his compassion (the Hebrew term is linked with "womb," v. 12). This promise to the community potentially opens a great future to the remnant, namely renewal and restoration as the people of God. *[Deliverance Oracles, p. 295.]*

On the other hand, most severe threats are associated with the choice of leaving for Egypt, even though the choice to escape war and hunger seems reasonable and sensible (vv. 13-18). The *trumpet* refers to the alarm sounded by watchmen to alert citizens to danger, or to call for troop mobilization. But these very dangers, *sword, famine and plague*, a trio of disasters, will bring total destruction (v. 17; cf. 27:8; 29:17). "In warning them Jeremiah invokes on the group some of the strongest denunciatory categories familiar to ancient Near Eastern peoples" (Harrison: 164). God's outpouring of wrath, which they have just witnessed on Jerusalem, will be their portion. *[Wrath, p. 313.]*

To the divine warning word Jeremiah adds his personal counsel not to go to Egypt (vv. 19-22). The fatal mistake ("deceived yourselves," NASB; "at the cost of your lives," RSV) is not their request for divine guidance, but their duplicity and insincerity, for in their hearts they do not care to follow the counsel given. According to the principles laid out in 18:1-10, the promise of verses 10-12 is clearly null and void if the group goes to Egypt. Every indication, then, is in favor of remaining in the land. *[Obey/Listen, p. 305.]*

### 43:1-7  The Decision: Off to Egypt

Contrary to all counsel, the decision is to press on toward Egypt. The charge against Jeremiah by Johanan, Azariah, and *all the arrogant men*, "You are an impostor," is hardly believable in the light of the man's integrity and the recent events which have clearly vindicated his prophecy (cf. 26:9). Note that Azariah has the same father as Jezaniah (cf. 42:1) and may indeed be the same person, if the Greek text reading is adopted.

The group dismisses Jeremiah's message on two counts: (1) the message was not of divine origin, and (2) Jeremiah had been influenced by Baruch. *[Baruch, p. 292.]* Their techniques of evasion supposedly left them free to go back on their word (cf. 34:1ff.) and to continue toward Egypt.

The emigration to Egypt is depicted as a wholesale one which included several groups: (1) the army officers as leaders, (2) refugees who had returned from surrounding nations, (3) the Mizpah group taken hostage by Ishmael and then set free, and (4) Jeremiah and Baruch. Whether Jeremiah joined of his own will or whether he was compelled is not stated. *Tahpanhes* is an Egyptian border fortress in the East Delta region of the Nile.

(For comments on *guidance* see page 243.)

## 43:8-13   The Threat: Babylon Once More

A symbolic action underscores the dangers the remnant, now in Egypt, will face. Several large stones are to be put in the pavement in front of a royal (government) building, probably the residence of an Egyptian governor where the Pharaoh may have stayed on a visit. *Pharaoh's palace*, though a permissible translation, is problematic since Tahpanhes was a border town. Moreover, Pharaoh's capital was Sais. Nebuchadnezzar, king of Babylon (Chaldea), is designated *my servant* also elsewhere (25:9; 27:6). Ultimately, God is recognized as the great actor in history: I [God] *will set fire to the temples of the gods of Egypt.* Some versions however read "he" (i.e., Nebuchadnezzar). *[Symbolic Action, p. 311.]*

The verb in verse 12b is translated here as *wrap*, but judging from the Septuagint, it has an alternate meaning also, "to delouse." The preferable translation is, "As a shepherd delouses his cloak, he shall delouse the land of Egypt and depart victorious" (NAB). King Nebuchadnezzar will plunder at will. Obelisks or "sacred pillars" are slightly tapered square granite shafts which are common to Egyptian temples. Those in the *temple of the sun* (Beth-Shemesh = Heliopolis, located five or six miles to the northeast of Cairo), Nebuchadnezzar will break in pieces.

Such a specific prediction raises the question of fulfillment. Existing fragmentary records do tell of Nebuchadnezzar's attack on Egypt in that king's thirty-seventh year (568-567). The result of this battle with Pharaoh Amasis (Ahmosis II) is unclear, and so is the extent of the invasion, since it seems to have been a punitive expedition.

## Idolatry in Egypt   44:1-30

Since the messages to the nations in chapters 46—51 are likely from another period, this chapter represents the final word from the prophet. According to tradition, Jeremiah died in Egypt at the hands of fellow Jews. He would have been in his seventies. In his final message, as in his first, Jeremiah combats apostasy—the falling away from God and resorting, as in this instance, to idolatry. From the prophet's viewpoint, the spiritual scene is grim.

## 44:1-14   Provoking God with Idolatry

Idolatry in Egypt sparks a lively argument on the pros and cons of idolatrous practices. The heading sentence suggests that sufficient time has elapsed after entering the land of Egypt for the immigrants to settle, not only in the Nile delta region, or Lower Egypt, but also south, as far as 300 miles, in Upper Egypt, also called Pathros. Migdol, meaning "tower," is in northern Egypt east of Tahpanhes; and Memphis or Noph was 13 miles south of modern Cairo (cf. Ezek. 29:8-16; 30:13-19). From archaeology we know that Jewish people lived in these places. Elephantine, a Jewish colony on an island in the Nile in Upper Egypt, is not mentioned here; but archaeologists have discovered Aramaic documents describing the religious life, at best an aberrant Yahwism, dating from the fifth century. Jews likely lived there soon after 587 B.C. [Map, p. 317.]

The Lord's speech addressing the idolatry of the Jewish community is in three parts (vv. 2-6; 7-10; 11-14). Each is introduced with the messenger formula, This is what the Lord God Almighty, the God of Israel, says, an unusually "full" title. The first segment reviews the catastrophe which came on Jerusalem (vv. 2-6). The reasons for this disaster are stressed: (1) worshiping other gods and burning incense to other gods, despite God's "urgent and persistent" dispatch of prophets (cf. 7:25; 25:4; 26:5); (2) disobedience, they did not listen or pay attention; and (3) provoking God to anger. [Lord of Hosts, p. 304; Obey/Listen, p. 305; Wrath, p. 313.]

The second segment poses a series of questions. God probes the people's conscience: "Why are you doing this great harm to yourselves?" (vv. 7-8a). The conclusion is serious: by their actions they will cut themselves off from the nucleus with whom God will continue his purposes. God appeals to Judah's memory: "Have you forgotten what happened to your fathers?" (v. 9). The accusation states by inference what God is looking for: (1) humility, (2) reverence (cf. 5:24), and (3) obedience to God's law (v. 10).

The third segment announces pending disaster: I am determined (lit., "have set my face") (vv. 11-14). Unlike earlier ones made to Judah, this announcement makes no mention of survival through exile. Sword and famine will make for total destruction. The term few fugitives emphasizes how utterly final will be the blow. This entire group, then, is effectively written off. The future will not lie with them. And so it happened. Later resettlement of Palestine and the preservation of the tradition came via the Babylon group and not at all via the Egyptian community.

Overall, the form of the divine speech is an oracle of judgment with an accusation (vv. 7-10), followed by an announcement (vv. 11-14), all of which is preceded by a stage-setting historical review (vv. 2-6). [Judgment Oracle, p. 299.]

## 44:15-19  A Defense of Idolatry

The people protest; idolatry is reasonable in their situation. The gravity of the people's spiritual waywardness is evident in what they say: *We will not listen* (cf. 6:17). Their intent to fulfill their vows to Asherah, *Queen of Heaven*, is self-conscious and deliberate. Their reason for the worship of the Queen of Heaven is their recent harsh experience. The argument was plausible.

Severe disasters had come on them following 621: beloved Josiah had died in battle; famine had come; their country had been invaded and their people exiled. *At that time*, presumably before Josiah's reformation of 621, when such idolatrous practices were suppressed, or even from the time of King Manasseh, who had introduced the worship of this fertility goddess, they had prospered. That their return to idolatry had become a family affair is clear in that the women lent their support by "making crescent-cakes marked with her image" (v. 19, NEB). *[Asherah, p. 291.]*

## 44:20-30  Disaster for the Idolaters

Jeremiah answers such an affront to God in his own words. He essentially reviews once more what happened to Jerusalem and why (vv. 20-23; cf. vv. 2-6). His words are followed by the Lord's speech (vv. 24-30). Note that Jeremiah does not refute but ignores the practical argument about the Queen of Heaven.

In the Lord's speech the people's actions and words are rehearsed (vv. 24-25). On that basis, the announcement of annihilation, already given in verses 7-10 as a threat, is repeated by oath. The sarcastic *Go ahead then* (v. 25d) may be compared with 7:21 and Romans 1:24-25. This last word from Jeremiah harks back to his initial call via the word *watching* (v. 27; 1:12). God superintends his promise both for good *and* for evil. God meets this community on their own terms. If they proceed with the experiment, then they shall have reason yet to own God's sovereignty (v. 28). *[Swearing, p. 311.]*

In addition to an oath, God offers them a sign. As Zedekiah, king of Judah, was handed over to Nebuchadnezzar (52:6-11), so will the Egyptian Pharaoh Hophra, fourth king of the 26th dynasty (589-570), be handed over to the enemies. Hophra is pictured on an Egyptian stele making an offering of bowls of wine. Hophra's army had come to help Judah in its last days, but then withdrew (37:5). The prophecy was fulfilled. Hophra was executed following a conflict with Amasis ( = Ahmose II), his army commander in chief (for three years a co-regent).

## A Message for Baruch  45:1-5

The date of this message to Baruch, Jeremiah's scribe, is 605. That year Babylon defeated the Egyptians at Carchemish, Jeremiah came forward to review his 23 years of preaching (25:1-11), and a scroll was dictated, read, and sliced into the fire (36:1-31). Chronologically, the passage belongs with chapter 36. In the Septuagint it appears at the very end of the book. In its present location it incorporates and concludes the judgment oracles against God's people.

God's message to Baruch comes in response to Baruch's complaint. His problem, if not "burn-out," is "worn-out." The *sorrow* may be his emotional response to Jehoiakim's scroll-burning, or a burden in addition to that disappointment. The complaint is like Jeremiah's "confessions" (e.g., 15:15-18). *[Baruch, p. 292.]*

The words *overthrow* and *uproot* are familiar not only from Jeremiah's call, but are found throughout the book (1:10; 24:6-10; 31:28). If Baruch is out of sorts, how must God feel when breaking up what he had built? Behind Baruch's groans lies frustration of personal ambitions. It is to Baruch's credit that he records the Lord's word, even if it casts him in an unfavorable light. Still the message is intended, no doubt, not so much as a biographical note but as another announcement that disaster will come. God does not leave his own unattended, however. Baruch is promised safety and will escape with his life. A similar promise was made to Ebed-Melech (39:15-18).


### THE TEXT IN BIBLICAL CONTEXT

*Two Deadly Sins.* In medieval times the "seven deadly sins" were pride, envy, wrath, greed, lechery, gluttony, and sloth. Chapters 40—45 identify two deadly sins, disobedience and idolatry, against which Jeremiah has railed throughout the book. Both are cast in bold relief in the two well-described exchanges between Jeremiah and the remnant: disobedience (42—43) and idolatry (44). In each case the discussion is not theoretical but involves concrete actions (e.g., crossing to Egypt, burning incense, and making cakes). The two deadly sins of disobedience and idolatry caused havoc in the Garden of Eden, later in the Israelite camp (Exod. 16:20; 32), and became the reason for Israel's punishment by the Assyrians (2 Kings 17:7-23).

Each of these two deadly sins is directly related to covenant thinking. Idolatry with its openness to other gods is contrary to the first commandment, which calls for exclusive loyalty to God. Disobedience is flying in the face of a covenant relationship established between God and his people. The Jewish community in Egypt, however, tried to make both the deadly sins look respectable through rationalization. The objections to going to Egypt (disobedience) were explained away (43:2-3). Idolatry was defended through a sophisticated (or simplistic?) theory of history (44:15-18).

*Blind and Deaf to History.* At least two glaring examples of not learning from history are given in Jeremiah. The Jerusalemites did not learn that sacred objects would not avert wrath: that as God had destroyed Shiloh despite the tent and the ark, where God's presence was said to be, so he would also the temple (chapter 7). Second, the remnant refused to believe that disobedience and idolatry, though it had brought destruction on Jerusalem, would bring destruction on them (chapter 44). Similarly, the history of Hebrew kings shows that many did not learn from history. Jeroboam looked for military help from Egypt, and so later, did Hezekiah, and, later still, Zedekiah. Each was disappointed.

## THE TEXT IN THE LIFE OF THE CHURCH

*Guidance.* That God offers guidance is illustrated in Jeremiah 42:1-19, but that incident also illustrates the falsity of a frequently heard notion that God will not disclose his will unless there is human readiness to do it. Not always so! The decision of the remnant to go contrary to God's will also shows all too well how personal preferences and inclinations get in the way of following God's offered guidance (cf. Num. 14:41-45; Matt. 19:16-24).

It is striking to note that when the people refused God's guidance and went to Egypt, Jeremiah went along. The principle here would be that having clearly pointed out God's word, a leader has a further duty to the people not to forsake them even when they stray from that word.

*Conflicting Interpretations of History.* The Jewish community in Egypt reasoned that the disasters that had come on Judah resulted from a failure to worship the Queen of Heaven (44:15-18). Jeremiah held that catastrophe had come because of Judah's sin against God (44:1-6). Which was correct? " . . . Jeremiah identifies the central issue: argument about the past is inconclusive; the real test of an hypothesis is the future" (Freedman: p. 37).

Conflicting interpretations of history continue. Some see the crucifixion of Jesus as inconsequential; others see the display of God's power (1 Cor. 1:18). What reasons are assigned by historians to the collapse of world empires, to North American prosperity? Does the God-aspect figure in these explanations? Should it?

*Sanctified Ambition.* Baruch is exhorted not to seek great things for himself. Shakespeare has Cardinal Wolsey say, "Cromwell, I charge thee, fling away ambition: By that sin fell the angels." There is, however, an ambition which God sanctions. "A God-approved ambition must be pure and noble, tinged with self-abnegation and self-sacrifice" (Chambers: 99). David Brainerd, missionary to North American Indians, wrote in his diary: "I cared not where or how I lived, or what hardships I endured, so that I could but gain souls for Christ."

Part 7

# Oracles Against Other Nations

# Jeremiah 46 – 51

This section holds a further political statement: a collection of nine oracles against nine nations. The form is poetry, alive with powerful images. The messages are primarily oracles of judgment, with an occasional statement of hope. Generally, they are in chronological order: 46:1—49:33, from the fourth year of Jehoiakim (605); 49:34-39, at the beginning of Zedekiah's reign (about 598); and 50:1—51:64, from the fourth year of Zedekiah (594). Some may be later, even post-587.

In our English versions, which follow the Hebrew text, these oracles against foreign nations are placed at the end of the book. The list of nations begins with Egypt in the west, and moving eastward, ends with Babylon. In the Septuagint, however, they are found after chapter 25:13, and in the order of importance. [Septuagint, p. 308.]

Putting the oracles at the end of the book has the effect of giving the book an apocalyptic flavor. While each oracle does depict not the final wrap-up of history, and many deal with events of the more immediate future, the net effect is to end on the note of a universal theme. Other oracles against nations are found in Isaiah 13—23; Ezekiel 25—32; Amos 1—2; Obadiah; and Nahum. [Apocalyptic, p. 290.]

The present arrangement of these oracles is both systematic and symmetrical. The first two nations, one geographically large (Egypt) and the other geographically small (Philistia), are balanced by the two nations at the end of the roster, one small (Elam) and the other large (Babylon). In between, three oracles deal with the trans-Jordan countries of Moab, Ammon, and Edom. Beyond these, moving northward, the subjects are Damascus and Kedar/Hazor. [Map, p. 317.]

EGYPT Philistia   Moab   Ammon   Edom   Damascus   Arabs   Elam BABYLON

Jeremiah 46–47

# Oracles Against Southern Nations: Egypt, Philistia

## PREVIEW

In the seventh century, as today, the fate of one people affected the policies and national security of surrounding nations. Egypt was a superpower to the south of Judah; Philistia was a small neighboring country directly west. The oracles announce disaster for both with the result that Judah need not fear or be threatened. But these oracles are not self-serving; they are grand and penetrating statements on how God assesses national powers.

## OUTLINE

For Egypt: Defeat Abroad; Distress at Home, 46:1-26
    46:1-12   A Military Defeat at Carchemish
    46:13-26  Distress at Home, Lower and Upper Egypt

For Israel: A Salvation Word, 46:27-28

For Philistia: A Relentless and Overpowering Onslaught, 47:1-7

## EXPLANATORY NOTES
### For Egypt: Defeat Abroad; Distress at Home 46:1-26

The oracle against Egypt is in two parts. The first is directed primarily to the army and centers on the decisive battle fought at Carchemish, in which the Babylonians defeated the Egyptians and so had opened to them Syria and Palestine (vv. 3-12). "For vividness and poetic quality, [the poem is] unexcelled by anything in the book" (Bright: 308). In the second, the focus is on the land of Egypt with a poetic announcement against Lower Egypt (vv. 14-24) and a prose announcement for Upper Egypt (vv. 25-26).

### 46:1-12 A Military Defeat at Carchemish

Like the Battle of Waterloo in the nineteenth century, the battle of Carchemish (605) was a clash between two superpowers—in this instance Egypt and Babylon. The two armies met at Carchemish, an important city on the east-west trade routes located on the Euphrates River, 60 miles west of Haran. Egypt was defeated. Accounts of this battle are varied; some scholars think the outcome was a draw. [*Babylon/ Babylonians, p. 291.*]

In the crisp staccato style of an army commander, the prophet barks out the customary orders for war preparations (vv. 3-4). Immediately, perhaps suggesting the surprise attack which Nebuchadnezzar sprang on the Egyptians, we are at the scene of battle (v. 5). *Terror on every side* is a term used in Jeremiah in war settings (6:25; 49:29) and in names (20:3, 10). It may have been a proverbial expression.

Pharaoh's aggressive ambition, compared to the rise, surge, and annual spillover of the Nile, is the only hint offered as reason for the destruction to come upon Egypt, unless by inference one includes Egypt's worship of its gods (vv. 7, 25). The *Nile*, 3,500 miles long, was the life vein of Egypt, inundating the desert regions to make them productive (Isa. 23:10; Amos 8:8; 9:5).

Cush, or Ethiopia, is in the upper Nile region. The location of Put, an African country, is disputed. Lydia is not a region of Asia Minor, but an unknown African nation; some scholars amend to "Lubim" (Libya, cf. Nah. 3:9). *That day* is the "day of the Lord" which will impact Israel, and also nations (Joel 1—2; Zeph. 1:14—2:15). It is the day when God visibly takes charge either to render judgment or to bring salvation. For Egypt it is judgment. At Carchemish on the Euphrates, the Egyptian army will be the Lord's *sacrifice* (v. 10, cf. Isa. 34:5-7; Zeph. 1:7). [*Vengeance, p. 312.*]

The advice about securing medicine is ironic. It may be paraphrased, "Go get balm in Gilead, but of course, it won't help" (cf. 8:22; Ezek. 30:22). Moreover, Egypt had ambitions to occupy Gilead in the northeast of Palestine and did so between 609 and 605. Like Napoleon at the gates of Moscow, she fought far from her borders, but lost. The irony lies also in that Egypt itself was known for its skills in medicine. The metaphor of sickness and healing, one of Jeremiah's favorites, has also been used for Israel (8:22; 14:19; 30:12-13).

### 46:13-26  Distress at Home, Lower and Upper Egypt

Several years after the Carchemish battle, Nebuchadnezzar attacked Egypt at her borders (601). Jeremiah's prophecy about the event describes precisely how the Egyptians will fare (i.e., badly). Babylon inflicted heavy losses but did not manage to take control. Babylon took the following year to refit the army.

In this passage the setting is clearly on Egyptian soil. Migdol is in the east Nile delta region; Tahpanhes was a border fortress; and Memphis, also known as Noph, near modern-day Cairo, was the capital of Lower Egypt. For the summons to battle-readiness, compare 46:3f; 49:14; 50:14f, 21; 51:11. It is mercenaries who say, Let us go back (v. 6; cf. v. 21). A textual unclarity can possibly be resolved by dividing a word to yield the attractive reading: "Why has Apis fled? Why did not your bull stand?" (v. 15, RSV, following the Septuagint). Apis, the chief god of Memphis, was worshiped as a black bull. He has missed his opportunity is a wordplay on Pharaoh Hophra (588-569), on the order of, so it has been suggested, "The Duke of Lambeth is a lame duck." Hophra, despite his boasts, was losing power (v. 17). [Wordplay, p. 313].

The poet reaches for comparisons and metaphors. First, the Babylonians are compared to towering mountains. Mt. Tabor is a conspicuous, isolated mountain with steep slopes, rising about 2,000 feet above sea level above the plain of Jezreel. Carmel, memorable for Elijah's contest, is a mountain jutting into the Mediterranean near modern Haifa. At the mercy of such a power, the prospect for Memphis is to lie in ruins (v. 19, "burned down," NASB, reading a different Hebrew root). Next, the animal and insect metaphors single out the laughable aspects of the coming match, as well as the disparity between the two superpowers (vv. 20-23). The Egyptian royal insignia was a serpent. The Babylonians are compared to woodchoppers—an apt figure since certain regions along the Nile are thick with palms.

Upper Egypt lies southward; its capital was Thebes, also known as No. Amon, a sun-god, was its patron deity. Thus both Upper and Lower

Egypt will be the object of Nebuchadnezzar's attacks. We know of two, possibly three, military engagements of Egypt with Babylon: one in 601, perhaps more like a foray; another in 568; and if Josephus, a Jewish historian, is to be trusted, one also in 582.

## For Israel: A Salvation Word  46:27-28

This assurance-salvation oracle, fits more easily in the context of 30:10-11. The reason for its placement here is not obvious. A contrast may be intended between a crumbling Egyptian Empire and a restored Israelite people. *[Doublets, p. 296; Deliverance Oracles, p. 295.]*

## For Philistia: A Relentless and Overpowering Onslaught  47:1-7

Israel's close neighbor, Philistia, had earlier been overrun by the Egyptians moving north. It will now be conquered by the Babylonians moving south. The time of this oracle, *before Pharaoh attacked Gaza,* likely dates to 609, when the Egyptians under Pharaoh Neco II moved northward, there to rebuff the westward push of the Babylonians. The Greek historian Herodotus tells of such an attack on Kadytis, widely believed to be Gaza. The Lord's speech is given in verses 2-5; the Philistines are quoted in verse 6, and the prophet replies in verse 7.

The figure of the flood, this *overflowing torrent* (v. 2; cf. Isa. 8:7-8), refers to the *noise of enemy chariots,* namely the Babylonians, rolling southward after the decisive battle at Carchemish in 605. The sense of helplessness in the face of such large numbers and impressive equipment is captured in the phrase *hands will hang limp* (v. 3; cf. 6:24; 50:43). *Tyre and Sidon,* Phoenician cities on the Mediterranean coast to the north, were commercial allies with the Philistine cities. Nebuchadnezzar conducted a thirteen-year, but largely unsuccessful siege against Tyre. *[Babylonians, p. 291.]* Caphtor or Crete is the place of origin for the Philistines, who were among the "sea peoples" who settled along the coast in the twelfth and eleventh centuries (Amos 9:7). Two of the five key cities, Gaza and Ashkelon, were within ten miles of each other. Three are not mentioned (Gath, Ekron, and Ashdod, cf. 25:20).

The baldness of Gaza can be either the baldness on its citizens *in mourning* (v. 5; cf. 16:6; 41:5) or the city itself: "Gaza is shorn bare" (NEB). The conjectural "remnant of the Anakim" (v. 5, RSV) is better rendered "remnant of their strength," since the word in question can be "strength" as well as *plain* (NIV), as a discovery from Ugaritic, a language related to the Hebrew, shows.

In the cry accompanying their self-inflicted gashings, the Philistines, though here unnamed, become weary of the relentless toll of the *sword of the Lord* and call for some relief. The prophet answers: it is the Lord who directs the conquering forces (v. 7). This prophecy was fulfilled in 605/4 when, according to the Babylonian Chronicle, Nebuchadnezzar sacked Ashkelon because the city had refused to pay tribute. Other prophets also spoke against the Philistines (Isa. 14:29-31; Ezek. 25:15-17; Amos 1:6-8).

## THE TEXT IN BIBLICAL CONTEXT

*Egypt.* For Israel Egypt was both a haven and a prison. In times of famine Jacob's family located there to survive (Gen. 46:1ff.). After the fall of Jerusalem, refugees settled there (Jer. 43:4-7). Our Lord escaped Herod's wrath by going to Egypt (Matt. 2:13-15). But for Israel, Egypt was the oppressor, too, like a furnace of affliction (Jer. 11:4).

The prophets warn Israel not to rely on Egypt (Isa. 31:1-3). Egypt is consigned to judgment, sometimes through natural disorders/disasters such as drought (Isa. 19:5-10) and at other times through war. Reasons for this judgment are not given at length, but include idolatry (Isa. 19:3; Ezek. 30:13), unreliability (Ezek. 29:6-7), possessiveness (Ezek. 29:9), ruthlessness (Ezek. 30:10), and pride (Ezek. 31:10, 18). In spite of all the denunciations, Isaiah anticipates the conversion of Egypt to become for God "my people" (Isa. 19:25).

## THE TEXT IN THE LIFE OF THE CHURCH

*Agents in God's Service.* Both Egypt and Philistia are to suffer severely at the hand of Nebuchadnezzar of Babylon, who is clearly God's agent (46:14-23, 26; 47:7).

That God uses warring nations to accomplish his purpose is not a justification for war, any more than God's use of Judas in the betrayal of Jesus exonerates Judas'. Judas remains responsible. So does Babylon, who will later be judged, not for being God's agent, but for gloating over Israel's destruction. According to the New Testament, believers are to be agents of reconciliation, not destruction (2 Cor. 5:18-20). Modern states will continue to engage in war, but such death-dealing is no work for Christians, for at least two reasons: (a) God chooses whatever agents he will to bring about justice—not necessarily "Christian" agents; and (b) followers of Christ are committed to pursue peace, not war.

Jeremiah 48 – 49

# Oracles Against the
# Trans-Jordan Countries

## PREVIEW

This group of oracles continues God's word to the nations surrounding Israel; it is directed to the countries east of the Jordan. Three of these lay to the south: Moab, Ammon, and Edom. To the north was Damascus, and in the remoter eastern areas were the desert peoples of Kedar and Hazor. Much further east beyond Babylon was Elam. Common themes are those of judgment and destruction. In several oracles the country's patron deity is noted. Greater attention is given to a description of the destruction than to the causes of punishment. The date of these oracles, sometimes composite, is unclear, although 604, the year Nebuchadnezzar came southward to Ashkelon, has been suggested.

## OUTLINE

For Moab: Calamity and Disgrace, 48:1-47
    48:1-10    Destroyed and Disgraced
    48:11-25   Shamed and Shattered
    48:26-39   Ridiculed, Yet Lamented
    48:40-47   Captured and Exiled

For Ammon: Terror for Its Boasting and Aggression, 49:1-6

For Edom: A Thorough Stripping and a Complete Overthrow, 49:7-22

For Damascus: Bad News—Panic, Anguish, and Pain, 49:23-27

For Desert Arabs: A Sudden Scattering, 49:28-33

For Elam: A Broken Bow, 49:34-39

The greatest space is devoted to Moab, an ancient antagonist of Israel. The reason for the disproportionate length is not clear. Three of the group will eventually be restored: Moab, Ammon, and Elam.

## EXPLANATORY NOTES
### For Moab: Calamity and Disgrace 48:1-47

Several themes in this symphony of poems are repeated in a doleful minor key: destruction of cities, cries of anguish, the flight of refugees, the pride of a people, the helplessness of the gods, and disgrace generally. With varying degrees of elaboration, most of these are found in each of the four sections for Moab. The four sections have a certain symmetry about them. The first and the last, of similar length, center on the destruction and are marked by an inclusio, namely "woe" (vv. 1, 46). The middle two each begin with references to wine and are marked by the inclusio "smashed jars" (vv. 12, 38). [Inclusio, p. 298.]

Moabites were the descendants of Lot (Gen. 19:37). They refused permission to the northward-traveling Israelite tribes under Moses to pass through their land (Judg. 11:17). As under Solomon and Omri, Moab was from time to time, subject to Israel. The major prophets each have oracles of judgment against this country (Isa. 15—16; Jer. 48:1-47, cf. 9:26; 25:2; 27:3; Ezek. 25:8-11). Since identical phrases, verses, and even sections occur in them, some of these oracles had likely been in circulation for some time—parts almost certainly from the middle of the seventh century. The major complaints against Moab are her pride (Isa. 16:6; Jer. 48:29), her disparagement of Judah (Ezek. 25:8; Zeph. 2:8, 10), and her insults to Edom (Amos 2:1-3).

Moab lies east of the Dead Sea and consists of a high plateau and some deep, rather rugged river-cut valleys, the Arnon in the north and Zared in the south. Many of Moab's cities are named—a striking feature—but only a few can now be located. Some believe that the Babylonians attacked Moab and Ammon in 598. Along with Israel, Moab was party to a planned rebellion in 594, but nothing came of it

(27:3). Josephus, a Jewish historian from the first century A.D., records that the Babylonians invaded Moab and Ammon in 582 (cf. the third Judean deportation, Jer. 52:30). Attacked by desert peoples, Moab soon after ceased to exist as a nation. Our knowledge of Moabite history is scanty. However, there are two possible times for the fulfillment of these prophecies: 599/98 and/or 582. [Map, p. 317.]

## 48:1-10 Destroyed and Disgraced

Verse 1 sets forth the dominant themes of "destroyed and disgraced." The cities listed are Nebo, its location unknown but presumably near Mt. Nebo (cf. Num. 32:38); Kiriathaim, 10 miles due west of Medeba; and Misgab, unknown, perhaps not a city, but as the name suggests, the stronghold. Heshbon was the capital for Sihon, the Amorite king (Num. 21:25-30; Josh. 13:16f.). It is identified with modern Hesban. A double wordplay occurs with the names of two cities: Heshbon and plot each contain the consonants h.s.b.; in Madmen and silenced the main consonants are d.m. Luhith and Horonaim are located on one single road leading from the plateau to the southwest of the Dead Sea. [Wordplay, p. 313.]

Nebo, Kiriathaim, and Horonaim are mentioned on the Moabite stone, a ninth-century basalt inscription left by Mesha, king of Moab. It commemorates a revolt against Israel (2 Kings 3:4-5). The three-foot-high stone, found at Dibon by a German missionary in 1868, contains 34 lines of writing.

The cries of the captured, the fleeing up to and away from cities, and the shouting of instructions are described in verses 3-6. Chemosh, the god of the Moabites, is known from the Moabite stone which reads in part, "Chemosh was angry at his land." King Mesha honored Chemosh by building a high place at Qarhoh (cf. vv. 13, 46; cf. 1 Kings 11:7). A problem Hebrew word in verse 6b has now been resolved on the basis of an Arabic cognate with the translation: "Like a sand grouse in the wilderness" (NEB). Misplaced trust in deeds (or "fortresses" following the Septuagint) and riches is an initial reason for the disaster, but more basic is pride (v. 29). The destroyer is likely Nebuchadnezzar. Above the visible destroyer, however, stands the Lord who has spoken.

Verse 9 is highly problematic. To the various suggestions one might add: "Set a flower for Moab; its petals will disappear." To put salt on Moab is a practice noted in Judges (9:45). A curse on halfhearted or negligent action concludes the oracle against Philistia, which ends on the subject of sword (47:5ff.); but it is also fitting here for Moab to indicate that at God's command the sword will pursue you (v. 2).

## 48:11-25  Shamed and Shattered

An easygoing and complacent, if not stale and stagnant, society is pictured in images from the vine industry, for which Moab was known (cf. vv. 32, 33; Isa. 16:8-11). Wine was left on its dregs to improve the flavor; it was then poured to strain the sediment. If left too long the wine would spoil, becoming insipid—"that tastes the same as ever and its scent mellows never" (Moffatt, cf. Zeph. 1:12). The "lees" or sediment may point to the god Chemosh, on whom Moab had depended. Pouring Moab into exile would remove the bad flavor.

Bethel may refer to the place where calf worship was introduced (1 Kings 12:28f.; cf. Amos 5:5; 7:10-17). Bethel is also a god, known to have been worshiped in Syria, and, as records show, by the Jews in the Egyptian colony of Elephantine in the fifth century B.C. The title of God as King is used comparatively sparingly, but is most suitable in the foreign nation oracles, especially to upstage the patron deities (v. 15; 8:19; 10:7; 46:18; 51:57; cf. Isa. 6:5; 33:22; Ps. 24:7-10).

Moab's arrogance is implied by Come down from your glory (cf. v. 29). Note the imperatives: console (v. 17); stand (v. 19); wail (v. 20). Wail and cry out continues the woe sentiment with which the poem opens, as does the sinister drumbeat of "shamed" and shattered (vv. 1, 20).

Of the cities mentioned, Dibon is modern Deban where the Moabite stone was found. Aroer is just north of the Arnon River; Bozrah is eight miles northeast of Medeba. These places can be located with certainty, though several others are mentioned on the Moabite stone. The Arnon River cuts through the rugged mountain terrain east of the Dead Sea to form Moab's north border. Moab's strength is gone—as symbolized by an animal's horn (cf. Ps. 75:5), now broken, and the arm, now severed.

## 48:26-39  Ridiculed, Yet Lamented

Make her drunk recalls the cup of wrath passed from one nation to the other, including Moab (25:15-21). For the call to flee (v. 28), compare verse 6; and for the pitfalls of such a flight, see verse 44.

The chief reason for Moab's destruction is pride, the Lord declares in a stack-up of synonyms (v. 29, cf. Isa. 16:6). Several of the terms derive from a Hebrew root which means "to rise." Two other words come from the root "to lift up" (cf. 2 Chron. 26:16; Ezek. 28), and are incorporated in the Hebrew idiom "the high of eyes," namely a "high look" or "haughty eyes" (Ps. 101:5; cf. Isa. 10:12). Pride has to do with "making (oneself) great," that is, magnifying oneself, hence they defied the Lord (vv. 26, 42 NIV). Evidence of that pride is their insolence and boasts (v. 30), and also their misplaced trust (v. 7).

*I wail . . . I moan . . . I weep* are expressions of lament and mourning, a subject which dominates in verses 31-39. For outward signs of mourning, such as shaving the head, see 41:5. A preferred translation for verse 32 is: "I will weep for you more than I wept for Jazer"(NEB). Once located in Ammonite territory, Jazer was conquered by King Mesha of Moab. The reason for grief is (1) that the vines, particularly luxuriant and far-spreading, have been despoiled; there is no fruit, no joy (vv. 32-33); and (2) that the citizens' wealth is gone (v. 36). It has been suggested that in verses 29-39 there is an antiphonal relay, perhaps between the Lord and the people. People's responses are in verses 31c, 34, 37, 39 (Thompson: 710).

As for the cities, Kir Hareseth has been identified with el-Kerak south of the Arnon, 11 miles east of the Dead Sea. Zoar was one of the "cities of the Plain" with Sodom and Gomorrah in the southern region of the Dead Sea (Gen. 13:10). Heshbon is modern Hesban, where excavations have uncovered an Iron Age city (1200-600 B.C., cf. v. 2). Other place names are not readily located.

### 48:40-47 Captured and Exiled

The takeover of Moab cities by the enemy is pictured in the metaphor of an eagle's swoop (cf. Ezek. 17:1ff.). The figure of soldiers becoming frightened and weak like travailing women is common (30:6; 49:22). The plight of refugees is handled with three similar-sounding words: *paḥad* (terror), *paḥat* (pit), and *paḥ* (snare) (v. 43). Each is then expanded (v. 44). For a similar point, see Amos 5:19; 9:1-4. In this section the reason for the captivity and exile is hinted at in the expression *noisy boasters* (cf. vv. 26, 29, 42). The expression *the people of Chemosh* has its counterpart in the expression (rarely used) "the people of Yahweh." Finally, there is a hope message even for Moab (v. 47). *[Restoration Formula, p. 307.]*

### THE TEXT IN BIBLICAL CONTEXT

*Pride Goes Before a Fall.* God abhors pride in nations: Assyria (Zech. 10:11), Babylon (Isa. 13:19), Moab (Jer. 48:29), Egypt (Ezek. 30:6), and Israel (Amos 6:8). On the "day of the Lord," God's acts of judgment will be against all that is proud (Isa. 2:12-18). In the three prophetic books (Isaiah, Jeremiah, and Ezekiel), plus the wisdom books (Psalms, Proverbs, Job), 53 examples of the condemnation of pride occur. Particularly noted for their pride were the king of Tyre (Ezek. 28), the kings Nebuchadnezzar and Belshazzar (Dan. 5:18-23), and the self-righteous Pharisees (Luke 18:9ff.). Jesus warned of pride (Mark 7:22), as did Paul (1 Tim. 3:6).

*Compassion for Enemies During Judgment.* Empathy with a despoiled people as described in 48:33-36, comparable to Jesus' compassion for people deserving judgment (Matt. 23:37), is a Spirit-given quality and is the direct opposite of that attitude which rejoices in another's evil (1 Cor. 13:6).

## THE TEXT IN THE LIFE OF THE CHURCH

*National and Denominational Pride.* Modern "high tech" nations, comparable to Moab with its fortresses and riches (48:7), readily become smug and arrogant because of their resources. Pride will make for insensitivity and disregard of the needs of others (Ezek. 16:47). "Prosperity commonly brings pride with it, and those who excel in dignity and power become self-willed and insolent" (Calvin IV: 592). Similarly, denominations with striking heritages or outstanding achievements may easily fall into the we-are-number-one trap. Celebration of achievements is appropriate; self-glorying is not. (See comments on "Pride" at Jeremiah 13.)

## For Ammon: Terror for Its Boasting and Aggression 49:1-6

Ammon comes under God's judgment for her ambitious program of territorial expansion. This small country was situated in central Transjordan east of the Jabbok River. Israel had claimed that territory upon coming into the land under Joshua (Josh. 10:6—12:6). It belonged to Israel under David (2 Sam. 12:26-31). Ammon's occupation of Gad came after Tiglath-pilezer the Assyrian had raided Israel in 733. With Israel's collapse, Ammon moved in. Late in the seventh century Ammon joined others against Jehoiakim (2 Kings 24:2). Later her king Baalis hired Ishmael to assassinate Gedaliah (40:14—41:10). Ammon is addressed by: Ezekiel (25:1-7), Amos (1:13-15), and Zephaniah (2:8-11).

The short oracle is pleasingly symmetrical, as the outline indicates:

> Judgment speech, vv. 1-2
> accusation, v. 1
> announcement, v. 2
> Summons to mourning, v. 3
> Judgment speech, vv. 4-5
> accusation (question and indictment), v. 4
> announcement, v. 5
> Salvation announcement, v. 6

The accusations in the judgment speeches revolve around Ammon (1) taking over the territory of Gad, east of the Jordan from Israel—land to which Gad's heirs were entitled; and (2) boastfully trusting in her wealth and security ("resources," so NEB for "valleys," v. 4, following an insight from excavated texts at Ugarit, cf. 47:5). Amos charges the Ammonites with grave atrocities in her conquests (1:13-14). Molech is the Ammonite god Milcom (meaning "the king"), in whose name the conquests were undertaken (cf. 1 Kings 11:5, 33, 2 Kings 23:13). The Hebrew is "Malcam" (so NASB) which can be rendered "their king"; but "Milcom," supported by major versions, is preferable. Like Chemosh, the Moabite deity, this patron deity will go into exile (cf. 48:7). [*Judgment Oracle, p. 299.*]

In each of the two announcements, a declaration of God's intervention (e.g., *I will bring terror*, v. 5) is followed by the effect of such action (e.g., *ruin*, v. 2; helpless fugitives, v. 5). Rabbah, modern Amman, was the Ammonite capital. The call to lament is a natural response to the fall of a great city (cf. 9:17-21). Heshbon was once the royal city of the Amorite king Sihon. At one point it was held by Gad, but later it belonged to Moab (48:2, 45). For Ammon as for Moab there is a salvation word (v. 6). [*Restoration Formula, p. 307.*]

## For Edom: A Thorough Stripping and a Complete Overthrow 49:7-22

Edom's history illustrates the proverb that "pride goes before destruction" (Prov. 16:18). The Edomites, descendants of Esau, occupied a region which stretched about 100 miles south of the Dead Sea to the Gulf of Aqabah (Gen. 36:1-19). The bitter hatred between the descendants of the two brothers, Esau and Jacob, was intense and of long-standing (Gen. 27:41; Amos 1:11-12; Ps. 137:7-9, especially if "Daughter of Babylon" is a reference to Edom as Babylon's ally). Edom at first collaborated with Zedekiah in a planned rebellion against the Babylonians (27:3), but later sided with the Babylonians (Ezek. 25:12-14; Obad.; Ps. 137:7). With the removal of the Judeans by the Babylonians in 587, the Edomites, pressed by desert Arab peoples, entered and settled Judah. The region came to be known even into New Testament times as Idumea, homeland of King Herod the Great.

The date of this oracle, which incorporates stanzas from other books, is uncertain. The oracle is rich with simile and metaphor. Another prophet, Obadiah, is concerned exclusively with Edom. Some of the text there is found in this passage (e.g., Obadiah 1-4 = Jer. 49:14-16; Obad.

5-6 = Jer. 49:9-10). Ezekiel also is severe with Edom, whom he names Mt. Seir (Ezek. 35:1-15; cf. Mal. 1:2-5).

## 49:7-12  Edom Stripped Bare

The question *Has counsel perished?* apparently concerns defense strategies (cf. v. 20). The best of human scheming is inadequate in the face of God's advance. The *disaster* by strict definition is the final disaster which awaits Edom at her "final audit," *the time I punish him* (v. 8). Though its location is disputed, Teman, may be in North Edom. Dedan is identified with an oasis area and lies southeast of Edom in Arabia, though at certain periods it belonged to Edom. Bozrah was Edom's chief city, 25 miles southeast of the Dead Sea.

Thieves who loot don't take all. Grape pickers leave gleanings. These two images provide the background for God's work with Edom which, by contrast, will be a total ransacking, a thorough stripping bare (Obad. 5-6). For the Edomites there will be no *hiding places.* Mention of surviving widows and orphans seems strange. Hence the New English Bible translates, "What! Am I to save alive your fatherless children? Are your widows to trust in me?" But the sense is rather that God is touched by compassion, even in his work of judgment (cf. 48:31-32; 31:20). Or perhaps the harshness of coming judgment is underscored: no survivors will be there to care for widows.

Edom should not think to be exempt. In fact Edom is the more guilty in that Judah, whom Edom raided, is a son of "Jacob," Esau's brother. God states on oath that Edom is destined to drink from the wine cup of God's wrath (cf. 25:17-28). *[Swearing, p. 311.]*

## 49:14-22  Edom Overthrown Completely

Edom's sin, repeated from Obadiah, is pride (v. 16; Obad. 1-4; cf. Jer. 48:29). Her position in rocky terrain led to a belief that she was invulnerable to attack. Petra, "the red-rock city" with homes and temples cut into rock—an attraction for modern tourists—was accessible only through a narrow gorge. This hidden city was an example of Edom's mountain fastnesses. The root word for pride means "high" and "lifted up"; the reference to *heights of the hill* and a *nest as high as the eagle's* draws a correspondence between Edom's dwellings and her inner arrogance. Edom's power, which now intimidates, will be made small (cf. Hannah's song, 1 Sam. 2:6).

The complete overthrow of Edom is sketched with the help of several images, beginning with Sodom and Gomorrah, continuing with the proverbially vicious and irresistible *lion from Jordan's thickets* (5:6; in

50:44-46 the same image applies to Babylon), and concluding with the third image, well known to these rock-dwellers, the *eagle* or vulture swooping toward its prey, in this case *Bozrah* (cf. v. 12). The overthrow will be so decisive that Edom will fall with a great thud. *What the Lord has planned* and *purposed*—a clean sweep of the Edomite territory—contrasts ironically with the counsels of its leaders in their schemes to defend the land (v. 20; cf. v. 7). Bozrah today lies in ruins. The nation has long since vanished.

### For Damascus: Bad News—Panic, Anguish and Pain 49:23-27

Large cities rise and wane. Damascus, one of the oldest cities in the ancient Near East, had been the capital of the Aramaen state east of Jordan to the north. Situated on the east bank of the Orontes River, Hamath was on a main route to the south of Asia Minor. According to the Babylonian Chronicle, it was at Hamath that the fleeing Egyptians were overtaken following the battle at Carchemish in 605. Arpad lies 25 miles northwest of Aleppo. Both Hamath and Arpad were small city states in the eighth century. Along with Damascus, they were annexed by the Assyrians between 740-732 and virtually ceased as independent territories. Hence the connection with Jeremiah is unclear.

The oracle stresses the consternation of Damascus, using the figure of a restless sea. Her enfeebled condition is vividly portrayed by the image of a *woman in labor*. She is in acute distress, even panic. Ben-Hadad ("son" of Hadad) was the name of several kings of Syria (1 Kings 15:18-20; 2 Kings 13:24). Hadad, known in Canaan as Baal, was the storm-god worshiped by the Aramaens.

### For Desert Arabs: A Sudden Scattering, 49:28-33

*Kedar* were nomadic tribespeople frequently mentioned in the Old Testament who occupied the Syrian-Arabian desert more remotely east of the Jordan. The Arab tribes had given the Assyrians difficulty in the seventh century. In the sixth century, more precisely in 599/8 B.C. according to the Babylonian Chronicle, Nebuchadnezzar attacked them and held these desert powers in check. A fulfillment of the prophecy against these nomads, perhaps spoken by Jeremiah in 604, comes from the Babylonian records, which state that their companies were sent out, and "scouring the desert, they took much plunder from many Arabs, their possessions, animals and goods."

*Hazor* was not the strategic northern Palestine city, but another Arab tribe of the eastern desert. It has been suggested that Hazor could also be the name of clustered unwalled encampments (v. 31, cf. Isa. 42:4; 60:7) and for *kingdoms of Hazor* one might more accurately read "village chieftains of Hazor" (Bright: 336). A third group, *the people of the East*, is mentioned elsewhere (Gen. 29:1; Judg. 7:12). They were responsible for the demise of Ammon and Moab in the middle sixth century (cf. Ezek. 25:1ff.).

The short war poem is constructed symmetrically with the second "summons to attack" (vv. 31-33) parallel to the first (vv. 28b-29), each with a "call to attack" followed by a listing of the consequences. Between these is a "summons to flee" (v. 30). *Terror on every side* is a favorite phrase of Jeremiah (6:25; 20:4, 10; 46:5).

## For Elam: A Broken Bow 49:34-39

God may lay a nation low at the point of its strength. Elam was situated east of Babylon in southwest Iran. In the seventh century it assisted Babylon in its overthrow of the Assyrians. Then it became independent; and, judging from a fragmentary text in the Babylonian Chronicle, in 596/4 it clashed with Nebuchadnezzar. Later it played a role in the overthrow of Babylon (540/39) and was then absorbed into the Persian Empire. The connections of Elam with Judea are not readily clear since our knowledge of Elamite history is so meager. The oracle makes clear that if the Jews hoped Babylon would be undone by an Eastern power and the 70 years announced by Jeremiah cut short, they were mistaken.

*The bow of Elam*: the renown of the Elamites for their prowess in archery is attested to in Scripture (Isa. 22:6) and in bas-reliefs at Nineveh, which show the Elamite army mainly as bowmen. Conquering kings set their throne within the conquered area (v. 38; cf. 1:15; 43:8-13). The poem is weighted in the direction of the Lord's intervention, as shown by the frequent *I will* statements. "But when it is all over, I will restore the fortunes of Elam" (Bright: 335). *[Restoration Formula, p. 307; Wrath, p. 313.]* Concerning Zedekiah, see *Kings of Judah, p. 300.*

### THE TEXT IN BIBLICAL CONTEXT

*War Poems and Prophecy.* War—fighting, torture, killing—has marked both primitive peoples and modern civilizations, pagan people and God's people. Abraham, Moses, Gideon, David, and Josiah knew about warfare firsthand. Warfare figures in the prophets' war poems (e.g., Zech. 9) and in the oracles against the nations (Amos, Isaiah, Jeremiah, Ezekiel, Obadiah, Nahum). The prophets almost always stress God's role (not Israel's) as decisive to the outcome.

Moreover, the arena of God's power is large. "The Prophets then represented as in a mirror the power of God, that the Israelites might know that it extended to the whole world and to every nation" (Calvin IV: 603). God decides the destinies of world powers like Assyria (Isa. 10:5) and Egypt (Exod. 14:11-12).

In one sense the war poems are uninterpreted; they are simply there as a record of the way it was predicted things would work out. In another sense they are their own interpretation: the long history of war is its own commentary, for war has repeatedly yielded destruction. War efforts are defeatist efforts. The victories have been temporary and often hollow. Jesus describes (thankfully, he does not prescribe), "There shall be wars and rumors of wars." Taken together, these war poems shout an anguished appeal, "Who will deliver us from this body of death?" To that cry, Jesus and the kingdom of God are the answer.

## THE TEXT IN THE LIFE OF THE CHURCH

*Oracles Against the Nations: Treasure Trove of Theology.* The messages of these oracles against the nations are useful for more than reconstructions of ancient history or the determinations of fulfillment, though these have their place. As poetry, they evoke feelings: they can express righteous indignation or grief. They also supply grist for theological reflection. Example: Calvin gave 14 lectures on Jeremiah 46—49, which extend to 165 pages. The following observations are pertinent to the modern situation.

1. Often harassed by most of the nations named, Israel could be consoled with the knowledge that oppressive powers would ultimately be dealt with. God had not ceased to care for his people. He would bring recompense. *[Vengeance, p. 312.]*

2. While they were a consolation to Israel, these oracles predicting the fall and/or demise of states make a strong statement about God's sovereignty. He superintends a nation's destruction; it does not occur by chance. Like a tree cursed at the roots, an evil nation may temporarily stand, but sooner or later it will topple. By the same token, at God's pleasure, nations are restored to prominence.

3. Whether Egyptian chariot or Elamite bow, the power of the enemy is not only oppressive but seems irresistible. But, as Calvin says, to form a judgment at a higher plane, "not according to the flesh, but according to the spirit [is to] see that all this is frail and evanescent" (Calvin IV: 576).

4. Pride, aggression, violence, trust in national resources, exploitation

of another's weakness—these bring about the collapse of nations and empires. "It is the divergence between the divine plan and the pagan intention which often provides the basis for the divine judicial decision against such nations" (Freedman, 1967: 39).

5. The greatest and the richest powers, those "inebriated with false confidences"—Egypt and Babylon—do not escape God's judgment.

6. Engagement with God means engagement with the world, and that means engagement with societies organized as nation-states.

7. The purpose of these war poems is not to abet war but to help us see war's futility.

## Jeremiah 50 — 51

# An Oracle Against Babylon

**PREVIEW**

Babylon has been the backdrop for much of Jeremiah. In the early chapters the mysterious "foe from the north" is a reference to Babylon, which is later made clear. In the central section of the book Babylon's expansionistic designs worry several of Judah's kings, especially Zedekiah. Events of the final siege by Babylon against Jerusalem and the aftermath dominate in chapters 39—44. A set of oracles against nations follows, and the book virtually ends with an oracle on the fate of Babylon and its empire.

This oracle differs from previous oracles against the nations in its length: it almost equals all the others combined. It is also more intense— God's vengeance is primary. Unlike preceding oracles, it frequently gives the reasons for destruction.

The date is uncertain. If, as some scholars hold, the oracle consists of separate pieces composed at various times, then the time of composition could range from 590 to 562. If a single date is to be selected, 580 is a suggestion.

The main burden of the oracle is that Babylon will be destroyed and consequently the captives from Israel will return home. Babylon will be destroyed because of her sins against God and against Israel. But this bland summary, like a single-sentence summary of a detective story, drains the color from the exciting drama and does not do justice to its sweeping, world-impacting action. The oracle has complex internal features as well. For example, note the unusual switch in which Babylon, who for Israel is the "foe from the north," will herself suddenly be threatened by a "foe from the north." The protagonists are God, who is the decisive agent, and the mighty Babylon. The oracle bounces back and forth among three subjects: Babylon, the "foe," and Israel. Rather than a complete outline, the gist of the oracle is given in the outline.

## OUTLINE (By Subject)

**Babylon:** God's case against her (50:11-13, 31-32)
the coming sword and army (50:35-44)
her imminent overthrow (51:7-9)
God's guarantee of her end (51:13-19, 29)
her fall (51:52-58)

**The Foe:** repeatedly summoned for the attack (50:14-16, 21-30)
clearly identified as God's agent (51:11-12, 20-23)
pressing on to victory (51:27-32)

**Israel/Judah:**
coming to terms with their sin (50:4-6, 17-20)
delivered from captivity by God (50:33-34)
urged to flee home from Babylon (51:6, 45, 50).

The structure of the poem, said to be "illogically arranged," is instead highly complex, involving skillfully balanced sections within movements (Aitken: 25-63; his helpful insights on structure have been adapted in what follows). At the surface level, the oracle is in two halves, roughly corresponding to the chapter divisions: 50:4-44 and 51:1-53. The framework of the oracle consists of an introduction (50:1-3), an intermediate conclusion for the first half (50:45-46), and a final conclusion (51:54-58). The oracle is followed by a symbolic action (50:59-64).

In each half of the oracle the three topics— Babylon, the "foe," and Israel—are discussed separately. In the first half the discussions are fewer but longer; in the second the pieces are shorter and fairly tumble over each other. The figure of sheep is carried through in the first half. Harvest and drunkenness (especially prominent) are recurring figures in the second. The first half is punctuated with a sword song (50:35-38); the second, a warclub song (51:20-23). In each half one finds a wordplay on "Babylon" (50:21; 51:1, 41), the phrase "I am against you" (50:31;

51:25), announcements of Babylon's capture (50:2, 46; 51:8, 31), and a description of the news reaching the king (50:43; 51:31-32). Various identical expressions occur in each half.

## EXPLANATORY NOTES

### Babylon's Fall Pictured  50:1-46

Throughout the two chapters beginning in 50:1, the Hebrew text distinguishes between the city of Babylon and the Babylonian people (=Chaldeans). Various translations of this passage differ in terminology. For example, for the term Chaldeans, scholarly and popular usage has substituted Babylonians (NIV, RSV). [Babylon/Babylonians, p. 291.] The translations also differ in verb tenses. NIV regards the verb as "prophetic perfect"—e.g., Babylon will be captured. RSV and NASB employ past tense, "Babylon has been captured." Although the prophet placed himself beyond the event and therefore spoke of actions as completed, the verb is best given as future, as in NIV.

### 50:1-3  Banner Headline: "Babylon Will Fall"

The call to *announce and proclaim among the nations* sets the oracle apart from other oracles in this sequence: none of the others have such wide-ranging, even universal, impact. The content of the message extends beyond verse 2 (contrary to NIV) to all of chapter 50, and so includes the reasons for her fall (cf. 50:46). *Bel* ("lord") is an older title of the chief Babylonian deity. *Marduk* ("Merodach" RSV, NASB) was a creator-god, the patron god of the city of Babylon. The downfall of a god meant the downfall of his people (51:44; cf. 46:25; 48:7; 49:3). Babylon fell to Cyrus the Persian in October 539 B.C.

The *nation from the north* seems to be Jeremiah's standardized way of speaking of an enemy who conquers. Earlier, it referred to Babylon, the destroyer of Israel (4:6; 6:1; 15:12), but now it signifies a northern power, possibly the Medes, the destroyer of Babylon (51:11, 27-28). Or perhaps the designation means the Persians, who, though located east of Babylon, not only entered the city from the north, but whose vassal people included groups from the north.

### 50:4-20  Israel's Guilt/Babylon's Guilt

This section speaks of Israel/Judah, the foe, and Babylon. The first and last of five sections deal with Israel (vv. 4-7; 17-20); the second and fourth, with the foe (vv. 8-10; 14-16); and the center section, with Babylon (vv. 11-13). As for **Israel,** Babylon's capture will mean the release of those held captive. They will return to *Zion*, to *Carmel* in the Mediterranean mountain range, and to *Bashan*, a region east of Jordan and north of *Gilead* (vv. 4, 19). As united peoples they will spiritually *bind themselves to the Lord* (v. 5). *[Covenant, p. 294.]*

Using the figure of sheep, the people's historical situation is reviewed (vv. 6-7, 17; cf. 23:1-4). *Assyria* captured Samaria in 722. Under Ashurbanipal Assyria reached its greatest territorial extent, but then crumbled after 630. *Babylon* captured Jerusalem in 587. The conquerors correctly said of Israel, *They sinned against the Lord* (v. 7; cf. Nebuzaradan, 40:3). But at the time of Babylon's fall and the captive's release, Israel's guilt will be forgiven (v. 20; cf. Micah 7:18). The opening and concluding verses of this section deal with Israel and explain her return to the land, despite her guilt, on the basis that (1) the people of their free will have returned into a covenant relationship with God (v. 5), and (2) God in his gracious initiative has forgiven them (v. 20).

As for the **foe,** we learn of him in two subsections: verses 8-10 and verses 14-16. God has stirred up *an alliance of great nations* (v. 9; cf. 51:1-2, 27-28). A prominent place is given in this oracle to the *arrows of skilled* warriors, a term which may refer especially to the Elamites (50:29; cf. 49:35). The Lord, as a commander in chief, orders the troops and directs the battle: *Shoot at her!* (v. 14). *[Vengeance, p. 312.]* She surrenders: in 539 Babylon surrendered peaceably—"without a battle," according to an extra-biblical record. *Her walls are torn down* therefore represents conventional war language. While it could refer to the invader's sword, *the sword of the oppressor,* also conventional war language, more likely refers to Babylon's sword—another reason for her fall. The coming of an attacker opened the way for flight (v. 8). It was Cyrus who issued the proclamation *Let everyone return to his own people* (v. 16, cf. 2 Chron. 36:22-23).

As for **Babylon,** she is addressed directly about her punishment and the reason for it: *Because you rejoice* (vv. 11-13). Her guilt is one of pillaging God's *inheritance,* namely Israel. Her joy and gladness in another's misfortune, compared to the frisking of *heifers* and the neighing of *stallions* is unwarranted (v. 11), so that the claim, *We are not guilty* (v. 7) does not hold up. Great Babylon will be *disgraced* and diminished in size to be a "mere rump of the nations" (v. 12, NEB; cf. 49:15). *[Wrath, p. 313.]* Your mother denotes either the older Babylon under Hammurabi in the second millennium or simply the city.

## 50:21-32 Babylon Hasn't a Chance.

Four sets of powers are arrayed against Babylon: the primary foe (vv.

21-24), a distant alliance (vv. 25-28), archers (vv. 29-30), and God himself (vv. 31-32). Each of these subsections ends with more than a hint of severe damage to Babylon: *captured* (v. 24), victory for the enemy (v. 28), all her *soldiers silenced* (v. 30), and *fire in her towns* (v. 32). Each also suggests or states outright why such trouble has come.

The summons to attack is addressed by God, presumably the commander in chief, first to the armies from the north, who are instructed to destroy them (i.e., the Babylonians) completely (v. 21). The Hebrew word *herem*, used in connection with God's war in the early Israelite conquest period, refers to a city as a sacrifice, wholly devoted and hence irretrievably given over to destruction, as was Jericho (Josh. 6:17). "Pile up her goods in heaps and doom it" (v. 26, NAB).

The names for Babylonians, more like nicknames, are two word-plays: *Merathaim*, (Twofold Rebellion) and *Pekod*, (Punishment.) The first is a wordplay on a district in southern Babylonia, known as *Marratim*; the second, on an east Babylonian tribe, *Puqudu*. The taunt in the form of a lament, *How broken and shattered is the hammer of the whole earth*, is not only mocking in tone, but suggests that Babylon's sin lay in its bid for world dominion. To that evil is added, *you opposed the Lord* (v. 24).

God's *arsenal* contains additional nations as *weapons of his wrath*—whole alliances of them—to join in the assault against Babylon (vv. 25, 27-28). Part of Babylon's disgrace will be that fugitives, and not renowned spokespersons, will announce her fall (v. 28). *[Vengeance, p. 312.]* The *young bulls* is figurative for Babylon's soldiers. The assaults on Babylon are for cause: because "she has proudly defied the Lord" (v. 29, RSV).

The theme of arrogance is continued in the next subsection, where God himself is the antagonist. The arrogance is apparent in the claims of Nebuchadnezzar and Belshazzar (Dan. 4:29, 5:23). Against such arrogance and all arrogance God resolutely sets himself. With the northern foe, an alliance of nations, archers, and God himself against her, Babylon does not have a chance of victory.

### 50:33-46 Breaking Babylon's Grip

Israel is in Babylon's grip, but God is Israel's power (vv. 33-34). For the rest, the Lord pounds away at Babylon. Babylon's sin is against God (vv. 14, 24, 29, 31), but more immediately against Israel, Babylon holds Israel in her grip, as did Egypt formerly, and refuses to release her. Such a situation sets the stage for a contest.

The first and last subsections assert the Lord's power, which resides in his name and his action. Like a lion from the forest or like a lawyer pleading his case, God is irresistible (v. 44, 34). Working inward from both ends, the next two sections describe the instrument which is coming against Babylon: a sword (vv. 35-38) and the army from the north (vv. 41-43). The center section, verses 39-40, like a stage in a coliseum visible from every quarter, shows the desolation following the downfall by comparing Babylon's overthrow with that of Sodom and Gomorrah, the ultimate picture of destruction (v. cf. 49:18). No one will live . . . in it is a refrain slightly varied in wording throughout (v. 3; 51:29, 37, 43, 62; cf. Isa. 34:13-14). The reaction to bad news is caught in the expressions (1) hands fall helpless, (2) pain in the loins like a woman's labor pains, and (3) the melting of the heart (cf. 6:24; 49:23; Isa. 13:7-8).

The sword song (v. 35), which has its counterpart in the "war club" song of the second half (51:20-23), isolates political, religious, military, and economic strengths which the sword will cut down. The military power includes foreigners, "that motley throng," namely hired soldiers or mercenaries.

God's people, both Israel and Judah, are oppressed. [Oppression, p. 305.] The captors, namely the Babylonians, hold them fast, ḥazaq (v. 33). This key root word ḥazaq, "to hold" or "to seize" or "be strong," which appears three times, sharpens the issue. But God is strong (ḥazaq), to loosen their hold (v. 34), so that in the end anguish has gripped ḥazaq, the captor, and the king of Babylon is helpless (v. 43). His grip has been broken.

Verses 45-46 both show who has whom in his grip and so conclude the section which begins in verse 33. Also, with the mention of Babylon's capture and the nations' response, we have reached an interim conclusion to part one of this two-part song (cf. vv. 2-3, 49:20-21). Verse 46 is best rendered more dramatically: "At the cry, 'Babylon has been captured!' the earth quakes" (NAB).

## Babylon's Fall Guaranteed  51:1-60

If the first part of the song pictures Babylon's fall, the second part takes pains to guarantee it. While the message continues to alternate between Babylon, the foe, and Israel (cf. chapter 50), greater attention is paid to Israel, and the certainty of Babylon's fall is more strongly emphasized.

### 51:1-19  God's Determined Purpose Against Babylon

Leb Kamai, literally "the heart of those who rise up against me," is a code name for the Babylonians (v. 1). The destroyer is named as the

king of the Medes (v. 11), assisted by alliances (vv. 27-28). The instruction to the foe is to move in a surprise attack so that the Babylonian
archer will be unable to string his bow (v. 3). With the word winnow, the
note of harvesting is struck, which, along with drinking, dominates in the
second half (vv. 7, 33, 39, 57; cf. the figure of sheep in the first half). The
drinking cup recalls the earlier scene of successive nations drinking of
God's wrath (25:15-29). Babylon was initially the cup from which various
nations drank. As God's agent of punishment, Babylon overran the nations. But now the cup itself will be broken.

God's purpose to destroy Babylon is explicitly stated (vv. 11-12) and
is reinforced both by an oath (v. 14) and by his position as Creator (vv.
15-19). [Swearing, p. 311.] The poem about God's creative power, is
directed earlier against Israel's false gods. Here it is reused and directed
against the Babylonian idols (cf. 10:12-16 and the comments there). The
Lord's vengeance for his temple, namely the temple of Jerusalem, is part
of the larger vengeance against the Babylonians, whose guilt is specified
throughout the extended oracle. [Vengeance, p. 312.] Like Egypt,
Babylon is urged to get healing for her wound (cf. 46:11). The
respondents are unnamed, though they could be Israelite captives along
with others (v. 9).

The Hebrew captives are definitely the speakers in verse 10. God is
on Israel/Judah's side. His covenant connections to his people shine
through in [they] have not been forsaken, literally "widowed" (v. 5; cf.
God's bride, chapter 2). The many waters is a reference to the Euphrates
River and the network of canals around the city (v. 13).

### 51:20-33 Babylon's Foe: Pressing to Victory

The "song of the war club" insists that God is the ultimate agent behind the immediate agent (cf. the corresponding sword song in 50:35-
38). That is, the enemy from the north is God's "battle-ax" against
Babylon. A less likely interpretation is that Babylon itself was God's war
club, a statement which, though true, is not here in view (cf. v. 24). I am
against you is motivated by the charge that Babylon destroys the whole
earth (v. 25; cf. Ezek. 35:3).

The strange phrase, destroying mountain, stands for Babylon, which
though built on a plain had an artificially constructed temple mountain
or ziggurat within it. Ararat is ancient Urartu, modern Armenia; Minni or
"Mannai" were hill folk whose territory lay southeast of Lake Urmia. The
Ashkenaz, identified as Scythians, occupied an area between the Black
and Caspian seas. They, along with the others mentioned, were
defeated by the Medes in the early sixth century and later formed part of

the force which then came against Babylon. The military engagement is not described, but the massiveness of forces on both sides is suggested by *the land trembles and writhes* (v. 29). Soldiers become weak *like women* (cf. 30:6; 48:41). News of the city's defeat is in stereotyped phrases: (1) hands fall helpless, (2) loins are weak like those of a woman in labor pains, and (3) the heart melts (vv. 30; cf. 50:43).

In summary, Babylon is *like a threshing floor* with earth beaten flat, swept clean for the coming harvest activities, pounded and shattered by the Lord's war club. A description of Babylon's guilt (vv. 24-25) is followed by (1) summons for the enemy (vv. 27-29), (2) allusions to battle (vv. 29-30), and (3) an announced outcome (vv. 31-33).

### 51:34-53 Avenging Israel; Babylon's Dire Destruction

Israel rehearses her situation—one in which she is at the complete mercy of Nebuchadnezzar (vv. 34-35). *[Nebuchadnezzar, p. 304.]* The seriousness of his aggression is caught in the curse-like wish that as he has brought havoc on Israel, others would equally bring havoc on him (v. 35). Such an evil situation moves God to act. Earlier God brought a case against Israel (2:9), but now the case is in her behalf.

Babylon's fate is described by picturing a feast at which the Lord makes these already worked-up people intoxicated and so drunk that they sleep forever (v. 39; cf. 25:15-29). *Sheshach* is an alternate name for Babylon "Babel." The name is formed by substituting for B.B.L. a corresponding consonant in the Hebrew alphabet numbered from the opposite end of the alphabet SH.SH.K.

*Bel* (=Lord) is the older name for Marduk, the patron god of Babylon (v. 4; cf. 50:2). *What he has swallowed* refers to Israel, whom Nebuchadnezzar has devoured (v. 34). Disgrace to an idol came when the people it was to protect succumbed to attack (vv. 47, 52). To Babylon applies the principle of *lex talionis*, i.e., an eye for an eye.

The spotlight turns on the captives from Israel/Judah, whose flight from the city is to proceed despite numerous and even conflicting rumors of advancing armies (v. 46). To *remember the Lord*, however, brings disgrace, since they remember why it was that Babylon was allowed by God to enter and desecrate their temple (v. 51).

### 51:54-58 Babylon Is Repaid in Full

Various figures of speech describe the enemy's advance: *(waves like great waters)*, his attack *(a destroyer)*, and Babylon's eternal sleep *(drunk)* (vv. 55-57; cf. 50:2-3). *Babylon's thick wall will be leveled* poses a problem since, when the Persians conquered her, they did so peaceably. In poetry, however, such expressions can be figurative. Strong Babylon was no more!

## 51:59-64 The Symbol of a Sinking Scroll

Unlike other symbolic actions performed at the Lord's express command, this sign act consists of instructions by the prophet. [Symbolic Actions, p. 311.] Seraiah, the brother of Baruch, Jeremiah's scribe (32:12), was an officer, a "quartermaster" responsible for bivouac arrangements when the party stopped to camp. The purpose of the visit to Babylon was for King Zedekiah (after his planned rebellion of 594/3) to pledge his loyalty to Nebuchadnezzar. Listening and looking on, the captives must have found the sinking of the scroll in the Euphrates, which flows through the city of Babylon, both strange and reassuring. Though not in chronological sequence, the account is placed here for its topical fit.

### THE TEXT IN BIBLICAL CONTEXT

*Babylon as a Symbol.* Two national powers, Edom and Babylon, but Babylon more than Edom, symbolize evil in the Old Testament. Already in the Babel story and especially later in the prophets, the portrait of Babel (Babylon) is one of an arrogant power which sets itself against God (Gen. 11; Isa. 13:1—14:23; 21:1-10; 46:1-2; 47:1-5). While it is true that for a little time she was unmistakably a servant of the Lord, for the most part she is described as strongly opposed to God and in need of punishment. That negative portrait is repeated in Revelation, where Babylon symbolizes the world power of Rome—in fact, all world powers (Rev. 17:5-18; 18:10, 21). "Her sins are piled up to heaven" in Revelation 18:5 echoes Jeremiah 51:9. The cry, "Fallen! Fallen is Babylon the Great" (14:8; 18:2) recalls Jeremiah's oracles (50:46; 51:8; Isa. 21:9).

*Fulfillment of Prophecy.* This oracle makes clear the important fact that Babylon will fall. Strong combat language is used of the coming undoing of Babylon (50:15; 51:30). Yet when the Persians took the city it was a peaceable takeover, since Babylon surrendered (539 B.C.). The talk about thick walls being broken is a conventional literary technique. Prophetic prediction, frequently written in poetry and thus often figurative, should not be unduly pressed to be literal.

### THE TEXT IN THE LIFE OF THE CHURCH

*On Whose Side?* God's judgment of Babylon, the superbly rich empire, is a further example that God is on the side of the poor. For it is they, the Israelite captives, who benefit from the crushing blow to Babylon. But such a statement must be qualified. Prior to 587 God was, so to speak, not on the side of the Hebrews, though they were clearly underdogs, but on the side of the aggressive Babylonians, who were the Lord's agents. The principle can be better put: God is on the side of justice. Since the rich most easily overstep prerogatives, God is indeed often (but not always) ranged against them. Those who are held fast and exploited by alien powers have reason to hope that God's power will be exercised in their behalf.

*The Rise and Fall of Empires.* Historians have proposed a variety of theories about the rise and demise of empires—theories having to do with economies, politics, wars, and geographies. While the demise of empires is complicated, this oracle gives basically one reason for Babylon's fall: a catalog of moral evils.

> Babylon worshiped Marduk and was a "land of idols" (50:2,38; 51:52).
> Babylon rejoiced at, even gloated over, the misfortunes of others (50:11).
> Babylon was arrogant (50:29).
> Babylon did wrong in Zion to Israel (51:24, 49).
> Babylon sinned against the Lord by defying him (50:14, 29).
> Babylon rebelled (50:24).

Part 8

# An Appendix: Historical Documentation

# Jeremiah 52

The words of (and about) Jeremiah end in 51:64. In the appendix to the book (52:1ff.) we are given greater detail about Jerusalem's fall than in 39:1-10. The chapter is largely parallel to 2 Kings 24:18—25:30.

This added chapter not only balances the introductory chapter (1:1ff.), but highlights once more the key event around which the entire book clusters, i.e., that there would be grave disaster if Judah would persist in her evil ways. The prose sections document the evils of leaders, both of kings and prophets, but also of the people. The ultimate disaster is not only that a capital city is destroyed, but that the temple, the symbol of Israel's spiritual life with God, is burned, its national structures are dismantled, and its people, intended to be a united people of God, are unceremoniously scattered in exile.

Jeremiah 52:1-34

# The Fall of Jerusalem and Exile

## PREVIEW

Some events have an awesome finality to them. Before we take leave of the book, we are led to cast one more look at the tragedy of Jerusalem, a city in ashes. The story of the toppling of throne and temple, king and priest, could be a book in itself, yet it is told with a minimum of detail. An explanation for the events is given: "Jerusalem and Judah so angered the Lord" (v. 3, NEB). Otherwise the account proceeds in a highly restrained, matter-of-fact style. Chronologically out of place, the chapter is put at the end of the book as an historical record to certify the reliability of Jeremiah's prophecy and so vindicate the prophet. He had said the city would fall to the Babylonians. It did!

## OUTLINE

Jerusalem Falls, 52:1-27a

In Exile: The Many and the One, 52:27b-34

EXPLANATORY NOTES

## Jerusalem Falls  52:1-27a

### 52:1-3  The Background: Zedekiah's Rule and Rebellion

The eleven-year reign of Judah's last king stretched from 597 to 587 B.C. (2 Kings 24:18-20). Hamutal, the wife of Jonah, was the mother of both Jehoahaz and Zedekiah (2 Kings 23:31; 24:18).

Zedekiah *did evil in the eyes of the Lord.* Two examples are the breach of faith with the slaves, and his breaking of covenant with Nebuchadnezzar (34:1ff.; Ezek. 17:13-18). The rebellion against Babylon planned in 594 did not take place (27:2-3). However, Zedekiah rebelled in 589. The writer pinpoints a moral and theological reason for the disaster, rather than a political one. *[Kings of Judah, p. 300; Wrath, p. 313.]*

### 52:4-27a  Jerusalem Taken, Its Temple Sacked, Its Leaders Executed

The Babylonian siege of Jerusalem lasted one and a half years, from January 588 to July 587. Starvation compounded the distress (cf. Lam. 2:20-22; 4:1-20). The story of Zedekiah's flight was sketched earlier; the new information here is that Zedekiah's sons as well as other royal princes were executed (see comments at 39:1-10; cf. 2 Kings 25:1-7).

Once the city walls were broken through and the city captured, it remained for the invaders to deal with property and people. Nebuzaradan, commander of the imperial guard, entered Jerusalem in August 587. The temple was looted for its gold, silver, and bronze—thus Jeremiah's prophecy was fulfilled (27:19-22). Temple, palace, and houses were burned. The temple vessels removed by the Babylonians in 597 had earlier been the subject of prophetic controversy (28:1-3).

Details about the temple portray its wealth and contribute to a sense of the extent of the tragedy. The two bronze pillars, Jachin and Boaz, were 27 feet in height and 18 feet in circumference, with a decorative bronze capital 7 1/2 feet high (1 Kings 7:15-37). The Sea of Bronze was a large basin 18 feet in diameter (1 Kings 7:23-26). As for the utensils, *shovels* were used for placing ashes into *pots; wick trimmers* or snuffers for trimming the wicks of lamps; *sprinkling bowls* to dash blood on the altar; *ladles* to burn incense; *basins* to store blood of sacrifice (cf. Exod. 12:22-23); *censers* or firepans to carry live coals to and from the altar; and *bowls* for pouring out libations (Exod. 25:29).

Two leading officials are mentioned. *Seraiah,* the chief priest, was a grandson of Hilkiah, priest at the time of Josiah and grandfather to the high priest Joshua, who served after the exile (1 Chron. 6:13-15; Ezra 3:2; Zech. 3:1-10). *Zephaniah* might be the person mentioned in 21:1 (cf. 29:29). The *sixty* may have been representatives of the army, or "sixty men of the landed gentry" (Bright: 369).

## In Exile: The Many and the One  52:27b-34

There is more sadness still: deportation. The census of captives is from three separate Babylonian campaigns over a 16-year period. The largest number were taken in the initial campaign of 598. The number may represent males only since, according to 2 Kings 24:14-16, the total was 18,000. In the second military campaign of 588/7 Jerusalem was sacked and burned. The Babylonian campaign in Nebuchadnezzar's *twenty-third year* (582) was likely a reprisal for Gedaliah's assassination (40:7; 41:18). Despite the comparatively limited number of exiles, the writer can say, *Judah went into captivity.* As Jeremiah maintained throughout, the future did not lie with either those who had remained, or with those who had gone to Egypt, but with the relatively small group exiled to Babylon.

The names of the many exiles were not preserved. They were clustered in colonies, and judging from Babylonian archaeological material, fared reasonably well. In later years some established business enterprises. After Cyrus conquered Babylon in 539, exiled peoples, including those from Israel/Judah, were given freedom to return (cf. Ezra 1:2-4).

*Jehoiachin,* a legitimate king from the Davidic dynasty, is given special notice—he is the one person named—possibly because hopes for a future kingdom were still pinned on him. Or perhaps because in an otherwise grim picture, the treatment given Jehoiachin was a ray of hope. The note about his *regular allowance* is illumined by sixth-century tablets from the Babylonian Ishtar gate which mention the rations for the king (Ya'u-kim) and his five sons. *Evil-Merodach,* also known as Amel Marduk, succeeded Nebuchadnezzar his father upon that ruler's death in 562, but ruled for only two years (cf. 2 Kings 25:27-30). *[Kings of Judah, p. 300.]*

With the fall of Jerusalem a 400-year old dynasty ended , and a Hebrew national existence was terminated. Except for a brief period following the Maccabees around the first century B.C., Jewish national life was not to be revived till the middle of the twentieth century A.D. Politically speaking, 587 marked the end for Judah. Jeremiah's book remains to tell us why.

## THE TEXT IN BIBLICAL CONTEXT

*Dismantling a System.* The royal family of Josiah, and more broadly that of David, was brought to an end with the deaths of Zedekiah and Jehoiachin. The magnificent temple built by Solomon in the tenth century was burned. Two long-standing institutions, the throne and the temple, both sanctioned by God, had been dismantled, and that at God's directive. The events might have been anticipated in Jeremiah's call, which spoke of uprooting and tearing down.

Institutions are not sacrosanct, and certainly not eternal. Israel's form of government changed from a theocracy, the rule of God; to a monarchy, the rule of kings; to a hierocracy, the rule of priests (post-exilic times). The old covenant was superseded by the new. It is sobering to realize that the institutions of monarchy, temple, and covenant were each terminated because of human evil. The deep pain which such dismantling brought is recorded in the book of Lamentations.

## THE TEXT IN THE LIFE OF THE CHURCH

*Systems—An Endangered Species.* The Western world places hope in such systems as the United Nations, a democratic form of government, courts of justice, national banks (and credit cards), the Red Cross, and informational systems. Our lives are built on these institutions. We have the feeling they will exist to serve us forever. But it is not impossible that changing times, if not the changing forms of evil, will erode one or the other. Indeed some, like the two-parent family, seem to be giving way. In the end our hope is not in institutions but in God.

# Outline of Jeremiah

## Part I:
## God's Personal Message to Jeremiah  1:1-19
1. An Editorial Heading    1:1-3
2. Grasped for Ministry    1:4-19
    1:4-10    God's Call to Jeremiah
    1:11-12   The Vision of the Almond Rod
    1:13-16   The Vision of the Boiling Pot
    1:17-19   God's Charge to Jeremiah

## Part II:
## Sermons Warning of Disaster  2 — 10
A. From Honeymoon to Divorce    2:1—3:5
    1. An Early Portrait: The Lord and His Bride    2:1-3
    2. A Court Lawsuit: The Charge of Unfaithfulness    2:4-13
    3. The Court Evidence    2:14—3:5
        2:14-19   Israel Has Turned to Other Nations
        2:20-28   Israel Has Turned to Baals
        2:29-37   Israel Has Forgotten the Lord
        3:1-5    Israel Presumes on the Lord

B. Appeals to Two "Ever-Turning" Sisters   3:6—4:4
   1. Comparison of the Two Sisters, Israel and Judah   3:6-10
   2. God's Appeal to Israel to Repent   3:11—4:2
      3:11-13   God's First Appeal to "Defecting" Israel
      3:14-22a   God's Second Appeal to "Ever-Turning" Israel
      3:22b—4:2   Israel's Confession and God's Reaction
   3. God's Appeal to Judah to Repent   4:3-4

C. Calamity and Collapse for a Sinning Society   4:5—6:30
   1. Announcements to Judah and Jerusalem   4:5—5:19
      4:5-9   An Alarm, "The Enemy Is on His Way"
      4:10   Jeremiah's Protest
      4:11-18   An Interpretation as the Enemy Nears
      4:19-22   Agonizing Responses
      4:23-28   A Look at the Apalling Ruin
      4:29-31   Jeremiah's Commentary
      5:1-2   The Lord's Dare
      5:3-6   Jeremiah's Researched Report
      5:7-19   God's Retort: You Force My Hand
   2. Announcements to Jacob and to Judah, 5:20—6:30
      5:20—6:9   God's Citations and the Coming Siege
      6:10-11a   Jeremiah's Exasperation
      6:11b-23   God's Orders: "Pour It On"
      6:24-26   Jeremiah's Counsel
      6:27-30   Once More: Testing, Testing

D. Straight Talk About Worship   7:1—8:3
   1. The Temple Sermon   7:1-15
      7:1-2a   Instruction to Jeremiah
      7:2b-15   A Word to the People
   2. Perversions and Precepts Involving Worship   7:16-26
      7:16-20   Instruction to Jeremiah
      7:21-26   A Word to the People
   3. Carcasses Everywhere   7:27—8:3
      7:27-28a   Instruction to Jeremiah
      7:28b—8:3   A Word to the People

E. A People's Sins, an Enemy's Siege, and a Prophet's Sorrow
      8:4—10:25
   1. Round I: Sin, Siege, and Sorrow   8:4—9:2b
      8:4-13   "No One Repents"

# Part III:
# Stories About Wrestling with Both People and God, 11 — 20

Part V:

## The Book of Consoltation   30–33

A. Recovery of What Was Lost—and More!   30–31
  1. The Recovery of the Land   30:1-24
    30:1-3   "Write a Scroll"
    30:4-9   "I Will Break the Yoke"
    30:10-11   "I Am with You and Will Save You"
    30:12-17a   "I Will Restore You to Health"
    30:17b-22   "I Will Bring Them Honor"
    30:23-24   Guaranteed!
  2. The Recovery of a Relationship   31:1-40
    31:1-9   "I Am Israel's Father"
    31:10-14   "Like a Shepherd the Lord Will Watch over His Flock"
    31:15-22   "I Have Great Compassion for . . . Rachel, for
             Ephraim, and for Virgin Israel"
    31:23-26   "I Will Refresh the Weary"
    31:27-30   In Coming Days: A Solid Society
    31:31-34   In Coming Days: A New Covenant
    31:35-37   Guaranteed by Oath!
    31:38-40   In Coming Days: A Rebuilt City

B. Reversing a People's Fortunes   32–33
  1. About Real Estate and Renewal   32:1-44
    32:1-15   A Prisoner's Purchase
    32:16-25   It Doesn't Add Up—a Prayer
    32:26-35   Jerusalem Will Burn!
    32:36-44   Jerusalem Will Flourish!
  2. About Repopulation and Rulers   33:1-26
    33:1-13   The Resettlement of Jerusalem
    33:14-26   The Reinstatement of Leaders

Part VI:

## Narratives About Wicked Leaders, a Suffering Prophet, and a Destroyed City   34–45

A. Repeat Message: Disobedience Dooms   34–36
  1. Going Back on One's Word   34:1-22
    34:1-7   Bad News and Good News for Zedekiah
    34:8-22   The Making and Breaking of a Pact

2. Testing for Obedience   35:1-19
   35:1-11   A Family Obeys
   35:12-16   A People Disobeys
   35:17-19   To Each a "Reward"
3. Rejecting the Word of God   36:1-32
   36:1-7   Preparing the Scroll
   36:8-26   Reading the Scroll
   36:27-31   Judgment on Jehoiakim
   36:32   Rewriting the Scroll

B. A Leader Falters, a City Falls   37—39
  1. King and Prophet: A Final Showdown   37—38
   37:1-10   A Royal Inquiry of Jeremiah
   37:11-16   Officials Arrest and Beat the Prophet
   37:17-21   Zedekiah's Personal Inquiry of the Prophet
   38:1-13   Officials: "Death to the Prophet"
   38:14-28   Zedekiah's Further Inquiry of the Prophet
  2. Jerusalem Falls   39:1-18
C. After the Catastrophe   40—45
  1. Tragedy Among the Survivors in Judah   40—41
   40:1-6   Jeremiah Is Freed
   40:7-12   Gedaliah Begins as Governor
   40:13—41:3   Gedaliah Is Assassinated
   41:4-10   Ishmael's Murder Rampage
   41:11-18   Johanan's Rescue Operation
  2. Decision-Making by the Remnant   42—43
   42:1-6   The Remnant Seeks Counsel
   42:7-22   The Counsel: Don't Go to Egypt
   43:1-7   The Decision: Off to Egypt
   43:8-13   The Threat: Babylon Once More
  3. Idolatry in Egypt   44:1-30
   44:1-14   Provoking God with Idolatry
   44:15-19   A Defense of Idolatry
   44:20-30   Disaster for the Idolaters
  4. A Message for Baruch   45:1-5

# Part VII:
# Oracles Against Other Nations   46—51

A. Oracles Against Southern Nations: Egypt, Philistia   46—47
　1. For Egypt: Defeat Abroad; Distress at Home   46:1-26
　　46:1-12   A Military Defeat at Carchemish
　　46:13-26   Distress at Home, Lower and Upper Egypt
　2. For Israel: A Salvation Word   46:27-28
　3. For Philistia: A Relentless and Overpowering Onslaught   47:1-7

B. Oracles Against the Trans-Jordan Countries   48—49
　1. For Moab: Calamity and Disgrace   48:1-47
　　48:1-10   Destroyed and Disgraced
　　48:11-25   Shamed and Shattered
　　48:26-39   Ridiculed, Yet Lamented
　　48:40-47   Captured and Exiled
　2. For Ammon: Terror for Its Boasting and Aggression   49:1-6
　3. For Edom: A Thorough Stripping and a Complete
　　Overthrow 49:7-22
　　49:7-12   Edom Stripped Bare
　　49:14-22   Edom Overthrown Completely
　4. For Damascus: Bad News—Panic, Anguish, and Pain   49:23-27
　5. For Desert Arabs: A Sudden Scattering   49:28-33
　6. For Elam: A Broken Bow   49:34-39

C. An Oracle Against Babylon   50—51
　1. Babylon's Fall Pictured   50:1-46
　　50:1-3   Banner Headline: "Babylon Will Fall"
　　50:4-20   Israel's Guilt/Babylon's Guilt
　　50:21-32   Babylon Hasn't a Chance
　　50:33-46   Breaking Babylon's Grip
　2. Babylon's Fall Guaranteed   51:1-60
　　51:1-19   God's Determined Purpose Against Babylon
　　51:20-33   Babylon's Foe: Pressing to Victory
　　51:34-53   Avenging Israel; Babylon's Dire Destruction
　　51:54-57   Babylon Is Repaid in Full
　　51:59-64   The Symbol of a Sinking Scroll

# Part VIII:
## An Appendix: Historical Documentation   52

# Glossary Notes
# on Terms and Themes

**APOCALYPTIC** "To uncover," understood technically as uncovering or re-vealing events at the end of time. In apocalyptic outlook there are pictured two contesting forces, God and Satan. World history, often divided into epochs, will come to an end with a cosmic showdown between God and Satan resulting in terrible catastrophe. Evil will be decisively punished. The world will be radically changed . . . perhaps soon.

As literature, "apocalyptic" refers to visionary writing in intertestamental and early Christian times (200 B.C.—A.D. 100). It includes such books as Baruch, Esdras, and Ethiopic Enoch, and in the New Testament, Revelation (the Apoc-alypse). Old Testament literature that anticipates the fuller apocalyptic em-phasis and is in part itself apocalyptic in character is Isaiah 24—27, known as the "Isaiah Apocalypse"; Ezekiel 38—39; and Daniel. The literature is rich in images and symbolism and is often pseudonymous. Books are written in the name of a past hero.

Since in apocalyptic thinking, nations were not agents in the hand of God, but objects of his anger, it is possible that the chapter arrangement in Jeremiah which puts nations last in the book is a deliberate way of suggesting an apoc-alyptic note to the whole book. By contrast, the oracles against the nations in Isaiah and Ezekiel occur in the middle of the book, and in general they precede and therefore prepare for salvation oracles for Israel (Isa. 13—23; Ezek. 25—32).

**APOSTASY** A spiritual falling away, specifically the falling away from God of a people who once knew God. Israel fell away from God and among other per-versions followed Baal or turned for resources to other nations (2:17-19). Leaders, priests, and prophets were usually held accountable for a people's

290

apostasy (2:8b; 5:1-5; 7:23-26). Sporadically God's people recognized their apostasy or backsliding. Upon true repentance God promised restoration of the apostate to himself (Jer. 31:18ff.; cf. Hos. 14:1-4). *[Baal, p. 291.]*

**ASHERAH**   A goddess of the ancient Near East known as Ishtar (Babylon-Assyria), Astarte (Canaanite), Aphrodite (Greece), and Venus (Rome). She was known in Jeremiah's day as the Queen of Heaven (7:18; 44:18). In the Canaanite pantheon, as the discoveries at Ugarit have shown, Asherah was the mother-goddess, consort of the aged deity, El.

Israelites turned to the worship of the Canaanite Ashtaroth (a plural form) upon arriving in the land (Judg. 2:13; 10:6). Solomon sanctioned such idolatry (1 Kings 11:5). Manasseh in the seventh century reintroduced her worship, which was also associated with the "heavenly host." Worship of Asherah was forbidden as part of Josiah's reform (2 Kings 23:4ff.). Women were especially attracted to the worship of this mother-goddess; they poured out wine in her honor and made crescent or five-point star cakes. The refugee group in Egypt resorted to Asherah worship. Southwest of Kadesh-Barnea in the Sinai a jar handle has been found with a drawing of two figures and the inscription "Asherah." Jeremiah strenuously objected to such worship (7:16-20; 44:7-10, 20-29). *[Baal, p. 291.]*

**BAAL**   A term signifying "lord"; also a Canaanite storm-god and fertility-bringing god, especially attractive to the Israelites. Excavation at Ugarit, along the Mediterranean coast, has uncovered literature extolling the exploits of this youthful and aggressive deity, who was second only to the aging Canaanite god, El. Baal does battle with the sea, has a wife/consort called Anat, and engages in wars, violence, and sex of all descriptions. Elijah engaged in a contest with the prophets of Baal. As the god of the weather, Baal could be expected to answer with fire (lightning)! The stress on fertility is dominant in Hosea (2:8ff.).

Jeremiah rails against prophets prophesying by Baal, which suggests that in the Southern Kingdom, Baal was approached primarily for the sake of oracles (2:5; cf. 23:13). Fifty years prior to Jeremiah, Manasseh from Judah introduced a form of Baal worship (2 Kings 21:3-7). An Assyrian understanding of Baal may date from Ahaz, Manasseh's grandfather, who brought measurements for an altar from Damascus. In Judah, then, the Baal religion may have been of the Assyrian variety where Baal was the head of the pantheon. In Jeremiah's time Baal, or Baal-Shamen, lord of fields, stars, and heaven, was worshiped along with Yahweh (the Lord).

**BABYLON/BABYLONIANS**   An important political and religious city and people situated on the Euphrates River about 60 miles south of modern Baghdad, Iraq. It was founded, its residents believed, by the god Marduk. Babylon was the central city for the Old Babylonian Empire (2000-1595 B.C.) and also of the Neo-Babylonian Empire (626-539).

The Neo-Babylonian Empire followed the Assyrian Empire (900-612), which at its height stretched from Elam in the east to Cilicia in the west. Tiglath-pilezer III (744-727) had subjugated Israel by 732 (2 Kings 15:20), and Sargon captured Samaria in 722 . The strength of this large empire was challenged from within when Nabopolassar, a Chaldean, took the city of Babylon in 626 and not only broke away from Assyrian control, but, joined by Medes, attacked Assur in 614 and captured Nineveh, the capital, in 612. Nahum and Zephaniah had so foretold it.

In an expansion westward, the forces of Babylon made an assault on Haran in 609. In a surprise attack in May 605, the Babylonian army under the command of Nebuchadnezzar attacked the Egyptians at Carchemish on the northern Euphrates. In this battle Babylon gained the upper hand, the Egyptians were defeated, and Syria-Palestine came under Babylonian domination. There it was decided that the east should rule the west.

Jehoiakim, the Israelite king, till then a vassal of Egyptian Pharaoh Neco II, became vassal to Nebuchadnezzar (605). The Babylonians sacked Ashkelon because it refused to pay tribute (Jer. 47:5-7), and also carried off Jewish hostages (including Daniel) to Babylon. In 601 the Babylonians fought the Egyptians on their soil with heavy losses on both sides (Jer. 46:14-26). About two years later the Babylonians raided certain Arab tribes (Jer. 49:28-33). Jerusalem was seized, according to the record of the Babylonians, on March 16, 597 (cf. 2 Kings 24:10-17). Because of King Zedekiah's later revolt, the Babylonians captured and sacked Jerusalem in 587. The temple was destroyed by fire; Jewish people were taken into exile. Back home, the Babylonians marched on Elam in 596 (49:34-38). Later they attacked the Egyptians once more and invaded the country in 568/7, according to a fragmentary Babylonian text (cf. Jer. 43:8-13). [Nebuchadnezzar, p. 304.]

Nebuchadnezzar, the brilliant king, was succeeded by Amel-Marduk (Evil-Merodach) in 562 (2 Kings 25:27). He was assassinated after two years and was succeeded by Neriglissar (=Nergal-sharezer), who ruled 560-556. The last rulers, co-regents, were Nabonidus and Belshazzar. The empire dissolved as quickly as it had formed. Cyrus, the Persian, entered the city of Babylon in October 539, slew Belshazzar, and so brought a great empire to its end. Its fall was announced by Isaiah (14:1-23; 21:1-10; 46:1-2; 47:1-5), Jeremiah (50—51), and Daniel (5:17-28).

In Jeremiah it was the Babylonians who came to be identifed with the "foe from the north" so frequently mentioned in 4:5—6:30 and 8:14-17. The Babylonians, usually designated in Jeremiah as Chaldeans, are the subject of the longest oracle against the nations (50—51). They were to be devastated in turn by a "foe from the north," apparently a traditional expression for an undefined enemy. The name "Sheshach" is an "atbash" designation (using alphabetical displacements numerically) for Babylon (25:26; 51:41).

**BARUCH** The scribe who recorded Jeremiah's dictations and read some of Jeremiah's messages to the people (36:4, 8). Baruch is assumed to be the major informant if not the author of the so-called "Baruch Narrative" (26—29, 34—45), since Jeremiah is there referred to in the third person.

Baruch, certainly emotionally involved in the life of his people, was perceived by others as having some influence on Jeremiah (43:3). He was with Jeremiah in prison when the prophet purchased a field (32:1-16), and later was taken with Jeremiah to Egypt (43:6). Baruch came from a prominent family—a royal line, according to Josephus, a first-century Jewish historian. Baruch's brother Seraiah was an officer of high rank under King Zedekiah (51:59).

**CHIASMUS** A literary device in which words or ideas are listed first in serial order and then in reverse order, thus:

A       B       C       //       $C^1$       $B^1$       $A^1$

Chiasmus, an arresting form of repetition, serves to emphasize the content. In Jeremiah chiasmus occurs in 11:18-20; 12:1-3; 14:7-9; 15:15-21. An example of chiasmus is Isaiah 6:10 (RSV):

A Make the heart of this people fat
B and their ears heavy
C and shut their eyes;

C¹ Lest they see with their eyes
B¹ and hear with their ears
A¹ and understand with their hearts

and turn and be healed.

## CHRONOLOGY

| Year | Event | References |
|---|---|---|
| 640 | Josiah begins to rule (640-609) | 2 Kings 22:1 |
| 627 | Jeremiah is called to be a prophet | Jer. 1:1-2 |
| 621 | Josiah repairs the temple | 2 Kings 23:1-25 |
| | scroll is discovered, reform begins | 2 Chron. 34:8-18 |
| 609 | Pharoah Neco rules in Egypt (609-594) | |
| | Battle of Megiddo, Josiah dies | 2 Kings 23:29ff. |
| | Jehoahaz rules three months in Judah | 2 Kings 23:31 |
| | | 2 Chron. 36:2 |
| | Jehoiakim rules in Judah (609-598) | 2 Kings 23:36 |
| | Jeremiah's temple sermon | Jer. 7:1-15; 26:1-24 |
| 605 | Battle of Carchemish (Babylon and Egypt) | Jer. 25:1, 3; 46:2 |
| | Nebuchadnezzar becomes ruler in Babylon | |
| | Daniel is taken captive to Babylon | Dan. 1:1 |
| | Jeremiah's dated sermon | Jer. 25:1-14 |
| 604 | King Jehoiakim burns Jeremiah's scroll | Jer. 36:9 |
| 602 | Jehoiakim rebels against Nebuchadnezzar | 2 Kings 24:1 |
| 598/ | Babylon's armies besiege Jerusalem | |
| 597 | Jehoiachin rules three months in Jerusalem | 2 Kings 24:8-16 |
| 597 | Jehoiachin and others deported to Babylon | 2 Kings 24:12ff. |
| | Zedekiah set as king of Judah (597-587) | 2 Kings 24:18 |
| | | 2 Chron. 36:11 |
| | Jeremiah wears a yoke | Jer. 27:1-2 |
| 594 | Stirrings of insurrection against Nebuchadnezzar | |
| | Seraiah visits Babylon | Jer. 51:59 |
| | Jeremiah's letter (?) | Jer. 29:29-32 |
| 595 | Pharaoh Psammatichus II in Egypt (595-589) | |
| 589 | Pharaoh Hophra (Apries) in Egypt (589-570) | |
| | Jerusalem besieged | 2 Kings 25:1 Jer. 32:1f.; 52:4 |

| 587 | Jerusalem falls to Babylon | 2 Kings 25:2-10 |
| | | Jer. 39:1ff. |
| | Deportation from Jerusalem | Jer. 52:5-30 |
| 586 | Gedaliah is assassinated (?) | Jer. 41:2 |
| 585 | Jeremiah goes to Egypt (?) | Jer. 43:5-7 |
| 582 | The third deportation | Jer. 52:30 |
| 561 | Jehoiachin released from prison | 2 Kings 25:27 |
| | | Jer. 52:31 |

—(Adapted from Kitchen/Mitchel, 1980:271ff.)

**COVENANT**   An arrangement between two or more parties that involves mutual obligations and has as its goal mutual relationships. A covenant relationship represents a close bonding, whether between persons, or between people and God. Loyalty is basic to covenant.

Research since the 1930s has shown the similarities between political treaties in the ancient Near East and covenant. Political treaties of the second millennium followed a stereotyped form: self-identification, historical prologue, stipulations, list of witnesses, blessings, and curses. The stipulation, essentially one of loyalty, was couched in such words as, "With my enemy you will be an enemy and with my friend you will be a friend." Scholars suggest that certain biblical passages have a similar format, at least in part: Exodus 20; Joshua 24:2-24; and the entire book of Deuteronomy.

Threats for breaking the covenant are found in these ancient political treaties; they are also listed in biblical covenants. Curses, in the form of evils, will follow disregard of covenant duties (e.g., Deut. 27:15-26). Blessings in the form of desirable benefits and especially empowerment for fruitfulness will follow adherence to the covenant (e.g., Deut. 28:1-14).

It is customary to catalog covenants in the Bible as *unconditional,* that is, consisting entirely of God's promises (e.g., the Abrahamic covenant, Gen. 12:1ff.; the Davidic covenant, 2 Sam. 7:8ff.; and the new covenant, Jer. 31:31ff.); and others as *conditional* (e.g., the Mosaic covenant, Exod. 19—20). But that loyalty is an unspoken condition throughout is clear from the condition noted for both the Abrahamic covenant (Ezek. 33:23-29) and the Davidic covenant ("if" in Ps. 132:12; Jer. 22:4). The covenant arrangement between God and Israel was unique in the ancient Near East, where gods were attached to territories, not to people as in Israel's case.

Prophets use the term covenant quite sparingly, presumably because God's people had one-sidedly fastened themselves to the security of covenant promises without attention to obedience and loyalty. Jeremiah refers to a covenant between human parties (chapter 34), and between people and God (e.g., chapter 11). Jeremiah charges that God's people have broken the covenant (11:10; cf. 14:21; 33:20; Deut. 31:16, 20; Ezek. 16:59; 17:15-17; 44:7; Zech. 11:10). But Jeremiah is the first to announce a new covenant (31:31-33; 32:40; cf. 33:20-21, 25; 50:5; Matt. 26:28; 1 Cor. 11:25; Heb. 8:7-16; 9:15; 10:16). [*Covenant Formula, p. 294.*]

**COVENANT FORMULA**   A label for the expression "I will be your God, and you shall be my people." Since covenant has to do with bonding, God's overtures in covenant are crystallized in this refrain. The formula appears in Jeremiah more often than in any other book. It occurs some 20 times in the Bible, though not with the identical word order (Exod. 6:7; Lev. 26:12; Jer. 7:23; 11:4; 24:7; 30:22; 31:1; 31:33; 32:38; Ezek. 11:20; 14:11; 36:28; 37:23; 37:27; Zech. 8:8; 13:9; to which could be added Deut. 14:1-2; 26:16-19; Rom. 9:25-26; 2 Cor. 6:16; 1 Pet. 2:10; Rev. 21:3-7).

The covenant formula has two parts. One is a promise: God takes the initiative and offers himself to be a people's God. The second, while including promise overtones, hints strongly of demand: You shall be my people. Of God's people certain loyalties and behaviors are expected.

**DELIVERANCE ORACLES** Oracles from God through a prophet that promise deliverance and salvation. Basic to many oracles is God's promised intervention on behalf of a person or a people, with announcement of a consequent transformation and a goal-statement about the establishment of a close relationship with God. Four speech forms of deliverance oracles can be identified, the last two of which may be modifications of the second.

*Assurance of Salvation.* The distinctive features are two: (1) the word of consolation, "Do not fear," and (2) the substantiation or the motivation for the announcements, characteristically "I am with you," known as the divine assistance formula. Examples of this form in Jeremiah are 30:10-11; 42:11-12 (cf. Isa. 43:5).

*Announcement of Salvation.* Characteristically this oracle opens with an allusion to a lament, followed by a statement of the Lord's position (stance) on the matter, or a word about intervention, and the consequences which flow from that action. Occasionally the goal is given in conclusion. Examples: Isaiah 41:17ff.; Jeremiah 30:17b-22; 31:2-6.

*Pronouncement of Salvation.* This oracle opens with a description of an evil or difficult situation, not necessarily having to do with a lament. More important, it has about it a tone of dispute, as though a rebuke, sometimes via a question, should bring the party addressed more quickly to accept the oracle. Examples in Jeremiah are 29:10-14; 30:5-9; 12-17a; 32:36-44.

*Portrayal of Salvation.* In this form, without any reasons or direct questions/ reproaches given, the details of the new or promised situation are listed, as in a catalog. One may think of it as the "consequence section" from the "announcement of salvation" now made free-standing. Examples: Jeremiah 31:23-25.

**DISCIPLINE** Correction or chastisement *(musar). Musar,* one of Jeremiah's favorite terms, is "the learning done in suffering . . . the pain inflicted for a purpose, calculated to produce amendment." *Musar* is not so much punitive action as it is educational (Blank: 196-199, 228). For occurrences of the term *musar:* 2:30; 5:3; 7:28; 15:7b; 30:14; 32:33; 35:13. For the concept, see 30:10-11; 31:18.

**DIVINE ASSISTANCE FORMULA** The label given to the oft-repeated "I am with you" and its expanded form ["to deliver you"]. The expression is associated with the divine call to God's servants (Exod. 3:12; Jer. 1:8, 19) and is an extension, so to speak, of the divine name, I AM.

A form of the expression occurs frequently in a setting of prayer or wish (Gen. 28:20; 48:21; Exod. 10:10; 18:19; Num. 14:43; Deut. 20:1). It is also found as a direct promise of God (Judg. 6:12, 16; Isa. 43:5; Jer. 15:20; 30:11; 42:11; 46:28; Matt. 28:20). As an assertion or confession it is found in Num.

23:21 (cf. Josh. 6:27; 1 Sam. 16:18; Ps. 46:7, 11). It has been suggested that in ancient times it belonged to the holy war tradition in which the Lord of hosts promised victory with the guarantee of his presence, "I am with you."

**DOUBLETS**   Identical sets of verses which appear in more than one place. Examples are:

6:13-15 = 8:10c-12
10:12-16 = 51:15-19
15:13-14 = 17:3-4
16:14-16 = 23:7-8
23:19-20 = 30:23-24
30:10-11 = 46:27-28

One context sometimes seems a better "fit" than does another. The reasons for the repetition are not always clear. Doublets have raised questions about the how and when and the who of the editorial work of the book.

**FALSEHOOD/DECEPTION**   Words used to translate the Hebrew *sheqer,* a common term for lies, which refers essentially to statements which are groundless or misleading and to false or faithless dealing. *Sheqer* is a perverted discernment of life. For example, the people have a false sense of security: they hold to the temple and to sacrifice (chapter 7) and to covenant and the promise of God's presence (chapter 11) at a time when God is moving against them.

"The term *sheqer* implies the operation of a destructive power" (Overholt: 101). Of its 119 occurrences in the Old Testament, 37 are in Jeremiah, 24 in the Psalms, and 20 in Proverbs. An important setting for the word is in treaty-making (Gen. 21:22-31). Lying is forbidden in speech (Exod. 20:16; cf. Prov. 6:19), and especially in oath (Lev. 19:12).

In Jeremiah the term is applied in three ways. (1) Jeremiah accuses the people of *dealing falsely (sheqer)* even when turning to God (3:10), and when taking oath (5:2), so that deception rather than integrity prevails in the land (9:3, 5). (2) Prophets who are unauthorized by the Lord are *lying prophets (sheqer)* against whom Jeremiah repeatedly warns (14:14; 23:26; 27:10, 14-16; 29:9). Their deception consists of preaching peace when there is no peace (6:14). Prophets and priests alike practice deceit (6:13). They walk in lies (23:14), which means either that they are hypocritical or that they go after idols, the big fraud. Five opponents are labeled by Jeremiah as *sheqer*: Hananiah (28:15), Ahab and Zedekiah (29:22f.), Shemaiah (29:31), and Pashhur (20:6). (3) *Idols* are deceptive *(sheqer)* by reason of their empty promises. The people's trust in them is one of the reasons for their punishment (13:25).

**FORMATION OF BOOK**   An issue in the study of Jeremiah which deals with the way in which the book was composed. Theories abound, compelling conclusions are few.

The book appears scrambled. Several incidents are dated (e.g., 25:1), but the chronological references are not sequential (e.g., chapter 24, dated 597, precedes chapter 25 with the date 605). Moreover, the account is sometimes written in first person as in 28:1. Such a note suggests a personal record. Jeremiah is often mentioned in third person; this gives the impression that someone is writing about him. Occasionally in the same text unit one finds both (e.g., 28:1, 5; 25:13, 15).

This set of data suggests the conclusion that Jeremiah is not necessarily himself the "author" of all that is in the book by his name. That conclusion is supported by the appendix (chapter 52 = 2 Kings 24:18—25:30), which follows the statement in 51:64: "The words of Jeremiah end here." Furthermore, the heading specifies that the book contains words of Jeremiah through the reign of Zedekiah (1:1). Is this perhaps intended as the heading for chapters 1—25? Some material is definitely post Zedekiah (e.g., chapters 42—44). The frequency of doublets raises further questions. *[Doublets, p. 296.]* The material, it seems, was brought together and edited. Some scholars hold that Jeremiah himself edited the book; others believe that chiefly Baruch or later editors are responsible.

There is still other data. Baruch wrote one scroll which was burned by King Jehoiakim (chapter 36). Baruch then recorded a second scroll which Jeremiah dictated (36:27-28). Where in the present book is that material located? The first 25 chapters are prime candidates, but suppositions—some based on lengths of scrolls and word columns—are numerous. One of the more helpful, though still debated suggestions, is that of William Holladay. He notes that the scroll read before the king provided for repentance. The oracle that is given in connection with the second scroll does not (36:26-31). Furthermore, some oracles in chapters 1—10, and in the prose sermon of chapter 11, hold out a hope, but others stress the finality of God's judgment. So the proposal emerges: the first scroll is imbedded in chapters 1—11 and can be identified by sifting out those units that allow for repentance, such as: 1:4-10; 2:1-37; 3:1-5, 12-13, 19-25; 4:1-4, 13-18, and so on. Material from the second scroll would be included in chapters 12—20 but would also be in 1:11-19; 4:9-12, 19-28; and so on (Holladay, 1980). Another alternative is to regard chapters 1—20 as comprising the original scroll.

Working on the hypothesis that the original scroll lies within 1:1—25:13, John Miller has proposed that the material which consists of prose is the original "book." These prose accounts are on the order of personal memoirs (e.g., 1:4-19; 3:6-11; 7:1—8:3; 11:1-14). This material represented the summary of the Lord's Word to him over a 23-year period (25:3). Into this prose account there were later inserted poetic oracles at various places (e.g., 2:1—3:5; 3:12-18; 8:4—9:24). (John Miller) Certainty as to the formation of the book eludes us.

Additional data deal with style. The poetry is usually succinct; the prose expansive. A widely regarded suggestion is to attribute the poetic material to Jeremiah, the biographical material (perhaps as much as 26—29 and 34—45) to Baruch, and the prose discourses to a source "stamped by a Deuteronomic hand." *[Style, p. 309.]* Critical in this theory is the affinity between Jeremiah and Deuteronomy and the date of Deuteronomy, which these theorists put in the seventh century. That affinity has recently been both sharply challenged and dogmatically affirmed.

The mention within Jeremiah of several books or scrolls could be a clue to the composition and the present arrangement of the book. Chapters 1 to 25 end with "all that are written in this book" (25:13a). The writing of a scroll (book) is commanded in 30:1f.; this mini-scroll extends from 30—33. A narrative might once have been a separate scroll(s): chapters 26—29; 34—45 (or 26—36; 37—45). The oracles against the nations, which seem to have been a movable section, would be a fourth scroll. *[Septuagint, p. 308.]* Could these four scrolls, presumably from Jeremiah (with the possible exception of the biographical material), have been brought together, perhaps by the prophet himself? How the book came to be in the present form is without doubt a complex issue.

There is validity, however, to the recently heard claim that the present shape of the book is our primary target of study. Not the process, but the product is all-important. Attention to the process, however, puts us in touch with the way God's message was delivered in a given culture and time, and how in preserving it, God saw fit to use not only Jeremiah, but Baruch and possibly others. The believing community recognizes in the words of this book the authoritative word from God.

**FUTURE-TIME FORMULAE** Several stereotyped expressions used by the prophets to lead into oracles about a future time. Examples: "Days are coming," "In that day."

"Days are coming" is a standard way of pointing to what is ahead, which may, but need not be, end-time events. For example, in future times the return from exile will rival in significance the Exodus from Egypt (16:14-15; 23:7-8); one such return is dated to 539 B.C. Salvation oracles, so introduced, cluster in chapters 30—33 (30:3; 31:27, 31, 38; 33:14). Judgment oracles introduced by this expression are for Israel (7:32; 19:6) and for nations (9:25; 48:12; 49:2; 51:47, 52). The expression is found sparsely in Isaiah and not at all in Ezekiel.

"In that day" or "in those days" can mean a future dreadful time either for Israel (4:9) or for nations (48:41; 49:22; 50:30), or a propititous time (30:8; 3:15-16; 50:4, 20), depending on what precedes. In any event the expression points to a new situation, one which the Lord has brought about.

**INCLUSIO** A literary device in which a section's opening and closing are identical or at least similar. An inclusio by definition ties the end to the beginning; it recapitulates. One might think of an inclusio as a sandwich: material is placed between identical phrases. The effect of such a device is to give unity and emphasis to the passage. For a discussion see J. Lundbom.

Larger sections in Jeremiah structured on the inclusio pattern, with the key words in parentheses, are:

1—20 (came forth from the womb . . . 1:5; 20:18)
1—51 (words of Jeremiah . . . 1:1; 51:64)
8:13—9:22 (gathering . . . 8:13; 9:22)
14:2—15:9 (languish . . . 14:2; 15:9)
26—36 (Jeremiah's message and rejection, chapters 26; 36)
30—31 (male[female] . . . soldier/strong man, 30:5-6; 31:22b)
30—33 (I will restore the fortunes . . . 30:3; 33:26)

In shorter units, examples of inclusio can be observed in:

3:1-5 (behold, vv. 1, 5)
5:26-31 (my people, vv. 26, 31)
10:6-7 (there is none like you, vv. 6a, 7c)
20:7-10 (you/he deceived, vv. 7a, 10c)
23:11-15 (godlessness/pollution, vv. 11, 15)
29:10-14 (bring back to this place, vv. 10, 14)
25:15-38 (wrath, vv. 15, 38)
34:1-22 (I will hand . . . over to Babylon, vv. 2, 21)
48:1-47 (woe, vv. 1, 46)

**JUDGMENT ORACLE**   A patterned speech form often employed by the prophets to announce divine judgment. It has two parts: an accusation and an announcement. The accusation lists the sins and the evils of the person or group. "Therefore" (e.g., Mic. 3:4) marks the transition to the announcement, which is usually of an unpleasant, even dreadful, future, and shows the cause-effect relationship between the accusation and the announcement.

The classic judgment speeches, so called because they are crisp and uncluttered, are found in the eighth-century prophets: Amos (4:1-3), Micah (3:1-4), Hosea (2:5-7), and Isaiah (8:6-8). An example of a short judgment speech form is Hosea 8:7 RSV (cf. Jer. 14:10).

> For they sow the wind ( = accusation)
> and they shall reap the whirlwind ( = announcement).

The significance of this speech form is that the accusation, also called "indictment," provides the reason for the announcement. The accusation convicts people of their sin. The announcement is not some arbitrary prediction out of the blue, but is connected with a situation in the present. Sometimes the announcement predicts events at the "end time," but more often it is an immediate warning for the audience.

Jeremiah departs from the strict form, for he embellishes with variations. For example, the accusation part may include rhetorical questions, "Why should I forgive you?" (5:7; cf. 5:29). The announcements have mixed into them a summons to action (6:1) or warnings (6:8) or additional accusations. The announcement section is sometimes more like "future instruction" or even a judicial "sentence." A law court as the setting for the judgment speech is questionable. Perhaps the "if . . . then" of the covenant, more than the law court, is the background for the judgment speech (Deut. 28:15; Josh. 24:20).

Examples of the prophetic speech oracle with the transition to announcement listed in parentheses are:

| | |
|---|---|
| 5:7-19 (14) | 11:21-23 (22) |
| 5:20—6:9 (6:1) | 13:20-26 (24) |
| | 23:11-15 (12), (15) |
| 8:4-13 (10) | 25:3-14 (8) |
| 9:4-9 (7) | 28:15-16 (16) |
| 9:3-11 (7) | 44:7-14(11) |
| 11:9-13 (11) | |

One may think of the oracles against the nations (46—51) as further adaptations of the judgment oracle. It is a useful exercise to study the accusation sections by itemizing God's reasons for censure.

**JUSTICE**   Honorable action which preserves well-being *(shalom)* all around, especially an action which sets right a disturbed situation. While it is linked with a ruler's responsibilities and refers therefore to God and to kings, its practice is required of God's people generally. God is one who proceeds in justice (Gen. 16:5; Jer. 11:20). He loves justice (Ps. 37:28). Justice, along with righteousness, is the foundation of God's throne (Ps. 89:14). Kings are repeatedly called to rule justly, i.e., they are to care for those whose rights are overlooked and who are easily exploited (Jer 21:12).

God's people are to do justice. This means they should show concern for the oppressed. *[Oppression, p. 305.]* Doing justice means coming to the defense of those who are helpless, the victims of mistreatment: strangers, orphans, widows. Justice includes fair decisions in the courtroom, but for the Hebrews more often it refers to fair dealings in everyday social life, including the proper protocol in all relationships: king/citizen, employer/employee, parent/child, and so on.

Justice in the Old Testament means considerably more than the English word suggests:

| Old Testament | Modern |
| --- | --- |
| Practice, "do" justice | "Get" justice |
| Used in legal, social, religious sphere | Primarily, legal sphere |
| A central concern everywhere | Restricted, even a marginal concern |

The noun "justice" *(mishpat)* occurs 422 times in the Old Testament, 32 of which are in Jeremiah (e.g., 4:2; 5:1; 7:5; 9:24; 33:15; see comments in 21:11—22:9). For a comparison/contrast, see Isaiah (e.g., 1:17; 5:7; 9:7; 10:2).

**KINGS OF JUDAH**    Jeremiah ministered during the reigns of the last five kings of Judah. Several have two names, a regal or throne name, as well as a personal name (listed below) (cf. 2 Sam. 12:24f.). Similarly today, the Roman Catholic pope assumes a new name when elected.

*Josiah* (640-609). During his reign the "book of the law" was discovered in the temple (621). Josiah launched a program of religious reforms (2 Kings 22:1—23:27). He tried to halt the Egyptian army which passed through Palestine on its way to resist the westward-moving Babylonians. In that attempt (at Megiddo in 609) Josiah was killed (2 Kings 23:29). Jeremiah presents him in a favorable light as one who upheld justice and righteousness (22:15-16).

*Jehoahaz (Shallum)* (609). He was the third-oldest son of Josiah. At age 23 he ruled for three months, incurred the disfavor of the Egyptians, and was taken captive by Pharaoh Neco, first to Riblah and then to Egypt, where he died (2 Kings 23:31-34; 2 Chron. 36:1-4; Ezek. 19:4; Jer. 22:10-11).

*Jehoiakim (Eliakim)* (609-598). His rule of 11 years was exercised in the shadow of the ever-expanding Babylonian Empire. Midway through his reign, the Babylonians engaged the Egyptians in military battle at Carchemish in 605 (Jer 46:2). Jehoiakim became a vassal to Nebuchadnezzar of Babylon (2 Kings 23:36—24:5) but rebelled in 601 B.C.

Jeremiah censured Jehoiakim severely. Jeremiah had harsh criticism for the king's elaborate palace and his oppressive measures (22:13-23). Jehoiakim was the king who, while hearing the reading of Jeremiah's words, cut the scroll and tossed it into the fire (Jer. 36).

*Jehoiachin (Jeconiah* and also *Coniah)* (598-597). Jehoiachin, son of Jehoiakim, was 18 when he began to rule. During his three-month rule (December 598 to March 597), the Babylonians took Jerusalem. The king was taken captive along with the queen mother and the officials (1 Kings 24:8ff). Though captive in Babylon, he was accorded respect and allowed to eat at the king's table. God's words against him are harsh because he did evil (22:24-30; 2 Kings 25:27-30 = Jer. 52:31-34).

*Zedekiah (Mattaniah)* (597-587). Zedekiah, an uncle to Jehoiachin, was a puppet king installed by Nebuchadnezzar (2 Kings 24:17). Zedekiah was torn in his decision-making between advisers who counseled that he get help from Egypt and those like Jeremiah who advised submission to the threatening Babylonians. Twice he himself consulted the prophet privately (37:17-21; 38:14-

28). Twice he sent officials (21:1-7; 37:3-10). At one point Jeremiah requested from Zedekiah a transfer from jail (37:20-21).

Zedekiah was Judah's last king—as a punishment for his revolt against Babylon, Nebuchadnezzar besieged Jerusalem, burned the temple, deported a portion of the people, and ended Judah's 335-year existence. Jeremiah announced that Zedekiah would be taken captive if he attempted to escape, and that he would see his sons slain before his eyes. And so it happened (2 Kings 25:21).

### Family Chart of the Last Kings of Judah

Josiah (648-609, ruled 640-609)

| Johanan (1 Chron. 3:15) | Jehoiakim 634-598, ruled 609-598 | Jehoahaz 632-? ruled 609 | Zedekiah* 619-587 597-587 |
|---|---|---|---|

| Zedekiah* (2 Chron. 36:10) | Jehoiachin 616-? ruled 598-597 |
|---|---|

*Zedekiah, the son of Josiah, was the uncle of Jehoiachin (2 Kings 24:17), but 2 Chronicles 36:10 describes him as brother of Jehoiachin. The discrepancy is not easily resolved.

**KNOWING GOD**  To have information about God, to be acquainted with him, and/or to experience him. "To know" may express casual acquaintance (Gen. 29:5), but at a deeper level it signifies close familiarity (cf. "to know" as the idiom for sexual intercourse, Gen. 4:1, KJV). "To know" has links with covenant, so that to know God is to have a positive and right relationship with him. While knowing God may include the mystical dimension, it decidedly includes the practice of social justice (22:15-16). "To know God" is also to "acknowledge God," as NIV translates.

"Knowledge of God" figures prominently in the message of both Hosea and Jeremiah (Hos. 4:1, 6; 6:6; Jer. 9:23-24). The people's problem lay in a failure to know God, his ways and his law (5:4; 8:7; 9:3, 6). In this respect they were hardly better than pagans (10:25). Even the priests and the scribes who handled the Torah did not know God (2:8; 8:12).

Not knowing God will be remedied when God gives his people a new heart "to know me" (24:7). In the age of the new covenant, teachers will no longer be needed, for the experience of God will be direct and immediate. "They shall all know me" (31:34). "Here is his [Jeremiah's] prophecy of the new covenant compressed into one sentence" (von Rad: 212).

**LAMENT**  A sad or mournful response to sickness, death, or some disaster. Professionals, usually women, would lead in giving expression to grief by wailing, shrieking, and beating the breast.

Technically, a literary poem setting out a complaint or responding to a disaster. A much-used form included: (1) an address, (2) a complaint, (3) a prayer, (4) a statement of confidence, and (5) a praise response. Psalms 13 and 22 are classic examples of laments. In fact, one third of the Psalms are laments, though not all follow the above forms. All of them with the exception of Psalm 88 contain praise. Some are individual laments; others are community laments. The poetry in a lament is of the 3 + 2 meter pattern, called *Qinah* ( =lament). An example of such meter, though awkward, in translation is:

My eyés are spént with weéping;
  my soúl is in tuḿult. Lam. 2:11, RSV.

In Jeremiah there are seven "laments," also called "confessions" (Jer. 11:18-23; 12:1-6(13); 15:10-12; 15-21; 17:14-18; 18:18-23; 20:7-13). Several include a "statement of innocence." Jeremiah 20:7-13 is the most striking for its bluntness, though Jeremiah vents his feelings in each of them. Laments bemoan hardship, but they often seek change. In three laments there is an answer by God: 11:18-23; 12:1-6(13); 15:15-21. They portray the tensions, the inward struggles, the frustrations and despondencies of a prophet.

The laments are unique in prophetic literature. A condensed composite from Jeremiah is presented for further comparative study.

| | |
|---|---|
| **Complaint** | "They said, 'Let us cut him off' " (11:19)<br>"Why do wicked prosper?" (12:1)<br>"Everyone curses me" (15:10)<br>"Why is my pain unending?" (15:18)<br>"Lord, you deceived me" (20:7) |
| **Petition** | "Let me see your vengeance on them" (11:20; 20:12)<br>"Drag them to be butchered" (12:3)<br>"Avenge me of my persecutors" (15:15)<br>"Save me" (17:14, 18) |
| **Statement<br>of Innocence** | "You test my thoughts" (12:3)<br>"What passes my lips is open to you" (17:16)<br>"I spoke in their behalf" (18:20) |
| **Statement<br>of Confidence** | "You judge righteously" (11:20)<br>"You are always righteous" (12:1)<br>"I will deliver you" (15:11)<br>"The Lord is with me" (20:11) |
| **Praise** | "Give praise to the Lord" (20:13) |

One student, following the lament form, wrote a 20th-century version entitled "A Modern Lament of Desperation."

O God of my salvation, why have you deserted me?
My desperate cry for help echoes back from the ceiling.
My loneliness is complete, for you also have ceased to care.
I sit engulfed in black despair,
My whole being weighed down so I cannot move.
The tears are ceaseless, yet I have only emptiness inside.
I am worthless and a burden to my family.
My only longing is to cease to exist.
Afflict those glib ones who say they also have blue days.

Blast their ears with their empty words, "Have more faith!"
"Count your blessings!"
They increase my sense of failure and guilt.
Show me yourself or I die.
Heal my spirit or I will destroy myself.
Awaken me again to the loving care of my family and friends.
Teach me to delight in myself, for I am wondrously made.
Praise God, my Creator and Redeemer.
O Lord, you are our God; we will give thanks to you forever.
—Nancy Schell (Used by permission)

**LAND** Defined as the "Promised Land," Palestine figures prominently in Jeremiah. In rehearsing Israel's past (chapter 2), "Jeremiah tells the whole story of Israel as the story of land" (Brueggemann: 121).

Repeatedly, Jeremiah warns his audience that only if they reform their ways will God let them dwell in the land (7:3, 7). God will remove, uproot, even hurl his people from the land (16:13; 24:6).

Beyond judgment, however, salvation will be experienced as a return to the land. The promise of return is compared with the Exodus from Egypt. God will bring the exiles out of captivity in a manner that will greatly exceed the earlier Exodus for impressiveness (16:13; 24:6; cf. Ezek. 11:17). One of the points of dispute between Jeremiah and the false prophets is the interval between judgment and salvation—two years or seventy years (25:12; 29:14; 28:1-4).

Return to the land is couched in at least two catch phrases. "I will restore their fortunes" is coupled with coming back to the land (30:3; cf. 32:42ff; 33:10-11). [Restoration Formula, p. 307.] A second catch phrase, "I will plant them in the land" (32:41; cf. 24:6; 42:10; 45:4), suggests firmness and security.

The reasons for a return to the homeland are not sentimental or economic but religious. The reasons are not, as popularly supposed, because God promised Abraham the land originally. There are at least four sets of reasons why such a return is significant. One reason for such a return rests in the nature of God. He is compassionate. He intends to do his people good. The Book of Consolation, in which promises for the return cluster, is punctuated with statements about God's compassion (31:3; 31:15-20; cf. 24:6; Isa. 14:1).

A second reason lies in covenant, not a former covenant such as the Abrahamic, but in the goal of covenant: "I will be their God, and they shall be my people" (24:7; 30:22; Ezek. 36:28; 37:27). "The covenant formula is not the ground for the return in the sense that an existing relationship of covenant calls for such a return, but instead, realization of intimacy with Yahweh is to be the outcome of the return" (Martens, 1972: 283). [Covenant Formula, p. 294.]

Another reason for the return to the land lies in God's holy name. God will intervene in deliverance and act "for the sake of my holy name" (Ezek. 36:22). By her shameful conduct, Israel has profaned the name of the Lord. The nations interpret her exile as God's inability to save her (Ezek. 36:20). God's reputation has been blemished. But God will safeguard that reputation, sanctify that name, clear that name, so to speak, by rescuing the people and returning them to the land. "Land is a tool, a visual aid in the educative process of the nations" (Martens, 1981: 246).

More strange to our ears is another reason for their return: worship. God delights in the worship of his people, but that worship was jeopardized in a foreign land. They will be spiritually qualified to worship in their homeland through repentance (3:13, 18; 24:7; 31:18-19) and a new heart (Ezek. 36:24ff.). The two themes of a spiritual restoration to God and the restoration to the land belong together (see comments on chapters 30—31).

In summary, return to the land is important because it will reveal God's goodness, it will sanctify God before the nations, it will implement God's design for peoplehood, and it will facilitate a people's worship. Historically, the return began with the decree of Cyrus in 539 B.C. For a variety of reasons, some Bible students hold that this return in 539 did not exhaust the promise but that we may look for yet a future return. For some, the formation of the state of Israel in 1948 represents, not altogether inappropriately, a further fulfillment of that promise.

**LORD OF HOSTS**    A title for God which has royal and military overtones. The "hosts" (lit., *tsebaot)* refer to Israel's armies of which the Lord (Yahweh) is the leader (1 Sam. 17:45), or heavenly beings such as angels (1 Kings 22:19), or the astral bodies of sun, moon, and stars (Deut. 4:19). Yahweh Tsebaot is God's name, a point made by Amos in a hymn (4:13; 5:27), by Isaiah in a taunt on Babylon (47:4; 48:2), and eight times by Jeremiah (31:35; 10:16; 32:18; 48:15; 50:34; 51:19, 57). In no book is the expression "Lord of hosts" found more often than in Jeremiah. Of 285 occurrences in the Old Testament, 82 are found in Jeremiah.

The "Lord of hosts" is a royal title. It refers to a kingly figure who "dwells between the cherubim" in majesty (1 Sam. 4:4; 2 Sam. 6:2; cf. Isa. 6:2). In ancient times kings were portrayed on thrones with cherubim on either side. This royal aspect, not directly linked to armies, appears in worship psalms, and often in conjunction with Mt. Zion (46:7, 11; 48:8; 84:1, 3, 12).

The title is also a military title, for the addition of "hosts" to the name Yahweh (Lord) underlines his power and combativeness. The aspect of power can be heard in such declarations as: "O great and powerful God, whose name is the Lord of hosts" (32:18; NIV translates "Lord of hosts" as "Lord Almighty"). In Jeremiah the expression "Lord of hosts," or "Lord of hosts, God of Israel" appears most often in warlike or combative contexts. More than 20 times this weighty title occurs in conjunction with other nations. The Lord of hosts is a total match for every power whether Moab (48:1), Elam (49:35), Ammon (46:25), Edom (49:7) or the larger powers of Egypt (46:10) and Babylon (50:25, 31; 51:57-59). The title is frequent in disputation-type passages such as Jeremiah 27:17-22.

The Lord directs his military power against nations and idols, but also—and here is irony—against his own people. More than 30 times sentences of judgment begin or conclude with the formidable expression "Lord of hosts" (e.g., 11:22; 23:15; 28:16). God's work is a work of judgment primarily, since of the 82 occurrences of this title in Jeremiah, 50 are associated with judgment (e.g., 6:6; 9:7). Only a dozen times is the title in a redemption context, but even there the combative note is heard (e.g., 30:8; 50:18).

**NEBUCHADNEZZAR**    The crown prince who succeeded his father, Nabopolassar, as ruler of the Babylonians in 605 B.C. Nabopolassar, who rebelled against the Assyrians and took Nineveh in 612, ruled as the first king of the neo-Babylonian empire (626-605). *[Babylon/Babylonians, p. 291.]*

Nebuchadnezzar, his son, secured the north and northwest frontiers, sealing the victory in a marriage alliance with the daughter of the king of the Medes. In his westward expansion he attacked Jerusalem in 598 and captured it on March 16, 597. The king and officials, along with craftsmen, were taken hostage to Babylon. Zedekiah was made a vassal king. Following a raid on Egypt Nebuchadnezzar returned because of Zedekiah's revolt, to lay siege to Jerusalem and destroyed it by fire in 587.

The name Nebuchadnezzar is spelled in Jeremiah as Nebuchadrezzar everywhere except in chapters 27—29. In Accadian, the language of the Babylonians, it is Nabu-kudurri-usur and apparently means "may the god Nabu protect the boundary." In Jeremiah this king is designated by God as "my servant" (27:6). Daniel describes his dream, pride, illness, and repentance (Dan. 2—4). Nebuchadnezzar was succeeded after his death in 562 by Evil-merodach (Amel-Marduk), who treated Jehoiachin with kindness (2 Kings 25:27-30).

**OBEY/LISTEN** A compound which captures the sense of the Hebrew term *shema‘*, which means both physically to listen and morally to obey. *Shema‘* is the primary term for "obey"; another word *(natah)* is, literally, "to stretch (the ear)."

The verbal form of *shema‘* occurs in the Old Testament 1,159 times, and of these 184 (=15 percent) occur in Jeremiah. In 32 instances the verb is in the command form. The charge, "You (they) have not listened (obeyed)" is found more than 30 times, especially in chapters 7, 11, 26, 35, and 42. The Recabites who honor their ancestor's instruction not to drink wine are held up as models of integrity, in contrast with the Judahites who do not listen (obey) (35:12-16).

An illustration of the meaning of obey/listen comes from the third world. A missionary who was searching for an appropriate native word meaning "obey," left a village, but his dog stayed behind. The missionary whistled and the dog came running at top speed. An old native at the roadside said in admiration: *"Mui adem delegan ge!"* which means in free translation: "Your dog is all ear." The appropriate word for "obey" had been found.

**OPPRESSION** Hardship brought to bear by those in power upon those who are in their grasp, often the poor. There are in the Old Testament ten basic Hebrew words and ten less frequent ones that deal with oppression (Hanks: 5-26). The most frequent term is *ashaq*, which means "harshness" or "roughness." Force and violence are embodied in this word (Eccles. 4:1). In half the usues of *ashaq* the context is poverty (cf. Prov. 14:31). The connection between *ashaq* and justice is clear from Psalms 103:6-7.

Another significant term is *anah*, which means "to humiliate" or make to feel dependent. Noting that the term is found in Genesis 15:13, Hanks observes, "In view of the covenantal structure . . . it is important to note that *liberation from oppression is one of the fundamental provisions . . . of the Abrahamic covenant"* (Hanks, *God So Loved*, p. 15, italics his).

Certainly from the Sinai covenant onwards, the command to be advocates of the unprotected and dependent, the orphans and the poor, is specified (Exod. 23:6; Deut. 10:18; 16:11, 14; 24:20-22; Ps. 109:9; 146:9; Jer. 7:6; 22:3). The eighth-century prophets, especially Amos, bear down hardest on the evil of oppression. Upper-class women, for instance, who goad their husbands to provide them more luxuries, indirectly oppress the poor and will be punished (Amos 4:1-3). Business persons are confronted with taking advantage of the poor (Amos 2:6-7; cf. Micah 3:1-4). Israel was not to oppress nor enslave the poor and the needy (Ezek. 22:29). The appropriate response to the poor is outlined in Isaiah 58:6-8.

Jeremiah also speaks out against the oppressive treatment of the poor and the unprotected by the rich and those in power. The rich are described (though not uniformly in the Bible) as having become rich through deceitful and devious means. They have dominated and exploited the poor (5:20-29). Sharp words

are spoken against those who murder the "innocent poor" (2:34). King Zedekiah took appropriate steps toward the slaves, but because he went back on his
word, this man of power and authority was severely censured (34:8-22). Yet the
poor are no more to be romanticized than the rich are to be always condemned,
for Jeremiah accuses also the poor of "not knowing the way of the Lord" (5:4).

**PROPHET/PROPHECY**   One who is called by God to serve as a herald or
authorized spokesperson in God's behalf. Designations for such a person in the
Old Testament are "man of god" (Deut. 33:1; 1 Kings 13:1-31), "seer" *(ro'eh)*
(1 Sam. 9:9), "seer" *(ḥozeh)* (2 Sam. 24:11), and "prophet" *(nabi')* (Exod. 7:1;
Deut. 18:14-22). The root meaning of *nabi'*, it is now generally agreed, is "to
call" or better, "to be called." Some Bible scholars speak of the "office" of a
prophet; others emphasize the characteristics of ecstasy or charisma. It is best to
describe prophets according to their role.
     First, prophets were to speak the Lord's words. These words might deal with
forthcoming destructions, either of Israel (5:14-17) or of the other nations (Jer.
51). Or they might be words of salvation, perhaps to Israel (30:1ff.) or to nations
(48:47). The prophet proclaimed the word which he had heard given in the
divine counsel (23:18, 22). Second, the prophet, because he stood between God
and the people, was to influence his audience Godward (cf. Amos 5:14f.). Third,
the prophet was to influence the deity by interceding for the people (1 Sam.
12:19; Amos 7:1-6; Jer. 11:14). The prophetic assignment was multiple, but the
presentation of God's message was primary.
     The prophets frequently targeted their message to the king and to his royal
house. In the divine ordering of accountabilities, it was the prophet who held the
king accountable and not vice versa (Lind, 1980). Elijah confronted King Ahab
(1 Kings 17:1) and Jeremiah critiqued King Jehoiakim (22:18-23). They were
forthright in their critique of their peers (Micah 3:5-7; Jer. 23:9ff.), as well as of
the priests (Amos 7:10-17). At other times the prophets' messages were targeted
to the people. Occasionally they had messages for individuals (28:15-16).
     Often the prophets identified the shape of evil in their society. Sometimes
they came with a message of hope. The prophets spoke the word of God into
their historic situations for the most part; prediction, especially to the distant future, was less common. Prophets occasionally lifted the veil disclosing the future.
"Prophecy moves present behavior into the light of future events, and it does so
in the name of God" (Wolff: 63). More often prophets lift the mask, uncovering
pretension and evil.

**REPENTANCE**   A "turning" and hence a change of spiritual direction. The
Hebrew word *shub* quite generally means "to turn back" (from something or
someone) or "to return to" (something or someone). In everyday speech the
word is used of walking in one direction and then changing or reversing direction
(cf. Ruth 1:15; 1 Sam. 26:25). In a covenantal or spiritual sense *shub* is "change
of loyalty on the part of Israel or God each for the other." (Holladay, 1958; 2).
For example, " 'If you return *(shub)*, O Israel, return *(shub)* to me,' declares the
Lord" (Jer. 4:1). Jeremiah's appeals to repentance are concentrated in chapters
2, 4, 7, and 18. *[Summons to Repentance, p. 310.]* Jeremiah has rightly been
called "the prophet of repentance." There are 164 usages of covenantal *shub* in
the Bible, 48 of which ( =30 percent) are in Jeremiah.
     Repentance is much more than saying, "I am sorry," or "If I have offended,"
or even "I have sinned" (cf. 14:20). The people may say so, but because they still
"love to wander" (14:10), they are not forgiven. Repentance for sin means a

spiritual turnabout, a change of direction. That implies a stop to the behavior or attitude in question and an embrace of God (cf. 31:15-22).

In the early phase of his ministry Jeremiah singled out evil worship practices from which Israel needed to repent. Forsaking God for idols is a repeated theme (2:13, 17, 32). Turning to Baal and the worship of idols are contrary even to common sense (2:11, 23, 27). Later in his career, so it seems, Jeremiah placed greater emphasis on social injustices, specifying oppression of aliens, murder, and adultery (5:28; 7:6-9), though rejection of the Lord, false worship, and the alliance with false prophets were constant problems.

Charles G. Finney, revivalist preacher and American thinker of note in America in the nineteenth century, asked in a letter why there were no longer revivals. "Is it possible, my dearly beloved brethren, that we can remain blind to the tendencies of things—to the causes that are operating to produce alienation, division, distrust, to grieve away the Spirit, overthrow revivals, and cover the land with darkness and the shadow of death? Is it not time for us, brethren, to repent, to be candid and search out wherein we have been wrong and publicly and privately confess it (Finney)?"

**RESTORATION FORMULA**    A designation for the expression "I will restore the fortunes *(shub shebut)* of. . . ." English translations which render the Hebrew expression *shub shebut* as "return the captivity of," or something similar, are based on an older view which held that the Hebrew word in question derived from "take captive" (cf. Jer. 30:3, NIV). But now new insights have come from studies of Hebrew parallelism and from archaeological Aramaic inscriptions at Sefire. It is increasingly clear that the expression is anchored in the word "turn," so that its sense is "turn the turning" = "reverse the fortunes" (Bright: 269) or "restore the fortunes." "The phrase *shub shebut* is to be understood as carrying the meaning, 'bring about the restoration'" (Martens, 1972: 181). It is an expression dealing with the recovery of what was lost (cf. Job 42:10), and can refer, though it need not, to the restoration of exiles from captivity.

Of the more than 25 occurrences of the expression in the Old Testament (e.g., Deut. 30:3), 12 are found in Jeremiah, most in the "Book of Consolation." The "Book of Consolation" opens with the restoration formula as a theme to introduce both restoration of land to a people and a people to their God (30:3, 18; 31:23; 32:44; 33:7, 11, 26; cf. 29:14; 48:47; 49:6; 49:39).

**REVELATION FORMULA**    The label given to phrases such as "the word of the Lord came to me [Jeremiah] from the Lord." The "word" is visualized as something tangible. It originates with God and comes from alongside him to the prophet. The word of the Lord is an event happening through words. The expression prepares the way for the New Testament statement, "And the word became flesh and lived for a while among us" (John 1:14).

The repeated use of the prophetic revelation formula emphasizes that the message is not man-originated but is from God. One might conveniently divide the book according to the occurrence of this formula: 1:4; 7:1; 11:1; 14:1; 18:1; 21:1; 27:1; 30:1; 34:1; 35:1; 36:1; 40:1; 46:1; 47:1; 50:1).

A closely related formula is "Thus says the Lord." The introductory statement in the ancient Near East of a messenger who relayed a message from his king to a foreign dignatary would be: "Thus says King X to Y." Hence the formula "Thus says the Lord" is commonly known as the prophetic messenger formula. In Jeremiah this formula or a similar phrase occurs more than 150 times.

**SEPTUAGINT**    The name given to the earliest translation of the Hebrew Old Testament into Greek, made in approximately the third century B.C. in Alexandria, Egypt. Whereas the Septuagint generally agrees with the Hebrew text, there are striking divergencies between the Greek and Hebrew texts in first century B.C. fragments from Qumran, and in books like Samuel and Jeremiah. In the Septuagint the book of Jeremiah is one seventh shorter than in the present Hebrew version.

These facts have raised questions. Did translators into the Greek follow a different Hebrew manuscript than the one we know? Did they deliberately eliminate material? Did the Hebrew writing which we follow expand an earlier text? Despite painstaking comparative studies, there are no clear-cut answers. Most scholars favor the Masoretic Hebrew text, from which our English Bible is translated, as closer to the original. The research has shown, however, that while the Greek version is a less reliable one generally, in individual instances it is helpful to clear up a difficulty.

Some examples of Septuagint differences in Jeremiah are: the section on the nations, which appears at the end in the Hebrew text, appears in the Septuagint following 25:13; the Septuagint omits "first" in 16:18; it omits the question mark in 23:23 and thus reverses the sense. It omits all references to Nebuchadnezzar as "my servant" (25:9; 27:6; 43:10). The RSV uses a Septuagint reading more often than does the NIV.

**SEVENTY YEARS**    An expression of a time span in Jeremiah specifying chiefly, but perhaps not exclusively, the duration of Babylonian rulership. For example, nations "will serve the king of Babylon 70 years" (25:11; cf. 29:10 and 27:7). To take this figure literally leads to calculation. Counting from the first siege in 598, 70 years would bring one to 528, an unimportant date. Some refer to the 70 years as the captivity and calculate from 586, when the temple was destroyed, to 516, when its rebuilding was completed; but the calculation leaves out of consideration the announcement that it is the duration of Babylon that is in question. It is best, if one must count, to count from 605, the year when Nebuchadnezzar became king (cf. wording of 29:10). The 70 years would conclude in 535, within range of 538, the year Babylon was overthrown by Persia and Cyrus decreed liberty for exiles to return.

It may also be that 70 is a figure more symbolic and approximate than exact. Support for this view is the text that cites three generations (27:7). Moreover, two score years and ten (70), the length of a full life, represents a full time period and may refer specifically to the duration of Babylon's power in the Mediterranean and less specifically to the duration of Judah's exile. Further exegesis of the 70 years which points to a further and larger meaning is given by Daniel (9:24; cf. 2 Chron. 36:20).

**SHALOM**    A Hebrew term for peace which describes comprehensive well-being. Shalom, while used in a daily greeting among the Hebrews, is a weighty theological term in the Old Testament. Shalom embraces concepts of harmony, security, serenity, right relationships, wholeness, health, prosperity, and even success. The term may refer to a condition or a relationship, and in the latter designates a right relationship to God.

God is the source of shalom and offers shalom to those who trust him (Ps. 29:11; Isa. 26:3). Shalom has a social dimension; it is understandably linked with righteousness (Isa. 32:17). "The prophets' positive call for justice (see Amos 5:15, 24) is not a call of individual charity but to establish the structures of justice—the prerequisites for shalom" (Yoder: 47).

Shalom is a repeated theme in Jeremiah. A group of prophets, whom Jeremiah branded as deceitful, promised shalom or peace (14:13f.; 23:17). This promise for shalom was made in the face of gross unrighteousness in Judah and despite the approach of an enemy power, the Babylonians. But shalom was not in store for God's people because of their social injustices and their disregard for, even defiance of, God. With society so thoroughly characterized by evil, the prophetic word could not be one of peace (28:9). God had withdrawn his shalom from his people. To make that point memorable, Jeremiah was not to socialize by attending funerals or joyous celebrations (16:5).

Yet God desired to bless his people with shalom. Following judgment on his people, he declares, "For I know the plans that I have for you . . . plans for welfare [shalom] and not calamity to give you a future and a hope" (29:11, NASB). In the book of comfort is included the promise, "I will bring health [shalom] and healing to it. . . ." (33:6).

**SHAPHAN**   A royal scribe who served under King Josiah and who sympathized with that king's religious reform (2 Kings 22:3-14). He and his family were helpful to Jeremiah. Ahikam, Shaphan's son, lent his support at Jeremiah's trial (26:24; cf. 2 Kings 22:12, 14). Elasah, a second son, carried Jeremiah's letter to the exiles (29:3). It was from the temple room of Gemariah, another of Shaphan's sons, that the scroll was read by Baruch to the crowds that gathered on the fast day. Gemariah was a scribe. His son Micaiah brought the news of the reading to the officials at the palace.

Gemariah was one of those who attempted to dissuade King Jehoiakim from slicing up Jeremiah's scroll and tossing it into the fire (36:10-12, 25). After the Babylonians crushed the Israelite monarchy, it was Gedaliah, Shaphan's grandson, who was given custody of Jeremiah (39:14; 40:5). Gedaliah was appointed governor but was assassinated by Ishmael (41:1-3). A signet ring has been unearthed in the ruins of Lachish, destroyed in 587 by the Babylonians, with the words "of Gedaliah, who is over the house."

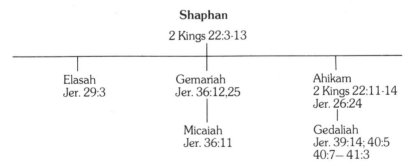

**Shaphan**

2 Kings 22:3-13

| Elasah | Gemariah | Ahikam |
|--------|----------|--------|
| Jer. 29:3 | Jer. 36:12,25 | 2 Kings 22:11-14 |
| | | Jer. 26:24 |
| | Micaiah | Gedaliah |
| | Jer. 36:11 | Jer. 39:14; 40:5 |
| | | 40:7– 41:3 |

**STYLE**   In this context the literary characteristics of a book, and the matters which touch on prose, poetry, vocabulary, and genre. Poetry predominates in the first half of the book; prose in the second half.

Hebrew poetry is characterized by parallelism of thought, rather than rhyme.

A lion has come out of his lair;
    a destroyer of nations has set out (4:7).

Jeremiah is a prophet of great poetic skill. His poetry is laced with simile and metaphor, drawing heavily in this respect on Hosea.

Death has climbed in through our windows
and has entered our fortresses;
it has cut off the children from the streets
and the young men from the public squares (9:21).

Jeremiah reaches for a daring mode of expression as he describes the adulterous practices: "They are well-fed lusty stallions, each neighing for another man's wife" (5:8). Jeremiah's poetry is often emotionally intensive and personal.

Oh, my anguish, my anguish!
I writhe in pain.
Oh, the agony of my heart!
My heart pounds within me,
I cannot keep silent (4:19).

Points of literary finesse include chiasmus structuring, inclusio, and word-play. *[Chiasmus, p. 292; Inclusio, p. 298; and Wordplay, p. 313.]*

If the poetry is poignant, the prose, by comparison, is sometimes rambling and repetitious (e.g., 32:30-44). Scholars have often pointed to the similarities of style between parts of Jeremiah and so-called Deuteronomic materials (Deuteronomy-Kings). Jeremiah 11 is a prime example of this affinity, for here words and phrases hark back to Deuteronomy. Examples: "iron furnace" (v. 4; Deut. 4:20); "terms (words) of this covenant" (vv. 2, 3, 6; Deut. 29:1); "cursed is . . . (v. 3; Deut. 27:15); "followed other gods" (v. 10; Deut. 6:14; 8:19; 11:28; 13:2; 28:14).

Jeremiah consists of diverse genre (kinds of literary writing). Earlier prophets followed a genre such as the judgment oracle quite strictly. Jeremiah works with greater freedom; he rearranges the components of a given form. A sample listing of genres with an example follows. Those genres with an asterisk indicate a separate treatment in this glossary.

| | |
|---|---|
| *lament, 20:7-13 | *judgment oracles, 11:9-13 |
| letter, 29:1ff. | sermon, 7:2-15 |
| biography, 37:1ff. | vision, 1:11-16; 24:1-10 |
| *symbolic action, 13:1-11; 32:1ff. | *summons to repentance, 3:12-13 |
| | *deliverance oracles, 30:4-11 |

**SUMMONS TO REPENTANCE**   A standardized speech form which calls people to a change of their ways and their beliefs. It consists of four parts: an admonition (e.g., seek me, return); a promise (e.g., you will live); a threat (e.g., you will go into exile); and an accusation (you have forsaken the Lord). Not always are all parts represented, nor are they always in the same sequence. A concise form of the summons to repentance as noted by Raitt is found in Jeremiah 3:12-13.

| | |
|---|---|
| (admonition) | "Return, faithless Israel . . . |
| (threat) | I will not be angry forever . . . |
| (promise) | For I am merciful . . . |
| (accusation) | You have rebelled against the Lord your God." |

In a summons of repentance people are addressed directly. Clear alternatives are set out and there is a call for a decision. In Jeremiah the admonition is almost always combined with *both* the promise and the accusation or threat (Raitt: 39).

Examples of summons to repentance are found in 2 Kings 17:13; Nehemiah 1:8-9; Isaiah 1:19-20; Joel 2:12-17; Jonah 3:7-9; and Jeremiah 3:12-13; 4:1-2, 3-4, 14; 7:3-7; 15:19; 18:11; 22:3-5; 25:5-6; 26:13; 31:21-22; 35:15.

**SWEARING**  The invoking of a greater power or reality, thereby giving a guarantee to one's commitment. King Zedekiah swore that "as surely as the Lord lives" he would spare Jeremiah's life (38:16). God himself swears, thereby binding himself securely to his promise (22:24). Swearing an oath, especially in connection with covenant, establishes the binding validity of the arrangement.

The phrase "as surely as the Lord lives," which might also be rendered "by the life of God," introduces an oath. The name of the god invoked is generally the god in whom one believes (e.g., Baal, 12:16). For this reason one of the marks of loyalty to God is to swear by his name (Jer. 4:2; 12:16). The opening formula could be expanded by some description, e.g., "who brought the Israelites up out of Egypt" (16:14//23:7), or "who has given us breath" (38:16), or it might be replaced by "as my lord the king lives" (2 Sam. 15:21). A shorthand introduction to an oath is literally, "If not . . ." translated as "surely" (15:11).

But to speak the oath phrase and to reject God's lordship in one's heart is mockery (5:2). Zephaniah, Jeremiah's contemporary, decries the syncretism of a people who swear both by the Lord and by Molech (Zeph. 1:5). Hosea even prohibits his disbelieving people from swearing by the Lord's name (Hos. 4:15).

Some religious groups, the Mennonites among them, hold on the basis of the New Testament that the swearing of oaths for Christians is uncalled for, even evil. "If you fear the Lord and are asked to swear, continue in the Lord's Word which has forbidden you so plainly to swear, and let your yea and nay be your oath as was commanded, whether life or death be your lot" (Quoted by Alan Kreider in *Heritage of Freedom*, p. 53).

**SYMBOLIC ACTIONS**  Actions which are signs—acted-out messages. Jeremiah and Ezekiel, who were both prophets associated with Babylon's takeover of Judah in 587 B.C., engaged in symbolic actions more than other prophets. Jeremiah purchased a linen girdle (chapter 13), smashed a pot (chapter 19), visited the potter's workplace (chapter 18), wore a yoke (chapters 27—28), and bought a field (chapter 32; cf. also 16:1ff.; 43:8-13; 51:63f.). Ezekiel prepared a model of Jerusalem (4:1-2) and cut his hair (5:1-17; cf. 12:1-7; 24:1-14; 37:15-28). Earlier in Israel's history Zedekiah made horns of iron (1 Kings 22:11), Isaiah walked "naked" (Isaiah 20), and Hosea married a prostitute as a sign.

The literary form of a symbolic action report is stereotyped and consists of (1) divine directives *(Befehl)*, (2) the report of compliance *(Bericht)*, and (3) the interpretation *(Bedeutung)*.

A reason for symbolic action was to reinforce visibly the oral word which people refused (Ezek. 12:2). Sign-acts arrested people's attention; they riveted the prophet's message in the memory. Though they were not "magic," it may well have been the belief that they set in motion that which they portrayed.

Swidler makes these applications for today: (1) social injustice should be confronted dramatically and not limited to "good taste"; (2) these signs are not liturgy, and so are nonrepeatable; (3) whenever there was destruction of property, it was the prophet's, not another's; (4) the prophet accepts and does not impose suffering on others; (5) neither the health nor life of a prophet was jeopardized by the act; and (6) the act was never used as threat against the people. (Arlene Swidler: 182-87).

**TOPHETH**    The name of a worship area, a "high place" in the valley of Ben Hinnom to the south of Jerusalem. Children were offered there to Molech, the national god of the Ammonites (32:35; 2 Chron. 28:3; 33:6). Topheth ("fire pit" in Syriac) later became known as *ge* (valley of) Hinnom, which in New Testament times became Gehenna.

Child sacrifice was introduced by Ahaz and Manasseh (2 Kings 16:3; 21:6), abolished by Josiah (2 Kings 23:10), and renewed by Jehoiakim. The practice was condemned by God (Lev. 20:2-5). It was apparently unknown in Assyria and Babylon. From Carthage in North Africa, which was settled by Phoenicians, we gather that parents placed children in the arms of the statue Baal-Hinnom. The bodies would roll or drop into the furnace. Later the charred bones would be gathered into pottery vases and buried. Jeremiah addressed the perversion of child sacrifice (7:31; 32:35).

**VENGEANCE**    The inflicting of pain or harm, either to oneself or another, in return for pain or harm done. Humanly speaking, vengeance is retaliation. When his eyes were put out by the Philistines, Samson wanted to settle accounts, and prayed, "O God, please strengthen me once more, and let me with one blow get revenge on the Philistines for my two eyes" (Judg. 16:28). It has been argued that proper vengeance belongs to the highest authority. Vengeance as retribution is essentially God's prerogative—"It is mine to avenge; I will repay" (Deut. 32:35; cf. Rom. 12:17-19; Heb. 10:28-31).

The prophets envision the day when God in his sovereignty will settle accounts:

> Say to those with fearful hearts,
> "Be strong, do not fear;
> your God will come,
> he will come with vengeance;
> with divine retribution
> he will come to save you." (Isa. 35:4)

Only rarely, and that when God specifies, are persons themselves entitled to take revenge (e.g., Num. 31:2-3). "Of the seventy-eight passages in the Bible where the [Hebrew] root *NQM* [vengeance] occurs, fifty-one involve situations in which the actor is either Yahweh Himself, or an agency to which the power to act is specifically delegated in a specific situation" (Mendenhall: 82). Since the act of vengeance belongs to God, those who sincerely believe in God do not take retaliation for evil into their own hands, but call on God to take vengeance (1 Sam. 24:12; cf. Ps. 18:47).

In Jeremiah one finds several assertions about God's role in taking vengeance on Israel and on nations (5:9, 29; 9:9; 46:10; 50:15; 51:6, 11, 36). The prophet also prays for God to take vengeance on his personal enemies (11:20; 15:15; 20:12). Jeremiah never speaks of "my vengeance." Here he is in accord with the scriptural teaching to leave the settling of accounts to God.

The Old Testament forbids the exercise of personal vendetta—"Do not seek revenge . . ."—and in the same breath sets a high standard, reiterated in the

New Testament, "but love your neighbor as yourself" (Lev. 19:18; Rom. 12:17-21; Matt. 5:44). While Jeremiah turned over his case for revenge to the Lord, it cannot be said, judging from his laments, that he moved to the second stage of loving his enemies.

**WORD/DEED**   A combination frequent in Jeremiah to emphasize that oral statement and practical action go together.

The inseparable relationship between word and deed is stressed from the outset when God is said to watch over his word to perform it (1:12). In broad outline, much of the first part of the book is a collection of words/messages; the second part contains a record of incidents (deeds). "They [the collectors] acknowledged by their inclusion of his life story that a complete understanding of his [Jeremiah's] ministry demanded elements of both speech and action" (Childs: 350).

Jeremiah confronts the people with the discrepancy of saying one thing and doing another (7:9-10). People are shown to be evil and deserving of punishment when both their speech and their actions are evil (3:5). Jeremiah therefore calls for a reform of both talk and walk (7:5; 18:11). The word/deed association is especially striking in chapter 2 where it is crucial for convicting Israel as guilty. She is guilty because of her sayings (2:20, 23, 25, 27, 31, 35; 3:4), as well as her actions, such as spiritual harlotry (2:20, 33; 3:2), worship of idols (2:27), violent disposal of prophets (2:30), and wicked oppression of the poor (2:34), not to mention reliance on Egypt and Assyria (2:18, 36). For additional word/deed parallelism in different contexts (though variously translated in English) see 4:18; 7:5; 23:22; 25:5; 26:13.

**WORDPLAY**   Interesting, clever, and sometimes highly significant "takeoffs" on words which sound the same, or roughly the same, but mean quite different things. It is a rhetorical device which not only brings surprise and sometimes a smile, but makes a memorable point. The effect, striking in Hebrew, can seldom be adequately represented in English. "He (God) looked for *right (mishpat)*, but behold a *riot (mishpah)*" (Isa. 5:7). Or, "If you will not confide *(ta'aminu)*, you shall not abide *(te'amenu)*" (Isa. 7:9).

Comparable examples from the English language are: "the creed of Christ and the greed of men"; "our seeing shapes our being"; and "In Jeremiah the gloom was evident, but the gleam shone through it" (Morgan, *Studies*, p. 281).

In Jeremiah examples are: almond branch *(shaqed)* // watching *(shoqed)* (1:11, 12); flask *(baqbuq)* // ruin *(baqqoti)* (19:1, 7); Zedekiah (the Lord our righteousness) (23:6); *shepherd* (verb) and *shepherds* (noun), (22:22); and oracle/burden (23:33ff.); throw//frost (36:30); Hophra//opportunity (46:17); Heshbon//plot and Madmen/silenced (48:2); and rebellion//punishment (50:21).

**WRATH**   An emotion of intense anger, ascribed both to human beings and to God. The major Hebrew words describing wrath have to do with "nose" and "heat"—anger is expressed physically in heavy breathing and in heated or intense emotions. Just as words for the physical body, such as arm and eyes, are used of God, so also are words of human emotions.

The word for anger *('ap)*, derived from "nose") is used in Jeremiah more often than in other books—24 times (e.g., 2:35; 15:14; 33:5). A second term for anger as a burning sensation and also as kindling a fire *(harah)* is used to describe Potiphar's feeling against Joseph (Gen. 39:19) and God's anger against a murmuring people (Num. 11:1). The noun form, always ascribed to God, is found 41 times in the Old Testament and often with 'ap to give the translation "fierceness (burning) of his anger" (4:8; 12:13; 25:37; 30:24). A third term *(ḥemah)* is also linked with heat as of fire and conveys the concept of an inner intense emotional disturbance. Of its 125 occurrences, 33 are found in Ezekiel and 17 in Jeremiah (e.g., 7:20; 25:15; 30:23). In Jeremiah 42 different verses or passages mention or elaborate God's anger.

Wrath is pictured as "breaking out and burning like a fire" (21:12). In another image it is as a tangible thing which leaves God's presence and is not diverted or turned until it has reached its target (30:24). Or, God's wrath is as a hurricane "swirling down on the heads of the wicked" (30:23). In still another image God's anger is in a cup to be poured out or taken as drink (21:15).

God's anger is aroused by the sin and the disbelief of his people (4:4; 32:31) or that of other nations (25:15-28 and comments there). His anger raged against the towns of Judah (44:6) and Jerusalem (42:18). His anger is pictured as devastating a region (4:26-28). God banished his people in anger (32:37). God's anger, as Luther said, is not against sinners but against unbelievers.

Wrath may be thought of as the energy of divine justice expressing itself. It is not an irrational outburst. It is God's concern which is the source of his anger. God's anger is protective of his interests, including the objects of his love. His anger is against evil and all that is not in keeping with his holiness. The measure of his anger is justice. Anger is not the opposite of love; love's opposite is apathy. One does well to remember that the God who put the sentence of judgment on Nineveh also lifted it off.

**YAHWEH** The personal name for the God of Israel. In English versions it is mostly rendered LORD, which strictly speaking is not a name but a title. Some older English versions employ Jehovah, but the latest consensus is that the tetragrammaton (the four consonants YHWH) were pronounced Yahweh.

Names in the Old Testament were often rich with meaning. The name Yahweh is linked to the Hebrew verb "to be." Some interpreters feel that this linkage stresses God's existence. The phrase "I am that I am," which is associated with God's name, say others, could be translated, "I cause to be that which I cause to be." Such an understanding would underline the creative activity of God. Noting that a distinction is made in the key passage of Exodus 6:1ff. between God Almighty and Yahweh (Lord), a Jewish scholar has suggested that the patriarchs knew God Almighty as a god of fertility but not as Yahweh, one who fulfilled promises. It has even been suggested that "I am that I am" is no name in the usual sense and that quite deliberately God did not reveal a personal name, as names are usually known, in order that people not manipulate the name.

While these explanations have merit, it is best to give close attention to the contexts of Exodus 3:12ff. and 6:2ff. The significance of the name for Moses lay in the promise of God's presence. God had said to Moses, "But I will be with you" (Exod. 3:12, NIV). The context is one in which deliverance is promised (3:17). Coupling these statements with the discussion in Exodus 6:2ff., which deal with covenant and deliverance, it becomes clear that the name Yahweh is linked with "saving." In short, Yahweh signfies a God who is present to save.

The event of the Exodus was *the* event by which to know, or experience, God, Yahweh (Exod. 6:2ff.). The name Yahweh, which occurs in the Old Testament more than 6,800 times, incorporates "salvation," "promise," and "covenant."

Palestine
In Jeremiah's Time

Sidon  Damascus

Mt. Hermon
Mt. Lebanon

Tyre  ARAM

Dan

Hazor

Acco  BASHAN

Mt. Carmel

Mt. Tabor

GILEAD

Megiddo
Jezreel  Beth-shan

ISRAEL

Samaria
Shechem

Aphek  EPHRAIM
Joppa  Shiloh

AMMON

BENJAMIN  Bethel
Mizpah  Ai  Jericho  Rabbath-Ammon
Ekron  Ramah  Heshbon
Ashdod  Gibeon  Anathoth  Mt. Nebo
Jerusalem  (Anata)  Medeba
Beth-shemesh  Beth-hakkerem  Baal-meon
Bethlehem
Ashkelon  Gath  Azekah  Tekoa
Lachish  Dibon
Gaza  Hebron  Dead  Aroer
Sea  Wadi Arnon

JUDAH
MOAB

Beersheba  Kir-heres

Honoraim

The Negev  Zoar  Ije-abarim

Bozrah

EDOM

Mediterranean Sea

Sea of Galilee

Wadi Yarmuk

Jordan River

The Arabah

The Arabah  Wadi Zered

Map by Jan Gleysteen and Paula Johnson

316

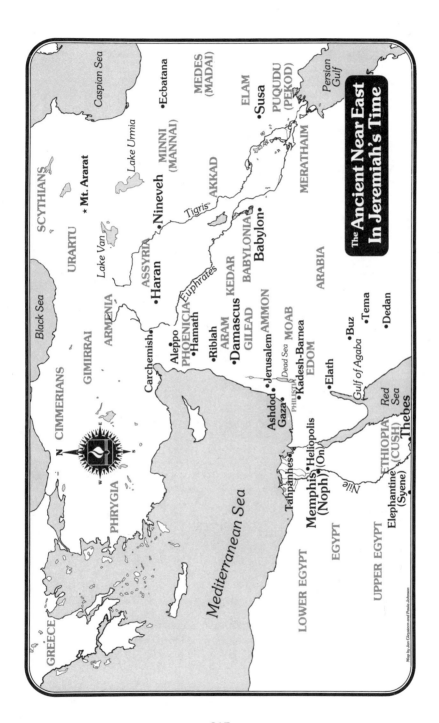

The Ancient Near East In Jeremiah's Time

Map by Ann Colquetson and Paula Johnson

# Sources Quoted

Achtemeier, Elizabeth
1983

"Imposes and Ideology." *The Presbyterian Outlook* 165/39 (14 November): 6-7.

Aitken, Kenneth T.
1984

"The Oracles Against Babylon in Jeremiah 50-51: Structures and Perspectives." *Tyndale Bulletin* 35:25-63.

Beuken, W. A. M.,
and H. M. W. van Grol
1981

"Jeremiah 14:1—15:9: A Situation of Distress and Its Hermeneutics. Unity and Diversity of Form-Dramatic Development" in *Le Livre de Jeremie*. Ed. by P.-M. Bogaert. Leuven: University Press. Pp. 297-342.

Blackwood, Andrew
W., Jr.
1981

*Jeremiah*. Waco, Tex.: Word Books.

Blank, Sheldon H.
1961

*Jeremiah: Man and Prophet.* 1st ed. Cincinnati: Hebrew Union College Press.

Boadt, Lawrence
1982

*Jeremiah 1-25.* Wilmington, Del.: Michael Glazier, Inc.

Braght, Thieleman
Janzoon van
1951

*Martyrs Mirror.* Scottdale, Pa.: Mennonite Publishing House.

Bright, John
1965

*Jeremiah.* 1st ed. Garden City, N.Y.: Doubleday.

Brueggemann, Walter
1977

*The Land: Place as Gift, Promise, and Challenge in Biblical Faith.* Philadelphia: Fortress Press.

Calvin, John
1948

*Commentaries on the Prophet Jeremiah and the Lamentations.* Vols. II and IV. Grand Rapids, Mich.: Eerdmans.

Carson, D. A., ed.
1982

*From Sabbath to Lord's Day. A Biblical, Historical, and Theological Investigation.* Grand Rapids, Mich.: Zondervan.

Chambers, Oswald.
1958

*A Spiritual Clinic.* Chicago: Moody Press.

Childs, Brevard S.
1979

*Introduction to the Old Testament as Scripture.* Philadelphia: Fortress Press.

Clines, David J. A.
and David M. Gunn
1978

" 'You Tried to Persuade Me' and 'Violence and Outrage' in Jeremiah 20:7-8." *Vetus Testamentum* 28: 20-27.

Dahood, Mitchell
1977

"Word and Witness: A Note on Jeremiah 29:23." *Vetus Testamentum* 27:483.

Driver, G. R.
1957

"Difficult Words in the Hebrew Prophets." *Studies in Old Testament Prophecy.* Ed. H. H. Rowley. Edinburgh: T&T Clark.

Durnbaugh, Donald F.
1968

*The Believer's Church, The History and Character of Radical Protestantism.* New York: Macmillan.

Finney, Charles G.
1976

"The Pernicious Attitude of the Church on the Reforms of the Age." Donald W. Dayton, *Discovering an Evangelical Heritage.* New York: Harper & Row.

Fitzmyer, J. A.
1967

*The Aramaic Inscriptions of Sefire.* Biblica et Orientalia, No. 19. Rome: Pontifical Biblical Institute.

Freedman, David Noel
1967

"The Biblical Idea of History." *Interpretation* 21:32-49.

Freehof, Solomon B.
1977

*Book of Jeremiah: A Commentary.* New York: Union of American Hebrew Congregations.

Fry, Peter
1976

*Spirits of Protest.* Cambridge University Press. Quoted in B. O. Long, "Social Dimensions of Prophetic Conflict." *Semeia* 21:36-37.

Green, Alberto R.
1982

"The Chronology of the Last Days of Judah: Two Apparent Discrepancies." *Journal of Biblical Literature* 101: 57-73.

Hanks, Thomas D.
1983

*God So Loved the Third World: The Biblical Vocabulary of Oppression.* Maryknoll, N.Y.: Orbis Books.

Harrison, Roland Kenneth
1973

*Jeremiah and Lamentations; An Introduction and Commentary.* 1st ed. Downers Grove, Ill.: InterVarsity Press.

Hartfeld, Hermann
1980

*Irina.* Chappaqua, N.Y.: Christian Herald Books.

Heschel, Abraham
1962

*The Prophets.* 1st ed. New York: Harper & Row.

Hillers, Delbert R.            *Covenant: The History of a Biblical Idea.* Balti-
1969                           more: Johns Hopkins Press.

Holladay, William Lee         *The Architecture of Jeremiah 1-20.* Lewisburg,
1976                           Pa.: Bucknell Univ. Press.

                              *A Concise Hebrew and Aramaic Lexicon of the*
1971                          *Old Testament.* Grand Rapids, Mich.: Eerdmans.

1980                          "The Identification of Two Scrolls." *Vetus Testa-
                              mentum* 30:452-467.

1958                          *The Root "Subh" in the Old Testament, with
                              Particular Reference to Its Usage in Covenantal
                              Contexts.* Leiden: E. J. Brill.

1974                          *Jeremiah: Spokesman Out of Time.* Philadelphia:
                              Pilgrim Press.

Hyatt, James Philip          "The Book of Jeremiah." *The Interpreter's Bible.*
1956                         Vol. V. Ed. by George Arthur Buttrick. Nashville:
                             Abingdon Press.

Isbell, Charles D.           "Rhetorical Criticism and Jeremiah 7:1—8:3."
and Michael Jackson          *Vetus Testamentum* 30:20-26.
1980

Kitchen, K. A.,and           "Chronology of the Old Testament." *The
T. C. Mitchell               Illustrated Bible Dictionary.* Vol. I. Wheaton, Ill.:
1980                         Tyndale House Publishers.

Kreider, Alan                (Essay in *Heritage of Freedom.*) Lion Publishing
                             PLC, Tring, Herts, England, 1984.

Kuist, Howard Tillman        *The Book of Jeremiah, the Lamentations of
1960                         Jeremiah.* Richmond, Va.: John Knox Press.

Labuschagne, C. J.           *The Incomparability of Yahweh in the Old Testa-
1966                         ment.* Leiden: E. J. Brill.

LaSor, William S.,           *Old Testament Survey: The Message, Form and
et al.                       Background of the Old Testament.* Grand
1982                         Rapids, Mich.: Eerdmans.

Lind, Millard                "The Anomaly of the Prophet." In *the New Way
1980                         of Jesus.* William Klassen, ed. Newton, Kans.,:
                             Faith and Life Press.

Luckenbill, Daniel           "The Rassam Cyclinder." *Ancient Records of
David                        Assyria and Babylonia.* Vol. II. Chicago: University
1927                         of Chicago Press.

Lundbom, Jack R.
1975

*Jeremiah: A Study in Ancient Hebrew Rhetoric.*
Missoula, Mont.: Society of Biblical Literature and
Scholars Press.

Luther, Martin
1955

*Works.* Ed. by Jaroslav Pelikan. Vol. 46. St. Louis:
Concordia Publishing House.

McKane, W.
1980

"Poison, Trial by Ordeal and the Cup of Wrath."
*Vetus Testamentum* 30: 474-482.

Martens, Elmer A.
1981

*God's Design: A Focus on Old Testament
Theology.* Grand Rapids, Mich.: Baker Book
House.

1972

*Motivation for the Promise of Israel's Restoration
to the Land in Jeremiah and Ezekiel.* Claremont,
Calif.: unpublished dissertation.

Martin, Ernest D.
1978

*Jeremiah: A Study Guide for Congregations.*
Scottdale, Pa.: Herald Press.

Mbiti, John S.
1969

*African Religions and Philosophy.* New York:
Praeger.

Mendenhall, George E.
1973

*The Tenth Generation: The Origins of the Biblical
Tradition.* Baltimore: Johns Hopkins University
Press.

Menno Simons
1956

*The Complete Writings of Menno Simons, 1496-
1561.* Scottdale, Pa.: Herald Press.

Miller, John W.

In a forthcoming publication.

Morgan, George Campbell
1969

*Studies in the Prophecy of Jeremiah.* Old Tappan, N.J.: Revell.

Nicholson, Ernest W.
1973

*The Book of the Prophet Jeremiah, 1-25.*
Cambridge University Press.

1975

*The Book of the Prophet Jeremiah, 26-52.*
Cambridge University Press.

Olan, Levi Arthur
1982

*Prophetic Faith and the Secular Age.* New York:
KTAV Publishing House, Inc.

Overholt, Thomas W.
1970

*The Threat of Falsehood: A Study in the
Theology of the Book of Jeremiah.* Naperville, Ill.:
A. R. Allenson.

Philip, Dietrich
1978

*Enchiridion or Handbook of the Christian Doc-
trine and Religion.* Lagrange, Ind.: Pathway
Publications.

Pritchard, James B.,     *Ancient Near Eastern Texts Relating to the Old*
ed.                      *Testament.* Princeton, N.J.: Princeton University
1955                     Press.

Raitt, Thomas M.        *A Theology of Exile: Judgment/Deliverance in*
1977                     *Jeremiah and Ezekiel.* Philadelphia: Fortress
                         Press.

Shriver, Donald W.      "Jeremiah, Prophet of the Eighties." *Review and*
1981                     *Expositor* 78:397-408.

Spurgeon, C. H.         *Sermons of Rev. C. H. Spurgeon.* Vol. I. New
                         York: Funk and Wagnalls.

Sutcliffe, Edmund F.    "A Note on Jer. 5, 12." *Biblica* 41:287-290.
1960

Swartley, Willard M.    *Slavery, Sabbath, War, and Women: Case Issues*
1983                     *in Biblical Interpretation.* Scottdale, Pa.: Herald
                         Press.

Swidler, Arlene         "Prophets and Symbolic Acts Today." *The Bible*
1981                     *Today* 19:182-187.

Thompson, John Arthur   *The Book of Jeremiah.* Grand Rapids, Mich.:
1980                     Eerdmans.

Von Rad, Gerhard        *Old Testament Theology.* Vol. II. Trans. by D. M.
1962-1965                G. Stalker. New York: Harper.

Wiesel, Elie            *Five Biblical Portraits.* Notre Dame: University of
1981                     Notre Dame Press.

Williams, Charles       *The Descent of the Dove: A Short History of the*
1939                     *Holy Spirit in the Church.* Grand Rapids, Mich.:
                         Eerdmans.

Wiseman, D. J.          "Abba—AN and Alalah." *Journal of Cuneiform*
1958                     *Studies* 12:124-129.

Wolff, Hans Walter      *Confrontations with Prophets: Discovering the*
1983                     *Old Testament's New and Contemporary Signifi-*
                         *cance.* Philadelphia: Fortress Press.

Yoder, John H.          *The Legacy of Michael Sattler.* Trans. and ed. by
1973                     John H. Yoder. Scottdale, Pa.: Herald Press.

Yoder, Perry            "Toward a Shalom Biblical Theology." *The*
1983                     *Conrad Grebel Review* I: 39-49.

# Selected Bibliography

Blackwood, Andrew W., Jr., *Commentary on Jeremiah*. Waco, Tex.: Word Books, 1977. A Presbyterian pastor comments, often phrase by phrase, on those points that would be important to a pastor preaching. Cryptic, but frequent pointers to relevant truths.

Bright, John, *Jeremiah*. New York: Doubleday, 1965. Arranges Jeremiah chronologically. A fresh translation. A standard work, judicious. Attention to linguistic matters.

Calvin, John, *Commentaries on the Book of the Prophet Jeremiah and the Lamentations*. Grand Rapids, Mich.: Eerdmans, 1948. Popular, expansive, with good insights; dates from the Reformation.

Feinberg, Charles L., *Jeremiah: A Commentary* (Vol. 6 of Expositor's Bible Commentary). Grand Rapids. Mich.: Zondervan, 1982. A verse-by-verse commentary with an occasional section "Notes" remarking on linguistic matters from the Hebrew. Conservative. Includes biblical text.

Harrison, R. K., *Jeremiah and Lamentations*. London: Inter-Varsity Press, 1973. A paragraph comment on 3-to-6-verse sections. Crisp, sound scholarship.

Holladay, William, *Jeremiah: Spokesman out of Time*. Philadephia: Pilgrim Press, 1974. A well-known scholar presents themes from Jeremiah, often with a new insight, in a lively, chatty manner. Not comprehensive.

_____. *Jeremiah*. Vol. I. Philadelphia: Fortress, 1986. Extensive historical and critical comment (752 pp.) for chapters 1-25, in the erudite Hermeneia Series.

Hyatt, J. P., "Jeremiah." *Interpreter's Bible*. Vol. V. New York: Abingdon, 1956. Technical comments by a well-known scholar; a separate section on exposition by Stanley R. Hopper.

Morgan, George Campbell, *Studies in the Prophecy of Jeremiah*. Old Tappan, N.J.: Revell, 1969. Comments at a popular level in preaching style. Devotional.

Nicholson, E. W., *Jeremiah 1-25; 26-52*. Cambridge University Press, 1973, 1975. Commentary for students and laypersons by a British scholar. Proposes that Deuteronomic writers supplemented Jeremiah's words to explain the catastrophe of 587.

Rudolph, W., *Jeremiah*. Tuebingen: J. C. B. Mohr, 1968. The standard work in German.

Thompson, J. A., *The Book of Jeremiah. New International Commentary on the Old Testament*. Grand Rapids, Mich.: Eerdmans, 1980. Expansive, often incorporates views from other commentaries. Encyclopedic. New translation; full indices. Helpful select bibliography of journal articles. Recommended.

# Helps in Teaching Jeremiah

Habel, Norman, *Are You Joking, Jeremiah?*. St. Louis: Concordia, 1967. Extended poetry in teenage language imaginatively rehearsing Jeremiah's experiences.

Kinsler, F., *Inductive Study of the Book of Jeremiah*. Guatemala: Presbyterian Seminary, 1971. A self-help guide via comments and questions with space for answers. Assumes little or no background knowledge.

Martin, Ernest D., *Jeremiah: A Study Guide for Congregations*. Scottdale, Pa.: Herald Press, 1978. A book of 13 lessons and outlines together with fill-in-the-blank questions. Written by a pastor.

Miller, John W., *Judgment and Hope*. Scottdale, Pa.: Herald Press, 1972. An able specialist in Jeremiah presents eight plays, five from Jeremiah, which focus on the prophet's call, temple sermon, confessions, symbolic actions on judgment and hope. Written originally for a local congregation.

Sire, James W., *Jeremiah Meet the 20th Century*. Downers Grove, Ill.: Inter-Varsity, 1975. Twelve studies of the fill-in-the-blank variety with 30 pages of helps for leaders. Intended to point up contemporary relevance.

Wainright, J. A., and Muriel Hardill, *The Fall of a City: The Book of Jeremiah*. London: SCM, 1962. Eight imaginative 4- to 6-page dramatized scenes, each followed by helpful explanatory notes and discussion questions. High school level.

# The Author

Elmer Martens is a Bible teacher with a concern for the spiritual well-being of the church at large. His eight years of pastoral experience have given him a love for God's people and a desire to see believers maturing in Christ in order to carry forward God's mission. His invitations to the churches and conventions for a Bible-teaching ministry are not limited to his own denomination.

For 16 years he has taught Old Testament at the Mennonite Brethren Biblical Seminary in Fresno [California], where he has served as president for nearly a decade. His teaching experience dates back to public school in Saskatchewan, where he was born.

He is the author of *God's Design: A Theology of the Old Testament*, published in the United States by Baker and in Britain by InterVarsity under the title *Plot and Purpose of the Old Testament.* Martens was on the translation team of the New American Standard Bible and assisted with the New King James Version.

Martens holds a doctorate in Old Testament from the Claremont Graduate School, where he completed a thesis on "Motivations for the Promise of Israel's Restoration to the Land in Jeremiah and Ezekiel." He has a B.A. degree from the University of Saskatchewan, and a B.Ed. from the University of Manitoba. He is a graduate of the Mennonite Brethren Biblical Seminary in Fresno, California, and a member of the North Fresno Mennonite Brethren congregation.

Martens is married to Phyllis Hiebert Martens, herself a writer. They have four children: Lauren, Frances, Vernon, and Karen.